THE LAST LIBERAL GOVERNMENTS

THE LAST
LIBERAL GOVERNMENTS

THE PROMISED LAND
1905–1910

by

Peter Rowland

THE MACMILLAN COMPANY
NEW YORK

Library of Congress Catalog Card Number: 69—11065

First Printing
FIRST AMERICAN EDITION 1969
FIRST PUBLISHED IN GREAT BRITAIN IN 1968
BY THE CRESSET PRESS, LONDON

The Macmillan Company, New York
Collier-Macmillan Canada Ltd., Toronto, Ontario

Printed in Great Britain

CONTENTS

To Jan, with all my love

PREFACE

On December 5th, 1905 Sir Henry Campbell-Bannerman, the leader of the Liberal Party, accepted King Edward VII's commission to form a Government: six weeks later he and his colleagues were confirmed in office by the greatest landslide victory at the polls ever known in Britain's history. It was a radiant beginning to what was to prove, ironically enough, the final chapter in the Liberal Party's role as a major political force: on May 24th, 1915 King George V acquiesced in Asquith's proposals for a new Ministry "on a broad and non-party basis", and the last Liberal Government came to an end.

Distance invariably lends enchantment and the years immediately preceding 1914 have come to be wistfully regarded as the sunshine days of the twentieth century. January 1906 was, it seems, the most blissful of dawns in which to be alive, and the spectacle of some three hundred-and-eighty Liberal M.P.s marching to Westminster with heads held high and burning with ardour is one which still works its magic. A Ministry of All the Talents was now in command and, so the legend runs, every moment of its time was devoted to implementing social and constitutional reforms in every sphere. Labour exchanges, trade boards and old age pensions were introduced and restrictions were lifted on trade union activities. The Unionists, baffled and enraged, turned in anguish to the House of Lords, but with the aid of "the People's Budget" the reformers battered down the barricades and swept on to triumphs of a still greater nature. The Upper Chamber was shorn of its powers, while the members of the Lower Chamber introduced a scheme of national insurance against sickness and unemployment and, in passing, awarded themselves salaries. South Africa was granted her independence, an act which was generally regarded until recently as the Ministry's most enlightened achievement, and constitutional reforms were introduced in India. A new model army and a new model navy were created and, as everybody knows, were ready for battle in 1914. A Home Rule Bill, together with a Welsh Disestablishment Bill, reached the Statute Book in the autumn of that year and, had it not been for the coming of Armageddon, would have been carried into effect without further ado. All in all, runs the general conclusion, this was an impressive list of achievements.

Somewhere along the line, however, the story does not ring quite true. Much was undoubtedly accomplished by the Campbell-Bannerman and Asquith administrations, but events—in the standard accounts of this period—fall into place rather too neatly. Was it really a case of roses, roses all the way? The mere fact that the Liberal Party should have come such a cropper in the two 1910 elections, after having been so supremely successful at the polls in 1906, does not in itself dispose of this theory. Radical administrations—though lauded in the history books—are rarely popular when actually in office, and it might be argued that this was simply another instance of an ungrateful and ungracious electorate indicating (twice over for good measure) that enough was enough so far as social reforms were concerned. When looked at more closely, however, a rather different picture emerges, and one is driven towards the conclusion that the erosion of support for the Liberal Party in the years which followed 1906 arose from the fact that it was doing too little rather than too much. After a steady stream of by-election disasters in 1908 an attempt was made to retrieve the situation, and (as I hope to show in a subsequent volume) the general election of December 1910 proved to be more of a turning-point than that of January 1906.

I am grateful to Mr John H. MacCallum Scott, for many useful comments and suggestions, and to Mrs Hilary Strudwick for undertaking the very laborious task of compiling an index. I must express my thanks to Marjorie, Lady Pentland, Mr C. A. Gladstone and the Trustees of the British Museum for allowing me to make use (respectively) of the Campbell-Bannerman, Gladstone and Balfour papers in the British Museum, and to Mr Randolph S. Churchill for allowing me to quote from certain letters written by Sir Winston Churchill which have not previously been published.

I must also acknowledge my indebtedness to G. Bell & Sons Ltd. in respect of quotations from *Arthur James Balfour* by Kenneth Young; to Ernest Benn Ltd. in respect of quotations from *John Burns: Labour's Lost Leader* by William Kent (originally published by Williams & Norgate Ltd.) and *The Rule of Democracy* by Elie Halévy, translated by E. I. Watkin; to the author, in respect of a quotation from *Frederick Edwin, Earl of Birkenhead* by the second Earl of Birkenhead (originally published by Thornton Butterworth Ltd.); to Anthony Blond Ltd. in respect of a quotation from *Proconsul in Politics* by A. M. Gollin; to the Cambridge University Press in respect of a quotation from *The Cambridge History of the British Empire, vol. III*; to Cassell & Co. Ltd. in respect of quotations from *Fifty Years of Parliament* by the Earl of Oxford and Asquith, *Life*,

Journalism and Politics by J. A. Spender, *Politics from Inside* by Sir Austen Chamberlain, *The Life and Letters of the Right Hon. Sir Austen Chamberlain* by Sir Charles Petrie, and *Northcliffe* by Reginald Pound and Geoffrey Harmsworth; to William Collins Sons & Co. Ltd. in respect of quotations from *Asquith* by Roy Jenkins; to Constable & Co. Ltd. in respect of quotations from *Lord Crewe, 1858–1945* by James Pope-Hennessy; to Country Life Ltd. in respect of quotations from *More Pages from My Diary, 1908–1914* by Lord Riddell; to the Cresset Press in respect of a quotation from *Memoirs* by Lord Samuel; to Eyre & Spottiswoode (Publishers) Ltd. in respect of quotations from *Autobiography* by Margot Asquith, *Reginald McKenna, 1863–1943* by Stephen McKenna, *The Unknown Prime Minister* by Robert Blake and *My Brother and I* by William George; to Faber and Faber Ltd. in respect of quotations from *Haldane, 1856–1915* by Sir Frederick Maurice and *The Irish Parliamentary Party, 1890–1910* by F. S. L. Lyons; the Syndics of the Fitzwilliam Museum, Cambridge, in respect of quotations from *My Diaries* by Wilfred Blunt (published by Martin Secker and Warburg Ltd.); to George Allen & Unwin Ltd. in respect of quotations from *The Advent of the Labour Party* by Philip P. Poirier, *Haldane of Cloan* by Dudley Sommer and *The Supreme Command, 1914–1918* by Lord Hankey; to the author, and Longmans, Green & Co. Ltd., in respect of a quotation from *Under Six Reigns* by G. P. Gooch; to the author, and to George G. Harrap Ltd., in respect of quotations from *The Life of John Redmond* by Denis Gwynn; to Hamish Hamilton Ltd. in respect of a quotation from *Politics in Wartime* by A. J. P. Taylor; to Rupert Hart-Davis Ltd. in respect of a quotation from *John Buchan* by Janet Adam Smith; to William Heinemann Ltd. in respect of quotations from *Carson* by H. Montgomery Hyde, *Mr Balfour's Poodle* by Roy Jenkins and *Lord Derby, "King of Lancashire"*, by Randolph S. Churchill; Her Majesty's Stationery Office in respect of quotations from *British Documents on the Origins of the War*; to Hodder & Stoughton Ltd. in respect of quotations from *The Life of the Right Hon. Sir Henry Campbell-Bannerman* by J. A. Spender, *Twenty-Five Years* by Viscount Grey of Fallodon, *An Autobiography* by R. B. Haldane and *All the Way* by Viscount Cecil of Chelwood; to Hutchinson & Co. Ltd. in respect of quotations from the *The Life and Letters of George Wyndham*, edited by J. W. Mackail and Guy Wyndham, *The Life of Herbert Henry Asquith, Lord Oxford and Asquith* by J. A. Spender and Cyril Asquith, *Walter Long and His Times* by Sir Charles Petrie, *Arthur James Balfour, First Earl of Balfour* by Blanche E. C. Dugdale, *David Lloyd George, the Official Biography* by Malcolm Thomson, *My Political Life* (vol. I) by L. S. Amery and *Tempestuous*

Journey, Lloyd George, His Life and Times by Frank Owen; to the author, and Nisbet & Co. Ltd., in respect of quotations from *A Liberal Attorney-General, The Life of Lord Robson of Jesmond* by G. W. Keeton; to Longmans, Green & Co. Ltd. in respect of quotations from *The History of England during the Reign of Victoria (1837–1901)* by Sidney Low and Lloyd C. Sandars, *Grey of Fallodon* by G. M. Trevelyan, *Beatrice Webb's Diaries, 1924–1932,* edited by Margaret Cole, and *Edward Marsh, Patron of the Arts* by Christopher Hassall; to Macmillan & Co. Ltd. in respect of quotations from *Recollections* by John, Viscount Morley, *James Bryce* by H. A. L. Fisher, *Lord Lansdowne, A Biography* by Lord Newton, *India, Minto and Morley, 1905–1910* by Mary, Countess of Minto, *The Life of Neville Chamberlain* by Keith Feiling, *The Life of Joseph Chamberlain (vol. IV)* by Julian Amery, *Labour and Politics, 1900–1906* by F. Bealey and Henry Pelling and *A Short History of the Labour Party* by Henry Pelling; to Methuen and Co. Ltd. in respect of quotations from *The Condition of England* by C. F. G. Masterman and *Lloyd George's Ambulance Wagon: the Memoirs of William J. Braithwaite, 1911–1912*; to the author, in respect of a quotation from *General Smuts* by Sarah Gertrude Millin (published by Faber and Faber Ltd); to John Murray (Publishers) Ltd. in respect of quotations from *The Life of the Right Hon. Sir Charles W. Dilke, Bart.* by Stephen Gwynne and G. M. Tuckwell, *The Letters of Queen Victoria (3rd Series, vol. II)*, *King George V, A Personal Memoir* by John Gore, *Master and Brother: Murrays of Elibank* by Arthur C. Murray and *King Edward the Seventh* by Sir Philip Magnus; to Thomas Nelson & Sons Ltd. in respect of quotations from *Lord Minto* by John Buchan and *The End of Isolation: British Foreign Policy, 1900–1907* by G. W. Monger; to the Warden and Fellows of the New College Oxford, and Cassell & Co. Ltd., in respect of a quotation from *The Milner Papers, vol. II, South Africa 1899–1905,* edited by Cecil Headlam; Nicholson & Watson Ltd. in respect of quotations from *An Autobiography* by Philip, Viscount Snowden, *Journals and Letters of Reginald, Viscount Esher* (vols. II and III) and *C. F. G. Masterman, A Biography* by Lucy Masterman; to the author in respect of quotations from *Lord Carnock, A Study in the Old Diplomacy* and *King George V, His Life and Reign* by Sir Harold Nicolson (published by Constable & Co. Ltd.); to Odhams Press Ltd. in respect of quotations from *The World Crisis* and *Great Contemporaries* by Winston S. Churchill and *War Memoirs* by David Lloyd George; to the Oxford University Press in respect of quotations from *England, 1870–1914* by R. C. K. Ensor, *Randall Davidson, Archbishop of Canterbury* by G. K. A. Bell, *The Struggle for Mastery in Europe, 1848–1918* by A. J. P. Taylor, *The Unification of South Africa,*

1902–1910 by L. M. Thompson, *"The Observer"* and *J. L. Garvin, 1908–1914* by A. M. Gollin, *Britain in India* by R. P. Masani, *From the Dreadnought to Scapa Flow (vol. I)* by Arthur J. Marder, *The Evolution of India and Pakistan, 1858 to 1947, Select Documents*, edited by C. H. Philips, and *Lives of the Lord Chancellors, 1885–1940* by R. F. V. Heuston; to the Passfield Trustees in respect of quotations from *Our Partnership* by Beatrice Webb (published by Longmans, Green & Co. Ltd.); to the Public Trustees in respect of quotations from *King Edward VII, A Biography* by Sir Sidney Lee (published by Macmillan & Co. Ltd.); to Routledge & Kegan Paul Ltd. in respect of quotations from *The Shaping of Modern Ireland*, edited by Conor Cruise O'Brien, and *Chief Whip, the Political Life and Times of Aretas Akers-Douglas* by the third Viscount Chilston; to Lord Shaw's executors, and Cassell & Co. Ltd., in respect of quotations from *Letters to Isabel* by Lord Shaw of Dunfermline; and, finally, to The Times Publishing Co. Ltd. in respect of quotations from *The History of The Times (vol. III)*.

London,
December 1967   Peter Rowland

PROLOGUE

(1)

Great Britain, in 1906, was a land in which the traditional bastions of society were still firmly entrenched. Despite the industrial revolutions through which she had passed, despite the growth of towns, the development of trade and the impoverishment of agriculture, despite Reform and Education Acts and despite the zeal of John Stuart Mill and others, Britain was still a country in which Land, while fighting a rearguard action, remained predominantly the largest single factor in the structure of society. The gentlemen of England (and of Scotland, Wales and Ireland, for that matter) had not disappeared in 1846 nor even in 1894; they were fewer in number than they had been, perhaps, but their estates were larger and twenty years of almost unbroken Conservative government had ensured that their power was as great as ever. Half of the total national income went to one-ninth of the population and one-third of it went to one-thirtieth, while half the national capital belonged to one-seventieth of the population.

Of the 43 million inhabitants of the United Kingdom, some 30 million lived in towns and more than 6 million in the Greater London area alone. The total number of adult males amounted to 14 million, of whom only 2 million were at any one time without some kind of employment, while the total number of adult females amounted to 16 million, of whom 5 million were wage-earners—almost half of them in domestic service. Among the men, the industries which attracted the greatest individual labour forces were metal manufacture (1,600,000); transport and communications (1,500,000); agriculture (1,400,000); building and construction (1,200,000) and mining and quarrying (1 million). In 1899 Seebohm Rowntree had calculated that the minimum weekly sum needed to maintain a family of five was twenty-one shillings, while a family of six would need twenty-six shillings. The average weekly wage at this time, however, was no more than twenty-nine shillings, that of the agricultural labourer being sixteen shillings, while the average wage for a woman was fifteen shillings. There were no safeguards against dismissal or sickness nor were there any old age pensions, although the latter had been vaguely talked about by politicians from the mid-1890s onwards. If one fell upon hard times, the best that the State could offer in the way of relief was the work-house. Trade unions did their best to secure better working conditions and higher wages for their members, although the total union member-ship at this time was little more than two million, and friendly societies also did much valuable work. The largest single ameliorator of poverty remained private philanthropy, but there were limits to what even this could do. "Ten millions," wrote C. F. G. Masterman in 1909, "disinherited, out of a doubtful forty, shiver through their lives on the verge of hunger: to the bulk of the remainder existence presents no certain joys, either in a guaranteed prosperity or in any serviceable and illuminating purpose of being."[*1]

(2)

The introduction of new industrial techniques, combined with an unrivalled ability to open up new markets, were the means whereby Britain had established her paramount position in the world during the nineteenth century, but by 1906 she had ceased to be a pace-setter and was, indeed, finding herself outdistanced by competition from Germany and America. Her three great industries, coal, steel and cotton, were still flourishing, but their days of triumphant expansion were over. New in-dustries such as rubber, gas, aluminium, rayon and, in particular, engineer-ing, had appeared on the scene, however, and shipbuilding continued to be of considerable importance. On the face of it, moreover, Britain's trade remained prosperous: her exports, so it was calculated, amounted to 30% of her national production, as opposed to 20–25% in the 1890s. By 1907 the value of her cotton exports would be 50% higher than the aver-age for 1901–3, while the increase in the exports of coal, machinery and iron over the same period would be even higher.

Joseph Chamberlain, as we shall soon see, was pressing at this time for closer trade relations with the colonies by means of a tariff on goods from Europe, America and the Far East, but the whole concept of a self-sufficing Empire was little more than a pipe-dream which had little or no relevance to the economic realities of the day. Britain was, admittedly, a steady consumer of colonial wheat, wool, cotton, cocoa, tea, timber, rubber, tin and other metals, but when in need of petroleum, raw cotton, meat or even sugar she was obliged to rely on foreign suppliers. Between 1904 and 1907, the three years which saw a marked expansion in her trade and investment, imperial trade increased by 23% as opposed to a 53% rise in foreign trade. Only a quarter of her imports were of colonial origin

* Small raised numbers refer to source references which appear at the end of the book. Footnotes are signalled in the text by asterisks, etc.

and only one-third of her exports were destined for colonial markets. The 1900s witnessed, moreover, a steady decline in the mother-country's share of Empire trade, and by 1914 she would be almost on a par with Japan in the east and Germany in the west. The Dominions did, however, provide a profitable sphere for investment: by 1910 Britain would have capital of £373 million in Canada, £365 million in South Africa, £301 million in Australia and £78 million in New Zealand, most of which would be devoted to railway construction.

Overseas investment was, indeed, the means by which Britain was chiefly enabled to carry her nineteenth-century prosperity into the twentieth. Between 1880 and 1900 Australia, Argentina and the United States had borrowed more heavily from her than ever before, and during the early 1900s Canada and several South American states also took advantage of her position as the world's banker. Capital investment had risen from £25 million in 1904 to £63 million in 1905 and it would soar to £105 million in 1906. Britain's total foreign investments at this time were in the region of £2,500 million, and the annual interest from them served to bridge the ever-widening gap between her exports and imports. The prices of imported foodstuffs and raw materials had fallen, moreover (although they were soon to rise again), and this too meant that the rise in real incomes was continuing.

(3)

Self-sufficiency breeds contempt, and throughout the greater part of the nineteenth century Britain had been a law unto herself so far as the political affairs of Europe were concerned. The maintenance of the balance of power was, admittedly, the guiding light of her foreign policy, and it was with this end in view that she had bestirred herself to intervene in the Crimea in 1853 and in the "Eastern Question" some twenty-five years later, but by and large her attitude towards other European countries had been a mixture of tolerance and boredom. At no time was this feeling of non-involvement more acute than in the 1890s, the period when Lord Salisbury presided over the Foreign Office like some weary Titan. Britain revelled in her "splendid isolation", and it was not until the South African War was running its dismal course that she came to realise, with something of a jolt, just how great were the reserves of unpopularity which she had accumulated for herself on the Continent. The victories of the Boers were greeted with ill-concealed delight, and Britain found that she was isolated with a vengeance. Apart from her alliance with Portugal, concluded in 1373 and of minimal importance, she had no real friends in

Europe. At the turn of the century, however, with interests in all parts of the globe in need of defence and with her military and naval resources extended to their utmost, she could no longer afford to pursue a wholly independent course.

The European Powers were, at this time, divided into two great rival camps: Germany, Austria-Hungary and Italy on the one hand, bound together in a Triple Alliance since 1882, and France and Russia on the other, linked in a Dual Alliance since 1894. Britain's one great fear was that she would be attacked by the latter, and she tried to guard against this by seeking, albeit half-heartedly, some kind of alliance with Germany. Germany decided to play for time, confident that better terms would eventually be offered her, but the Foreign Office confounded her expectations by looking elsewhere for security. In 1902 Britain signed an alliance with Japan, thus freeing her Far Eastern fleet for service in home waters. This was something of a bombshell for the Wilhelmstrasse, but worse was to follow. Two years later came the conclusion of an *entente cordiale* between Britain and France. This agreement was not an alliance but represented a genuine attempt to settle all outstanding differences between the two countries. It had been brought about by a mutual desire not to become involved in a war between Russia and Japan which had started some weeks before and owed little or nothing to fear of Germany. As we shall see, however, the latter resented the existence of such an agreement and lost no time in challenging the validity of the assumptions on which it had been made.

By the end of 1905, therefore, Britain's position as a great Power was once again relatively secure. Her relations with France were good, while her fears of Russia were now banished as a result of the latter's humiliating defeat at the hands of Japan. It was only with Germany, towards whom her attitude had stiffened since 1902, that friction threatened to develop, but the possibility of war between them was not taken very seriously and there seemed, indeed, no reason why any differences of opinion should not be smoothly resolved by normal diplomatic means. She had no particular axe to grind in the world, having acquired all that she needed in the way of colonial possessions during the four preceding centuries, and wanted nothing more than to enjoy the fruits of her conquest in peace. That anyone could be so ill-natured as to grudge her the right of repose seemed, on the face of it, inconceivable.

CHAPTER ONE

THE PRELUDE, 1902–5

Few would have predicted, when Arthur James Balfour succeeded his uncle, Lord Salisbury, as Prime Minister on July 10th, 1902, that within the space of three and a half years his party would have suffered the most overwhelming defeat over recorded in British electoral history, that he himself would have been rejected by the constituents he had represented since 1885 or that his opponents would sweep into office and remain there for ten triumphant years. The outlook, after all, seemed reasonably bright. A long and arduous war had finally been brought to a victorious, if somewhat belated, conclusion and the joys of Mafeking night had resulted in the Conservative Party and the Liberal Unionists, generally known as the Unionists, being returned with a majority of 134, a gain of three seats, in the "Khaki" election of 1900. Lord Salisbury, with the exception of two short interludes, had presided over the destinies of his country for seventeen years and there seemed no good reason why the Unionist supremacy should not continue. With Balfour in control of domestic policy, Joseph Chamberlain at the Colonial Office and Lord Lansdowne managing foreign affairs, the patriarch's retirement need make no more than a gracious ripple upon the waters of Britain's political history.

Salisbury's departure, however, marked the start of a steady decline in Unionist fortunes. This was partly due to the character of the new premier, who had played the role of languid heir-apparent for so many years that people found it difficult to accept him as a leader in his own right. "Prince Arthur's" policies did not receive the same unquestioning support as those of his predecessor. There was also, perhaps, a general feeling that it was time for changes of a more positive nature. What did more than anything else to hasten the downfall of Balfour's administration, however, was the fact that Chamberlain was anxious to embark upon one more crusade before he died.

Since 1860 Great Britain had been to all intents and purposes a Free Trade country. During those forty years her income had increased, her industries had expanded and her overseas trade and investment had broken all records. It seemed reasonable to suppose that the dismantling of her old protective barriers had been largely responsible for this growth in prosperity, but towards the end of the nineteenth century came murmurs of dissent. Farmers and landowners, having weathered what they regarded as a period of severe depression, were now sceptical of Manchester economics, while Germany and America were proving serious rivals in the battle for world markets. Neither the Unionists nor the Liberals would admit that the Free Trade gospel stood in need of revision, and one can therefore appreciate the excitement aroused when Chamberlain, in a speech at Birmingham on May 15th, 1903, urged his countrymen to abandon it and concentrate, instead, on building up the Empire as a self-sufficient unit. This could be achieved by imposing duties on foreign goods while allowing those from the Dominions and colonies to enter the country at a much lower rate or even duty-free.

This speech produced tremendous reactions. It was, in fact, the political bombshell of the year. Liberals immediately rushed to the defence of Free Trade, reaffirming their belief in the doctrines of Cobdenite finance and launching into furious denunciations of anyone who dared to think otherwise. A considerable number of Unionists, on the other hand, felt that Chamberlain had put into words what they themselves had long been thinking and responded to his clarion call for action by banding together in a movement which soon became known as the Tariff Reform League. Their leader, however, had forged too far ahead of the Cabinet. Balfour, while guardedly sympathetic towards Tariff Reform, felt that neither the country nor his colleagues were ready for it. "To make it part of the Government's programme would be to break up the party," he wrote to the King.[1] The Unionist Free Traders were incensed and there soon developed a party split of the first magnitude. The Prime Minister's refusal to state his own views, beyond the fact that he had "unsettled convictions", did nothing to improve matters and Chamberlain resigned from the Government in the autumn. So did several Tory Free Traders, including the Duke of Devonshire. The ex-Colonial Secretary, with all the relentless vigour of his earlier days, flung himself into a campaign for Imperial Preference and Balfour's administration, abruptly shorn of its extremist wings, was left to struggle on as best it could.

The Prime Minister made what were, in the circumstances, valiant efforts to preserve a semblance of unity throughout his party. Austen Chamberlain, the son of the self-appointed prophet, was made Chancellor of the Exchequer, although he was not allowed to deviate from Free Trade principles. Balfour's niece and first biographer tells us that the Prime Minister was anxious to retain office in order to carry through several important tasks. These included the signing of the *entente cordiale*, the renewal of the Anglo-Japanese Alliance, the firm establishment of the Committee of Imperial Defence and the efficient production of the 18-pounder gun. "He was less obsessed by the tariff controversy than most of his colleagues and his followers," writes Mrs Blanche Dugdale somewhat loftily; ". . . the general tone of his correspondence reinforces the impression that he felt it an interruption of more fruitful meditations."[2]

So far as the Government were concerned, the Tariff Reform controversy did not exist. Its members adopted the simple expedient of sauntering out of the House of Commons whenever a debate upon the subject began. So far as the parliamentary party was concerned, however, this was the one issue that really mattered, and its members split into three camps: the "whole hoggers" led by Chamberlain, those temporising with Balfour (known as the "little piggers") and the Tory Free Traders, of whom Lord Hugh Cecil and Winston Churchill were the most prominent. The latter felt so strongly on this issue that, in May 1904, he crossed the floor of the House and joined the Liberals.

Other factors were also responsible for the Government's unpopularity. The Education Act of 1902, while an admirable measure in many respects, enraged the Nonconformists by the privileged position which it accorded to Church of England schools,* while the Licensing Act of 1904 aroused the fury of temperance reformers.† The issue of "Chinese slavery" was another stick with which to beat the Ministry‡ and so was the mysterious resignation of the Chief Secretary for Ireland, George Wyndham, in March 1905.§

The Licensing Act was virtually Balfour's last triumph. Early in 1905,

---

* See footnote on page 77.

† The Licensing Act provided that compensation for brewers and publicans for the withdrawal of their licences should come from a fund levied on the trade. This enraged temperance reformers, who pointed out that there were 160,000 convictions for drunkenness each year and that the annual amount spent on drink came to almost £200 million. They saw no reason why compensation should be paid to those who had previously benefited from this state of affairs.

‡ The Government decided early in 1904 to allow the importation of nearly 5,000 Chinese labourers into South Africa to work the mines. They were paid miserable wages, separated from their families and enclosed in compounds from which escape was almost impossible. This grim state of affairs gradually became known in Britain, thanks largely to the efforts of Miss Emily Hobhouse. The Liberal Party launched a campaign on behalf of the coolies and Campbell-Bannerman declared that it was all "very like slavery".

§ Wyndham's Permanent Under-Secretary, Sir Antony MacDonnell, had (due to a misunderstanding with his chief) announced to the Press the preliminary details of a scheme for giving Ireland a certain degree of independence. There was an immediate outcry from the Unionist ranks and Wyndham was obliged to resign. It was widely believed that the Cabinet had been toying with a Home Rule scheme and that Wyndham had been made a scapegoat.

obliged at long last to take formal note of the splits in his party, he produced a formula "on a half-sheet of notepaper" designed to re-unite them: duties to be imposed on foreign goods for the purposes of negotiation, retaliation and the prevention of dumping, and a Colonial Conference to discuss closer commercial union between the mother-country and her off-spring. The Free Traders were angry and the Chamberlainites were not impressed. During the months which followed, which were marked by successive Unionists defeats at by-elections, it became clear that the Government could not continue much longer. "The session of Parliament which comes to an end today," commented *The Times* on August 11th, "leaves behind it a record of futile debates and disappointing achievement . . . [Mr Balfour's] credit and influence are scarcely what they were, even in the House of Commons, and out of doors they have certainly been impaired."

The Liberals were overjoyed by this wholly unexpected turn of events. Chamberlain's campaign was nothing less than an invitation to fight on their favourite battleground, and the defence of Free Trade proved a rallying cry for Gladstonians, "Little Englanders", Liberal Imperialists and Radicals alike. They became, for the first time since Gladstone's resignation, a united body of men. Since 1895 they had, in fact, passed through a singularly unhappy period. Wrenched this way and that by internal dissensions and with divisions slashed in all directions, they had ceased to be an effective Opposition and had become simply an anti-Unionist coalition. Lord Rosebery led them for only two years after Gladstone's retirement, surrendering his authority in the autumn of 1896, and Sir William Harcourt undertook the thankless task for what proved to be two more. Both of them were discouraged by lack of support and Harcourt, resigning towards the end of 1898, complained bitterly of "sectional disputes and personal interests" which had made his job impossible. John Morley, his friend and ally, shortly afterwards announced his own withdrawal from "the formal councils of the Liberal Party". For almost two months they had no official leader. H. H. Asquith was sounded, but he could not afford to throw up his lucrative practice at the Bar and devote himself wholly to politics. Finally, by a process of elimination, the post devolved upon the modest, amiable and unambitious Minister of War in Gladstone's last administration, Sir Henry Campbell-Bannerman.

Sir Henry, who was elected to the leadership on February 6th, 1899, was determined that there should be no further splits in the party. Home Rule, he announced, would no longer be at the forefront of their programme. This declaration produced sighs of relief from many quarters, but the

South African War momentarily wrecked his efforts to re-establish the Liberal Party as a cohesive political force. This conflict, which began only a few months after his accession to the leadership, proved a testing time for Radical politicians. Campbell-Bannerman himself, in company with Morley and Harcourt, was sympathetic towards the Boers and thought that an armistice should be concluded without delay, while David Lloyd George made his reputation by declaring that the war was wholly unjustified and was waged simply to satisfy the ambitions of Joseph Chamberlain. Those who denounced the affair were dubbed "Little Englanders"; those who supported it became known as Liberal Imperialists. This latter group, which had Asquith, Sir Edward Grey and R. B. Haldane as its most prominent members, turned to Rosebery for assistance and his lordship obliged by establishing, in 1902, an organisation called the Liberal League. He himself was President and the others, together with Sir Henry Fowler, served as Vice-Presidents.

The ending of the South African War did much to restore harmony in the Liberal camp, and Chamberlain's Tariff Reform campaign now completed the process. The quarrels over the war were not forgotten, however, and for the Vice-Presidents of the Liberal League the near-certainty of Unionist defeat at the polls posed serious problems. Early in September 1905 Asquith, Grey and Haldane reached an understanding (the "Relugas Compact") to the effect that unless Campbell-Bannerman, if called upon to form a Government, agreed to take a peerage and leave the leadership of the Commons to Asquith, they would not accept office under him.[*]

Campbell-Bannerman soon learned something of this agreement. "I hear it has been suggested", he told Asquith on November 13th, "by that ingenious person, Richard Burdon Haldane, that I should go to the House of Lords, a place for which I have neither liking, training nor ambition."[†][4] Asquith, who was always distressed by frontal attacks, said that an acceptable alternative would be for Haldane himself to go to the Upper House as Lord Chancellor. Campbell-Bannerman said that this was out of the question: the Woolsack had already been earmarked for Sir Robert Reid. He made it clear, however, that Asquith and Grey would both occupy

---

[*] Haldane wrote to Lord Knollys, the King's secretary, on September 12th, informing him of their decision. Knollys pointed out that the King would be placed in an awkward position if the three Roseberyites refused to serve under Campbell-Bannerman. Further exchanges ensued, and on October 17th and 22nd Haldane actually sent Knollys, for the King's perusal, a suggested distribution of offices in the event of the Liberal Party being returned to power.[3]

[†] The suggestion was by no means a new one. Henry Labouchere, for example, had written to Campbell-Bannerman on February 21st, 1905 informing him that "my very opportunist friend Lloyd George was explaining to me a plan for you to go to the Lords. I said to him that as his object was to be in the Cabinet, he would do well to stick to you."[5]

important posts in the next Liberal Government—the first as Chancellor of the Exchequer and the second as Foreign Secretary*—and it seems probable that Asquith, from this time onwards, began to have second thoughts about the advisability of the Relugas Compact.

The President of the Liberal League was meanwhile striking out on his own account. Rosebery had, by 1905, drifted far to the right of his erstwhile colleagues, though never formally changing sides. With the Liberals he was whole-heartedly devoted to the cause of Free Trade: with the Conservatives he was whole-heartedly in favour of Imperialism and the Act of Union. We find him, to quote a contemporary, "in a curiously detached position, lying a little outside both political camps, formidable to one side as a candid critic, more formidable to the other as a candid friend."[7] As a personality he was far more interesting than the slow, plodding, good-humoured but unimpressive Campbell-Bannerman: on the other hand, he was completely out of touch with the rank and file of the Liberal Party and his failure to comprehend this fact forced the ultimate issue between himself and its nominal leader. It was not that the battleground was ill-chosen but simply that the real battle had already been won without anyone realising it.

Rosebery had constantly proclaimed, since 1896, that he had no desire to return to an active role in the party, but this had not prevented him from periodically delivering weighty judgments as to what ought or ought not to be Liberal policy. The creation of the League, moreover, could hardly be regarded as anything less than a challenge to Campbell-Bannerman's authority, and matters came to a head when Rosebery firmly rejected (in a speech on October 25th) the idea that Home Rule should continue to form part of the Liberal programme. He presumably hoped to forestall any other pronouncements on the subject but his hopes, alas, were doomed to disappointment. Campbell-Bannerman, speaking at Stirling on November 23rd, expressed his desire to ultimately place "the effective management of Irish affairs in the hands of a representative Irish authority." Furious at his wishes being brushed aside so casually, Rosebery drove the final wedge between himself and Sir Henry in a speech at Bodmin on November 25th. "The responsible leader of the Liberal Party," he declared, "has . . . hoisted once more in its most pronounced form the

---

* Campbell-Bannerman had also considered Lord Elgin for the Foreign Office, but Harcourt (very much in the royal confidence) reported on November 30th that the King "does not think Elgin would do. . . . Edward Grey will be pressed on you probably. I said impossible in House of Commons: too poor for peerage: the answer was not too poor as he has no children: not impossible to have Foreign Minister in H. of C". Not since 1868, in fact, had a Foreign Secretary sat in the Commons.[6]

flag of Irish Home Rule." After announcing his intention of not uttering, even now, one jarring note which could "conflict with the unity of the Free Trade party," he went on "to say emphatically and once for all that I cannot serve under that banner."

There was general consternation at this speech in most sections of the Liberal Party. It was, after all, Rosebery himself who had revived the issue of Home Rule, and it seemed that his declaration could not have come at a worse moment. "Is R. clean off his head?" exclaimed Campbell-Banner-man,[8] and Herbert Gladstone, the Liberal Chief Whip, told him, five days later, that "R.'s monstrous outbreak" had ruined the effect of the Stirling announcement: "letters have been coming to me from all parts of the country reporting disturbed minds."[*9] The other representatives of Liberal Imperialism were especially dismayed and Grey, writing to Rosebery on November 27th, explained that the substance of Campbell-Bannerman's speech had been agreed beforehand with Asquith.[†10]

Meanwhile, following a triumph at the annual Conservative Conference, at which a motion in favour of Imperial Preference had been carried with only one dissentient, Chamberlain had delivered a stinging attack on the Prime Minister's vacillation. When the Cabinet met on November 24th Balfour announced his intention of resigning without further ado. Lansdowne welcomed the decision but the other members were horrified and urged him to reconsider. Acland-Hood, the Chief Whip, saw Jack Sandars, Balfour's secretary, a few hours later and was told "that the Chief was rather upset, still believed his own opinion was right, but hesitated to act in view of the evident feeling of the Cabinet."[12] The following day Balfour sent his colleagues a memorandum in which he made it plain that, although his own leanings towards a December resignation had taken shape before Chamberlain's speech, he was now fully convinced that the time had come to depart. "We may meet Parliament," he wrote, "and go on until we are beaten or until our majority is reduced to such obviously exiguous proportions that even the most vehement supporter of the 'holding-on' policy must feel that resignation is inevitable. . . . In the present state of the party such a course is most undesirable."[13]

---

* See page 345 for a fuller version of Gladstone's letter.

† "Rosebery," wrote Labouchere to Campbell-Bannerman on November 30th, "is making a desperate effort to embroil matters. His connections begin and end with his desire to come in at the head of a central party. He is angry at Asquith, Grey and his former associates not standing by him and wishes to make things difficult for them. I suspect that our friend Haldane was with him for his overtures mean that he wants to be Chancellor. His friends—with the exception, perhaps, of Grey, who is very obstinate—prefer a bird in the hand. As for Grey, it is never possible to know what he may do. But I do not see that it much signifies, for he is an invention of the Press, and has no hold on Liberal opinion which is with you."[11]

It is important to note that Balfour's decision to resign had been taken before he knew of any fresh crisis in the affairs of the Liberal Party: it was Chamberlain, not Rosebery, who forced his hand. He no doubt believed, however, that the Liberal Party was embarking upon yet another of its domestic quarrels and evidently doubted whether Campbell-Bannerman would be able to form a satisfactory Government. Rather than seek a dissolution he would force his opponents to take office at a moment's notice, if they could, and leave them to cope with the affairs of State on the one hand and a general election on the other. With the reluctant acquiescence of his colleagues, therefore, he motored from No. 10 Downing Street to Buckingham Palace on the afternoon of Monday, December 4th, and submitted his resignation to King Edward VII.

CHAPTER TWO

FORMING A GOVERNMENT, DECEMBER 1905

"The storm signals are flying," wrote Asquith to Campbell-Bannerman on November 25th, "and everything points to an early break-up."[1] Sir Henry, however, was resting at his home at Belmont Castle in Scotland and remained in the north until absolutely certain that Balfour's resignation was imminent. Urgent telegrams requesting his immediate presence in London, sent by Morley and Gladstone, were placidly ignored. Not until the evening of December 3rd did Campbell-Bannerman leave Belmont Castle and he reached London early next morning, the Monday on which Balfour resigned.

There had been much anxious debate, during the previous two weeks, as to whether or not it would be wise to take office in the event of Balfour's resignation. Disraeli had refused to do so in 1873, when Gladstone resigned rather than seek a dissolution, and the latter had been obliged to return to office for another nine months with his position gravely weakened. Asquith, in the letter to Campbell-Bannerman quoted above, had made it plain that he was strongly opposed to accepting office under such conditions: "it is obviously right", he wrote, "that these people should themselves dissolve and the Liberal Party should not be compelled to form a Government until the country has given its decision and the composition of the new Parliament is ascertained."* Gladstone agreed, but Campbell-Bannerman was not convinced and sought the opinion of Lord Ripon, the party's chief representative in the Upper House since the illness of Lord Spencer. "Many of our people," he wrote on November 25th, "appear to be impressed with the disadvantage of accepting office after a resignation. Anyone can see that there would be inconveniences, and that as a mere move in the party game it would be clever to refuse. But it seems to me that these inconveniences would be outweighed by the damping effect on

---

* This was also (not surprisingly) Grey's view. Resignation, instead of dissolution, obviously threw a spanner into the works so far as the Relugas plan of campaign was concerned.[2]

our fighting men throughout the country, when after all our clamour we invited the Government to retain office."[3] Ripon, replying three days later, agreed that refusal to take office would be inconsistent with past attitudes, and thought that it might lead to "entanglements even worse than those with which we have now to deal." There was a chance that if Sir Henry declined to form a Government the King would send for Lansdowne or Chamberlain. The game of refusal, moreover, could only be played once. If Balfour resumed office, was defeated on the Address and resigned yet again, Sir Henry would be obliged to accept the premiership. A second refusal would not be fair either to the country or the King— "H.M. might justly complain that you were leaving him in the lurch and might conceive a strong dislike to the Liberals in consequence."[4]

Ripon's reply was probably a decisive factor in helping Campbell-Bannerman to reach his decision. There was also the possibility, albeit a remote one, that the King would send for Rosebery if Sir Henry declined to take office. "By all I see," wrote the latter to Gladstone on November 30th, "I am rather confirmed in my opinion of what we must do. This R[osebery] thing gives strength to the argument, for it would be said we could not agree and therefore could not form a Government."*[5]

Sir Henry, on his arrival in London, was driven straight to his home, No. 29 Belgrave Square. Morley was one of his first visitors, followed shortly by Lord Tweedmouth and Gladstone. Grey called after lunch and Asquith arrived a little while later, both offering Campbell-Bannerman their cordial support in any attempt he might make to form a Government. Sir Henry noted that they seemed "very amiable and reasonable on the subject of Ireland"[7] and they parted on friendly terms.† A little while later an emissary arrived from Rosebery in the person of J. A. Spender, editor of *The Westminster Gazette*. His lordship was now anxious to make amends for the awkwardness caused by his Bodmin speech and Spender explained that he was prepared to issue a public statement on the Irish question if Sir Henry would only meet him half-way. Campbell-Bannerman, wrote Spender many years later, "twinkled all over, as only C.B. could twinkle, and after some moments of apparent reflection delivered

---

* Cf. Bryce to Gladstone (December 2nd): "On the whole I incline to the view that the balance of argument is for accepting, and fancy somehow this is coming to be the general view. There are no doubt great inconveniences in taking the reins now, but with such opponents we can't tell what sort of a game might be played if we let them have a fresh start. Any harm the recent incident has caused seems to be passing off. It may have lost us a few Unionist 'waverers', but it has rather brought all Liberals into line behind C. B." Morley and McKenna (but not Harcourt) also counselled acceptance.[6]

† Morley had reported to Campbell-Bannerman on November 25th that Grey still thought Asquith ought to lead in the Commons, in which case "they supposed that *I* should wish to be C[hancellor] of E[xchequer]," but did "not press for F.O."[8]

his ultimatum: 'Will you please tell Lord Rosebery that within two hours from now I expect to have accepted the King's commission to form a Government, and that being so I can obviously say no more about the Irish question until I have had an opportunity of consulting my colleagues."9 Rosebery was thus placed gently but firmly to one side: his views had ceased to be relevant to the situation.

The hours slipped by, and eventually a letter arrived from Lord Knollys (the King's secretary) informing Sir Henry that Balfour had resigned and inviting him to call at the Palace the following morning. There was no doubt as to what such an invitation implied nor was there now any question of not taking office. All was not well, however, for at ten o'clock that evening Grey returned to Belgrave Square and bluntly announced that he would be unable to serve under Sir Henry unless the latter transferred both himself and his leadership to the House of Lords. He was, he explained, very reluctant to enter any Government of which Rosebery was not a member and could only do so if the leadership of the Commons were entrusted to Asquith. Sir Henry replied that he had no intention of leaving the Commons, at any rate not for a year or two. "We parted quite cordially," wrote Grey to his wife later that night; "he took my really outrageous (from me to him) proposal in perfect temper and said very nice things." He wrote to Asquith at the same time, warning him not to risk his personal position more than he thought absolutely necessary, since "C.B. gave me the impression that he was quite prepared to form a Government without any of us. . . . I shan't think it in the least wrong of you to go in."*10

Asquith himself called at Belgrave Square the following morning. He found Campbell-Bannerman "rather smarting" from Grey's remarks and did his best to smooth things over. He pointed out that, quite apart from anything else, Sir Henry (who was almost seventy) would find the task of leading the Commons and being Prime Minister a fearful labour, since they were practically the jobs of two men. The House of Lords, on the other hand, was without a leader and no one could possibly accuse him of deserting the battlefield at a crucial moment if he accepted a peerage.12 "The impression left on me," he wrote to Grey, "was that he would not be indisposed to yield, if something in the nature of a golden bridge could be constructed for him. Do you think you could do anything in that direction?"13

* He also wrote to Campbell-Bannerman, thanking him "for having listened so patiently and kindly to what I had to say this evening. It was not only difficult but very disagreeable for me to say it, but . . . [it is] really vital to me that under present conditions Asquith should lead in the House of Commons."11

Campbell-Bannerman left for his interview at the Palace in a very worried frame of mind. It was intolerable that, after all the stresses and strains he had withstood since 1899, an attempt should be made—now that the promised land was finally in sight—to bundle him off to the House of Lords. If he gave way the Government would cease to be his own administration except in name, yet if he remained in the Commons it seemed that at least two of the leading lights of the party would refuse to take office. Asquith's arguments, moreover, were not altogether unreasonable, and later that week a letter would arrive from his doctor making precisely the same point about the inadvisability of accepting a double burden. For the moment, however, he would reconcile himself to the idea of managing without Grey's services, and later that day a telegram was sent to Lord Cromer (then in Cairo) offering him the Foreign Office.

The invitation to form a Government was duly accepted, but King Edward—whose support for the Relugas Compact had been enlisted by Haldane—jovially exclaimed "We are not as young as we were, Sir Henry!" and reiterated the suggestion that he should go to the House of Lords. Campbell-Bannerman replied that he would prefer starting in the Commons, if only for a short time. This idea seemed to appeal to the King and the interview came to an apparent end. Sir Henry, knowing that he ought to kiss hands on his appointment as Prime Minister, advanced and waited expectantly. The King murmured something and Sir Henry advanced towards him yet again, intending to kneel. The King, however, said nothing but clasped him warmly by the hand, at which Sir Henry concluded that the interview was over. He was assured by Knollys, however, that all would be put right in the official record, and returned home to begin the task of officially forming a Government.[14]

A telegram arrived from Cromer, the following day, declining the Foreign Office on the grounds of ill health. Grey, intent upon the construction of "a golden bridge" in response to Asquith's appeal, had meanwhile returned to the idea that Haldane should become Lord Chancellor. On November 13th, as we have seen, Asquith had pressed Haldane's claim to the Woolsack on Campbell-Bannerman and had added, in a letter dated November 25th, that Sir Robert Reid (the other candidate) would make an admirable Home Secretary. Grey now suggested that, in addition to becoming Lord Chancellor, Haldane should be entrusted with the leadership of the Upper House. Asquith called on Campbell-Bannerman and put forward this alternative proposal, but Sir Henry declared that the Woolsack was definitely reserved for Reid and refused to give way.* Asquith then took the bull by the horns. "It is no use going over the ground again, my dear C.B.," he exclaimed. "I make a personal appeal to you, which I've never done before; I urge you to go to the House of Lords and solve this difficulty."[16]

Campbell-Bannerman said, after wavering, that his wife was arriving from Scotland that night and that he would abide by her decision, whatever it might be. In the event, his wife's advice—"No surrender!"—was brisk and decisive, and Sir Henry's self-confidence and cheerful spirits came flooding back. Everything was going to be all right! At breakfast next day (December 7th) he told his secretary of the decision. "I don't often make up my mind, Sinclair," he announced, "but I've done it now— I shan't go to the Lords."[17] Asquith arrived soon afterwards. Sir Henry, he noted, "looked white and upset and began like a man who, having taken the plunge, meant to make the best of it. He spoke in a rapid, rather cheerful and determined manner: 'I'm going to stick to the Commons, Asquith, so will you go and tell Grey he may have the Foreign Office and Haldane the War Office."[18] There was no more to be said. Asquith at last agreed to become Chancellor of the Exchequer and, leaving Sir Henry at 11.30, called upon Grey to inform him of what had taken place. Grey, however, still refused to enter the Government, since both his conditions had been rejected.†

Asquith returned to Belgrave Square, where a meeting of the embryo Cabinet was in progress. Various candidates for the Foreign Office were discussed, including Lord Crewe, Lord Burghclere and Lord Edmond Fitzmaurice, but no decision had been reached when the meeting ended at 1.30‡ Asquith later sent a note to Campbell-Bannerman stating that, on the regrettable assumption that both his and Grey's decisions were irrevocable, "Crewe seems to me for many reasons the best man for the F.O.,"[19] while Morley (in effect) urged Sir Henry to make another attempt to enlist Grey's services. "The more I think of it," Morley declared, "the more I am *dismayed* at the prospect of either L[ord] B[urghclere] or L[ord] C[rewe]. So far as the public goes, they are not well known; they have had no experience; and they are as yet lightweights. It is quite true that Grey is grossly overrated, and that he would be a doubtful diplomatist. Still, his name stands high—and you lose something

* "Asquith has told me of his talk with you," wrote Morley to Campbell-Bannerman later that day. "The 'new suggestion' did not strike me as brilliant."[15]

† He wrote to Campbell-Bannerman reaffirming his decision. This letter is quoted on page 346.

‡ Campbell-Bannerman eventually offered Burghclere the post of Under-Secretary. The latter accepted, but made so many stipulations as to the conditions on which he was to hold office (i.e., being accorded full Cabinet status) that the offer was withdrawn.

[otherwise] in the public weight of your Cabinet. If you fill his place by people of such second-rate public position as B. or C. it will be a heavy handicapping for us. ... You will not misunderstand my motive. My anxiety is wholly impersonal."[20]

"A possible solution to this tangle" was meanwhile put forward by Gladstone, who wrote to Sir Henry urging him to persuade Sir Arthur Acland, a man who held "more sway" over Grey and Haldane "than anyone except R. himself", to "bring these men to their bearings at the eleventh hour."[21] Acland, a much respected senior member of the Liberal Party who had left the Commons in 1899 on the grounds of ill health, could be offered the Board of Education or a peerage and the leadership of the House of Lords in return for his services. Gladstone had been in touch with Sir Arthur but he did not know that Acland had already declined any position in the new administration. Sir Henry did not pay much attention to Gladstone's suggestion, but Acland was destined, as we shall see, to play an important part in the drama now unfolding.

Haldane, late that afternoon, was presiding at a meeting in Kensington when two letters were brought to him, the first from Asquith and the second from Campbell-Bannerman. The former was apologetic but firm. Asquith explained that, despite Campbell-Bannerman's refusal to give way over the Woolsack or the leadership of the Commons, he had reached the painful conclusion that it was his duty to take office in the new administration. If he refused to go in the attempt to form a Government would either be abandoned (which did not seem likely) or it would be a weak body composed largely of "Little Englanders". In either event, victory at the polls would be imperilled. "I could not say," he wrote, ". . . that our group had been flouted, and the only ground I could take would be that I and not C.B. must from the first lead the new House of Commons. I could not to my own conscience or to the world justify such a position. If the elections were over, and Free Trade secure, different considerations would arise." He had been authorised to offer the Foreign Office to Grey and an offer of the War Office would soon be on its way to Haldane. "I need not say," he concluded, "what an enormous and immeasurable difference your co-operation would make to me."[22] Campbell-Bannerman's letter, which was much shorter, made no direct reference to the War Office. It contained an offer of the post of Attorney-General (involving what were "practically Cabinet reponsibilities though not Cabinet rank") but added that "if I am under a misapprehension as to your desires . . . I shall gladly make to you a proposition of a different nature which would bring you into the Cabinet."[23]

After the meeting Haldane called on Lady Horner, an old friend and confidante, to ask her advice. Lady Horner declared that—for the sake of both the King and the cause of Free Trade—it was his duty to enter the Government. Pleasantly encouraged by these sentiments, Haldane returned home to his flat in Whitehall Court, which he reached at six o'clock. "There I found Grey reposing on the sofa," he wrote later, "with the air of one who had taken a decision and was done with political troubles. But I put before him the thoughts which were passing through my mind, especially about resisting Protection. Were we not thinking too much of ourselves and too little of the public? . . . It was now about seven o'clock and we had promised to call on Acland at about half past seven. Grey gave his answer to these fresh points, but he was obviously troubled and he said, 'Let us walk to Acland's rooms and consider as we go along.' He added, 'You are not as clear as you were that we are right.' I replied that I was as clear as ever from a personal point. My doubt was whether we had sufficiently considered the ethical question. . . . There could be no question of either of us entering without the other. He was much troubled: I think he felt that we were acting somewhat selfishly."[24]

When they reached Acland's flat, however, Grey announced to their host that he had finally burnt his boats so far as entering the Government was concerned and Haldane said that he too had decided to stay out. "For a moment or two," writes Acland, who had promised Gladstone that he would do all he could to make them change their minds, "I considered whether I could say anything as it seemed hopeless—it was dinner-time and they were both weary of the subject. However, I began and Grey said 'What is the use? I have finally and absolutely closed the door.' I said I thought he was bound at least to listen to an old friend for a short time. After I had poured in all the gems that were in my battery they both promised to go away and think over what I had said."[25] Grey and Haldane left Acland soon after eight and dined in a private room at the Café Royal. Grey was now very uncertain what to do for the best and Haldane was careful to let his companion make the first move. "If we enter," said Grey at last, "it is not for pleasure's sake and we must take the most beastly things. I will take the War Office."[26] This was as good an admission of defeat as could be expected and Haldane quickly took advantage of it. He pointed out that the public interest demanded that Grey should have the Foreign Office and that he himself should take the War Office. "I will not do so unless you come into the Cabinet," protested Grey.[27] This was all that was needed. Leaving his companion still at dinner Haldane hurried out of the Café Royal, hired a hansom and in next to no time was at Belgrave Square asking to see Campbell-Bannerman. "I found that he was dining alone with his wife," writes Haldane. "I said I would wait for him in his study—he came at once. I asked him whether he still wanted Grey. He said he did indeed, but that G[rey] was very difficult. I replied that possibly I might help to bring G[rey] in. I had not answered his letter to myself, but that I could do so now. I did not want to be Attorney-General. He then offered me the Home Office. I said, 'What about the War Office?' 'Nobody,' answered C.B., 'will touch it with a pole.'* 'Then give it to me,' I replied; 'I will come as Secretary if Grey takes the Foreign Office, and I will ask him to call on you early tomorrow to tell you his decision, which may, I think, be favourable.' "28 Leaving Campbell-Bannerman, Haldane hurriedly scribbled a note to Asquith. "I have talked the matter over with E.G.," he wrote, "and have induced him to reconsider his position. . . . He is to see C.B. in the morning. My decision will follow his after he has seen C.B."29

Acland's account of Haldane's interview with Campbell-Bannerman is slightly different. While he himself has been informing Gladstone (via Spender) of the latest position, "Haldane had been by agreement with Grey to C.B. to say they were both really thinking it over and might the door be kept open till the next morning? Haldane was received in a very friendly spirit by C.B. and returned from there straight to my flat and told me what had taken place and that they really were seriously thinking over what I had said. In a few minutes, about 10.45, Grey arrived and said at once to me 'I have been thinking it all over since Haldane left me and I have come to the definite conclusion that you are *wrong*.' I then had to begin all over again and after about three-quarters of an hour he admitted that I had won and said about 11.30 p.m., 'I will go and see C.B. after breakfast tomorrow.' "30

The Relugas Compact was no more. That such an extraordinary agreement had ever been concluded in the first place was due, in fact, simply and solely to the driving force of Haldane, whose eloquence had borne down his colleagues' defences with no great difficulty. The need to keep faith with Rosebery and each other, to stand firm on Liberal League principles and not allow themselves to be swallowed up in a "Little Englander" administration were powerful shots from his armoury, and neither Asquith nor Grey felt strong enough to withstand them at the time. Asquith's enthusiasm for the scheme steadily decreased in the weeks that followed,

---

* He had offered it to Gladstone earlier that day. Since the Home Office had not been disposed of at the time of Haldane's visit it would seem that Gladstone (or Campbell-Bannerman) was waiting upon the course of events.

however, and his suggestion that Haldane should have the Woolsack was put forward as a compromise. Grey, although as stubborn as a mule once he had made up his mind to do something, was not a natural plotter and initially, in fact, he had offered greater resistance to the idea than Asquith. Haldane, on the other hand, was a born intriguer. The crucial factor in the whole situation was that Asquith and Grey were really indispensable for the success of any Government which Sir Henry might form, whereas Haldane's abilities were by no means so essential an ingredient.* He disliked Campbell-Bannerman and knew that the animosity was mutual. He thus hit upon the idea of bringing Asquith and Grey over to his side of the fence, so that it would seem that he was not alone in being separated from Campbell-Bannerman. His self-importance was the one thing for which he truly cared, yet it would suffer a horrid deflation if the other Vice-Presidents of the League were to be included in a Government from which he himself was excluded. The companionship in exile of Asquith and Grey was Haldane's insurance against not obtaining office.

When the invitation to Sir Henry to form a Government finally arrived, Asquith agreed, after a token hesitation, to sink his differences with Campbell-Bannerman.† Grey, however, who had no great desire to take office at all, had adopted a stance of passive resistance, in which he had been warmly supported by Haldane. Even the unsuspecting Sir Edward was mildly surprised by the latter's sublimity, since he was not yet "in the firing line",[33] and he never really understood how it was that he came to occupy the unpleasant position of chief opponent to Campbell-Bannerman.‡ The outcome of the situation must have been very satisfying for Haldane: he now assumed the role of martyr, agreeing to abandon (for the sake of Free Trade) his old pledge of holding aloof from the Government

---

* "The feeling against Haldane being in the Cabinet is *very strong* with our rank and file," Harcourt wrote to Campbell-Bannerman on December 5th. "I don't share it, though *I* have no reason to love him. Perhaps the K[ing] will want him somewhere in the inner circle."[31]

† He had taken good care to make himself as inaccessible as possible to Grey and Haldane while the crisis lasted. His earlier discussions with Campbell-Bannerman had made it extremely difficult for him to withdraw from the inner conclaves of the Liberal Party at this stage, and there is no real evidence to suggest that he wished to do so. "Asquith," Campbell-Bannerman told his old crony, Thomas Shaw, on December 8th, "was always uneasy: he walked back and forward . . . and said: 'Here we are, on every conceivable point of policy agreed, and yet somehow something wrong. Suppose I go down to my constituents, and they say to me: "Would you tell us, were you not asked to be in the Government?" and I reply, "I was." And then they say, "Did you not get a good enough offer?" and I reply, "Well, the fact is, I was offered the Chancellorship of the Exchequer!" And then they say, "What's wrong, then?" and I say, "Oh, but my leader was to be in the Commons!" How shall I look?' "[32]

‡ "Asquith's position is the more difficult and painful," Grey had written to his wife on December 6th, "but it seems to C.B. and the rest as if, had it not been for me, there would have been no difficulty. I am afraid they must think me a beast; in a way I feel one, but I am a beast in the right."[34]

and actually joining in the general chorus of advice to persuade Grey to accept the Foreign Office.* The feeling that he was sacrificing himself, even abandoning his hopes of the Woolsack, was evidently uppermost when Asquith wrote to him on December 8th, declaring that "by your action during the last two days you have laid the party and the country and myself (most of all) under an unmeasured debt of gratitude."[36] Haldane, far from being the villain of the piece, was treated as the hero! It was a most extraordinary outcome to a most extraordinary situation.

It is instructive, perhaps, to enquire why, in view of his earlier exchanges with Asquith about Haldane's suitability for the War Office, Campbell-Bannerman had found it necessary to offer him first the post of Attorney-General and then that of Home Secretary. The explanation seems to be that Sir Henry adopted a canny method of snaring his quarry: rather than make Haldane a direct offer of the War Office he had apparently tried to fob him off with posts of a lesser nature, thereby whetting his appetite for the fruit which was being withheld. Finally, by Haldane's own account, he was driven to the point of actually having to ask for the post. Campbell-Bannerman had, in fact, had him in mind for it since the beginning of December, "Lulu" Harcourt (Sir William's son) having reported that "the K[ing] thinks Haldane would do very well at the War Office. (So do I—and serve him right!)"[37] There is, moreover, the evidence of Lawson Walton who, anxiously waiting to hear whether he would be included in the Government, records that "nothing happened for some days, when suddenly I was summoned to Belgrave Square. Campbell-Bannerman said 'I have submitted your name to the King for Attorney-General, and do you know—I have got Haldane to take the War Office!' and he chuckled and chuckled."†[38]

Gladstone, at any rate, felt that Acland was the real hero of the piece, and (according to Acland himself) sent word to him via Spender, on the Thursday evening, that he was entitled to a post in the Cabinet and could claim, if he wished, the leadership of the Lords. Sir Arthur saw Gladstone the following morning, after Grey had agreed to take office, and was again told (so his own account runs) that he could have whatever post he liked. Acland said that he would call on Sir Henry that evening to see what proposals he had to make, but when he arrived at Belgrave Square he was left

* "Now that Grey has recognised his obligation," wrote Haldane to Campbell-Bannerman on December 8th in a typical mood of condescension, "he has accepted it very wholeheartedly, and in a spirit which would give you great satisfaction. . . . He has conveyed to me your offer of the War Office. This I accept, and will do all I can to serve you."[35]

† "I chose the War Office out of three different offices," Haldane told Beatrice Webb on December 14th. "Asquith, Grey and I stood together; they were forced to take us on our own terms. We were really very indifferent."[39]

"sitting, to speak metaphorically, on the doorstep," and did not see Campbell-Bannerman at all.[40] On December 10th Morley wrote to Gladstone asking him "to urge C.B. at once to send for Acland to thank him for his services in the matter of E.G. You told him that he deserved a 'stoup of gold'—quite true. Since then he has heard nothing from anybody and is, I think, considerably hurt. Something ought immediately to be said to him about H. of L., prospect of possible office, etc. (for some hint of that sort seems to have been dropped."[41] Gladstone did, in fact, urge Campbell-Bannerman to see Acland but failed to make the reason clear and Sir Henry did not realise for several days that he was supposed to be indebted to Sir Arthur. He eventually wrote to him on or about December 15th, and Acland (who had returned to his northern retreat) replied two days later, referring to the promises which he claimed Gladstone had made.[42] Gladstone, promptly taxed with these promises by Sir Henry, appears to have been genuinely astonished by this turn of events. "You got me into rare trouble with A.A. by not bringing off that interview with C.B.," he wrote to John Sinclair, Campbell-Bannerman's assistant private secretary, on December 28th, "although I urged it at every opportunity. A. will now nurse a grievance for the rest of his life. Of course I made him no such offer by Spender; still less did I make it myself. It is indeed odd that he entirely forgot that when I asked him if he was ready to accept Cabinet [office] in the Lords if it was offered he replied 'My health will not allow me to take Cabinet responsibility.' I have written to him and there the matter ends so far as I am concerned. . . . The fact remains that Acland himself saved the whole situation."[43]

The task of filling the other ministerial posts was comparatively easy. Morley became Secretary for India and Gladstone took the Home Office. Lloyd George, offered the choice between the Board of Trade and the Local Government Board, accepted the former while making it plain (in conversation with Harcourt on December 5th) that he would rather have liked to be Home Secretary.*[44] Lord Elgin, after obtaining an assurance that Home Rule did not form part of the Government's immediate programme, agreed to become Secretary for the Colonies and Crewe was made

---

* "Board of Trade with a seat in the Cabinet. . .," wrote Lloyd George to his brother on December 8th. "I am delighted. . . . Winston and McKenna think I have got the most important post of all in the Ministry at this juncture. I asked for pledges about education and the extension of self-government for Wales—and got both." Some accounts state that he had also been offered the Postmaster-Generalship but had accepted the Board of Trade because this would (despite a smaller salary) give him wider administrative scope. "He attaches great importance to being in some office which brings him into contact with Wales," Harcourt had noted on December 5th. According to McKenna, Campbell-Bannerman's initial views on Lloyd George had been "I suppose we ought to include him."[45]

Lord President of the Council. Churchill, who had personal and much-publicised experience of South African affairs, became Under-Secretary for the Colonies after declining the post of Financial Secretary to the Treasury (which went to Reginald McKenna) and Augustine Birrell accepted the presidency of the Board of Education. An amusing incident occurred when Campbell-Bannerman offered John Burns, one of the most strident of early Socialists, the presidency of the Local Government Board. "Naturally," said Sir Henry later, "I expected him to be somewhat overpowered by the announcement. But to my surprise, he seemed to think that the obligation was on my side. 'Bravo, Sir Henry!' he said, slapping me on the back. 'Bravo! This is the most popular thing you have yet done!'"[46]

The final list of appointments ran as follows:

The Cabinet

Sir Henry Campbell-Bannerman: First Lord of the Treasury
Earl Loreburn (Sir Robert Reid): Lord Chancellor
Marquess of Ripon: Lord Privy Seal
Herbert H. Asquith: Chancellor of the Exchequer
Sir Edward Grey: Foreign Secretary
Earl of Elgin: Colonial Secretary
John Morley: Secretary for India
Herbert Gladstone: Home Secretary
Richard Haldane: Secretary for War
Lord Tweedmouth: First Lord of the Admiralty
John Sinclair: Secretary for Scotland
Sir Henry Fowler: Chancellor of the Duchy of Lancaster
Earl of Crewe: Lord President of the Council
David Lloyd George: President of the Board of Trade
John Burns: President of the Local Government Board
Earl Carrington: President of the Board of Agriculture
Augustine Birrell: President of the Board of Education
James Bryce: Chief Secretary for Ireland
Sydney Buxton: Postmaster-General

Earl of Aberdeen: Lord Lieutenant of Ireland
Lord Justice Walker: Lord Chancellor of Ireland
Lewis Harcourt: First Commissioner of Works
Reginald McKenna: Financial Secretary to the Treasury

J. A. Pease ⎤
Herbert Lewis   ⎫ Junior Lords
F. Freeman-Thomas ⎬ of the Treasury
Cecil Norton   ⎭
R. K. Causton: Paymaster-General
Lord Edmond Fitzmaurice: Under-Secretary for Foreign Affairs
Winston Churchill: Under-Secretary for the Colonies
J. E. Ellis: Under-Secretary for India
Earl of Portsmouth: Under-Secretary for War
T. R. Buchanan: Financial Secretary to the War Office
George Lambert: Civil Lord of the Admiralty
Edmund Robertson: Secretary to the Admiralty
Herbert Samuel: Under-Secretary at the Home Office
H. E. Kearly: Secretary to the Board of Trade.*
Walter Runciman: Secretary to the Local Government Board
T. Lough: Parliamentary Secretary to the Board of Education
Sir J. Lawson Walton: Attorney-General
Sir W. S. Robson: Solicitor-General
Thomas Shaw: Lord Advocate
Alexander Ure: Solicitor-General
R. R. Cherry: Attorney-General for Ireland
Redmond Barry: Solicitor-General for Ireland

The composition of the new Government received acclamation from virtually every quarter, being generally regarded as a new "Ministry of All the Talents", and one well deserving of success. Rosebery made another petulant outburst on Ireland, in which he stated that he could not retreat from the principles proclaimed in his Bodmin speech, but no one really minded what he said any more and his effect on public opinion was negligible. Campbell-Bannerman had accepted the challenge flung down by Balfour, had stood firm against the Relugas triumvirate and had emerged as the true and undisputed leader of the Liberal Party. His Government was, by the standards both of that time and this, one of the most distinguished, not to say formidable, which has ever taken office: once a good working majority had been secured at the polls there seemed no reason why it should not go down in history as one of the greatest.

---

* "A first-rate businessman," wrote Lloyd George to his brother on December 11th, "but a poor speaker. Just the man for me."[47]

CHAPTER THREE

THE LIBERAL TRIUMPH,
DECEMBER 1905–JANUARY 1906

(1)

At noon on Monday, December 11th the out-going Ministers surrendered their seals of office and a few hours later the members of the new Government arrived at Buckingham Palace to kiss hands on their appointments. Dense fog had descended and the brougham carrying Grey, Haldane and Fowler from the Palace was obliged to halt in the Mall. Haldane, always intrepid, ventured forth and lost contact with the others. He found his way with difficulty to the War Office (then situated in Pall Mall) and clumped his muddy way into the building, much to the astonishment of the officials awaiting his arrival.[1] Grey, in the meantime, had been hopefully groping his way around the circular hoarding which surrounded the half-completed Victoria Memorial and almost an hour had passed before he found his way to the Foreign Office. Fowler, the least adventurous of the trio, remained in the brougham, which eventually returned to the Palace. John Burns, scorning such undemocratic aids to travel, walked briskly to the Palace under his own steam, where he was greeted with a feeble cheer from the little group of bystanders who waited at the gates. It was not an auspicious inauguration of the new Government, but that night Campbell-Bannerman gave a dinner party which no doubt helped to alleviate some of the distress. Rosebery, not to be outdone, gave a reception of his own, to which several of Sir Henry's guests slipped off later in the evening.

Ten days later, addressing an army of enthusiastic supporters at the Albert Hall, Campbell-Bannerman fired off a preliminary salvo in the election campaign. It was an occasion which had been eagerly awaited and the members of his Government turned out in force to give him full moral and vocal support. In the event, however, it proved a disappointing performance. Sir Henry, perhaps recalling the reception which had greeted Gladstone's "Newcastle programme" of 1891, devoted most of his speech

22

to an uninspired attack upon Balfour's administration. His own Government, it appeared, would stop the importation of Chinese labour into South Africa, continue the *Entente Cordiale*, tap fresh sources of revenue for domestic reforms and prepare Ireland for eventual Home Rule. His election address, issued on January 8th, was equally uninformative. This too began with an attack on Balfour's Government, went on to condemn Tariff Reform and then took refuge in a host of vague promises. Only too clearly, Sir Henry was feeling his way with great caution. "Our own policy," he wrote, "is well known to you and I need not here repeat the terms of the public declaration which it fell to me to make shortly after assuming office. Should we be confirmed in office it will be our duty, whilst holding fast to the time-honoured principles of Liberalism—the principles of peace, economy, self-government and civil and religious liberty—and whilst resisting with all our strength the attack upon Free Trade, to repair so far as lies in our power the mischief wrought in recent years and, by a course of strenuous legislation and administration, to secure those social and economic reforms which have been too long delayed. As to the spirit in which foreign affairs will be conducted, it is satisfactory to be able to say that, by renouncing those undesirable characteristics which we formerly detected in their foreign policy, the Unionist Party have made it possible for us to pursue a substantial continuity of policy without departing from the friendly and unprovocative methods which, under Liberal Governments in the past, have determined the relations of Great Britain with her neighbours."

The Times thought it "a very remarkable document," declaring that all of it, "except an introductory sentence or two at the beginning and some twenty lines at the end, is devoted to a diffuse and inaccurate review of the acts of the late Government." Chamberlain, speaking in Birmingham on January 10th, declared that there was no more elusive phantom in the world than the Radical party at the present time. Something strange had come over them all. In all the verbiage of the Prime Minister's election address they would find only one single definite statement and that was the sentence where Sir Henry said he was going to continue the foreign policy of his predecessor. Upon all positive matters the Prime Minister was suddenly silent. Balfour, on the same day, remarked that the Radicals had not agreed upon a programme of reform and that their addresses were sadly out of step with one another. In his own manifesto, however, he noted that "Home Rule, disestablishment, the destruction of voluntary schools and the spoliation of the licence-holder have lost none of their ancient charms in the eyes of Radical law-makers."

(2)

It is as well, at this point, to take stock of the issues at stake in the general election of 1906. The first, and greatest, was Tariff Reform. The Unionist Party were, of course, hotly divided over Chamberlain's crusade for Imperial Preference, although they struggled hard to present a unified front. The Liberals meanwhile trotted out their standard Free Trade slogans and took full advantage of their opponents' embarrassment, claiming that Chamberlain's proposals would simply mean dearer food for the home consumer. "To hold our own," declared Asquith in his manifesto to the electors of East Fife, "our first necessity is to keep an open market here and to secure from every possible source a cheap and abundant supply of food and raw material."

The second was "Chinese slavery". At the end of 1905 the number of labourers on the Rand amounted to 47,218 and another 1,949 were on their way .The Liberal Party, much to the indignation of their opponents, gave this issue the full treatment. "What would you say," exclaimed Lloyd George, "to introducing Chinamen at a shilling a day into the Welsh quarries? Slavery on the hills of Wales!" In some places, in order to drive the point home beyond any shadow of doubt, there were processions of sandwich-board men linked together and dressed as coolies. It was revealed, moreover, that Lord Milner, who had only recently ceased to be High Commissioner of South Africa, had raised no objection to "slight corporal punishment of Chinese coolies," despite the fact that explicit assurances had been given to the Chinese Government that none of the labourers would be flogged without the approval of the Supreme Court. "For one seat lost by Tariff Reform," said Chamberlain on January 18th, "ten have been lost by libels and baseless stories about Chinese labour," and Balfour, writing to Lord Stanley on January 27th, remarked that "you probably had the same experience that I had, namely that the constituency did not the least want to argue any question at all except Chinese labour."[2]

The third issue, as yet little more than a tiny speck on the Liberal horizon, was Home Rule for Ireland. Campbell-Bannerman, while making it clear that, if the Liberals were returned to power, this matter would be held in abeyance until another appeal had been made to the nation, had nevertheless declared that "the opportunity of making a great advance on the question of Irish government will not be long delayed." Even Haldane had plumped for Home Rule on a "step by step" basis. The Unionists made what they could of this, but the subject as a whole did not attract much attention.

The fourth issue ought, by rights, to have been domestic reforms, but the Liberals were far from clear in their own minds what they intended to do in this field. The Education Act of 1902 would certainly have to be amended and fresh licensing proposals would have to be introduced, but beyond this point all was doubt and confusion. Campbell-Bannerman had referred to "those social and economic reforms which have been so long delayed" but refrained from specifying them, while Burns, at the other extreme, advocated abolition of the House of Lords, payment of M.P.s and full adult and female suffrage.* Grey came nearest to a comprehensive declaration of policy and even he was somewhat unsure of himself. "Higher education needs encouragement," he wrote, "the licensing system, the land question, especially as regards site values in large towns, and other matters, need reform and attention."

These, then, were the issues upon which the general election of 1906 was fought, but whether they were the issues upon which it was won is quite a different matter. It is doubtful whether "Chinese slavery" and the bogeys conjured up by Tariff Reform influenced the electorate to any significant extent. People voted against the Unionists because Balfour's administration had shown itself incapable of managing the nation's affairs and not because they were impressed by the vague policies of the Liberal Party. There was a general desire for new men at the helm and Campbell-Bannerman's Government was unlikely, at the very least, to be any worse than that which had preceded it. Many working-class voters, moreover, were convinced that the Unionists (despite the Royal Commission which Balfour had appointed) had no intention of trying to improve the legal status of trade unions.†

(3)

On January 8th Parliament was dissolved and the election campaigns got properly under way. The Conservatives sallied forth into battle almost gaily. They expected to lose but they were confident that the Liberal

---

* The King (January 7th) expressed surprise at Burns's declaration about the House of Lords. Sir Henry admitted, in reply, that this was "the worst of the abrupt appointment of men to the Cabinet without serving an apprenticeship in subordinate office," and took care to mention that he had had "two or three cases of want of discretion already from the 'novi homines', including the Secretary of State for War."[3]

† The Taff Vale judgment, which did more than anything else to increase the rate of affiliations to the Labour Representation Committee (see page 59), was the outcome of a dispute between the Taff Vale Railway Company and the Amalgamated Society of Railway Servants. The House of Lords ruled in 1901 that the union should pay the company £23,000 (including costs) in respect of damages caused by a strike the previous year. A union's funds, it seemed, were no longer protected, and this judgment—together with a similar one the same month and two more the following year—made it clear that the battles of the 1870s would have to be fought all over again.

majority would not be a large one. The 1900 House of Commons had consisted of 402 Unionists, 188 Liberals and 80 Nationalists. Joseph Chamberlain thought that the Liberal majority would not be more than eighty while the *Daily Mail*, on December 27th, made the following forecast: "Conservatives and Unionists, 247; Liberals 297; Labour (including Lib-Labs) 35; Nationalists 81."*

A general election, in the days before 1918, did not take place on a single day but was fought out over several weeks. Ipswich, on January 12th, was the first town to go to the polls and it was promptly captured by the Liberals. On the following day Lancashire held its elections and the startling result was a pointer as to the general course the contest would take. Twenty-nine seats out of a total of 56 fell to the Liberals, 12 to Labour candidates and 1 to a Nationalist, leaving the Unionists with 14. Manchester, possessing 9 seats of which only 1 had been Liberal, had both Balfour and Churchill among its candidates and attention was keenly focused on the great battle for supremacy. Balfour had represented the East division since 1885 but Churchill, relinquishing his claim to Oldham's affections and fighting the North-west division, was taking something of a risk. To charges that he had "ratted" on his old colleagues he was almost embarrassingly frank in his replies. "I admit that I have changed my party," he declared. "I don't deny it. I am proud of it. When I think of all the labours which Lord Randolph Churchill gave to the fortunes of the Conservative Party and the ungrateful way he was treated by them when they obtained what they would never have had but for him, I am delighted that circumstances have enabled me to break with them while I am still young and still have the first energies of my life to give to the popular cause."†

Manchester went to the polls on January 13th and early that evening the results were announced: Winston was in and Balfour was out. All the nine seats had been captured by Liberals. Balfour took his defeat calmly, but Churchill was in his seventh heaven. "Do Protectionists think," he demanded at the Reform Club that night, "that after sixty years Manchester cannot tell truth from falsehood and has forgotten the work of Cobden and Bright or that Lancashire is asleep and would be false to her traditions?

---

* "What the electors will do next month no one knows," wrote Haldane to Rosebery on December 19th. "I do not think much will be heard of Home Rule except from the other side . . . A narrow majority would be a great curse."[4]

† He was, at this time, receiving the plaudits of the Press for his biography of his father, and with the completion of *Lord Randolph Churchill* he succeeded in working off much of the resentment which had accrued during the previous ten years. His father's spirit had at last been avenged: honour was satisfied, and the young Hamlet need no longer fear the reproaches of a paternal ghost.

We have given the new Government a splendid send-off and the Liberal army will march on without pause to a complete triumph."

"Happy and brilliant Winston!" exclaimed Grey when he heard the news. "I still can't believe that everything will go like this."[5] From now onwards, however, nothing could halt the great Liberal advance. Seats which had long been staunchly Conservative capitulated at the first blast of the trumpet. Heads rolled in the dust and cries of anguish were heard amidst the ruins. Young men who had never expected to taste the fruits of victory were swept into power on the crest of a wave. The Unionist candidate at Peterborough, Sir Robert Purvis, was attacked by a large crowd and rolled in the mud while Sir J. F. L. Rolleston, the "much respected" Conservative candidate at Leicester, was dragged from his car and stoned by an angry mob. Among the prominent Unionists who lost their seats were Balfour, his brother Gerald, Sir Charles Dalrymple, Lord Hugh Cecil, Alfred Lyttleton, St John Broderick, Henry Chaplin and Bonar Law. Walter Long was defeated at Bristol but managed to get elected for Dublin County. Stanley Baldwin, fighting his first contest, failed to get in at Kidderminster.* "What a smash!" wrote Chamberlain to Mrs Asquith on the 23rd. "For once I was quite out in my estimate."[6]

Campbell-Bannerman, who had been returned unopposed for Stirling, rushed about the country making excited little speeches of joy, while Lloyd George, issuing his election address to Caernarvon Boroughs on the 16th, proclaimed that "the startling electoral results already recorded show how deeply the people of this country resent the mismanagement of their affairs and perversion of their confidence. ... The Minister mainly responsible for the misgovernment of the last few years, and the men who aided and abetted him therein, have been swept away by the electors." The manifesto, breathing avid nationalism, ended with the declaration that "the turn of Wales has come!" The turn had also come, it appeared, for master Richard Lloyd George to make his first public speech, which was brief and explicit. "I have nothing to say," he stated, "except to ask you all to vote for my father next Saturday." This request was received with loud cheers.

On January 19th, when the borough contests were almost at an end, the county elections began. These were a little kinder to the Unionists, but they still sustained heavy losses. In England 74 Liberals and 60 Unionists were returned, in Scotland 35 Liberals and 4 Unionists and in Wales the Liberals gained control of all 19 seats. On the side of the Government were

---

* He subsequently succeeded his father as M.P. for the Bewdley Division of Worcestershire in February 1908.

377 Liberals, 53 Labour members and 83 Irish Nationalists. The Opposition consisted of 132 Conservatives and 25 Liberal Unionists. The Government's majority thus amounted to 356, while the Liberal Party's alone was 129. Such a parliamentary majority has not been seen since the days of the younger Pitt. Small wonder that a force of this magnitude aroused consternation and awe in the ranks of the Tories! Small wonder that the House of Lords began to emerge from the comfortable stupor in which it had functioned for so long and take alarm at these dreadful happenings! It was, in many ways, a repetition of those exciting days of 1830, with Lansdowne and Balfour taking the place of Wellington and Peel and the prospect of Home Rule for Ireland taking the place of the 1832 Reform Bill. Balfour, speaking at Nottingham on January 15th, had already declared that it was the duty of everyone to see that "the great Unionist Party should still control, whether in power or whether in Opposition, the destinies of this great Empire." Once again, as will be seen in the pages which follow, a constitutional crisis of the greatest importance was about to open.

"I am keeping an analysis of the composition of our party up to date," wrote Gladstone to Campbell-Bannerman on January 21st. "The most striking thing about it is the preponderance of the 'centre' Liberals. There is no sign of any *violent* forward movement in opinion. In other words, apart from the extreme group of Labour men, the party as a whole seems to me to be more homogenous than in 1885 and '92. The only Whigs I can discover are D. Davies of Montgomeryshire (invited to stand by both parties!) and Eddy Tenant. There are some excellent young enthusiasts like Masterman. The dangerous element does not amount to a dozen."[7]

(4)

One of the most significant features of the new situation was the emergence of the Labour Party, the child of the Reform Acts of 1867 and 1884 and, to some extent, of the Education Act of 1870.* The total number of

---

* Balfour in particular was very preoccupied with this new phenomenon, which served as a welcome distraction from the plight of his own party, and he went out of his way to draw attention to it in a batch of letters which he wrote on January 17th. "I am horribly ashamed at feeling a kind of illegitimate exhilaration at the catastrophe which has occurred," he told Lady Salisbury. ". . . If I read the signs aright, what has occurred has nothing whatever to do with any of the things we have been squabbling over the last few years. C.B. is a mere cork, dancing on a torrent which he cannot control, and what is going on here is a faint echo of the same movement which has produced massacres in St Petersburg, riots in Vienna and Socialist processions in Berlin." Austen Chamberlain was informed that this probably heralded "the break-up of the Liberal Party" and Knollys learned that the general election had inaugurated a new era. "I never doubted," wrote Balfour to Lord Stanley on January 27th, "that your defeat was due to *Labour*."[8]

Labour members elected is generally reckoned as 53, but it is important to note that only 29 of them, a group which included Keir Hardie, Ramsay MacDonald, Philip Snowden, Arthur Henderson and J. R. Clynes, had been sponsored by the Labour Representation Committee (the L.R.C.).* The other 24, although describing themselves as Labour, were mainly miners' representatives who viewed the advent of the Labour Party, as it soon came to be called, with distrust. They had been known in the past as "Lib-Labs" and the oldest of them, Thomas Burt, had been present in the Commons since 1874. Fourteen of them would, however, be taking their seats for the first time and the sudden swelling of their ranks was generally regarded as part of the overall "Labour revolution".

The triumph of the Labour Party in this election was not a fluke but it was not, on the other hand, due simply and solely to its own efforts. The whole affair had been carefully stage-managed by MacDonald, the L.R.C.'s secretary, and Gladstone. It had been agreed (after negotiations which had begun in 1903) that 30 candidates put forward by the L.R.C. should not be opposed by Liberals.† Twenty-four of these were victorious, while only 3 of the 15 who faced Liberal as well as Conservative opponents were returned. Gladstone, in an undated memorandum, noted that preparation for the election "apart from routine was specially concerned with ed[uca-tion], Free Trade, finance and with the successful working out of an under-standing with the Labour Party. To this last was due the abnormality of the Liberal victory."[10] He did his best to convince Campbell-Bannerman of the wisdom of this transaction.

"It has," he wrote in the letter of January 21st referred to above, "pro-duced a solidarity in voting, especially in the big towns, which I scarcely dared to hope for. The L.R.C. know quite well how much support was given them by Liberals & this should have a steadying influence upon them. I am sure they will be a good element."[11]

---

* In all, the L.R.C. had sponsored 50 candidates.
† As early as March 1900 the secretary of the T.U.C. Parliamentary Committee had sug-gested to MacDonald that Gladstone "might be disposed to set aside a reasonable number of fairly hopeful constituencies and to give his general assistance to the running of a goodly number of Labour candidates, provided they were run under the auspices of your committee." Gladstone himself, speaking in May 1902, had expressed a hope that "the Liberal Party will be able to make an arrangement by which Labour will have greater and fairer opportunities of fighting seats at the next election than it has had before." There was, as by-election results during the next few months were to show, an urgent need for such an arrangement and Mac-Donald at length opened negotiations, making it clear that the L.R.C. had a fighting fund of £100,000 and could influence the votes of almost a million men. "In the great majority of cases," wrote Gladstone to Campbell-Bannerman on August 7th, 1903, "there is no friction or danger. . . . People are talking great nonsense about the need for an understanding and arrangement, but if they would only hold their tongues and allow us to work the thing quietly we should be all right."[9]

(5)

The Liberal Party had triumphed with a vengeance. The promised land had finally been reached and the fruits of victory were at last within their grasp. It all seemed too good to be true and the feeling of insecurity which still existed among the members of the new administration is revealed in a letter from Churchill to Bonar Law dated February 6th. "The wheel," he wrote, "has swung full circle in the country and we may be at work for some time. I resist all temptation to say 'I told you so.' Perhaps if you had had a clear run you might have got across your fence, but the double objective was fatal. It would be fun to be a Tory now. I expect you will not be out of the House for long. The wheel may swing again as suddenly and completely as before."[12]

One can hardly escape the conclusion that the victory was largely undeserved. There had been a reaction against the ineptitude of Balfour's administration rather than sudden swing to Liberalism which was, at this time, a very incoherent creed. It is all too easy to assume, as so many writers have done, that the team of talented men who now occupied the Treasury Bench had long before prepared a comprehensive programme of reforms and measures which they now proceeded to put into action. The truth is, however, that they possessed no definite programme, no definite ideas and no definite plan of campaign. If anything, they were conservative in their outlook in that they desired to preserve the good old nineteenth-century pattern of Liberalism without making any concessions to the demands of the twentieth. Free Trade was to remain undefiled, the Education Act of 1902 and the Licensing Act of 1904 were to be repealed and Home Rule for Ireland to be granted at some unspecified date in the far, far future. The ephemeral issues, such as the abolition of Chinese labour and the introduction of legislation to return trade unions to their pre-1901 financial status, helped to cloud the fact that the Liberal Party's immediate programme was both reactionary and negative.

CHAPTER FOUR

THE NEW PARLIAMENT

(1)

The myth of the two-party system has not yet, one fears, been fully exorcised from our textbooks. It never existed in the eighteenth century, it never quite appeared in the nineteenth and has only occasionally been glimpsed in the twentieth. The 1906 House of Commons, as we noted in our last chapter, was composed of the representatives of five parties: 377 Liberals, 132 Conservatives, 83 Nationalists, 53 Labour members and 25 Liberal-Unionists. These parties can, of course, be sub-divided almost indefinitely into smaller groupings: the Liberals into Gladstonians, Imperialists and Radicals, the Conservatives and Liberal Unionists into Tariff Reformers, Unionist Free Traders and Balfourites, the Labour members into Lib-Labs, trade unionists and Socialists. Even the Nationalists were not wholly united, Timothy Healy and William O'Brien having cut themselves adrift from the official organisation. In order to understand the account which follows, therefore, it is necessary to consider these factors a little more fully, bearing in mind that, quite apart from the scale of the Liberal triumph, the new House of Commons was one of the most exceptional assemblies of this century: 318 of the 670 members were taking their seats for the first time.*

(2)

The Liberal Party, like any Radical party at any time, was a mixture of factions. Potential reformers who wished to see their ideas actually implemented or who were personally ambitious had been left with no real alternative but to sail into power on the Liberal tide. The Labour Party represented only a small section of the community in the 1900s and the prospects of its capturing real political power in the near future were, to say the least, somewhat remote. The term Liberal, then as now, was vague

---

* The new members consisted of 220 Liberals, 46 Unionists, 25 Labour men, 14 Lib-Labs and 13 Irish Nationalists. This Parliament also goes down in history as having contained the largest-ever number of Nonconformists: 157, including 65 Congregationalists and 37 Wesleyan Methodists.

enough to allow unlimited latitude and respectable enough to attract support from all levels of society. High Churchmen and Nonconformists, fiery Radicals and cautious reformers, Imperialists and Little Englanders, staid suburbians and the apostles of anarchy, were able to pull together in the same boat without too many questions asked about individual destinations.

The party's real origins go back to 1859, when Gladstone joined with Palmerston and Russell in forming a ministry pledged to support Italian unification. The Peelites and the Whigs thus fused together and Derby and Disraeli, for the twenty years or so which followed, led the Tory opposition in Parliament and the country. This did not mean, however, that parties in the modern sense had come into existence. Personalities, as in the eighteenth century, were still the dominant factor and there was little to choose between policies until 1886. None the less, from the mid 1870s onwards the Whig patricians were overshadowed by Radical reformers such as Chamberlain and Dilke, and with the party's base thus broadened and an object for suitable moral denunciation having been found in the "Turkish atrocities" Gladstone was free to stump the country with the fervour of an Old Testament prophet, calling down the wrath of heaven upon his opponents. The importance of his Midlothian campaign is that it represented the first direct contact between a great politican and the people. None of his predecessors had found it necessary to campaign throughout the country in such a fashion. Gladstone's action was unprecedented and thought by some of his contemporaries to be grossly undignified. The people, however, loved it. Not only was the party returned to office in the general election of 1880 but it was identified, henceforth, with a domestic policy of social and constitutional reforms and a foreign policy of support for oppressed minorities, whatever their race and creed. In practice it proved difficult to live up to these standards and, with Ireland coerced and Egypt invaded, the image became rather tarnished. Gladstone, perhaps in an unconscious attempt to restore the balance, shocked his supporters and aroused the derision of his opponents in 1886 by announcing his conversion to the cause of Home Rule. The conversion was genuine but the timing unfortunate: the Chamberlainites promptly renounced his leadership and so, for that matter, did most of the Whigs. What remained of the parliamentary Liberal Party was simply a band of Gladstone's personal adherents. With the support of the Irish Nationalists he was able to form a third ministry but this only lasted a few months and in the general election of 1886 the Liberal Home Rulers were reduced to 191. The Chamberlainites continued to sit with them in the House for a few more years but their votes were generally cast in favour of Salisbury and the party divisions did not mend. Although Gladstone was able to form another ministry in 1892 he failed to win the day for Ireland and the Liberals were defeated in the general election of 1895. The Newcastle programme of 1891 had, however, launched them on other missions of a Radical character: besides Home Rule, they were now committed to disestablishment of the Church in Scotland and Wales, reform of the liquor laws and the general improvement of working conditions. There were also vague promises to reform the House of Lords and introduce payment of M.P.s. During the 1890s the party thus found itself reinforced by Nonconformists, temperance reformers and Lib-Labs and by 1906 a phoenix was arising which bore little or no resemblance to the Liberal Party of 1886. One hesitates to suggest that every Liberal was necessarily a Nonconformist and temperance reformer, but it was probably the case that every Nonconformist and temperance reformer was a supporter of the Liberal Party. If we are to look for a common denominator among the parliamentary party it is to be found in a detestation of war and a desire to see limitations placed upon the construction of armaments: a reduction of expenditure on the army and the navy was not the least of the reforms which the new Government was expected to effect.

Mr Roy Jenkins has analysed the 377 members of this reinvigorated party as consisting of 80 businessmen from good homes, 74 self-made businessmen, 64 practising barristers, 69 "gentlemen", 25 writers and journalists, 22 service officers, 21 solicitors, 9 teachers, 8 trade unionists and 5 doctors of medicine. A third of them had been to public schools and rather more than a third to Oxford or Cambridge.[1] "In so far as their occupations are a guide," writes Mr Jenkins, "the Liberal members of this Parliament had clearly not become a true cross-section of the nation . . . but they had for the first time become a real cross-section of the middle and upper classes; and as such they were more broadly based than their opponents."[2] This comment is only partially true, since it must be emphasised that the links with property, trade and industry were overwhelmingly strong, to a much greater extent than Mr Jenkins' analysis would suggest, and that "the people" had but a small voice in the counsels of the parliamentary Liberal Party. It included among its ranks 57 landowners, 97 manufacturers, 47 large merchants and financiers and 12 newspaper proprietors. Bankers, colliery owners, shipping magnates and men famous in every sphere of commerce were well to the fore and it was obvious that the new Government would do all in its power to keep the world safe for capitalism. Social reforms were needed, but not Socialism; the extremes of poverty and wealth would be abolished, but the idea of a classless society was firmly rejected.

Of the various strands which twined together to make up the new Government, it is possible to distinguish three that were thicker than the rest. The first of these, and by far the most prominent, was the "Gladstonian" strand, composed of Campbell-Bannerman, Morley, Herbert Gladstone, Birrell and Bryce; to the second, the "Imperialist" strand, we shall consign Asquith, Grey and Haldane; and to the third, the "Radical" strand, Lloyd George, Churchill and—for the moment, at any rate—Burns. These were the main figures in the main groups, but this must not be regarded as a watertight classification. Churchill, for example, was as much a disciple of Rosebery and Morley as of Lloyd George, while Grey received a freer hand at the Foreign Office from Campbell-Bannerman than he did from Asquith.

The "Gladstonians" remained true to the nineteenth-century pattern of Liberalism: Home Rule, Free Trade, economy wherever possible and social reforms when necessary.* They had condemned the South African War and detested jingoism. Their leader, and the head of the new Government, was a homely, round-faced, podgy little man, his eyes rarely losing their twinkle and his small moustache bristling benevolently on all occasions. Born in Glasgow in 1836, the son of a wealthy draper, and educated at the universities of Glasgow and Cambridge, Campbell-Bannerman was elected M.P. for Stirling Boroughs in 1868 and held minor posts in the Liberal Governments of the 1870s and early 'eighties. He entered the Cabinet as Secretary of State for War in 1886, an office which he held again in the administrations of 1892–5, and it was his admission in June 1895 that the cordite reserves were inadequate which led to the Government's defeat and Rosebery's resignation. Campbell-Bannerman's unexpected candour was the occasion, rather than the cause, of the Government's collapse and his colleagues bore no resentment. He was tempted, a few months later, to apply for the Speakership, but was persuaded not to withdraw from active participation in the parliamentary fray. The Liberal Party needed, at this time, all the Front Bench talent it could muster, and he was elected to the leadership in 1899 simply because no one else wanted the job.

By 1906 he had proved himself indispensable. His political philosophy was not, perhaps, very profound, but he clung to what he regarded as the

---

* "Our people," wrote Sir Robert Reid to Campbell-Bannerman on October 20th, 1905, "are very keen about social reform and economy." He evidently saw no conflict between these two objectives.[3]

basic tenets of Liberalism through thick and thin: freedom for all wherever possible, fairness in public dealings and a thorough respect for human rights. He was capable of upholding them in a manner which sometimes embarrassed his colleagues, but the secret of his success lay in the fact that he managed the party without imposing too heavy a hand upon the activities of its members. "It is because I have no fault to find with anyone," he once remarked, "that I am where I am."[4] Unlike Rosebery or Harcourt, he recognised that a Radical party is always prone to internal dissensions and, while not concealing his own views on various issues, made no attempt to muzzle the adverse comment of his colleagues. He went his own way and those who wished to join him were welcome to do so.

John Morley was a shrewd observer and an original thinker, but never quite the elder statesman that he always wanted to be. Born in 1838 and educated at Oxford, he came to London in 1860 and succeeded in earning a substantial income as a free-lance journalist and author. He entered Parliament in 1882 and had two spells as Chief Secretary for Ireland (1886 and 1892-5). His *Life of Gladstone*, the most outstanding political biography of its day, occupied much of his time from 1898 onwards, but his ringing denunciations of the Boer War brought him back to the political arena. By 1906 he had earned himself a dignified place both in literature and politics, but he resembled an ageing prima donna in that, while easily offended, he had become increasingly reluctant to leave the stage. None the less, there was something curiously likeable about this shrivelled, petulant, old-maidish little man, and his influence in Liberal circles, enhanced by his close association with Gladstone, remained undimmed for many years. As Secretary of State for India he would be responsible, as we shall see, for introducing some modest constitutional reforms.*

Herbert Gladstone, born in 1854, was educated at Eton and Oxford. He entered Parliament in 1880 and became a party whip and Junior Lord of the Treasury the following year. In 1885 he shot into prominence when he announced his father's conversion to Home Rule and thus precipitated the first really big crisis in the Liberal Party. He held minor posts in his father's

---

* His opinion of himself, and of Campbell-Bannerman for that matter, is indicated by a letter which he wrote to the latter on August 2nd, 1906. "Yesterday," it runs, "Gokhale [a leading Indian Nationalist] rather surprised me by telling me he had had a long conversation with you. Of course, it is the undisputed prerogative of a Prime Minister to see anybody in the world whom he wishes to see. Still, I submit that on such extremely delicate ground as India, and the relations between the Congress people and the home Govt., it would have been a pleasant compliment, shall I call it, if the Prime Minister had said something to the S. of S. before seeing Gokhale, or after. It is not important in this case—but I think as a precedent it would be too dubious, and you will forgive me for saying so." Campbell-Bannerman, who often referred to Morley as "Priscilla", presumably bore this outburst with his usual equanimity.[5]

administrations and was First Commissioner of Works under Rosebery. In 1889 he became Chief Whip. His talents were not remarkable but he was a diligent worker and a good administrator.

Augustine Birrell, the President of the Board of Education, was a cheerful, modest personality who, as the history of the next ten years would show, was always willing to undertake the dreariest of chores. He had been born in 1850, the son of a Nonconformist minister, and after being educated at Cambridge entered the legal profession. He gradually became known for his abilities as a reviewer and essayist. In 1889 he entered Parliament, but his political career was subordinated to his literary and legal activities. Defeated in the general election of 1900, he now re-entered Parliament as the member for North Bristol. His political views were closely akin to those of Campbell-Bannerman, and while he voiced the views of Nonconformists his good humour and tolerant disposition endeared him to members of all parties.

James Bryce, the son of a Belfast schoolmaster, had been born in 1838 and grew up in the Ireland of the "hungry forties". In 1857, a young man with staunch Presbyterian views, he won a scholarship to Oxford where he went from triumph to triumph in the field of classical history. He was called to the Bar in 1867 and from 1870 until 1893 was Regius Professor of Civil Law at Oxford. *The Holy Roman Empire* (1864) and *The American Commonwealth* (1888) were two of his many books. In 1880 he entered Parliament, serving under Gladstone as an Under-Secretary at the Foreign Office (1886) and Chancellor of the Duchy of Lancaster (1892–4) and under Rosebery as President of the Board of Trade. After 1895 he found himself increasingly in sympathy with the views of Campbell-Bannerman and his opposition to the South African War won him much unpopularity. It was his misfortune, as an ardent Home Ruler, to serve as Chief Secretary for Ireland at a time when Home Rule was, for the moment, strictly taboo.

These, then, were the "Gladstonians". It is now time for us to examine the "Imperialists", of whom Asquith, Grey and Haldane were the principal, but not the only, representatives. These were the men who had supported Rosebery in his belief that the Boer War was justly waged and in his founding of the Liberal League. They were, it might be said, conservative in foreign policy and vaguely socialistic when it came to home affairs.

Herbert Henry Asquith, the leading figure of this group, was generally regarded as "the coming man". Born in 1852 and brought up in a middle-class Yorkshire home, he gained a Double First at Oxford, became President of the Union and was elected a Fellow of Balliol. He was called to the Bar in 1876, but his legal career got off to a slow start and he was obliged to practise rigid economy for several years. He married in 1877 and entered Parliament as the member for East Fife in 1886. His short but effective intervention in the Parnell libel action made him famous throughout the country and in 1890 he took silk. His wife, however, died the following year and he was left with five small children to bring up. His fortunes rose again in 1892, when he became Home Secretary, and his marriage to Margot Tenant, two years later, was one of the sensations of the season. No two people less alike in temperament could have been imagined. Where Margot was colourful, Henry was dowdy; where Margot was excited, Henry was bored; where Margot was virulent, Henry was tolerant. Nevertheless, they were deeply attracted to each other at this time and their marriage proved to be fairly successful. Asquith was never a rich man, but his life was a happy one. In private life, despite a certain reserve, he was kindly and good-humoured and (partly as a means of escape from Margot's more boisterous activities) somewhat addicted to correspondence with intelligent young women.

Asquith was competent rather than brilliant and more of a party politician than Campbell-Bannerman. His speeches were generally brief, generally lucid and generally dull, and frequently took the form of lectures rather than arguments.* His voice, we are told by Leo Amery, was "resonant, clear and pleasantly modulated" and he had a curious habit of stroking the front of his thighs up and down with the palms of his hands while speaking. Campbell-Bannerman thought that his brain was like a "faultless piece of machinery" and Lloyd George later professed admiration "for his unrivalled gifts of lucid and logical statement". He refrained, whenever possible, from stating his own views on controversial issues and Morley, who thought he would have made an ideal judge, later recalled "that although he discussed every proposition advanced by others with great intelligence and force, he never submitted any ideas of his own for our consideration."[7] As Chancellor of the Exchequer he played a nominally important but, in reality, not very influential part in the first of the last Liberal Governments.

Sir Edward Grey, a distant relative of "Grey of the Reform Bill", was born in 1862. The family home, Fallodon, was set in the bleak countryside of Northumberland, and he grew up with a deep attachment to Nature. He was a shy, dreamy youth, somewhat isolated from the world at

---

* "Asquith's lucidity of style is a positive disadvantage when he has nothing to say," Balfour once remarked.[6]

large, and his studies at Balliol, unlike those of Asquith, were not a success. In 1884 he was sent down for idleness and never summoned up the energy or enthusiasm to work his way back into favour. He married the following year and entered Parliament in 1886 as the member for Berwick. More than a year elapsed before he made his first speech. From this point onwards, however, he gained confidence and gradually emerged into public life as a quiet, reasonably intelligent young man, coming into close contact with Asquith, Haldane and Acland. He served as Under-Secretary for Foreign Affairs (1892–5) and, like Asquith and Haldane, found himself in sympathy with Rosebery's sentiments at the time of the Boer War. His reluctance to enter the Government, however, was due more to temperament than devotion to Rosebery: it was a last despairing attempt to avoid his destiny.

Balfour once described him as "a curious combination of the old-fashioned Whig and the Socialist," and the description is not a bad one.[8] He laboured, in fact, under the guilt of having been born an aristocrat in the century which saw the emergence of the common man, and while he felt it his duty to encourage the dissolution of class barriers he could never forget that he himself was the prisoner of a way of life from which escape was impossible. This is not to say, of course, that he did not make the attempt. Associating with the Fabian Society was a sincere effort on the part of Sir Edward to link hands with the new world rather than cling to the old, but he was not the stuff of which determined reformers are made. Shy, reserved, self-conscious and horribly aware of his defects in the field of sociology he eventually abandoned the attempt to join in the creation of Utopia and retired once more to his beloved Wordsworth, Fallodon and bird-watching. Everything else came as a burden. Time and time again he expressed the wish to relinquish his political career and devote himself to the pursuits of a country gentleman, but some inner compulsion drove him on, a tired visionary, until, at length, he could go no further and retired from the public scene altogether, blind, broken but, in the last analysis, at peace with the world: in working himself to death he had justified his existence, and this was all that mattered.

Richard Burdon Haldane, the third member of the Relugas triumvirate, had been born in Edinburgh in 1856. His family were prominent citizens and he thus obtained a good despatch into the whirlpool of public life. In 1872 he went to Edinburgh University, philosophy being the subject which interested him most, and in 1874 he spent several months at the University of Göttingen. He graduated in law and philosophy, came to London in 1877 and was called to the Bar two years later. From 1883 onwards his practice at the Bar prospered and in 1886 he was elected to Parliament as the member for East Lothian. Legal and political work took up much of his time but he nevertheless managed, in the late 1880s, to translate Schopenhauer's works into English. A broken engagement came as a great blow to him in 1890 and his failure to secure a position in Gladstone's administration of 1892 came as another. He occupied himself in non-political fields, especially university reform and lecturing, before becoming involved in the activities of the Liberal League.

"He loved power," wrote Beatrice Webb in 1928, "especially the power of the hidden hand, or shall I say of the *recognised* hidden hand."[9] Campbell-Bannerman, who had reason for complaint, had spotted this more than twenty years before. "Haldane is always climbing up and down the backstairs," he remarked, "but he makes such a clatter that everyone hears him."[10] There was, in fact, something vaguely pathetic about his plots and intrigues which, for all their ingenuity, always seem to have misfired, and it must be admitted that he had a capacity for sustained hard work that did much to atone for his defects. Once in harness he pressed forward with a will, driven on by a love of thoroughness and order. His War Office reforms, as we shall see, transformed the British army into an efficient fighting machine. Fate dealt him some unkind blows, but though he reeled he always came bouncing back for more, as cocksure and undeflatable as ever. An unshakeable belief in his own abilities acted as a permanent buffer between himself and the outside world.*

From the "Imperialists" we turn to the "Radicals", namely Lloyd George, Churchill and Burns, although only the first of these, and possibly not even he, possessed Radical convictions which were more than superficial. Churchill, as we shall see, was more of a rebel than a Radical, while Burns was more of a Tory than a Liberal.

Lloyd George, one of the two *enfants terribles* of the Liberal Party, was the exact antithesis of Asquith. Born in Manchester in 1863, brought up in humble conditions in a tiny Welsh village, he had forced his way up the ladder by sheer animal determination. He was the self-made man *par excellence*, shrewd, energetic and ambitious. He had begun his adult life as a solicitor at Criccieth, had soon gained a widespread reputation for his industry and ingenuity, and in 1890 was elected M.P. for Caernarvon Boroughs. During the 1890s he had been one of the foremost figures in the little group of Welsh Nationalists in the Commons, but with the coming

---

* His opinion of his colleagues was not high. Asquith, he felt, was "not a man of imagination", Morley "not really cut out for public administration", Lloyd George "an illiterate with an unbalanced mind", and Churchill "as long-winded as he was persistent". Only Grey, whom he described as "a first-rate statesman", seems to have measured up to his standards.[11]

of the Boer War turned his attention to the agreeable task of denouncing Chamberlain for plunging Britain into what he described as one of the most reckless and unnecessary adventures that she had ever experienced. He led the Nonconformist opposition to the Education Bill and by 1906 was one of the most prominent politicians in the country.

He delighted in making cheerful, slap-happy, exaggerated speeches, usually enjoying his performances but not taking his own arguments too seriously. It was much more fun to make an exciting speech than a dull one, and in his chosen fields—Welsh nationalism, Nonconformity, belligerent pacifism and the iniquities of the House of Lords—he charged about with cutlass waving and battle-cries galore. With his high-pitched voice proclaiming the days of triumph to come, he would lift his arms to the heavens and cry for victory or hurl them downwards and lash the wicked Tories with all the vigour and fury at his command. The "people's William" was to be duly succeeded by the "people's David" and the people were to be given as good a show it was possible to stage, bless their silly old hearts! All the paraphernalia of evangelistic oratory was cheerfully trotted out: all the drums were walloped and all the trumpets blasted. In private, as would soon be discovered, he was a smooth and tricky customer, adept at flattery and with a genius for getting his own way.

Lloyd George acted on intuition rather than principle: his philosophy was essentially one of short-cuts and splendid improvisation, but it did at least result in positive achievements. Contemptuous of "intellectuals" and motivated by opportunism, he was nevertheless usually sincere in most of his professed sentiments and had the dynamic energy that was needed to carry through reforms of any or every character. Asquith lost the premiership in 1916 because he had done too little: Lloyd George lost it in 1922 because he had done too much.

Churchill, the other *enfant terrible* of the Liberal Party, was an impetuous and somewhat reckless young man. He had been born in 1874, the son of Lord Randolph Churchill, and after showing little or no promise at Harrow had entered Sandhurst as a cavalry cadet in 1893. The death of his father two years later forced him into the position of family bread-winner and he set to work as a journalist, combining a literary career with his life in the army. In 1898, the year that he resigned his commission, the publication of *The Malakand Field Force* assured his future as a writer. It was all good patriotic stuff, written in a lively but sometimes stilted manner, with traces of Gibbon and Macaulay in nearly every line. Its purpose, so its author gravely asserted, was to relate events which "the philo-

sopher may observe with pity and the philanthropist deplore with pain."
He followed it up with similar books and a swashbuckling romance
entitled *Savrola*. His escape from the Boers, in 1899, made him one of the
most popular heroes of the day. In 1900 he was elected Conservative M.P.
for Oldham, but he soon found himself marching out of step with Balfour
and Chamberlain. Seeking revenge, it seems, for what he regarded as the
shabby treatment of Lord Randolph, he constantly went out of his way
to differ from the leaders of his party and to advertise his glorious independence to the world in general. His father's phrase of "Tory democracy"
was resurrected and Tariff Reform proved wonderful grist for the Churchillian mill. "Free Traders of all parties," he declared, "should form one
line of battle against the common foe." He launched an anti-protectionist
campaign of his own and when speaking at a meeting in Halifax exclaimed
"Thank God for the Liberal Party!" The Oldham Conservative Association promptly disowned their member. When he next rose to speak in the
Commons almost the entire Conservative Party, led by Balfour, got up
and walked out of the Chamber. It was undeniably a childish incident, but
the Prime Minister and his supporters had grown tired of the young rebel
in their midst. Two months later Churchill joined Lloyd George on an
Opposition bench below the gangway. The Liberal Party thus gained an
unexpected convert and the Unionists breathed a sigh of relief. "One
Winston is quite enough!" were the sentiments of Campbell-Bannerman
when it was suggested that a veritable army of Unionist Free Traders
should also be encouraged to cross the floor of the Commons,[12] but the new
member flung himself into the task of belabouring his erstwhile colleagues
with such zeal that his inclusion in the new Government was a foregone
conclusion.

The greatest defect under which Churchill laboured was his lack of
intellectual ability. He appeared, to all who met him, to be an electrifying
bundle of energy and excitement, but not much more than this. His
schooling had been patchy, the young Winston learning only the things
he wanted to and ignoring everything else, and he lacked the benefits
which a university education might have given him. He had not yet
learnt to endure discipline and in his impatience to get into the limelight
had hurled himself into the fray without experience or knowledge, sinking
his teeth into every bone of contention that came his way.* No matter!
It was all a jolly good free-for-all, and he revelled in it to his heart's content.

---

* The great tragedy of Winston Churchill, in fact, is that he started too soon and went on
too long.

Burns, the third member of our "Radical" trio, had been born in Lambeth in 1848 and brought up in very humble conditions. He started work at an early age and passed from job to job, educating himself as best he could. From the mid-1870s onwards he was a familiar orator in Battersea Park and Clapham Common and he stood as an independent Labour candidate for Nottingham in the general election of 1886. He played a leading part in the "Bloody Sunday" demonstration, being sentenced to six weeks' imprisonment for assaulting a policeman, but his greatest hour of fame came in 1889 when, in company with Tom Mann and Ben Tillet, he helped to organise the great dock strike. Thenceforth he was looked upon as a recognised leader of the working classes and it was widely supposed that he would play an important part in the Labour movement. In 1892 he was elected M.P. for Battersea, but from this point onwards his outlook began to change. Possibly this was prompted by jealousy of Keir Hardie; more probably it was because he enjoyed acting as an individual and did not relish close entanglement with either the Lib-Labs or Hardie's small band of pioneers. He still described himself as a Socialist and looked upon himself as the only authentic Working Man M.P., but his old Radical ideas were allowed to fade away. He refused to co-operate with Hardie and MacDonald and in 1904 he delivered a stinging attack upon the Labour Representation Committee.*

Campbell-Bannerman, who did not know Burns very well, obviously thought that he was doing a wise thing in making him President of the Local Government Board and Burns himself revelled with delight in his new position. It soon became apparent, however, that he was out of his depth in administrative work and had little or no idea what policies to put into action. John Burns, the supremely conceited, untruthful, arrogant and boastful "colossus of Battersea", was no more than a sheep in wolf's clothing.†

Three other members of the Government, although occupying comparatively junior posts at this time, were also destined to play an important

---

* This speech marked his formal severance from the Labour movement, although Keir Hardie does not seem to have thought him much of a loss.

† It is instructive to link his name with that of Charles Masterman, who had just been elected Liberal M.P. for West Ham (North). Masterman, in his early thirties, was an ardent social reformer and High Churchman. He had been educated at Cambridge and, unlike Burns, received enough financial backing from his family to secure him a good start in life. His talents as an author soon proved, however, that he could stand on his own feet. His books included *From the Abyss* (1902) and *In Peril of Change* (1905), two bitter attacks on the social conditions of the day. In 1908, to anticipate events, he became Parliamentary Secretary to the Local Government Board, an appointment with which Burns was none too pleased. Masterman soon discovered that the inertia of his chief was a barrier to any real progress and, after a year's futile struggling to initiate reforms, persuaded Asquith to transfer him to the Home Office.

part in the history of the next ten years, and it is convenient if we note them in passing at this stage of our narrative. They were Reginald McKenna, Herbert Samuel and Lewis Harcourt.

McKenna, the Financial Secretary to the Treasury and, for the next six years, Asquith's protégé, had been born in 1863, the son of an Irish businessman. He was called to the Bar in 1887 and succeeded in building up a prosperous practice. In 1895 he entered the House of Commons as the member for North Monmouthshire. Sir Charles Dilke took this promising young man under his wing and fed him, so rumour had it, on a diet of Blue Books. After 1900 he became a leading member of the Opposition, concentrating a steady stream of fire on the Tariff Reformers.

Samuel, who occupied the post of Under-Secretary for the Home Office, had been born in 1870,* the son of a wealthy City businessman. In 1889, when canvassing in the first L.C.C. elections, he had been horrified by the slums of Whitechapel and resolved then and there to embark upon a career as a social reformer M.P. He became friendly with the Webbs, Shaw and Graham Wallas, although he did not join the Fabians, and became a leading figure in Oxford University's Liberal Association. A member of the Commons since 1902, he was now regarded as one of the party's most promising young men.

Harcourt, commonly known as "Lulu", occupied a curious position in the Liberal Party. He was the only surviving son of Sir William Harcourt and had devoted twenty years of his life to the furtherance, by all possible means, of his father's career. He had acted as Sir William's private secretary and, as such, had been a kind of power behind the throne. He was largely responsible, it seems, for ensuring that the rift between Sir William and Rosebery never had a chance to heal and he evidently pulled a good many strings to ensure his father's election as leader of the party in 1896. It was not until Sir William's death that he felt free to pursue a political career of his own and in 1904, at the age of forty-one, he entered the Commons as member for a Lancashire division. He had played a prominent part in the Tariff Reform controversy, having been a founder of the Free Trade Union, but his reputation as an intriguer meant that he was still viewed with distrust in various quarters. For himself, however, he was far less ambitious than he had been for his father, and was quite content with his appointment as First Commissioner of Works.

We must take a look, finally, at other members of the parliamentary

---

* Fifty years later, in 1955, Churchill informed his Woodford constituents that he always listened with great attention to anything Lord Samuel had to say. He paused for a moment, and then added—"He's older than I am!"[13]

Liberal Party. Among those who had been re-elected were Felix Cobbold (the representative of a Suffolk family of brewers), Sir Charles Dilke, Sir Hudson Kearley (the partner in a well-known grocery concern), Sir Weetman Pearson (the future Lord Cowdray), Colonel John Seely (who, like Churchill, had left the Unionist benches in 1904), D. A. Thomas (the future Lord Rhondda), Charles Trevelyan and Samuel Whitbread, while the new members included Sir John Barker (the owner of a famous Kensington store), Hilaire Belloc, Horatio Bottomley, John Bright (the son of the famous Radical), Harold Cox, Lord Dalmeny (Rosebery's son, whose father threatened to disown him if he moved the reply to the King's Address at the start of the Session), G. P. Gooch, Hamar Greenwood, Cecil Harmsworth, Thomas Idris (the head of a famous soft-drinks firm), Percy Illingworth, Rufus Isaacs, R. C. Lehman, William Lever, A. E. W. Mason, Alfred Mond, Edwin Montagu, Sir George Newnes and his son Frank, Charles Price (the former partner of McVitie and Price), John Simon, Donald Smeaton and Josiah Wedgwood. The impressive array of talent on the ministerial side of the House was not, in short, confined to the members of the Ministry itself. The new Government, besides being stronger than any Liberal administration since 1880, would be supported by a rank and file of an exceptionally good quality. After the eclipse of 1895 and the dreary struggles for supremacy the party had, so it seemed, undergone a transformation, almost a renaissance, and had swept back to the Commons in one final blaze of glory.

(3)

The official Opposition consisted, in theory, of 132 Conservatives led by Balfour and 25 Liberal-Unionists led by Chamberlain. In practice, however, the original dividing line between the two sections had almost disappeared and it would be nearer the mark to say that the Opposition consisted of 109 Chamberlainites, 36 Balfourites and 12 Unionist Free Traders.* Seventeen of these members were also Ulster Unionists, who formed—despite their various allegiances in the Tariff Reform dispute— a distinct group in themselves. As we shall see in the following chapter, a hasty truce was concluded on the morrow of the election whereby fiscal reform theoretically ceased to be a bone of contention and became a

---

* *The Times* estimated on January 30th that the parliamentary party consisted of 109 Tariff Reformers, 32 Balfourites and 11 Unionist Free Traders (a total of 152, thus leaving five members unaccounted for), while the Duke of Devonshire, speaking on March 6th, gave the figures as 102 Tariff Reformers, 36 Balfourites and 16 Unionist Free Traders (a total of 154, thus leaving three members unaccounted for). The figures given above are thus to be treated as an approximation.

standard part of the Unionist creed. This did not mean, of course, that divisions no longer existed but it did mean that the cracks had been momentarily papered over.

The year 1906 was a turning point for the Unionist Party and it is probable that, amidst the widespread "re-thinking" which went on at this time, many of its chastened members were led to consider anew the basic tenets of Conservatism, wonderfully vague though they were, and to look back at the ground which their party had covered during the past seventy years. The year 1846 cannot, admittedly, be properly regarded as the formal birth-date of the Unionist Party, but it was amidst the flames of the Corn Laws crisis that the old Toryism perished and the new Conservatism emerged. Peel, as the leader of the first, and Disraeli, as the leader of the second, went their separate ways, each taking with them a band of stalwart supporters and both leaving behind a considerable number of bewildered gentlemen who knew not which way to turn. It was not until 1874 that the new Conservatism had a chance to show its paces, but Disraeli (with a working majority of 50) made the most of it. His Ministry put up an impressive show on the home front and a considerable number of useful Acts found their way on to the Statute Book.* These measures, so it was argued, showed that Tory Democracy could and did work. The acquisition of the Suez Canal and the bestowal on Queen Victoria of the title "Empress of India" elevated Imperialism to a prominent place in the party's creed. After these sparkling triumphs, however, disaster struck the party in the general election of 1880, and with Disraeli's death a few months later its chances of returning to power in the immediate future seemed remote. It was Lord Randolph Churchill who, by his leadership of the "Fourth Party" and valiant efforts to make "Tory Democracy" something more than a mere catch-phrase, did most to keep the flag flying during the next five years, but it is unlikely that Conservative fortunes would have prospered to any great extent had it not been for the disintegration of the Liberal Party over the issue of Home Rule. It was Lord Randolph who, speaking at Manchester in March 1886, referred to all the

---

* Disraeli, of course, realised that if the Conservative Party were to survive at all it would have to do so with the support of a substantial section of the middle and lower classes. He and Lord Randolph Churchill perceived, as Mr Paul Johnson has written, "that brutal economic self-interest need not necessarily be the decisive factor in determining how men vote; that even the poorest have conservative instincts; and that, by creating new political emotions, they could persuade men without property to keep its custodians in office." That Tory Democracy was a phantasm, a kind of confidence trick, as Rosebery later described it, should not be allowed to obscure the fact that in the 1870s and 1880s it did much to enhance the fortunes of Conservatism and seemed, indeed, to possess real possibilities. After 1895, with Chamberlain and Kipling sounding the trumpets on behalf of Imperialism, it was allowed to die a natural death.[14]

anti-Home Rulers as "the Unionist Party" and from that time onwards, although Chamberlain and his supporters did not finally merge with the Conservatives until 1895, a coalition between the two groups was an accomplished fact.

Defeat at the polls was a chastening experience in more ways than one for the gentlemen of England. "The nineteen years of Unionist supremacy," R. C. K. Ensor has written," . . . may be looked on as a successful rally of the governing families to maintain their position, propped and modified by their alliance with the ablest leader of the upstarts—Chamberlain. But from their standpoint the House of Commons elected in 1906 was far worse than that of 1880. Not merely were there the fifty-three Labour M.P.s—nearly all of whom had been manual workers, and all of whom without exception had been reared in working-class homes—but a large proportion of the huge Liberal contingent consisted of men with small means, and in the Cabinet itself sat Lloyd George, the orphan son of an elementary schoolteacher, brought up by his uncle who was a village shoemaker. To persons born like Lansdowne and Balfour (and only a little less to Rosebery) it appeared out of the question that a House of Commons so composed and led should effectively rule the nation."[15] The leaders of the Conservative Party were convinced, in fact, that they were the men whom Providence had chosen to govern.

In quality, as well as quantity, the party had suffered a severe reverse. Balfour himself was without a seat for several weeks; Bonar Law and Alfred Lyttleton did not return to the Commons for another four months and Lord Hugh Cecil not for another four years. All in all, only 110 of the Unionists who sat in the 1900 Parliament had been re-elected and 46 of the new members were without previous parliamentary experience. Among those who reappeared, however, were Walter Long, Edward Carson, George Wyndham, Hugh Arnold-Foster, Aretas Akers-Douglas, Jesse Collings and Sir William Anson, while the new members included F. E. Smith, Lord Robert Cecil, Arthur Lee and Sir George Younger. It would seem, following Mr Roy Jenkins's calculations, that the party as a whole consisted of 48 "gentlemen", 32 service officers, 26 businessmen who had started life in easy circumstances and 13 who were self-made, 21 barristers, 6 journalists and writers, 5 solicitors, 3 dons, 2 doctors of medicine and 1 accountant.[16]

The official leader of the Unionist Party was at this time in his fifty-eighth year. Balfour had entered the Commons in 1874 and had accompanied his uncle, Lord Salisbury, to the Congress of Berlin, but it was not until the defeat of the Conservatives in 1880 that he developed a real interest in politics. In company with the "Fourth Party" he delivered a series of unorthodox attacks upon the Government, but he broke away from Churchill after some five years and became more closely associated with his uncle. His ruthless campaign of terror as Chief Secretary for Ireland (1887–91) made his political fortune, and from the early 'nineties onwards "Prince Arthur" was regarded as Salisbury's inevitable successor. After 1895 he played an ever-increasing role in the management of his party and with Chamberlain's assistance he succeeded in welding the Government's majority into one that was virtually impregnable. He regarded the South African War as an unpleasant necessity but recognised, perhaps more quickly than his contemporaries, the need to overhaul the outdated machinery with which Britain had lumbered into battle. He was responsible, when he became premier, for the creation of the Committee of Imperial Defence and his last achievement had been that of securing the supremacy of the 18-pounder gun over its rival, the 13-pounder.

The image of Balfour assiduously fostered by both his biographers is that of a benign, courteous, serene though sometimes indolent statesman, wandering thoughtfully and happily through life, apparently oblivious to slings and arrows and never bothering to read the newspapers but very sensitive to changing conditions and evincing a keen interest in every new idea which came his way, whether it be the bicycle, the Labour Party or the Zionist movement. This was the man, who, one gathers, was responsible for the *Entente Cordiale* and the overhauling of the machinery of Britain's defences, the man who pioneered the cause of technology and the man who did more than anyone else to equip this country for the problems of the twentieth century. This was the man who, with a weary smile of disdain, bowed himself out of the Tariff Reform debate and concentrated on the really important task of securing the ascendancy of one particular type of gun over another. This was the man who put principle before party, the man who dwelt in rarefied heights but who was always willing, when necessary, to descend to the level of lesser mortals.

It is an agreeable, indeed an appealing picture, but it is one which his contemporaries would have had some difficulty in accepting as altogether accurate. The Balfour that most of them knew, although invariably courteous and charming, was made of tougher stuff than this. To speak of a mailed fist in a velvet glove is something of an exaggeration, but he was undeniably a shrewd, cunning, ruthless and sometimes spiteful politician. The waspish note of his earlier days had been replaced by layer after layer of urbanity and charm, yet few of those who came into close contact with him could fail to be aware that he was, withal, as hard as nails. Gladstone,

c

in 1891, privately described him as "the most unscrupulous man in public life" and Neville Chamberlain, writing almost forty years later, remarked that "I admired his intellectual gifts immensely, and realised his charm, but he always seemed to me to have a heart like a stone."[17] "Had he lived in the French Revolution," wrote Churchill in the early 1930s, "he would, when it was found absolutely necessary, have consigned a dangerous enemy of his Government or party or even an erring colleague to the guillotine with much complacency. But he would have done it in a thoroughly polite and impersonal manner."[18] Balfour was, in short, the personification of Conservatism. He had drifted into political life almost accidentally, partly because he was a member of the governing class and partly because it was something to do. Gradually, however, he had warmed to the game for its own sake and was destined, indeed, to continue in harness almost to the day he died. Yet what were the results of this unceasing activity? It may be granted that he was an enlightened administrator in foreign affairs and defence but he invariably turned a blind eye to the question of social reform. He was aware that poverty existed and, in his own elegant way, he deplored it, but he did not admit that anything could be done to bring about a happier state of affairs. These things would presumably sort themselves out and it was better that they should not be spoken of too often in polite society. Lord Randolph Churchill had, in 1889, likened him to Dickens's Mr Podsnap, "a person in easy circumstances who was very content with himself and was extremely surprised that all the world was not equally contented like him." The comparison may have been a little cruel: it was certainly not unfair.*

Joseph Chamberlain, the unofficial leader of the Unionist Party, was now approaching his seventieth birthday. He had entered the Commons in 1876, a wealthy Nonconformist Radical screw-manufacturer who had worked wonders in modernising Birmingham and had built up a powerful political organisation. He served under Gladstone as President of the Board of Trade (1880-5), but grew very depressed at the Government's lukewarm attitude towards social reform. Throughout 1884, the year of the

---

* *Foundations of Belief*, written in the early 1890s, provides the best guide to Balfour's political philosophy. "Reasoning," he declared, "is a force most apt to divide and disintegrate; and though division and disintegration may often be the necessary preliminaries of social development, still more necessary are the forces that bind and stiffen, without which there would be no society to develop." Authority, in the form of tradition and habit, ought not to be challenged and change, if change there must be, should develop naturally and not be forced. Having thus expounded the classic case for Conservatism—namely, that it is better to leave well alone than to meddle with the *status quo*—this owner of estates valued at rather more than £4 million presumably strolled happily off to his games of golf or tennis, or to amiable conversations with those charming young creatures who constituted the *couterie* known as "the Souls".

third Reform Act, he carried out a series of attacks on the Upper House, attacks which were specially notable when delivered by a Cabinet Minister. What ransom, he demanded, would property pay for the security it enjoyed? Questions such as this horrified Queen Victoria and alarmed Gladstone, but Chamberlain refused to be suppressed except at the price of not speaking at all. He also propounded an "unauthorised programme" which included, among other things, the disestablishment of the Church in England, Wales and Scotland, free primary education and payment of M.P.s* Home Rule for Ireland, however, was something he could not swallow, and in 1886 he and his ninety-odd followers left the official Liberal fold. Early in 1894 he announced he would have nothing more to do with the "new Radicalism" and the following year he entered Salisbury's administration as Colonial Secretary. The Boer War completed his transformation into a full-blooded Imperialist and his campaign for Tariff Reform now seemed to be turning the Tory clock back to a point where even Disraeli had hesitated to do battle. Like Lloyd George, however, he was chiefly concerned with getting things done, and it was as natural for him to seek to organise the units of the Empire into one all-powerful body as it had been to organise all the various Liberal associations into a National Liberal Federation. He sincerely believed, moreover, that Tariff Reform would result in both the creation of a self-reliant and tremendously powerful empire and the cure of poverty, sickness and unemployment.

Externally, at least, Chamberlain had altered very little with the passage of the years. He was still remarkably slim and agile and his clear-cut profile with eye-glass agleam, together with the inevitable orchid, had become so familiar to the public that it seemed almost inconceivable that he would ever vanish from the political scene. Already, however, there were signs that the fires were dying down and at least one member of the new Parliament was startled by the realisation that the Unionist demagogue was now an old and tired man. "I had not," wrote Philip Snowden later, "heard Mr Chamberlain since the days of his matured powers twenty years before. I was amazed and pained by the decline of these powers. . . . In voice and vigour and skill he was but a shadow of the Joe Chamberlain of former days."[20]

Chamberlain's son and political heir was Joseph Austen Chamberlain, born in 1863. The quip attributed to Churchill, that Austen Chamberlain "always played the game and always lost it," has been chanted so many

---

* "He is unquestionably the future leader of the people," wrote an admiring Lloyd George at this time. "He is a Radical and doesn't care who knows it." Ramsay MacDonald was another young man greatly impressed by Chamberlain.[19]

times by so many pop-historians, that one feels obliged to apologise for quoting it yet again. It is not, of course, strictly accurate, since Chamberlain *fils* was as great an intriguer as Chamberlain *pere*: the only difference was that the son's schemes rarely, if ever, succeeded. He did not possess his father's originality of thought or powers of leadership. He did possess the Chamberlain tenacity but, as it transpired, possessed it to rather too great a degree. Where the father, finding his way blocked on a certain issue, would manoeuvre and temporise until the obstacle disappeared, the son would stand firm on the rock of his principles and refuse to budge until he found that the tide of events had flowed on and left him high and dry. He suffered, of course, from being the over-groomed offspring of an outstanding personality. It had been generally accepted, from his childhood onwards, that he would follow his father into public life and no attempt was made to prepare him for any other career. He had entered Parliament in 1892, was a junior member of the Government from 1895 onwards and he served as Chancellor of the Exchequer in the last two years of Balfour's administration. Since 1903, if not earlier, his self-esteem had steadily increased, and it seemed only reasonable to conclude that Providence had marked him out to play a leading role in the fortunes of the Unionist Party. From July 1906 onwards, with his father's active career at an end, he would struggle to fulfil this role, blithely unconscious of the fact that his shortcomings rendered him hopelessly inadequate for such a position. "Austen," Mr Julian Amery has written, "was a born Conservative, punctilious to a fault. He was a capable administrator but, like many who have no clear vision of the end, he was ever preoccupied about the means. He copied his father in every detail of dress and manner, till he seemed almost to be his caricature. But the resemblance was only on the surface; even their bodies denied it. Chamberlain's features were questing and aggressive; Austen's were calm and smooth. The father's frame was taut and wiry; the son's upright and relaxed. . . . The surface similarities only served to underline the differences between the two men. Nor was Austen wholly unaware of them. He was intensely proud of his father, but sometimes he seemed embarrassed by a lingering doubt whether 'Joe' was really quite a gentleman."[21]

A truer disciple of Joseph Chamberlain was, perhaps, Andrew Bonar Law, a middle-aged Glasgow businessman who had entered the Commons in 1900 and served as Parliamentary Secretary to the Board of Trade under Balfour. He was a dour, humourless man with a habitual air of melancholy, although capable of giving vent to unexpected passions, and his pleasures were those which most of his associates in the party would have found rather too much like penance. During the five years which followed he would be little more than a shadowy figure hovering in the background of the political scene: no one could have suspected, in 1906, that this drab, "meekly ambitious" man, as Asquith described him, would five years later be replacing Balfour as leader of the Unionist Party. Still less, however, could anyone have imagined that, with the passage of yet another five years, he would be Lloyd George's second-in-command in a Coalition Government.

The Ulster Unionists who, as we have already noted, numbered seventeen, were led by Walter Long and Sir Edward Carson. The strength and importance of this group has often, as Mr R. B. McDowell points out, been underestimated. "For over a century," he writes, "the Irish supporters of the Union included the bulk of the landed interest, the Protestant clergy, very large sections of the professional and business classes and practically the whole Protestant community of the north. Their political, social and economic power was immense. Their intellectual strength was by no means contemptible and they were thoroughly convinced that their cause was righteous and rational. They believed that the Union offered to Irishmen a fuller and richer social life, while it enabled them to make a valuable contribution to the common development of the two islands. If their Nationalist opponents accused them of treachery to the national cause, they considered they were fighting for larger loyalties against the onset of a stifling provincialism. For they were in their own eyes the most intelligent and progressive element in Irish life."[22]

Walter Long, the unexpected leader of this little group, was a hot-tempered, loud-mouthed man in his fifty-second year, a splendid representative of the English squirearchy. His family had owned estates in Wiltshire since the fourteenth century. His limitations as a politician were also, to some extent, his strength. His sturdy Toryism and moderate attitude towards Tariff Reform commanded a considerable degree of support in the party and he could always be relied on to stand firm against any Radical innovation.* He had, moreover, a fair amount of administrative experience behind him, having served as President of the Board of Agriculture (1895–1900) and President of the Local Government Board (1900–5). His identification with the Ulster Unionists had begun when he succeeded George Wyndham as Chief Secretary for Ireland in March 1905, but it was now intensified by his election as M.P. for Dublin County.

Sir Edward Carson, although Long's contemporary in age, was a bird

---

* In 1907, for example, he would create his Union Defence League and two years later would be President of the Budget Protest League.

of a very different plumage. A distinguished legal record, at both the Irish and English Bars, had resulted in his becoming Solicitor-General for England in 1900. An M.P. for Dublin University since 1892, he was one of the most outstanding members of the Unionist Party and one of the best orators of the day. The secret of his power lay, perhaps, in the very restraint that he placed upon his passions, and in those cases where a fiery outburst and a torrent of invective might have seemed most fitting an icy calm would descend upon him and he would deliver his denunciations in cold, clipped sentences, fashioned with a clarity and logic all the more terrible for the suppressed emotions that lay behind them.

The Unionist Party as a whole at this time, however, was in a pitiable condition. Bereft of its official leader and its most talented members, the shattered remnant which assembled at Westminster in February 1906 was still scarcely able to take in the magnitude of the disaster which had befallen them. That the heavens had crashed about their ears was clear enough; that they would have to endure five, six, even seven years of exile from the corridors of power, with the prospect of more to follow if the country remained impervious to the blandishments of Tariff Reform, was a possibility which even the bravest of them scarcely dared to contemplate. Some ghastly mistake had evidently been made and the nightmare would no doubt end if only the right magic word could be uttered, but for the moment that word had eluded them. The "Valentine letters", to be dealt with in our next chapter, would settle the question of immediate strategy, but an uneasy alliance between Balfour and Chamberlain could hardly be regarded as a final answer to the leadership problem. Resilience in defeat, however, has always been a well-known characteristic of the Conservative Party, and the more far-sighted Unionist members could console themselves with the knowledge that, given the swings of the political pendulum, their plight was unlikely to become any worse.

(4)

The only party whose fortunes had not undergone any radical change at the general election was that of the Irish Nationalists. The eighty-three members who took their seats on the Opposition benches below the gangway were, with only thirteen exceptions, the same body of men who had occupied those benches during the Parliament of 1900. Seventy-three of them had, in fact, been returned unopposed. They attended Westminster, under the leadership of John Redmond, in the confident expectation that they would one day be in a position to compel a British Government to grant them Home Rule.

To appreciate the character and aims of the Nationalist movement it is necessary to remember that Ireland, ever since the passing of the Act of Union in 1800, had been a country governed by alien administrators and an alien parliament. Distant rule need not necessarily be bad rule but in this instance the Irish people had ample justification for what can, at the very least, be described as feelings of strong resentment. Poverty and famine had stalked the land for the greater part of the nineteenth century. Catholics had been freed from their political disabilities in 1829 and the Anglican Church had been disestablished forty years later, but the great estates of the country were nearly all in the hands of absentee Protestant landlords who had little or no interest in the welfare of the peasantry. Ireland, like Russia, was one of the last strongholds of feudalism and thousands of tenant farmers struggled, with varying degress of success, to meet their financial commitments to their landlords. Failure to do so resulted in eviction. Only the implementation of a large-scale programme of capital investment could have transformed their miserable holdings into paying concerns, but neither the landlords nor the State had any desire to launch such a programme.

From 1832 onwards there were several Irish members in the House of Commons opposed to the Act of Union but the real struggle against English rule came from the Young Ireland movement and later from the Irish Republican Brotherhood, two organisations which met their respective fates in the uprisings of 1848 and 1867. Fenianism, a form of guerrilla warfare, flourished during the 1870s and it was a leading Fenian, Michael Davitt, who in 1878 created a tenants' organisation known as the Land League. In 1874 there arrived at Westminster, under the leadership of Isaac Butt, a band of fifty-six Home Rulers pledged to act as "a separate and distinct party . . . united on the principle of obtaining self-government for Ireland." Their watchword, however, was moderation and the plea for independence was made in terms that were almost apologetic. The Commons barely noticed them nor were the more extreme elements in Ireland impressed by the group's activities. The situation changed in 1879 when Charles Stewart Parnell, a young Protestant landlord who had been elected to Parliament four years earlier, joined forces with Davitt and thus affected an alliance between the party at Westminster and the men responsible for perpetrating "agrarian outrages".

The story of the next ten years is well known. Sixty-one Home Rulers were elected in 1880 and the party cast moderation to the winds. Ireland, amidst scenes of mounting tumult, became the dominating issue of the day. In 1885 the Nationalists (now eighty-six strong) helped the Liberals to bring down Salisbury's administration. Later that year the first Home Rule Bill was defeated in the Commons by 341 to 311, but the Nationalists were jubilant. No matter that the Liberal Party was shattered and that, in the general election which followed, it secured only 191 seats as opposed to the Unionists' 394: the power of Gladstone's name was as great as ever, and an inevitable change in public opinion would sweep the Grand Old Man back into office at the next election. Liberals and Nationalists now spoke together on the same platforms and the Unionist policy of rigorous coercion only served to tighten the bonds between them.

Disaster, however, was fast approaching. In November 1890, faced with Parnell's failure to deny that he had committed adultery with Kitty O'Shea, Gladstone, as the stern custodian of the Nonconformist conscience, was obliged to condemn his continued leadership of the Nationalist cause. This declaration, coming as a bolt from the blue, dealt the Nationalist Party a mighty blow and one from which it never really recovered. A choice had to be made, it seemed, between Parnell and Home Rule, and after prolonged and terrible debates in Committee Room 15 at the House of Commons, forty-five members of the party reassembled elsewhere as a separate group: with Justin McCarthy as their leader, it was agreed that their policy should be close co-operation with the Liberal Party. Parnell was left with a band of twenty-eight followers, foremost among whom was Redmond, and there followed ten months of bitter and bloody warfare between the two groups, each of whom claimed to be the legitimate party. The "great Comedian's" death brought the first phase of the crisis to an end, but the party remained divided. Its four leading members, Redmond, John Dillon, Tim Healy and William O'Brien, were unable to settle their differences and each went his own way. Redmond took charge of the Parnellites, reduced to nine after the general election of 1892, Dillon (from 1896 onwards) assumed control of the seventy-odd anti-Parnellites, Healy ploughed a solitary furrow which culminated in the creation of his People's Rights Association (1897) and O'Brien, returning to agrarian agitation, launched the United Irish League (1898). Throughout the 1890s, in short, the Irish parliamentary party was only a shadow of its former self. The defeat of Gladstone's second Home Rule Bill and the subsequent eclipse of the Liberal Party deprived it of any immediate goal.

In January 1900, after ten wasted years, a reconciliation took place. Dillon handed over the leadership to Redmond and accepted the post of second-in-command. A few months later Redmond became President of the United Irish League, which was henceforth recognised as the official Nationalist organisation, and O'Brien himself came to exercise a considerable amount of influence behind the scenes. After the general election the Nationalists returned to Westminster in a mood of exultant fury which had not been witnessed for almost twenty years. It seemed as though the spirit of Parnell had returned to the scene and before long Irish members were on their feet demanding that the grievances of the peasantry be given proper attention and protesting against the Government's refusal to repeal the Crimes Act. The old tactics of obstruction were revived, together with agitation in Ireland itself, and during the next two years eleven Irish M.P.s suffered spells of imprisonment. Wyndham's Land Act led to fresh disagreements within the party, however, and O'Brien resigned from it in November 1903. He joined forces with Healy, who had been expelled from the party three years before, and the leadership of the Nationalists was henceforth concentrated in the hands of Redmond and Dillon, with T. P. O'Connor usually at hand to give advice and assistance.

Wyndham's resignation in March 1905 ended the influence of the moderate reformers in the Unionist camp. Hopes for an Irish University Bill, which he had intended to promote, were abruptly shattered and the Nationalists could do little more than console themselves with the reflection that the Liberals would probably be in power before another year had elapsed. Eight months later, with the prospects of a Liberal triumph at the polls very bright indeed, an expectant Redmond and O'Connor breakfasted with Campbell-Bannerman on November 14th. Sir Henry, however, while declaring that he personally was stronger than ever for Home Rule and did not mind "the Rosebery crowd", explained that it would not be possible to pass such a measure in the next Parliament. The party would adopt, instead, the policy of "Home Rule by easy stages", and his Government would pass an interim measure consistent with, and leading up to, complete self-government. Redmond and O'Connor, knowing the difficulties of Sir Henry's position, agreed that this was probably the best policy.*23

The actual meaning of the magic words Home Rule was, perhaps, something which no two Irishmen at this time would have been able to agree. A great conference held in Dublin in 1873 had not gone into details and those who attended took the words to mean the repeal of the Act of Union and the re-establishment of an Irish parliament which would have exclusive control of their country's affairs. The Bill of 1886 had envisaged a parliament which would handle everything except foreign policy,

---

* "The main thing that Redmond wants," wrote Labouchere to Campbell-Bannerman on November 30th, 1905, "is that there be some sort of general assembly elected by the Irish. If it be given very limited powers, he considers that in the nature of things it would gradually get more. But he will stand out for this assembly."24

defence, customs and excise, religious establishments, matter affecting the Crown, the post office and the coinage. Ireland would cease to be represented at Westminster but she would contribute towards the United Kingdom's expenditure on defence. This meant, of course, that there would be taxation without representation and this was one of the chief criticisms levied against the Bill by those who were otherwise favourably disposed towards it. By 1893 a compromise had been reached and the second Home Rule Bill provided for eighty Irish representatives at Westminster who would speak and vote solely on matters appertaining to Ireland. The Nationalists claimed to be satisfied with this measure and regarded it, henceforth, as the very least they could expect. Redmond, writing in 1910, declared that Ireland wanted legislative and executive control of all purely Irish affairs (land, education, local government, transport, labour, industries, taxation for local purposes, justice, police, etc.) "subject to the supreme authority of the Imperial Parliament." The latter, in which Ireland would probably continue to be represented, would retain control of defence, foreign policy, customs, Imperial taxation, matters concerning the Crown and all questions which were Imperial and not local in nature.[25]

One problem which none of the Home Rulers had seriously considered, however, was Ulster, the Protestant representatives of which had made it clear time and time again that the last thing they desired was separation from England and the domination of a Catholic parliament. Gladstone had promised in 1886 that "the Protestant minority should have its wishes considered to the utmost practicable extent" but had made it clear that those wishes should not be allowed to overrule the desires of the great mass of the Irish people. Lord Randolph Churchill, in reply, had coined the slogan "Ulster will fight and Ulster will be right!" which would now be heard again before many years had elapsed. The Irish Unionists, as we have already noted, were a formidable band: neither they nor the Nationalists were prepared to consider partition as a solution and neither side was prepared to make concessions to the other.

In February 1906 Home Rule was, admittedly, of academic rather than immediate interest, but the Irish members reassembling at Westminster were for this very reason determined that their grievances in other spheres would receive proper attention. "My idea of an Irish policy for the Liberal Party," wrote Dillon to Bryce on December 19th, "is that until they are able to propose their legislative proposals for the better government of Ireland they ought to govern the country, so far as the present system allows, in accordance with Irish ideas—ascertaining those ideas from the representatives of the majority of the Irish people, and when attacked in the House or in the Press, that they ought boldly to proclaim this policy. . . . the whole situation would be easier for us and it would be made possible for us to give the Government time to mature their proposals. . . . It is absolutely *vital* that Bannerman's Stirling speech should be allowed to stand as the definition of the position of the Liberal Party on the Irish question. Any attempt to explain away that statement by the Prime Minister himself—or by you—would lead to the most disastrous results. We are content with that statement, although it was, as the Prime Minister said, a *most moderate statement.*"[26] On December 31st Bryce warned Campbell-Bannerman that Redmond was "quite friendly but says that unless we do something to indicate a change of policy . . . his supporters in Ireland and in the H. of C. will not allow him to give us the support he desires to give, and in particular that he will be placed in the greatest difficulties over the Education Bill, in which he desires to oppose us as little as he can."[27]

The two largest individual groups represented in the parliamentary party were barristers and journalists, who made up nearly half its strength, but they did not form so great an element as they had before 1900. Mr F. S. L. Lyons has pointed out that after the "Khaki" election "the type of member who sat at Westminster for part of the year and attended to his business or his farm was being represented in increasingly large numbers"[28] and local merchants and farmers were, indeed, the third largest group in the party. The great majority of them never opened their mouths in Parliament, their duty being simply that of voting in whatever manner they were instructed. The leading lights of the party, it is interesting but rather saddening to note, were the men who had been Parnell's lieutenants in the 1880s: apart from Joseph Devlin no new figures had come to the fore. Redmond, Dillon, O'Connor, Healy and O'Brien had, despite their differences with one another, occupied the centre of the stage for so long that they were in danger of becoming permanent fixtures. They were certainly more at home at Westminster than they were in Ireland and knew little or nothing of the Gaelic League, the Gaelic Athletic Association or, last but very far from least, Sinn Fein. Herein, as we shall see, lay the seeds of ultimate tragedy.

(5)

W. H. Beveridge, writing in the *Morning Post* on February 1st, 1906, described the advent of the Labour Party as "the most outstanding feature of a remarkable election," and it must be admitted that there was ample justification for these words.

Labour had, in a sense, been politically active since the creation of the

Labour Representation League in 1869, an organisation concerned with securing the return to Parliament of "qualified working men". Two of the twelve candidates which it sponsored in the general election of 1874 had been successful. The League was dissolved soon after this, but Thomas Burt—one of the two members elected—had retained his seat ever since. He had been joined, as the years went by, by several other "qualified working men", the majority of whom (like Burt himself) were miners' representatives. They made no attempt to form a separate party but attached themselves to the Liberals and became known as Lib-Labs. As we noted in our last chapter, twenty-four of them had now been returned to Parliament.*

The year 1893 had witnessed the creation of the Independent Labour Party, a body of men who, led by Keir Hardie, were intent upon the general betterment of working-class conditions and believed in direct political action as the best means of achieving this goal. They agreed at the outset that their chief objectives should be "the collective and communal ownership of all means of production, distribution and exchange," but their programme also provided for the abolition of the monarchy, the House of Lords, overtime, piecework and child labour, together with the establishment of a forty-eight-hour week in all industries, State provision for the sick, disabled, aged and widows and the introduction of a graduated income tax. Its strength lay initially in Scotland and north-east England, but by 1896 it had 381 branches throughout Britain and 10,000 subscribing members. "Many young men who were Nonconformist local preachers," wrote Philip Snowlen later, "were attracted to the movement by the ethical appeal of Socialism. Their experience in speaking was a great help to the party propoganda. Working men who had toiled all day at arduous work went out at night into the streets to preach in their simple way the new gospel of emancipation. Men who had never before attempted public speaking were given courage and the gift of effective oratory by the new passion for social justice which consumed them. The movement was something new in politics. It was politics inspired by idealism and religious fervour."[29]

The twenty-eight candidates which the I.L.P., as it soon became known, put forward in the general election of 1895 were defeated and Hardie, who had himself sat as an independent Labour member from 1891 to 1895, grew despondent at his party's failure to win a single by-election during the five years which followed. He was gradually driven to the conclusion that the only way a Socialist organisation could gain a parliamentary foothold

* Enoch Edwards was the Chairman of this group and Richard Bell the Vice-Chairman.

would be by alliance with the trade union movement, but this was something easier said than done. Trade unions, despite their rapid growth in strength and importance since the early 1880s, had shown little or no interest in political action.* Fortunately for Hardie, however, recent judgments had left their legal status in doubt, and anxiety to change the law led to what is nowadays automatically described as "that fateful meeting" at the Memorial Hall, Farringdon Street, in February 1900. This meeting did *not* result in the creation of the Labour Party. What it did result in was the creation of a Labour Representation Committee, with Ramsay MacDonald as its secretary, which aimed at establishing "a distinct Labour group in Parliament." The Labour Representation Committee, or the L.R.C., was composed initially of seven trade unionists, two members of the I.L.P., two members of the Social Democratic Federation and one Fabian. It was an uneasy alliance, and during the year which followed no more than 40 unions out of the 1,200 or so then existing troubled to affiliate. The Taff Vale judgment, however, sent membership soaring: by 1906 only the miners were holding aloof. Success at the polls also helped to boost membership: Keir Hardie and Richard Bell, the secretary of the Amalgamated Society of Railway Servants, were triumphant in the general election of 1900 (in which the L.R.C. sponsored 15 candidates) and by-election successes in 1902 and 1903 brought the Committee into prominence and led to the pact between Gladstone and MacDonald.

The début of Labour politicians in the 1900 Parliament had not been altogether satisfactory. Hardie and Bell were soon at loggerheads and the latter joined forces with the Liberal Party, leaving Hardie to battle on alone. David Shackleton, who entered the Commons in 1902, found himself more in sympathy with the Lib-Labs than with Hardie, and so did Will Crooks and Arthur Henderson, who were victorious in by-elections the following year. In February 1905, however, a step towards unity was taken when the T.U.C. Parliamentary Committee, the Lib-Labs and the L.R.C. agreed to join forces in the battle to amend the legal status of trade unions, although Hardie glumly reflected that "my position as the only avowed Socialist in the group is not one of the pleasantest."†[30]

From January 1906 onwards it was evident that the Labour movement

* A Labour Electoral Association was set up in the late 1880s for the purpose of securing the return of more Lib-Labs, but this gave way in the 1890s to the T.U.C. Parliamentary Committee, which was simply concerned with lobbying both Liberal and Unionist M.P.s. The T.U.C. occasionally advocated, at its annual conferences, nationalisation of the land, the mines and the railways and the introduction of old age pensions, but it did not take any practical steps to secure these ends.

† At the time of dissolution there were 15 Labour M.P.s in the 1900 Parliament (11 Lib-Labs and the 4 L.R.C. members).

was a force to be reckoned with in British politics. Even so, this was not exactly the Socialist revolution which Balfour was gaily depicting to his friends since only seven of the twenty-nine victors had been sponsored by the I.L.P. and the Bible loomed larger than the Communist Manifesto in the party's affairs at this time. The majority of the other twenty-two members did, admittedly, belong to the I.L.P., but they were more concerned with promoting the interests of their respective trade unions than the cause of Socialism. In accordance with the 1900 resolution they elected their own whips and christened themselves "the Labour Party", but problems arose when it came to choosing a chairman. Hardie and Shackleton, the two candidates, tied on the first ballot. They tied again on the second and MacDonald, who had been appointed Secretary of the parliamentary party, gave his casting vote in favour of Hardie. Since the voting had been so close, however, Hardie was obliged to agree that his chairmanship would not be permanent during this Parliament. Shackleton became Deputy Chairman and Henderson was elected Chief Whip.

The I.L.P. section of the Labour Party was led by two Scotsmen and a Yorkshireman: Keir Hardie, Ramsay MacDonald and Philip Snowden. They were a formidable triumvirate, although the years had taken their toll of Hardie: with his long flowing beard and large sad eyes he was fast becoming a figure of veneration, albeit not yet fifty. Time, however, had not softened his tongue, as some of his colleagues were soon to discover, and he remained a powerful figure. Ramsay MacDonald, slim and aggressive, was looked upon as the angry young man of the party, a symbol of things to come,* but it was Snowden, the member for Blackburn, who attracted the greatest attention. This "frail figure with the top-heavy head," as one journalist described him, had somehow inherited the Gladstonian glare and the corresponding power of riveting members to their seats by the sheer intensity of his invective. Hardie represented the party's past, MacDonald its future and Snowden its conscience. Other members of the parliamentary party who had been sponsored by the I.L.P. were John Clynes, Fred Jowett, James Parker and Thomas Summerbell.

The most prominent of the twenty-one trade union members of the party were Henderson, Shackleton, Will Thorne, John Hodge and George Barnes. Where they differed from the I.L.P. section (although several of them belonged to the I.L.P.) was in their tendency to distinguish between questions that were specifically "Labour" and those that were "political".

---

* Beatrice Webb, writing in 1896, referred to him as "a brilliant young Scot" but one who was simply not much good at expounding Socialist principles to the uninitiated, since he had "never had time to do any sound original work, or even [to] learn the old stuff well."[31]

They preferred to keep an open mind on issues that did not directly concern them and voted as individuals, while the I.L.P. argued that the party
ought to present a united and positive front on each and every issue. The
trade union members were also more inclined to work in harmony with
the Liberals.

Mention should also be made of Will Crooks, the candidate of neither
the I.L.P. nor the trade unions but the Woolwich L.R.C. He had played
an important part in the 1889 dock strike and had been active in the municipal politics of Poplar for many years. In 1901 he became its mayor, the
first Labour mayor that London had ever known, and had been M.P. for
Woolwich since 1903. A towering figure with a black bushy beard, he
proved to be one of the best-loved members of the party.

These, then, were some of the members of the parliamentary Labour
Party. They formed at this period little more than a specialised pressure
group and, despite the I.L.P.'s declaration in 1905 that the ultimate object
of the L.R.C. was "the overthrow of the present competitive system of
capitalism and the institution of a system of public ownership of all the
means of production, distribution and exchange," Socialism did not play
any great part in their propaganda. Their immediate concern was the
reform of trade-union legislation while their general policy was the improvement of working-class conditions, which could best be brought
about by prodding the Liberal Party into action. The most optimistic of
these Labour representatives can scarcely have foreseen that they would,
eighteen years later, be forming a Government of their own or that the
leader-writer of the *Morning Post* would one day be providing them with
a blueprint of social reforms more extensive than anything Lloyd George
could have dreamt of.

(6)

A word must be said, finally, about the "unrepresentative assembly",
namely that august body of elderly nobleman whose combined intelligence enshrined, so it was confidently asserted, the wisdom of the ages,
whose debates were little short of pearls of perfection and whose actions,
however incomprehensible they might sometimes appear, were motivated
solely by a desire to legislate or pontificate in the interests of the public at
large. The House of Lords was regarded with pride as the oldest surviving
portion of the British Constitution after the Crown itself. Whereas the
Commons had not appeared on the scene until 1265, and then only nominally, the Lords had been the advisers of the King from time immemorial.
Even now, a De Clifford, a Grey de Ruthyn, a Herries, a Mowbray and

Segrave, a Norfolk, a Sayle and Sele and a Willoughby de Brooke, scions of the most ancient families of England, were present in their midst. Resplendent in the lustre of the ages, they met together to deliberate on the affairs of the nation secure in the knowledge that, whatever the views of the transient assembly in the adjoining chamber, here and here only was the final decision reached as to what alterations, if any, should be made to the Statute Book of the United Kingdom. It was, admittedly, argued in certain quarters that a Second Chamber was something of an anachronism and that true political power ought now to reside solely with the Commons, the authentic voice of the people.* The answer to this, however, was that the Upper House served as a permanent safeguard against any excesses which the Commons (in a temporary mood of misguided revolutionary fervour) might endeavour to perpetrate. For the most part, in any case, the two Houses found themselves in agreement—the Education Act of 1902 and the Licensing Act of 1904, for example, had occasioned no dissent whatever—and it was only on comparatively rare occasions, when the Radicals managed to seize control of the Lower House, that the Lords were honour-bound to exercise special vigilance. The last such occasion had been the Liberal Governments of 1892–5, and the peers had then been obliged (among other things) to act in the best interests of the country by rejecting the Home Rule Bill and drastically amending an Employers' Liability Bill and a Parish Councils Bill.

"Nearly the whole work of the Session has been wrecked," said Gladstone in March 1894, in the last speech which he ever delivered in the Commons. He went on to declare that what had long been a serious question "has arrived at a state of peculiar acuteness and peculiar magnitude. . . . The question is whether the work of the House of Lords is not merely to modify but to annihilate the whole work of the House of Commons." He was the only member of his own Cabinet, however, who desired to provide an answer to this question, and his successor, Rosebery, while bemoaning the activities of the Upper House in long letters to Queen Victoria, showed no desire to lead a crusade against his fellow peers.† Several members of the Liberal Party (including Labouchere) nevertheless expressed their anger in no uncertain terms, and the Queen felt obliged to warn Campbell-Bannerman, the deputy leader in the Commons, that al-

* Roebuck and Lytton Bulwer had campaigned in the mid-1830s for the reform of the House of Lords, but the first real onslaught of any importance (leaving aside the Cromwellian era) had been launched by Chamberlain in 1884.

† Rosebery did, admittedly, for want of any other subject on which to fight an election, endeavour to raise the issue in a speech at Bradford in October 1894. His efforts were so restrained, however, that they attracted little or no attention and his lordship soon relapsed into his usual attitude of helpless passivity.

though the House of Lords might require reform she could never agree to depriving them of their power to alter or reject measures, since this would leave "no force to resist the subversive measures of the so-called Liberals but better called destructives."* Campbell-Bannerman, in reply, had admitted that there was no strong feeling in the country at large about the powers of the Upper House but said that there did exist a strong and steady conviction (1) that the present position was neither solid nor safe; (2) that it was ridiculous to have an elaborate representative system and maintain a House to check its results; (3) that the check only applied, in any case, to legislation and not to the whole sphere of administration; (4) that so far as legislation was concerned the "more violent Bills of Tories are passed when moderate Liberal Bills are refused" and (5) that there was no check at all when the Tories were in power. The House of Lords, in short, was a partisan assembly functioning in a partisan manner.³³ The Queen was evidently impressed with these arguments, but the days of Rosebery's Government were numbered and no attempt was made by the Liberal leaders of that time to mount a full-scale attack against the Second Chamber. Eleven years later, however, Campbell-Bannerman found himself at the head of a Radical Government with an overwhelming majority in the Commons and in a position, at long last, to rectify the unequal balance between the two Houses.

The relative strengths of the two main parties in the Upper House were exactly the reverse of what they were in the Commons. Only 102 of the 607 peers were Liberals: of the rest, 349 were Conservatives, 123 were Liberal-Unionists and the remaining 33 had no particular affiliation.† The latter, however, included four members of the royal family (who were officially non-political), the Archbishop of York and 14 bishops,‡ and Asquith reckoned that at least 500 peers were Unionist supporters. The weakness of the Liberal contingent owed much to the events of 1886: before that date there had, admittedly, been clashes between the two Houses whenever a Radical administration held office, but the Lords had proceeded with caution since 1832 and the Reform Bill of 1884 had occasioned the first major collision between them for more than fifty years. A com-

---

* "The House of Lords," she had written to Rosebery some seven months earlier, "might possibly be improved, but it is *part* and *parcel* of the *much vaunted* and admired *British constitution* and CANNOT be *abolished*. It is the *ONLY REALLY* independent House."³²

† This assessment indicates the position as it was after June 1906 and not as it was when Campbell-Bannerman took office, at which time the number of Liberal peers only amounted to 86. One of the first things the new Prime Minister did was to secure the royal assent to the creation of 10 Liberal peers, and in June 1906 the King reluctantly agreed to the creation of a further half-dozen.

‡ The Archbishop of Canterbury was a Liberal-Unionist, as were 4 of the 11 remaining bishops. Another 4 bishops were Conservatives and the remaining 3 were Liberal supporters.

promise had then been reached, but two years later Gladstone's decision to support Home Rule led to a mass evacuation of the Liberal benches in the Upper House. The Conservatives, who in 1885 commanded the allegiance of not much more than half of the then 524 members, found themselves reinforced by a small army of discontented Liberals and in 1893 the Government was only able to muster a voting strength of 41 in support of the second Home Rule Bill as opposed to a Unionist vote of 419.

The new leader of the Liberal contingent in the Upper House (in succession to the ailing Lord Spencer) was Lord Ripon, the Lord Privy Seal. Ripon, at seventy-eight, was the oldest member of the new Government, and had been active in politics since 1853. He had served under both Palmerston and Gladstone and had been Governor-General of India in the 1880s. His chief assistant was Lord Crewe, Lord President of the Council and Rosebery's son-in-law, who at the age of forty-eight was already acquiring the prestige of an elder statesman. Efficient, untiring and uncomplaining, the burden of guiding the Government's bills through the Second Chamber would fall upon him with increasing intensity during the years which followed.

Ripon and Crewe were supported by Loreburn (previously Sir Robert Reid), the Lord Chancellor, Tweedmouth, the First Lord of the Admiralty, and Elgin, the Colonial Secretary (whose appointment, like Tweedmouth's, had been one of Campbell-Bannerman's less happy inspirations). The other members of the Government in the Upper House at this time were Carrington, President of the Board of Agriculture; Aberdeen, Lord-Lieutenant of Ireland; Fitzmaurice, Under-Secretary for Foreign Affairs, and Portsmouth, who was Under-Secretary at the War Office. The remaining ninety-three members of the Liberal Party, on whose support they theoretically relied, were something of a mixed bag. Spencer, for example, was rarely seen in the House these days; Rosebery, that spoilt child of fortune, was just as likely to vote for the Unionists as he was for the Government. Only from newly created Liberal peers could anything approaching regular attendance be expected, although the rest of the contingent would obviously do their best to provide support when needed. The Government's voting strength could be reckoned at no more than ninety, therefore, although this was an improvement on the situation in 1886, when it had been put at no more than thirty.

The Unionist leader in the Lords was the sixty-year-old Marquess of Lansdowne. He came of one of the great Whig families and had served under Gladstone before becoming Governor-General of Canada (1883–8) and Viceroy of India (1888–94). Home Rule alienated him from the

Liberals, however, and he had served under Salisbury and Balfour as Secretary of State for War (1895–1900) and Foreign Secretary (1900–5). He was responsible for the Anglo-Japanese Alliance and the *Entente Codiale*, two feathers which he was justly entitled to wear in his cap. Balfour, discussing Lansdowne with his niece in 1929, remarked that "I shouldn't call him very clever. He was—I don't quite know how to put it—better than competent."[34]

Lansdowne's chief colleague was the Earl of Cawdor, who had served as First Lord of the Admiralty in 1905. Other Unionist peers who played an active part in the politics of this period were Balfour of Burleigh (Secretary of State for Scotland from 1895 to 1903); Halsbury (Lord Chancellor from 1895 to 1905); James of Hereford (formerly Sir Henry James, who had served in Conservative administrations since the 1870s); Lytton (a young man of thirty, who had been a peer since the age of fifteen); Milner (fresh from his experiences in South Africa); Newton (who believed, as we shall see, in ploughing an independent furrow) and St Aldwyn (formerly Sir Michael Hicks Beach, one of Chamberlain's chief opponents, who had served under both Salisbury and Balfour as Chancellor of the Exchequer). The most illustrious figure on the Unionist side of the House was the Duke of Devonshire, now very deaf and slow-thinking, who, as Lord Hartington, had been one of Gladstone's right-hand men in the years before 1886.*

With the total number of Government supporters in the Upper House amounting to little more than a hundred, as opposed to a Unionist strength of at least 470, it was clear from the outset that there would be a repetition of the events of 1893 and 1894: the Commons proposed but the Lords disposed, and no one doubted that Liberal legislation would once again be weighed in the balance by the unrepresentative assembly and found wanting. There was, however, one important difference between the present position and that which had existed in the Parliament of 1892. On the latter occasion the Liberals had been obliged to rely on the Irish Nationalists for their support in the House of Commons and had been led first by an ageing Messiah and then by a Scottish peer who seemed sadly uncertain as to the direction (if any) in which they ought to be moving. In these circumstances, despite the pressure exerted by extremists, there was neither the spirit nor desire for a full-blooded crusade against the House of Lords. Possessing little more than 40% of the seats in the Com-

---

* Cromer did not play a part in the House of Lords debates until his return from Egypt in 1907; Curzon, whose peerage was an Irish one, did not become a member of the Upper House until 1908.

mons, they could scarcely claim to be the voice of the people. Now, however, the tables had been turned with a vengeance. Not only was the party solidly united at last, behind a capable leader; not only did they have some ideas (though still very nebulous) of what they wanted to do but, far more important than either of these factors, they now possessed an overwhelming majority in the Commons. A battle with the House of Lords, if it came, would be fought from a position of real strength for the first time since 1832.

CHAPTER FIVE

THE RISE OF THE OPPOSITION, FEBRUARY 1906

On the morrow of the general election the Unionists were in a sorry state. It was evident that drastic reorganisation and rethinking were necessary if they were to regain their ascendancy and equally apparent that the Tariff Reform controversy must now be settled one way or the other. Balfour's vacillation had led to disaster on a frightening scale and a settlement between the "whole hoggers" and the "little piggers" could no longer be postponed. "Everything," wrote Chamberlain to Long on January 30th, "seems to me to depend upon our being able to arrange for a firm, definite and united policy as the foundation of the new army we have to raise. There must be a reaction, but I cannot contemplate as possible another lengthened period of strenuous contest to secure a victory which, after it is gained, will still find the party at sixes and sevens on the main object of our policy."[1]

Superficially, it seemed that the rank and file of the party had drunk deeply of the Birmingham waters, but against this was the fact that the doctrine of Imperial Preference had not yet obtained a real hold upon the country at large. Strengthening the bonds of Empire was all very well in theory, but if it were to be presented to the electorate in the form of a tax upon foreign foodstuffs it was clear that the Unionist Party would have to abandon any hope of success at the polls for many a long day. Now or never was the time for Balfour to have the courage of what were thought to be his convictions and reassert himself by putting forward an alternative programme to re-unite the party and appeal to the electorate. If, on the other hand, he allowed this last great opportunity to pass him by, then Chamberlain and his ideas would predominate and the Unionists would find themselves committed to what might well, despite its colourful allure and majestic trappings, prove to be a sinking ship.*

* "Many of your best supporters," wrote Lansdowne to Balfour on January 29th, " 'stretched a point' when they went as far as you did, and will absolutely decline to go any further. . . . Surely we may, so far as the near future—certainly so far as this Session—is concerned, relegate the fiscal question to the background. . . . I particularly dislike the idea of tarring the H. of Lords with the brush of Protection."[2]

A meeting of the executive committee of the Liberal-Unionist Association Council was held on February 2nd and it was agreed that Balfour and the two Chamberlains should produce a formula defining the party's attitude to the fiscal question and that it should, when drafted, be submitted to a party meeting. Lansdowne, "filled with uneasiness" at this decision, warned Balfour (February 4th) that "any 'compromise' which the Chamberlainites are at all likely to accept would inevitably be regarded by the public and by your friends as a surrender on your part, and as an admission that we have said and allowed our supporters to say that your policy was a self-contained one and that it differed from Chamberlain's. . . . Almost any misfortune would be better for us than an alliance on these terms. . . . If he wrecks the party, or what remains of it, let him accept the responsibility and the consequences. He must lead in the H. of C. and one of his men in the H. of L. If he persists in his views and we in ours, I don't see how he can refuse."*[3]

Balfour reacted strongly to the suggestion that he might be willing to abandon his previous convictions. "I have never," he replied on February 6th, "thought it possible either to retract or to modify the public statement of my views which, in their essence, have undergone no alteration. And if Chamberlain insists upon this as the necessary price of unity, all hopes of unity must be abandoned."[5] Preliminary discussions with the Chamberlains had not, in any case, been markedly successful,† but on the same day that he wrote to Lansdowne he despatched a letter to Chamberlain in which he revealed that he had been reluctantly converted to the idea of a party meeting.

Balfour to Chamberlain, February 6th, 1906

You know how strong my objection is in ordinary circumstances to a party meeting, and how reluctant I am to have all our differences dealt with in a manner which is certain to be published, and will probably be irritating. But, on carefully thinking over the whole situation, I have come round to your view that, *if you desire it,* a party meeting must be held. . . .

There is no case in history, as far as I am aware, in which a party meeting has been summoned except to give emphasis and authority to a decision at which the

* This view was supported by Balfour's cousin, the fourth Marquess of Salisbury. "No attempt should be made," he wrote, "to unite the party by a formula designed to conceal their differences. I am afraid that policy has only led the electors to distrust us. They are stupid enough to suspect even verbal refinements. . . . I should announce the definite line in Parliament for the party to take it or leave it."[4]

† "Balfour showed himself so determined against any advance in my direction last night," wrote Chamberlain to Lord Northcliffe on February 3rd, "and was also [so] cold to my suggestion of joint organisation, that I was forced to the conclusion that he has finally decided to stand with the Free Traders rather than the Tariff Reformers." See also his letter of February 5th to Long, quoted on page 347.[6]

party have informally already arrived; still less is there an example to be found of a vote taken at such a meeting. How then are we to proceed on the present occasion? Are you and I to agree upon some question on which the meeting can vote Aye or No? If so, what is the question to be?...[7]

Chamberlain replied a few hours later, declaring that there would be no question whatever as to leadership, but that "the party as a whole should be asked to express freely their opinion as to the best policy for the future, and to vote between the alternatives suggested.... It will be clearly understood that the decision is not binding on the leaders ... but is merely taken for information."[8] Balfour, however, felt that he would be placing himself in an embarrassing position if he agreed to this arrangement. "If they choose the Glasgow speech," he wrote to Chamberlain on February 8th, "how can you refuse to become their leader? If they regret the 'Half-sheet of Notepaper' how can I continue to lead them?"*[9]

Having got his own way over the question of a meeting, Chamberlain could afford to be magnanimous. He replied on February 10th, explaining that he personally differed from Balfour only in what the latter did *not* say rather than what he did ."But ...," he added, "and this is serious, I object to the interpretations of what you have said by those who are, I think, more Balfour than Balfour himself." There was no personal rivalry between them and the time had surely come "to remove this suspicion of dual aims and to give the party a lead which will certainly be accepted by the great majority as an official policy." He and Austen had tried to produce "some kind of joint programme or declaration to which both of us can agree" and the draft of a resolution to be approved by the meeting was enclosed for Balfour's attention. "I do not think," Chamberlain's letter continued, "that there is anything in it which may not be found almost *verbatim* in your speeches and declarations; and, although it is not nearly as definite and does not go nearly as far as the Glasgow Programme, it *does* officially deprecate any premature decision against either a general tariff or a small duty on foreign corn. If ... in substance you are able to assent to it, I see no reason why it should not constitute the charter of our co-operation."[10]

On February 14th came the publication in the Press of correspondence, promptly dubbed "the Valentine letters", between Balfour and Chamberlain. The essential passage of these documents ran as follows:

* The "Glasgow Programme" referred to a speech which Chamberlain made in 1903, after leaving the Government, in which he declared that his proposals involved a duty of 2*s*. a quarter on foreign corn (excluding maize) and flour, a duty of 5% on meat and dairy produce (excluding bacon) and an average duty of 10% on all articles of foreign manufacture, colonial produce being allowed in duty-free. For the "half-sheet of notepaper" see page 4.

That fiscal reform is, and must remain, the first constructive work of the Unionist Party.

That the objects of such reform are to secure more equal terms of competition
for British trade, and closer commercial union with the Colonies.

That, while it is at present unnecessary to prescribe the exact methods by which
these objects are to be attained, and inexpedient to permit differences of opinion as
to these methods to divide the party, though other means may be possible, the
establishment of a moderate general tariff on manufactured goods, not imposed for
the purpose of raising prices or giving artificial protection against legitimate competition, and the imposition of a small duty on foreign corn, are not in principle
objectionable, and should be adopted if shown to be necessary for the attainment
of the ends in view or for purposes of revenue.

The party meeting took place at Lansdowne House the following day,
but the publication of these nicely worded letters had already produced
the impression that Balfour and Chamberlain were in harmony once more.
The meeting did nothing to dispel this impression. It was attended by
Unionist peers, members of the Commons and defeated candidates,
numbering about 650 in all. Chamberlain, according to one account, made
a speech in these terms: "Gentlemen, I will be very frank with you. I can
never lead the Conservative Party. There was a time when I thought I
might; but I am a Radical, and I disagree with you on points you would
regard as fundamental. I am not at one with you on the question of the
Church, nor yet of the land. With regard to Tariff Reform, I will assist
you in every way I can. I can never lead you."[11]

"My recollection is that the audience appeared to be almost wholly in
favour of Tariff Reform," wrote Lord Newton many years later: "that
the proceedings were amicable, and that Mr Balfour appeared somewhat
in the character of a captive, it being the general belief that he had yielded
at the last moment in consequence of the pressure put upon him by numerous members of the party."[12] The policy was, admittedly, so vague and
indeterminate that it could be twisted and stretched, read backwards or
forwards, to everyone's satisfaction, and Lord St Aldwyn saw nothing in
the "Valentine letters" which committed the Unionist Party to a general
tariff or a tax upon corn. Even the Duke of Devonshire seemed satisfied.
The general feeling, however, was that Balfour had given way. "I am
afraid it has been a capitulation," wrote one of the onlookers to Lansdowne. "Joe was able to say that he had surrendered nothing, that A.J.B.
agreed with him, and that the result was the official policy; and amid the
resounding cheers of Tariff Reformers, A.J.B. said nothing."[13]

On the face of it, what Lansdowne feared in his letter of February 4th

had come to pass: Balfour had sacrificed his own convictions and principles for the sake of party unity. The latter, on the other hand, evidently
felt that he had done no such thing. His own view on Colonial Preference,
as propounded in a letter to the King dated September 15th, 1903, was
that it was "eminently desirable in the interests of British commerce and
Imperial unity" but had not yet come within the sphere of practical politics.[14] He had clung tenaciously to this mid-way position ever since, and
even now it was difficult to gauge his true feelings on the subject. The
truth of the matter seems to have been that he did not actually have any.
He was far less interested in the merits or demerits of Tariff Reform than
his contemporaries, and the passions of the Chamberlainites and the "little
piggers" aroused no answering cry of excitement from their nominal
leader. He was bored by the whole subject, intent solely upon finding the
easiest way out of it. If party unity could only be obtained by the rejection
of Tariff Reform as a policy, he was willing to reject it; if it could only be
obtained by its acceptance, he was willing to accept it. "Nothing in this
world matters very much," he once said, "and there are very few things
that matter at all." His peculiar difficulty during the past few years had not
been so much that of concealing his own views upon the subject as of
hiding the fact that he had no views of his own to conceal. Balfour, sad to
relate, was a sphinx without a secret.

To what extent, then, were the Unionists at this time genuinely inclined
towards the beckoning siren of Imperial Preference? According to Neville
Chamberlain, writing to a friend on February 11th, "the majority of our
party both in and out of the House are in favour of Tariff Reform, and
would gladly follow if Balfour would only lead. . . . Unfortunately there
are still in the House and in the machine a good many representatives of
the old Tories who would never follow my father's lead even if he were
willing to give it."[15] Making allowance for the younger Chamberlain's
partisanship, it is probably true to say that the majority of Unionists had
been converted to Tariff Reform in a negative rather than an active sense,
being more concerned (like Balfour himself) with outward harmony than
the economic issues.* If unity could only be reached via the purgatory of
Imperial Preference then so be it, but they were not prepared, for the
moment, to shout aloud their conversion from the rooftops. The genuine
fiscal reformers remained a small but vociferous element in the party, but
while the Tory Free Traders fought a dogged rearguard action the great

* "The more I go about," Carson had written on December 17th, 1905, "the more I see
that Chamberlain has got hold of the bulk of our people. I don't mean so much our leading
men as those of the working classes that follow us."[16]

bulk of the Unionists allowed themselves to be propelled sluggishly forward in the direction of Chamberlain's goal.

At any rate, by the woolliest of compromise solutions the Conservative and Unionist Party was once more united, and for the next few months Balfour and Chamberlain would be pulling together in the same boat, pledged to prevent by all possible means the most important legislation of the new Government from taking effect. Tariff Reform, for the moment, had become a side-issue: all that mattered was presenting a united front to the enemy, and this they had at last succeeded in doing.*

---

* A struggle continued behind the scenes, however, for control of the Conservative Central Office. The Tariff Reformers had already gained control of the Conservative National Union and at the annual conference in November 1905 a resolution had been carried to the effect that it was desirable to strengthen the central management of the party "by the addition of a popular representative element in close touch with the constituencies." On February 25th the National Council of the National Union appointed a committee (eight Tariff Reformers and four Balfourites) to consider the means whereby this could best be done. On May 14th Sandars reported to Balfour that Acland-Hood was much alarmed at the way things were developing and "argues that to bring Joe into a position of appellate control of our election machine will be far from popular. . . . I told Alick that my idea would be to pursue a policy of dilatory tactics." Chamberlain's disappearance from the political scene early in July robbed the reforming movement of much of its vigour, and at a special party conference on July 27th approval was given to a somewhat meagre list of reforms which left control of the Central Office firmly in the hands of the Balfourites.[17]

CHAPTER SIX

DOMESTIC AFFAIRS, FEBRUARY–DECEMBER 1906

(1)

Parliament was officially opened on Tuesday, February 13th. In the Upper House the new Lord Chancellor took his oath as a peer, while in the Commons J. W. Lowther was re-elected Speaker.* After the oath had been administered the Houses adjourned until February 19th, when the King's Speech inaugurated the first Session. Apart from enumerating the steps to be taken in regard to South Africa, which will be dealt with later in this volume, it announced thirteen measures of prime importance to be placed upon the Statute Book. Pride of place was given to an Education Bill, which had a paragraph to itself, and this was followed by a Trade Disputes Bill and legislation concerned with amending the Workmen's Compensation and the Unemployed Women's Acts, extending Merchant Shipping Law and the Crofters' Holdings (Scotland) Act and altering the Labourers' (Ireland) Act. Other measures would check commercial corruption, improve the law regarding colonial marriages, abolish the property qualification required of County Justices in England, end plural voting in parliamentary elections and improve conditions in Ireland. "This list appears long," Campbell-Bannerman had written to the King on February 9th, "but many of the measures do not raise very disputable questions and need not occupy much time."[2]

The first important item debated by the Commons, thoughtfully timed to coincide with Balfour's reappearance in the House on March 12th as member for the City of London,† was a resolution in favour of Free Trade which specifically condemned the notion of a tax upon foreign corn or a general tariff on foreign goods. A full-dress debate upon Tariff Reform,

---

* In congratulating Lowther, noted Snowden, Campbell-Bannerman "betrayed a nervousness which was painful to see."[1]

† A cry of "Welcome, little stranger!" came from the Irish benches as he entered the Chamber.

the subject which had dogged him so unrelentingly during his premiership, was the most disconcerning welcome that ministerial ingenuity
could have devised.

The debate got under way and when the leader of the Unionist Party
rose to speak it seemed, to the uninitiated, that he had at last been forced
into a corner from which there was no escape. Either he must declare himself in favour of an out-and-out policy of protection or he must repudiate
the compromise reached in the "Valentine letters". Balfour, however, was
too old a hand to be caught so easily and his speech, though lengthy and
entertaining, skirted round the traps which had been laid for him with
comparative ease. He began by describing the resolution as a vote of censure upon the Opposition, which was a novel parliamentary procedure,
then went on to challenge its veracity and to chide the Government for
picking deliberate quarrels with the Opposition when it ought to be
bringing in its grand programme of reforms. He ended by putting five
questions to the Government, asking—among other things—whether it
intended to abolish existing protective duties (and if not, why not?),
whether it was refusing to deal with the protection of labour, and whether
it would be able, in times of great national emergency or for carrying out
some great social reform, to broaden the basis of taxation, even though it
be found practically impossible to do this without putting on Customs
duties that should not be exactly and nicely balanced by the Excise?

There was a moment's silence when he sat down. The Ministers remained in their places. "The right hon. gentleman," began Russell Rea,
the Liberal member for Gloucester, but he was interrupted by Balfour
demanding whether any member of the Government was going to reply.
Chamberlain rose in indignation, and there were cries of "Name, name!"
from the Opposition. The Speaker, amidst the ensuing hubbub, ruled that
he had called upon the member for Gloucester, who continued with his
speech. As soon as he had finished Chamberlain asked the Prime Minister
whether he intended to answer Balfour's questions, at which Campbell-
Bannerman shook his head. A Liberal member spoke next and then Balfour intervened once more. He expressed surprise at the Government's
silence and called upon the Prime Minister to clarify the situation.

Campbell-Bannerman at last rose to his feet, the light of battle gleaming
in his eyes. The opportunity had finally arrived for him to repay the insults
and jibes which he had suffered from Balfour in the past and he was determined to make the most of it. "The right hon. gentleman the member
for the City has been in the country since we last saw him," he began. "He
made it rather a matter of complaint that this was a vote of confidence in

himself and his friends moved by us. We moved the same want of confidence a few weeks ago in the country and the country voted the want of confidence. The right hon. gentleman is like the old Bourbans in the oft-quoted phrase—he has learnt nothing. He comes back to this new House of Commons with the same airy graces, the same subtle dialectics, the same light and frivolous way of dealing with a great question, and he little knows the temper of the House of Commons if he thinks that those methods will prevail here. He has put some questions to me on the resolution. He has split it and tortured it and pulled it to pieces and thinks he can put some posers to us."

"I put no posers," interrupted Balfour. "I asked for information which I thought the Government could give."

"It would be a very clever Government that could reconcile to each other the questions which the right hon. gentleman has put to us," retorted Campbell-Bannerman. "In the first place, he finds fault with us for having selected two principal courses of policy, the establishment of a general tariff and the taxation of foreign corn. They were selected because they were the main topics or features of the policy urged upon the country during the election. When the two right hon. gentlemen appeared at last to have come together it was on the ground of these two topics. . . . Then he says we are to stop the proceedings in this debate, and his amendments are not to be moved until we have answered these terrible questions. . . . I have no direct answer to give to them. They are utterly futile, nonsensical and misleading. They were invented by the right hon. gentleman for the purpose of occupying time in this debate. I say, enough of this foolery! It might have answered very well in the last Parliament, but it is altogether out of place in this Parliament. The tone and temper of this Parliament will not permit it. Move your amendments and let us get to business."

A motion for adjournment was defeated by 405 to 115 and the debate on the resolution continued. It was marked by a brilliant maiden speech by F. E. Smith, a latter-day Disraeli, but as the evening wore on it was very clear that the Opposition was getting the worst of the battle. The debate was adjourned that night and the resolution passed by 474 to 98 the following day. It had been an important occasion in many respects. It had shattered any hopes that Balfour might have cherished of regaining his old supremacy over the House, while it had done much to raise Campbell-Bannerman's prestige in the eyes of his supporters. From this point onwards, in fact, Sir Henry never looked back. The spectre of Tariff Reform had been laid, the Liberals were triumphant and their modest little leader had blossomed into an able and supremely confident parliamentarian.

With the decks cleared for action the long-awaited "Liberal reforms" began to put in an appearance. The first to arrive was the Merchant Shipping Act Amendment Bill, which was introduced into the House by Lloyd George on March 20th. It was designed to prevent overcrowding on merchant ships, to prohibit foreign seamen from serving on British ships unless they understood a certain amount of English, to fix a minimum standard of food for sailors and to arrange regular inspections by officials from the Board of Trade. On March 26th Gladstone introduced the Workmen's Compensation Bill, a measure designed to cover all classes not specified in previous Acts. Both measures passed their Second Readings without delay.

The Government's Trade Unions and Trade Disputes Bill, which was introduced into the House on March 28th, met with a poor response. It was phrased in so cautious a manner that the Labour members, who had given notice that they would be introducing a Bill of their own, announced their determination to press on with their measure. The latter had its Second Reading on March 30th and Campbell-Bannerman astounded his followers by voting for it in preference to the Government's own proposals. An Opposition motion that the debate be adjourned was defeated by 370 to 66 and the Bill duly passed its Second Reading by 416 to 66. Several Ministers and 60 or 70 Liberals abstained from voting and for the next month the matter was bitterly thrashed out at Cabinet meetings. Asquith was especially indignant at this jettisoning of the Government Bill but he was overruled, and when the latter received its Second Reading on April 25th it was announced that its final form would be settled in Committee. The Labour members, reassured by Sir Henry's action, abandoned their own Bill and awaited the result of these deliberations.

On April 27th the Plural Voting Bill was read for the first time. Leave to introduce this measure, which would make it illegal for an elector to cast his vote in more than one constituency at a general election, was granted by 327 to 66. Three days later Asquith, in a typically brief and lucid speech, introduced his first Budget. It was not a particularly exciting measure, its author having found "the field of possible action already to a very large degree limited and circumscribed," and its most attractive feature, from the Liberal viewpoint, was a cut of £1,500,000 in naval expenditure.

What was destined to be the most controversial measure of the year had been introduced into the Commons on April 9th. This was the Government's Education Bill, designed to remove all the religious difficulties created by the Act of 1902.* It proposed that every school maintained out of rates and taxes (which meant every Church of England school and a good many Catholic schools) should be under the exclusive management and control of the representative local authority. Religious tests for teachers would be abolished and staff would not be compelled to give religious instruction. The local authority would be responsible for the appointment of all members of staff and could use its discretion in regard to undenominational teaching, which might (if it approved) be given by members of the existing staff, qualified or not. In transferred schools denominational teaching might be given twice a week if this were a condition of the transfer, but not by regular members of staff. From January 1st, 1908 no schools would be recognised as public elementary schools except those provided by the local education authorities, which could take over existing voluntary schools by agreement with the trustees and, in some cases, by force. Rent would be paid for the use of Church schools.

However admirable the purposes of the Bill, it was framed in such a manner as to provoke the maximum degree of opposition from the outset and to leave the Government with very little room for subsequent manoeuvre. Several members of the Cabinet felt that it might have been softened but the Radicals were sternly against compromise in any form.† The Archbishop of Canterbury, Dr Randall Davidson, who was given a preview of the proposals, noted on April 4th that "some of the members are indignant at the line the majority has taken, and Asquith for one wished the matter to be reconsidered 'ab initio' but was overruled. The matter is not to go before the Cabinet again and Birrell is cross and despondent, saying that the Bill will be thrown out in the Lords."[4]

It passed its First Reading, at any rate, without a division, but Anglican and Roman Catholic opposition was very soon making itself felt, the cry being that parents had the right to secure specific religious teaching for

* The 1902 measure had abolished School Boards (nearly 3,000 in all) and placed the responsibility for all education, with certain exceptions, on the county and county borough councils. What infuriated the Nonconformists, however, was that Church or voluntary schools (which numbered 14,000 in 1902 as opposed to 5,700 Board schools) were incorporated into the new system without losing their separate indentities. The burden of their upkeep fell upon the rates, but the managers retained the right to select their own staff (hence religious tests for teachers) and religious instruction continued in accordance with the terms of original trust deeds. In "provided" schools (i.e., schools "provided" by the local authority) religious teaching (where given) was undenominational and the appointment of staff was the responsibility of the local authority. Nonconformists objected (*a*) to paying rates towards the upkeep of Church schools and (*b*) to sending their children to them in those parishes where no alternative existed.

† See Campbell-Bannerman's letter to Ripon of April 7th, quoted on page 348, for an indication of feeling among the Liberal rank and file at this time. Wilfred Meynell told Wilfred Blunt on May 9th that Birrell had repudiated the Bill as his own and described it as "really Lloyd George's drafting forced on Birrell by a Cabinet majority."[3]

their children. The Nationalists joined forces with the Unionists in opposing the measure, while Labour members argued that religious teaching
was the concern of the religious authorities and not the State. Protest
meetings were held throughout the country and the Bishops of London
and Manchester played a prominent part in stirring up the agitation. The
Archbishop of Canterbury wrote a long letter of protest to King Edward,
who was on a Mediterranean cruise, and the King reacted in a characteristic fashion. "The Bill," he noted, "is most unfair and dangerous, and instead of smoothing matters will produce violent dissensions between the
Church of England and Roman Catholics on one side and the Nonconformists on the other. In fact, a kind of political-religious warfare will ensue,
which is most undesirable, especially just now. The Prime Minister pro-
fesses to like the Archbishop and values his opinion. At least, he told me
so. But . . . the way he forces these violent measures with such haste on the
House of Commons does not augur well for the future.* The conduct of
the Government in the matter is, by the Archbishop's letter, most Jesuisti-
cal."[6] A seven-line account from Campbell-Bannerman of the happenings
of April 9th had the comment "What valuable information!" scrawled
across it.[7]

The Bill was read for a second time on May 10th, a motion for its rejection (which the Nationalists supported) having been defeated by a
majority of 206, and the Committee Stage began some ten days later. It
was soon found necessary to introduce "closure by compartments" to
speed the measure on its way, but it was not until July 30th, even so, that
the Third Reading could be carried by 369 to 177. Balfour, with unusual
candour, made it plain that he regarded these proceedings as nothing
more than a tiresome charade. "The real discussion of this question is not
now in this House," he declared, "and has not been for some time. The
real discussion must be elsewhere; and everybody is perfectly reconciled
to the fact that another place is going to deal with large tracts of the Bill
which we have not found time even to touch upon. . . . It is in the highest
degree improbable that the Bill will come back in the shape in which it
leaves us."

On August 4th the Commons adjourned for the summer recess, nearly
fifty measures having passed through their House since the beginning of

---

* "Between ourselves," Knollys had written to Lord Esher on March 23rd, "I don't think
the King will ever like C.B. politically. I do not believe that the latter understands him, any
more than Mr G. understood the Queen." The King himself, writing to Esher on April
14th, declared that he viewed "with considerable alarm . . . the way the Prime Minister is
going on, and needless to say, he never brings anything before me—never consults me in *any*
way."[5]

the Session. This was a marked contrast to previous years, but it was a moot point just how many of these measures would survive their passage through the House of Lords.

(2)

In a letter to Balfour dated April 5th Lansdowne had stressed the need for co-ordinating Unionist strategy in the two Houses. "In dealing with such Bills as the Trade Disputes Bill or the Robartes Bill,"* he wrote, "I cannot help thinking that the leaders in the House of Commons should have before them at the outset a definite idea of the treatment which the question might receive in the event of either of those Bills coming before the House of Lords later in the Session." He suggested the establishment of a small committee "including, say, four or five members of each House," which would meet at least once a week for an exchange of ideas.[8] Balfour replied a week later, agreeing in principle to the proposal and letting slip some interesting observations of his own.

Balfour to Lansdowne, April 13th, 1906

There is not the least doubt that your idea must, in some shape or other, be carried out. . . . I conjecture that the Government methods of carrying on their legislative work will be this: they will bring in Bills in a much more extreme form than the moderate members of the Cabinet probably approve: the moderate members will trust to the House of Lords cutting out or modifying the most outrageous provisions: the left wing of the Cabinet, on the other hand, . . . will be consoled for the anticipated mutilation of their measures by the reflection that they will be gradually accumulating a case against the Upper House, and that they will be able to appeal at the next election for a mandate to modify its constitution. The scheme is an ingenious one, and it will be our business to defeat it as far as we can.

I do not think the House of Lords will be able to escape the duty of making serious modifications in important Government measures, but, if this is done with caution and tact, I do not believe that they will do themselves any harm. On the contrary, . . . I think it quite possible that your House may come out of the ordeal strengthened rather than weakened by the inevitable difficulties of the next few years.[9]

Balfour's belief that the "moderate" members of the Government would rely upon the Upper House modifying or rejecting legislation put

* The "Robartes Bill" was a Land Tenure Bill introduced by Agar-Robartes, a Liberal member. It was designed to extend, cheapen and simplify the law of compensation for tenants' improvements. Before its Third Reading Agar-Robartes had lost his seat, as the result of an election petition, and the Government adopted the Bill, renaming it the Agricultural Holdings Bill. It received a rough passage in the Upper House and a considerable number of alterations were made to it. The Commons, however, protested against these changes and the Lords gave way at the last moment.

forward by their more Radical colleagues is not quite so extraordinary as it might seem at first glance. Already, as we have seen, several members of the Cabinet were unhappy about both the Trade Disputes Bill and the Education Bill and Loreburn, writing to Ripon on May 10th about an Aliens Bill approved by the Lower House, remarked that "the House of Commons seems disposed to let anything through, relying on the Lords to act as executioners."* The Unionists, he thought, were not altogether unjustified in assuming that the Liberal peers would automatically take charge of any measure, no matter how outlandish, that might be sent up to them.[11] Ripon, replying the following day, admitted that the Government would no doubt be in conflict with the Lords sooner or later, although he hoped that such a break would not take place during the current Session. "But if we are to break with them," he added, "it is surely most important that it should be on some large question in which strong public interest is felt and not on a small matter like the Aliens Bill."[12]

(3)

On July 7th Birmingham celebrated the seventieth birthday of Joseph Chamberlain, dispelling for all time the adage that a prophet is without honour in his own land. Dancing, feasting and revelry were the order of the day. Outwardly, at any rate, the old man himself appeared as energetic as ever, dominating the scene as he had done for so many years past. It was an occasion that Birmingham would long remember.

Ten days later Chamberlain suffered a stroke that put an end to his career. The power of movement departed from him almost entirely, although his brain remained as clear and alert as it had always been, and it was only with great difficulty that he was able to speak. He lived on until 1914, an uneasy spectator hovering in the wings, but to all intents and purposes he vanished from the scene in 1906. Without his zeal and energy behind it the movement for Tariff Reform, as we shall see, faltered, hesitated and ultimately dwindled away into a vague dogmatism rather than a living creed. The grand concept of Imperialism which had dominated Chamberlain in his later years was all but smothered before it could advance beyond the teething stage. The number of his genuine followers melted away into a faithful few and sullen petulance succeeded enthusiastic conviction. All this he saw, but he could do nothing to change the situation or bring back

---

* The Aliens Bill, introduced by a Labour member, was designed to prevent the entry of "blackleg" foreigners into the country during a trade dispute. It received an unopposed passage through the Commons but was rejected by the Lords by 96 to 24 on May 17th. "There is no need for the Government to intervene," wrote Campbell-Bannerman to the King on May 21st.[10]

the old magic. Chamberlainism, as a political creed, was extinct even before its founder: what remained was nothing but the dregs.

Ironically, Chamberlain's disappearance made Balfour's position more, rather than less, precarious. In partnership with the Birmingham messiah, each complementing the other's defects, he had formed part of an admirable combination: by himself, surrounded by sullen and frustrated Tariff Reformers, he was less than adequate. "His intelligent mind and his excellent dialetic are of immense value in the House," Arnold Foster had written to Bonar Law on April 24th. "But somehow he doesn't inspire—not me, at any rate—and his leadership is simply the public expression of his family affections and personal preferences."[13] This was the first faint murmuring of what was destined to become a holocaust of criticism.

On August 30th Sir Henry Campbell-Bannerman, like Grey earlier that year, found himself a widower. His wife, the stout-hearted old lady whose advice had persuaded him to become Prime Minister while remaining in the Commons, passed peacefully away at Marienbad. "She has been sacrificed to my public life," wrote Campbell-Bannerman to a friend. "We both wished and strove to get out of it, but could not. . . . Circumstances were too strong for us, and of course for the last two or three years her longing to escape was mingled with a keen desire to see me vindicated. . . . With God's help I will go on, as she would have had me go on, until such forces as without her I can muster fail altogether."[14]

There was, fortunately, much to occupy his attention. On September 29th Lloyd George delivered the first of many stinging attacks on the House of Lords, and King Edward (in whose eyes criticism of the Upper House was only one step removed from criticism of the Crown) remonstrated with Campbell-Bannerman via Knollys. A reprimand was duly administered and Campbell-Bannerman (October 16th) explained that "Lloyd George is essentially a fighting man, and he has not yet learned that once he gets inside an office his sword and spear should only be used on extreme occasions, and with the consent of his colleagues. In all business connected with his department and in House of Commons work he is most conciliatory, but the combative spirit seems to get the better of him when he is talking about other subjects."[15]*

---

* The "combative spirit" asserted itself again a fortnight later, much to the King's irritation. "H.M." wrote Knollys to Campbell-Bannerman on November 1st, "desires me to say that notwithstanding your remonstrance, he sees that Mr Lloyd George has made another indecent attack on the House of Lords. Mr Lloyd George is very anxious that the King and Queen should go to Cardiff next summer to open up some new docks there, and they have given him a half consent that they would do so, but the King says nothing would induce him to visit Cardiff unless Mr Lloyd George learns how to behave with propriety as a Cabinet Minister."[16]

(4)

The scene was now set for the crucial battle over the Education Bill. Matters were not helped by the fact that Liberal spokesmen in the Upper House were none too certain what kind of strategy they ought to be following. "Are we going to make any possible concessions as we go on," Crewe had written to Ripon on August 21st, "leaving the House of Commons to stand out for the Bill as we indicate it ought to be, yielding nothing else? Or are we going to fight everything, leaving the House of Commons to do the bargaining? Or are we going to combine the two plans, making some concessions and leaving others a matter of bargain between the two Houses? In this last case, what are the particular points to be?"[17] Ripon had replied two days later, on the day that the Bill received its Second Reading in the Lords, stating that "it would probably be advisable to make some minor concessions in Committee and to leave one or two larger questions for compromise at the last moment."[18]

The Second Reading was unopposed but notice was given that the Bill would have to be thoroughly revised before it could be read again. It soon became known that Balfour was drawing up a long list of amendments for Unionist peers to move. Crewe, not unnaturally, was somewhat disturbed at this news.

Crewe to Ripon, September 12th, 1906

If we find ourselves obliged to stick to the Bill exactly as it stands and to fight every amendment we shall be debarred from making any appeal to the more moderate opposition when the extreme amendments are brought up. If you refuse to agree to anything yourself, you can hardly make [an] appeal to other people for reasonable concessions.

The result will be, in my opinion, that almost every amendment that is put down, however extravagant, will be carried; and that the Bill will be returned to the Commons in a scarcely recognisable state.

If our object is to pass the Bill at all, this will add vastly to the difficulty of doing so. When there is a great mass of amendments to consider, a deal becomes far more difficult. . . .

I am confirmed, therefore, in the opinion that while it may be necessary to leave some of the biggest points for final concession by the Commons, we shall be more likely to get the Bill through if we can meet the moderate opposition on several minor points, thus preserving the power of invoking their aid against the fanatics.[19]

Parliament reassembled on October 23rd and the Lords promptly plunged into the Committee Stage of the Bill. It soon became apparent that its whole character was being drastically changed and Birrell announced that the Government would be unable to accept the revised measure the "unrepresentative assembly" were producing, a declaration that was regarded in many quarters as throwing down the gauntlet. King Edward was anxious to avoid a conflict and invited Campbell-Bannerman and the Archbishop of Canterbury to Windsor to discuss the situation in a cordial atmosphere. Nothing was settled, however, and the King's uneasiness increased. He urged Sir Henry, in a letter dated November 25th, to enter into further discussions with the Archbishop and Campbell-Bannerman called at Lambeth Palace the following evening. He reported to the King that "the Archbishop showed, as usual, the most fair and conciliatory spirit. Practically, the important point on which His Grace insisted as all-important was that the ordinary teacher should not be prevented from giving, if he were willing to do so, the special and distinctive religious teaching. Your Majesty's Government ... think that this would be inadmissible, in its full extent, because it would leave the voluntary denominational schools practically as they are now ... with all their powers and privileges notwithstanding their being nominally under the control of the local authority, who would pay rent to the Church for the schools." [20] Dr Davidson, for his part, noted that Sir Henry "had really nothing to say, and did not appear to me to be more familiar with the Bill than he was when I talked to him at Windsor. ... He showed no kind of wish of his own for an uncompromising or anti-Church school attitude, but simply kept referring again to his own majority and the need of satisfying it. Pleasant as he was, I felt this to be rather humiliating at such a juncture. ... When I suggested particular points ... he at once personally acquiesced, but kept saying 'These are points on which my people are very hot.' "[21]

The next day, in a letter to the Committee of the National Liberal Federation, Campbell-Bannerman stated his case in forceful tones. "The Education Bill as it passed the House of Commons," he declared, "was the Bill which the country demanded in unmistakable terms at the general election. It now seems to have been turned into a travesty of its original form. As amended, it perpetuates, if it does not extend, the very grievances and wrongs that were fixed upon the country by the Act of 1902. ... [If], without prejudice to the cause of education, an arrangement can be come to, well and good; if not, it will be for us to see that on this question of education and on others a way may be found by which the wishes of the country may be made to prevail."

Lloyd George, always straining at the bit, was quick to follow this declaration with a challenge of his own. "I think the time has come," he said at Oxford on December 1st, "if the House of Lords insists on maintaining a claim to reject legislation that comes from the representatives of the people, to consider ... whether this country is to be governed by King and Peers or by the King and his People."

King Edward, who by now had fallen into the habit of scrutinising the words of Lloyd George with an eagle eye, bubbled over with indignation as he read this speech the following day. Really, this was going much too far! Not only had his previous warnings been ignored, but this dreadful Welsh demagogue was now introducing the King's own name into his diatribes! Knollys despatched a stinging letter of rebuke to Campbell-Bannerman on December 3rd but the Prime Minister replied that, whether or not Lloyd George's language be thought exaggerated, "he had at least some excuse for fault-finding, when we have seen the Bill—in Committee, and even more in Report—not only seriously amended but turned upside down." He added darkly that, in view of the Opposition's treatment of the measure, they would have to "be prepared for forcible language being employed generally, and even by Ministers; for it will be hard to restrain the feelings certain to be legitimately aroused when a Bill so largely supported in the country, and passed in the Lower House by such a majority, is deliberately converted by the House of Lords into a measure whose purpose is the exact reverse."*[22]

There remained moderates on both sides anxious to reach a settlement and the Archbishop of Canterbury told Lansdowne on December 3rd that there was "a strong section of the Cabinet genuinely anxious to make some real concessions to us with a view to passing the measure."†[23] Balfour, however, was not interested in coming to terms and the amended version of the Bill passed its Third Reading by 105 to 28 on December 6th. The following day Crewe wrote to Lansdowne suggesting that, in view of the gravity of the situation, "exchanges of views might be valuable" at a small meeting of representatives of both sides.[25] "It must be doubtful if anything can come of it," he admitted to Ripon, "in view of what is universally stated as to Balfour's intentions. Still, Balfour is not quite omnipotent; and in any case we shall have done what we can towards a settlement."[26] No immediate response was forthcoming and the Cabinet resolved upon the

---

* For Knollys's letter of December 3rd and Campbell-Bannerman's reply see page 349.

† The Archbishop himself felt that the Bill should become law if the Government agreed, among other things, to "religious instruction in all schools within the school hours, with full protection of conscience" and "a reasonable expectation that our schools will (where fit) be taken over by the local education authority." For further evidence of the desire for compromise at this time, see Gladstone's letter to Birrell of December 8th, quoted on page 350. Campbell-Bannerman, writing to the King on December 12th, referred to several concessions which the Government might make, but pointed out that these could not be stated publicly "because they could only be recommended to the party as the price of saving the Bill and settling the controversy, at least for a time, and we must first know that this would be their effect."[24]

unusual course of rejecting the Lords' amendments *en bloc*.* On December 11th a Government spokesman moved "That this House do disagree with the Lords' amendments," which was carried the following day by 416 to 107.† On December 18th, however, an attempt was made to break the deadlock when Crewe, Asquith and Birrell met Balfour, Lansdowne and Cawdor in Balfour's room at the House of Commons, Dr Davidson being in the chair. It very soon became apparent that no agreement would be reached on the main issues, although both sides hinted that they were prepared to consider minor concessions. "The general impression produced upon us," wrote Lansdowne afterwards, "was that Lord Crewe and his colleagues felt that they had already gone too far, and were inclined to draw in their horns rather than to advance further."[28]

With the failure of these negotiations there was no course left to the Government except to abandon the Bill altogether. "At a meeting of the Cabinet today," wrote Campbell-Bannerman to the King on December 19th, "the unfavourable result of the negotiations regarding the Education Bill was reported, the demands of the Opposition being that liberty to teach dogmas should be given (*a*) to head teachers as well as assistants; (*b*) in all schools, large and small, in town and country; (*c*) with or without the assent of the local authority, and these three conditions being said to be essential, there could evidently be no settlement. Such a scheme would imply the continuance of all the present denominational schools, with the addition of a rent being paid for them. The purpose for which the Bill was introduced was the exact opposite of this, and therefore the Cabinet cannot hope to save the Bill."[29]

Next day the Lords decided, by 142 to 53, to insist upon their amendments and Campbell-Bannerman moved the abandonment of the Bill. "It is plainly intolerable, sir," he said, "that a second Chamber should, while one party in the State is in power, be its willing servant, and when that party has received an unmistakable and emphatic condemnation by the country, the House of Lords should then be able to neutralise, thwart and distort the policy which the electors have approved. . . . But, sir, the resources of the House of Commons are not exhausted, and I say with conviction that a way must be found, a way will be found, by which the will of the people expressed through their elected representatives in this House will be made to prevail."

* Birrell and Crewe both opposed this decision. "Birrell," noted Dr Davidson on December 14th, "said he had fully contemplated and desired the discussion of the amendments seratiam, and evidently he did not think there would have been any impossibility in doing this."[27]

† The Irish Nationalists supported this motion.

By now it was clear that the Upper House planned to reject or drastic-ally amend all important measures coming to it from the Liberal Party alone, while letting through those which also commanded the support of both the Labour and Irish members. Lansdowne, for example, had reluc-tantly advised the Lords on December 3rd that the Trade Disputes Bill, now remodelled to the satisfaction of the Labour Party, should be allowed to reach the Statute Book unmolested. He described it, in passing, as "fraught with danger to the community and likely to embitter the indus-trial life of this country," but concluded that "it is useless for us, situated as we are, to oppose this measure." The following week, however, the Lords had no hesitation in rejecting the Plural Voting Bill (a comparatively harmless measure, but one dear to Liberal hearts) by 143 to 43 at its Second Reading. There was no consistency in their actions except that dictated by party. It could certainly not be pretended that they were a cool and im-partial assembly judging each measure on its merits.

None the less, in destroying the Education Bill the Lords were on fairly safe ground. The country at large, if we ignore the hysterical protest meet-ings arranged by the Bishops of London and Manchester, was generally disinterested in the matter, and while the Labour and Irish members ex-pressed their indignation at the tactics adopted by the Upper House they did not intend to lose any sleep over the fate of the Bill itself. The feeling of the Commons appears to have been one of acute irritation rather than grief. Balfour, speaking on November 28th, blandly suggested that the anxiety shown by Liberal leaders to pick a quarrel with the Lords was due to a desire to conceal their general shortcomings and lack of constructive ideas, ending his speech with the confident prediction that the Govern-ment would not dare to dissolve Parliament and go to the country. This taunt was taken up by *The Times*, with a beguiling reasonableness, on December 21st, when it remarked that if the Government really believed that "their Education Bill represents the settled wishes of the nation, not of a combination of sects accidentally successful at the polls, their course is clear and simple. They have only to ask the country whether it really meant what it is now declared to have meant."

Lloyd George and Grey were both willing to accept the challenge, but the rest of the Cabinet overruled them. If the Liberal Party had gone to the country on the issue of the Education Bill alone it would have been court-ing disaster and an election might well have resulted, as it did in January 1910, in the disappearance of their overall majority. The Government had not been in office long enough to be sure of obtaining renewed support at the polls and there were already signs that the pendulum was beginning to swing back in the direction of the Unionists.* The wisest course appeared to be that of waiting until the "cup was overflowing" before trying to repeat the electoral triumph of January.

An interesting feature of this Session had been the deference paid to the Labour members by both the Liberals and the Unionists. Campbell-Bannerman's abandonment of the Government's original Trade Disputes Bill has been noted and he was equally anxious to ensure, as far as he could, that members of the Government refrained from launching attacks on the new party.† The Labour members, for their part, had proceeded with caution, speaking comparatively seldom but tabling some awkward questions. Their victory over the Trade Disputes Bill had been a notable triumph and this satisfied them for the moment.

Parliament was prorogued on December 21st. Far more work had been done in this first Session than in its two Balfourian predecessors combined, since Campbell-Bannerman had not only lengthened the number of hours that Parliament sat each day but had increased the Session to almost twice its normal length. The Education and Plural Voting Bills had, admittedly, failed to reach the Statute Book, but there were compensations. These included two small Education Acts, the first providing regular school dinners and the second regular medical inspection, a Justices of the Peace Act, the Trade Disputes Act, an Agricultural Holdings Act and a Town Tenants Act. Gladstone's Workmen's Compensation Act and Lloyd George's Merchant Shipping Act had received widespread praise. The South African settlement, which will be dealt with elsewhere, was another great achievement. "The general sense," wrote Bryce to Campbell-Bannerman on December 26th, "visible even in the comments of our

---

* The Unionists had captured a seat from them at a by-election in August and made considerable gains at the municipal elections in November.

† The Master of Elibank (Alexander Murray), who held an appointment in the royal household at this time, was the worst offender. Speaking on August 25th to his Peebleshire constituents, he referred to the desirability of a "crusade against Socialism", which he felt threatened both the Liberal Party and British commercial supremacy. A similar speech was delivered on October 5th. "Do let him be told," wrote Ripon to Campbell-Bannerman on October 12th, "that he has no business to meddle with questions of tactics, which must be regulated by you as you advise. If he speaks again in the same vein everyone will suppose that he does so by order." Campbell-Bannerman informed Gladstone that there was "a great flutter among my colleagues on seeing that the irresponsible Elibank is going to make a speech at Edinburgh on the 17th. I flutter myself. . . . A third speech would confirm the impression that he has my authority for what he says." Churchill, however, did something to redress the balance in a speech at Glasgow on October 11th. "I should like to see," he declared, "the State embark on various novel and adventurous experiments. . . I am very sorry we have not got the railways of the country in our hands. We may do something better with the canals, and we are all agreed . . . that the State must increasingly and earnestly concern itself with care of the sick and the aged and, above all, of the children. . . . I would recommend you not to be scared in discussing any of these proposals, just because some old woman comes along and tells you they are Socialistic."[30]

opponents, is that the Government had made an unusually full and good record for the Session is quite remarkable. I recollect nothing like it since 1871."[31]

It was nevertheless apparent, by the end of 1906, that the two Houses were set on a collision course. The Liberals, naturally enough, saw no reason why they should curb their enthusiasms for causes which were particularly dear to their hearts, while the Upper House, determined to stand firm against Radical reforms which were not, to their lordships' way of thinking, genuinely indicative of the wishes of the people, was prepared to meet the challenge with equal ardour. Balfour's dictum, that the Unionist Party should still control, "whether in power or whether in Opposition, the destinies of this great Empire," had been partially fulfilled: it remained to be seen whether the next round would prove more conclusive than the last.

CHAPTER SEVEN

THE EMPIRE, 1905–10

(1)

In 1905 the British Empire consisted of 10,990,000 square miles and almost four hundred million inhabitants. It occupied, that is to say, one-sixth of the world's land area and contained a quarter of its population. To the west lay Canada and the West Indies; to the east, the glittering trophy of India; to the south were sizeable possessions in Africa and, most distant of all, the Antipodes: these, together with colonies, settlements, outposts and mandated territories scattered over all parts of the globe, constituted the greatest Empire ever known to mankind. From Britain herself, a tiny island occupying one-hundredth part of it, there streamed forth an influence never witnessed since the golden days of Rome. The Royal Navy, basking in the sunshine of an unequalled though not unchallenged supremacy, patrolled the seas and British manufactures continued to reap the benefits of nineteenth-century pioneering. The envy of other nations, and a source of constant pride to herself, the Empire stood as the embodiment of British achievements in every sphere. In South Africa the wicked Boers had been defeated and Milner's "kindergarten" were doing their best to consolidate a system of British rule, while in India the Crown exercised direct control and refused to admit the principle of popular representation. Chamberlain regarded the British as "the greatest of governing races the world has ever seen" and was in no hurry to lighten the white man's burden.

The trouble was, however, that Britain had never really had time to make the most of her Empire. Throughout the greater part of the nineteenth century she had regarded her colonies as little more than millstones. The old mercantilist system had had its day and Free Trade doctrine, as Mr Keith Kyle has written, "was not in the least in favour of the acquisition of land or of the idea that a flag was necessary before the arrival of trade: indeed, quite the contrary."[1] Barely had it dawned upon Britain, towards the close of Victoria's reign, that the vast collection of lands under her nominal control offered a tremendous opportunity for asserting her authority as a world Power than the strings binding the mother-country to her children loosened and, like a gigantic iceberg disintegrating with painful slowness, cracks appeared in a thousand places. Chamberlain, in his efforts to hold the Empire together as an autonomous unit, had fought a losing battle: in a sense, its fate had been decided before he even began, although this was still far from clear in 1905. Canada, of course, had been a Dominion since 1867 and the six colonies of Australia had been welded into a Commonwealth in 1901, but it was not yet apparent that their policies could be anything but conductive to the welfare of Great Britain. With the right people in charge of the Colonial Office, so it was argued, the Empire's supremacy was undoubtedly assured.

The Liberals, alas, were not altogether the right people. Since the South African War "Imperialism" had held rather unpleasant connotations for them, and by making the word virtually synonomous with Tariff Reform Chamberlain and his associates had forced them to defend Free Trade at the expense of the Dominions. They were now firmly committed to the doctrine of no preferential tariffs for the Empire and in 1907 would be obliged, in Churchill's words, to "bang, bolt and bar" the door upon the pleadings of Dominion Prime Ministers. The Liberals, indeed, partly as a result of the labours of such men as E. D. Morel, Dilke, Masterman, G. P. Gooch and G. M. Trevelyan, together with the Hammonds, harboured something of a guilt complex concerning the actual possessions of an Empire. "Chinese slavery", despite the crudeness of the campaign to which it gave rise, represented genuine revulsion from the Unionist policy of securing quick material gains with no questions asked. Asquith, Haldane and Grey were admittedly, after Rosebery himself, the chief exponents of Liberal Imperialism, but their influence in the Cabinet was balanced by that of Campbell-Bannerman, Morley and Lloyd George. Lord Elgin, Colonial Secretary until April 1908, was largely a negative force and Churchill, Under-Secretary for the same period, was not a member of the Cabinet.

The colonial problems facing the new Ministry were multifarious, but it should be emphasised that the great majority were of a routine administrative nature and belong to the history of the colonies concerned rather than to that of the mother-country. Apart from the Morley-Minto reforms in India, which will be touched upon later in this chapter, we need only concern ourselves with matters influencing Great Britain's own development.*

---

* I have thought it advisable, however, in the light of later events, to put on record some extracts (page 351) from a very long letter which Churchill wrote to Campbell-Bannerman on October 15th, 1907 about Britain's policy towards Cyprus.

(2)

South Africa was the first item on the new Government's imperial agenda. Less than four years had elapsed since the Treaty of Vereeniging, during which time the Transvaal and Orange Free State, like Natal and the Cape, had been administered as Crown colonies. Lord Milner, the High Commissioner for South Africa and Governor of the Transvaal and (as it was now called) Orange River Colony, had worked hard to prove to the world in general that British rule in South Africa could yield dividends for all and sundry. "You must," he wrote to the Colonial Office, "give us time thoroughly to Anglicise the Transvaal. We must increase the British population first. We cannot afford to risk the experiment of self-government."[2] With an able team of young Tory administrators under his control, known as "Milner's kindergarten", he had done his best to reach this objective: roads had been built, railways constructed, lands irrigated and new settlements completed. Sad to relate, however, the expected influx of English settlers never materialised. Autocracy, for all its vigour, could not save the day, and towards the end of 1904 the Balfour administration reluctantly decided that steps would now have to be taken to implement in the Transvaal the "representative institutions leading up to self-government" promised at Vereeniging. Lyttelton, the Colonial Secretary, drew up a scheme for "constitutional changes", but it was designed to keep the effective control of affairs in Britain's hands and gave rise to much angry criticism in South Africa.

Milner was replaced by Lord Selborne in April 1905, but one of his last acts as High Commissioner was to persuade the British Government to pass an ordinance whereby licences could be issued for the entry of Chinese indentured labourers into South Africa to work the mines of the Rand. This led to a singularly unpleasant state of affairs, with (by the end of 1905) the establishment of some 47,000 coolies in the Transvaal who were paid deplorably low wages, beaten for their misdemeanours and enclosed in compounds at night. Campbell-Bannerman declared that it was "very like slavery", and the new Government lost no time in deciding (as Elgin cabled Selborne on December 20th) that the recruitment, embarkation and importation of Chinese coolies should be stopped.* They soon found,

* Elgin's telegram was not shown to the King before despatch and Knollys told him (December 22nd) that it was the King's "constitutional right" to see all despatches of any importance, "especially those initiating or relating to a change of policy." "I confess," wrote Elgin to Ripon two days later, "I don't quite see how to work that out so far as I am concerned. . . . Surely the Prime Minister would advise the King on any changes of policy and decisions of the Cabinet?" Ripon thought that the King was "technically right but in Queen Victoria's later time I do not believe that any complaint would have been made." Campbell-Bannerman had,

however, that this was easier said than done. Early in November licences had been issued for the importation of 14,700 fresh coolies and they were already on their way to the Transvaal. The licences could only be cancelled if there were a breach of regulations by the holder. Campbell-Bannerman wanted to introduce legislation revoking the licences and paying the mine-owners compensation, but was persuaded by Asquith that this would be too costly a business. "It would raise a tremendous hubbub both here and there," wrote the latter on December 27th, "would involve the British taxpayer (who is without available funds) in indefinitely large claims for compensation and would not be regarded as necessary to fulfil your pledge [to end Chinese labour]. The whole responsibility for this addition to the numbers ought to be thrown on the late Govt. I believe that anti-Chinese opinion here would quite acquiesce in this course."[4] Elgin took the same line, arguing that they could state "with absolute accuracy that we do interfere immediately the law enables us to do so, and that for all else the late Government is responsible. And if we couple this with some such provision as will abolish the charge of slavery, our whole policy becomes coherent."[5]

It was, therefore, not until June 1907 that General Botha could announce to the Transvaal Assembly that the ordinance would not be renewed and that the coolies would be sent home immediately their contracts expired. A loan of £5 million from the British Government enabled the magnates of the Rand to make up the immediate deficit arising from this termination of cheap labour and the last boatload of coolies left South Africa in February 1910.

The problem of "constitutional changes" for the Transvaal now had to be tackled. Letters Patent had been granted for the implementation of the Lyttelton constitution, but it had not been put into operation when Balfour resigned. The Het Volk Party took fresh heart with the news of the Liberal landslide and Jan Christian Smuts, who had distinguished himself in the war, was at once sent to England to press for more generous terms. A grant of self-government of some kind or another was never in doubt, but it was feared that the new Government, while making the executive responsible to the legislature, would not object to the Unionist electoral provisions. Smuts brought with him a persuasively worded memorandum which argued that the Boers simply desired fair rights under the new constitution and that Lyttelton's scheme did not favour the "permanent popu-

in fact, advised the King of the Cabinet's decision on December 20th. The King (via Knollys) suggested that the decision had been reached without sufficient consideration, and Campbell-Bannerman defended the Cabinet's action in a letter dated December 22nd. These letters are quoted on page 347.[3]

lation of the land". Instead of property qualifications there should be white manhood suffrage. Peace could only be secured by "the removal of all just grounds of discontent and the unreserved application of Liberal principles to the government of the new colonies, by showing a statesmanlike trust in the people of the land, of whatever race, and granting them a fair and equitable constitution under which they can work out their own salvation."*[6]

Smuts has left his own account of what transpired. "I went," it runs, "to see Churchill, Morley, Elgin, Lloyd George and Campbell-Bannerman. The only one I had met before was Churchill. . . . He asked me if I had ever known of a conquered people being allowed to govern themselves. I said no. But we did not want to govern ourselves. We could not govern ourselves without England's assistance. . . . Then I went to see Morley. Morley was very pro-Boer during the war and he was one of our strongest hopes. I was shocked when he said that, if it were in his power, he would go further than I asked, but he had his colleagues to consider, and to study public opinion. . . . The last man I saw was Campbell-Bannerman. I explained our position to him and said we were anxious to co-operate with the English. He asked me why, if that were so, we had refused to join Milner's legislative council. I answered: what would it have led to but friction? A Government appointed and not elected. An angry minority of Boers with no power except that of criticism. The Lyttelton constitution now proposed, a partly Boer legislature under Crown Colony administration, was hardly, I said, better. There was only one thing that could make the wheels run: self-government. . . . I went on explaining. I could see that Campbell-Bannerman was listening sympathetically. Without being brilliant he was the sort of sane personality—large-hearted and honest— on whom people depend. . . . Such men get things done. He told me there was to be a Cabinet meeting next day, and he said: 'Smuts, you have convinced me.' "[7]

The Boer leader's persuasion had done the trick. When the Cabinet met on February 8th the Prime Minister, in the words of Lloyd George, brushed aside in ten minutes "all the checks and safeguards devised by Asquith, Winston and Loreburn. At the outset only two of us were with him, John Burns and myself. But his speech convinced the whole Cabinet."†[8]

---

* The words "of whatever race", as events soon proved, were not to be taken too literally.

† It was evidently no easy task. "You must allow me to congratulate you," wrote Carrington to Sir Henry a few hours later, "on having so magnificently saved the South African situation today. The party would have been in arms if we had capitulated to Lyttelton and the mine-owners—and you pulled us through entirely and alone. Burns and I are very proud of our chief." Lloyd George added his tribute the following day: "I hope you will not regard it as presumptuous of me if I congratulate you on the way you saved the Government from inevitable disaster yesterday. It was a magnificent piece of work."[9]

Conversion, however, was not so instantaneous as this account suggests: Elgin, two days later, complained to Ripon that "the result of Thursday's Cabinet was unexpected and as it stands there is no very clear decision. While it is more than ever necessary that anything we say should be well considered, I don't know that the duty distinctly lies on me—for the Prime Minister rather took it out of my hands."[10] On February 13th, however, the Cabinet decided to cancel the Letters Patent for the Lyttelton constitution and send a commission to the Transvaal to report on the best means of securing an equitable constitution based on white manhood suffrage. This decision was formally announced in the King's Speech on February 19th, together with the promise of a constitution granting responsible government to the Orange River Colony.

The Unionists, greatly embittered at the part which "Chinese slavery" had played in the election,* listened to these announcements with mounting fury. Milner immediately launched a savage attack on the new policy, condemning it whole-heartedly in a speech in the House of Lords on February 26th. The rank and file of the Liberal Party cast about for some means to retaliate and on March 21st a private member introduced a resolution of censure on the ex-High Commissioner for "authorising the flogging of Chinese labourers, in breach of the law, in violation of treaty obligations, and without the knowledge or sanction of the Colonial Secretary."† Chamberlain angrily denounced the attack as ungenerous in every respect. Churchill then moved a Government amendment which, while not condoning the flogging, proposed that the House refrain from censure on individuals, but he did so in a manner which proved more galling to the Unionists than the original resolution.‡ "Lord Milner," he declared, "has gone from South Africa, probably for ever. The public service knows him no more. Having exercised great authority he now exercises no authority. Having held high employment he now has no employment. Having disposed of events which have shaped the course of history, he is now unable to deflect in the smallest degree the policy of the day. . . . Lord Milner has ceased to be a factor in public life." Nothing, in other words, could be gained by condemning the past actions of this indi-

---

* The subject proved rather embarrassing to the Government once the election was over. Crewe explained to the Lords that no one had actually spoken of Chinese indentured labour as slavery, although it came very close to it, while Churchill on February 23rd declared that it could not be "classified as slavery in the extreme acceptance of the word without some risk of terminological inexactitude."

† See page 24.

‡ "I would far rather have had the vote of censure passed," wrote John Buchan, an ex-member of the "kindergarten", on March 23rd, "than have it burked by the intolerable patronage of Winston."[11]

vidual: the Government, having no further interest in Milner, could afford
to be generous and overlook his mismanagement of South African affairs.
The amendment was carried by 355 to 135, but the wrath of the Unionist
Party knew no bounds. How dare Mr Churchill treat one of the most
illustrious figure-heads of the British Empire in such a fashion! Who was
he, that he could take it upon himself to forgive and forget the actions of
men far greater than himself? How dare he mete out such contemptuous
patronage! Shrill cries of passion rent the air and it was a long time before
the Opposition ceased to rage at the dreadful aspersions cast upon its idol.
Lord Halifax promptly announced that he would introduce a motion in
the House of Lords approving Milner's policy and conduct in South Africa.
Campbell-Bannerman, in a letter to the King dated March 26th, reported
that the Cabinet were unanimously agreed that further public discussion of
"this acrimonious subject" would be unwise at a time when feelings in
South Africa were running high, "harm having already been done by Lord
Milner's intemperate speech in the House of Lords a short time ago," and
that the Government would try to avoid a debate.[12] King Edward, however, made it plain that he shared the views of the Unionists on this subject. "I cannot consider Lord Milner's speech in the House of Lords was
intemperate," he replied. "If it was, what were Mr W. S. Churchill's
speeches in the House of Commons?"*[13] The Upper House duly repudiated the action of the Lower† while Mrs Asquith even went so far as to
apologise to Milner for the slur that had been cast upon his reputation. His
lordship, however, was "wonderfully nice" about the whole affair and the
conversation passed to happier topics.[16]

On April 5th Churchill explained to the Commons the Government's
reasons for jettisoning the Lyttelton constitution. "Equally with our political opponents," he declared, "we desire to see the maintenance of British
supremacy in South Africa. But we seek to secure it by a different method.
There is a profound difference between the schools of thought . . . in this
House. We think that British authority in South Africa has got to stand
on two legs. You have laboured for ten years to make it stand on one. We
on this side know that if British domination is to endure in South Africa
it must endure with the assent of the Dutch as well as of the British. . . .
We hope that it may be our fortune so to dispose of affairs that these two
valiant, strong races may dwell together side by side in peace and amity
under the shelter of an equal flag." Three months later on July 24th, with

* He answered his own question by describing them, in a letter to Esher, as "simply disgraceful."[14]
† "This is *most* satisfactory," wrote the King, "and a wholesome *snub* for the Govt!"[15]

the commission having completed its investigation, he was able to reveal the details of the Government's scheme. Manhood suffrage, coupled with a residential qualification of six months, would be granted to the white races. A legislative assembly composed of sixty-nine paid members would be elected for a period of five years. Dutch, as well as English, would be spoken at its sessions. A second chamber, composed of fifteen members nominated by the Crown, would also be established. This arrangement was provisional: the second chamber would eventually be remoulded on an electoral basis.

Churchill's speech ended with an appeal to the Unionists to pause before uttering "violent or rash denunciations of this great arrangement. I will ask them, further, whether they cannot join with us to invest the grant of a free constitution to the Transvaal with something of a national sanction. With all our majority we can only make it the gift of a party; they can make it the gift of England." Nothing would, presumably, have been more disconcerting than if they had taken him at his word, but the Unionists, running true to form, were shocked at such a "dangerous, audacious and reckless experiment." To have struggled three years through an unexpectedly difficult, costly and humiliating war, simply to have the fruits of victory presented to their opponents at the end of it all, seemed the very essence of stupidity. Balfour announced his "alarm and distrust" at "this most reckless development of a great colonial policy." There can be little doubt that, if the constitution had been subject to the approval of the House of Lords, it would never have become law. It was, however, promulgated by Letters Patent on November 16th and came into force on December 12th. A similar constitution for the Orange River Colony was granted by Letters Patent on June 5th, 1907.*

Thus, in eighteen months, the Campbell-Bannerman administration had accomplished a major revolution in South African affairs. Magnanimous and statesmanlike as its policy undoubtedly seemed at the time,† historians are nowadays rather chary of singing its praises. The Liberals had, in fact, simply chosen the lesser of two evils. Since Vereeniging it had been clear that the days of British supremacy were numbered and that sooner or

---

* "From my point of view," wrote Milner to a friend on April 17th, 1907, "all that has happened in the last eighteen months is wholly deplorable. People here—not only Liberals— seem delighted, and to think themselves wonderfully fine fellows for having given South Africa back to the Boers. I think it all sheer lunacy."[17]

† Even the King seems to have had second thoughts. "I see a good deal of H.M. here," wrote Churchill to Campbell-Bannerman on March 28th, 1907 from Biarritz, "for he lunches and dines nearly every day with Cassel. . . . He is quite reconciled to our African policy, and undoubtedly impressed by its increasing and evident success. Having been in disfavour for a long time, I am now apparently entirely forgiven!"[18]

later the Imperial Government would have to surrender its authority. Milner's reconstruction programme and Lyttelton's lopsided constitution had been desperate efforts to stave off this inevitable denouement but Campbell-Bannerman, taking the bull by the horns, not only acknowledged the day of reckoning but actually accelerated its arrival. His was a policy based on trust and the events of the immediate future apparently justified his faith. On the other hand, there was an unpalatable truth in Unionist accusations that the Government had been in too much of a hurry: the Unionists, of course, had the British settlers in mind, but the real victims of Liberal haste were the natives. The Treaty of Vereeniging had bound the British Government not to enfranchise the Africans but, at the very least, Britain should have insisted, while she was still in a position to bargain, on their enfranchisement within a certain period. By saying nothing on this subject the Liberals had, in fact, shuffled off responsibility, leaving Dilke and others to cry in the wilderness. In February 1906 the Government had agreed to a Commons motion that a South African settlement should include "the protection of native races excluded from full political rights" without realising, it seems, that the transfer of power to the Europeans would preclude their intervention on this issue.*

(3)

Since the Liberals had been obliged, during the election campaign, to emphasise that Imperial Preference was anathema to them, there was considerable speculation as to how they would cope in their relationships with other members of the Empire. They were granted something of a respite however, since the fourth Colonial Conference, due to take place in the spring of 1906, was postponed and it was not until April 15th, 1907 that the delegates eventually assembled at the Colonial Office. They included the Prime Ministers of Canada, Australia, New Zealand, the Cape, Natal and the Transvaal.† Elgin presided, assisted by Churchill and (at various

---

* Realisation, however, ought to have dawned without delay, since later that year Britain was criticized by Australia, New Zealand and the Cape for having protested to the Natal Government at the proposed execution of Zulu leaders after nothing more than a summary court martial. The sentence was changed to one of deportation, but the mother-country's rebuke was regarded as presumptuous interference and, startled and abashed, she resolved to tread more cautiously in future. In May 1908, nevertheless, the Under-Secretary for the Colonies, Colonel Seely, could still announce that the Government were committed to the view "that in any solution of the South African question some special representation must be found for the natives in order to safeguard their rights and with that, I am glad to say, all people in South Africa are now practically agreed."

† It had been proposed at one point that the Prime Ministers of all the Australian states should be asked to attend. Churchill, in a letter to Campbell-Bannerman dated January 24th, 1907, had urged this at some length. "Believing as I do," he concluded, "that the serious part of the Conference is the good relations which may be established between a Liberal Ministry

times) other members of the Government. After an opening speech from Campbell-Bannerman, who afterwards withdrew, they got down to business.

It was agreed, to start with, that the Conference should henceforth be known as the Imperial Conference and that it should meet every four years. A secretariat would be created, under the direction of the Colonial Secretary, which would prepare for each conference and attend to its resolutions. A subsidiary conference would, if necessary, be held during the four years to consider urgent business.

Matters of procedure and other business having been disposed of, it was not long before the question of Imperial Preference came up for discussion. Oddly enough it was not Canada, who had always been the foremost advocate of the idea on previous occasions, but Australia who raised this matter.* Arthur Deakin, the Australian Prime Minister, argued that it was doubtful whether the Dominions and the colonies could even retain their present trading position if no assistance was forthcoming from the mother-country. An angry discussion then ensued and it was left to Asquith, doing battle on his favourite front, to make it crystal-clear that no compromise was possible between Free Trade and "a penal duty directed against foreign produce."[20]

The other main topic for discussion was Imperial Defence, a subject which had been placed on the agenda by Britain. The mother-country's complaint was, quite simply, that she was bearing a disproportionate share of the burden. Contributions from the Dominions did not amount to very much and Canada, in particular, had reaped the benefit of naval protection while dodging financial responsibility. Britain was willing, indeed anxious to retain responsibility for the naval defence of the Empire, but material assistance was needed.† As for land forces, which were under the control of the Dominions, she desired a greater degree of co-ordination. No specific decisions were reached but it was agreed that a subsidiary conference should meet two years later to discuss the subject.

1909 proved, in the event, to be something of a watershed so far as Imperial Defence was concerned. The naval scare in Britain at the beginning of that year triggered off a chain-reaction. New Zealand offered to pro-

---

and Colonial Governments, I should greatly regret [it] if its most obvious result was to earn us the hatred of six Prime Ministers, to say nothing of their sisters and their cousins and their aunts."[19]

* Sir Wilfred Laurier, Canada's Prime Minister since 1896, was now contemplating the possibility of closer trade relations with the United States.

† She strongly resisted proposals by Canada and Australia that they should have fleets of their own during peacetime instead of contributing towards the cost of a single imperial navy.

vide the mother-country with two Dreadnoughts, "to be controlled both in peace and wartime by the British Admiralty," and the Federated Malay States made a similar offer. Australia grudgingly followed suit, while making it plain that she would much prefer a fleet of her own. Britain was gratified by these offers, and when the Imperial Defence Conference met she proposed an alternative arrangement which, in turn, went a long way towards satisfying the Dominions and proved generally acceptable. This was that there should be a special Pacific Fleet, the control of which would be shared.*

Progress was also made on the subject of military training. The Imperial Defence Conference agreed that the General Staff (hitherto a purely insular body) should extend its scope and become the Imperial General Staff. It would have its headquarters in London, under a single head, and divisions throughout the Empire which would, subject to Dominion consent, organise local defence and ensure a unified system of training. A substantial step would thus be taken towards the standardisation of forces, weapons and transport arrangements. "There was one problem, however," wrote Lord Hankey later, "which the Conference did not touch, namely the Supreme Command—the co-ordination and direction of the Empire's forces, and the continuous study together of the major problems of imperial defence."[21] Two years, in fact, were to elapse before this omission could be repaired.

(4)

India occupied a special position in the British Empire. She was, without doubt, a magnificent trophy and thanks to the labours of Disraeli and Kipling was justly venerated by the inhabitants of late Victorian England. Curiously enough, however, she was neither a national settlement nor the prize of conquest: Britain's overlordship, if not an accident, was at any rate largely unpremeditated. The East India Company, supervising her trade and administration from 1600 until 1858, had brought her under the mother-country's aegis, although it was always understood that the British were guardians rather than conquerors and that the Indian people would

---

* The fleet would consist of three squadrons, each comprising one battle-cruiser, three light cruisers and three submarines. The Dominions, who would bear part of the cost, would control their respective vessels in home waters during peacetime, but the Admiralty would control them during wartime or manoeuvres outside home waters. Australia agreed to maintain the whole of one of the squadrons and to meet most of the cost of one of the battle-cruisers, while New Zealand undertook to meet the cost of another battle-cruiser. Canada, in the event, decided to build a force of light cruisers and destroyers, and the scheme as envisaged never quite materialised. During the five years which followed, however, enough of it came into effect to satisfy the mother-country and Dominions alike.

eventually be allowed to manage their own affairs. Throughout the nineteenth century the prospect of their doing so remained agreeably remote and the self-appointed trustees were confident that so many races and sects, who quarrelled more readily with each other than with the British, would never reach a level of real political maturity. The mutiny of 1857, a short-lived but cautionary reign of terror, provided the custodians with a good excuse for not allowing Indians anything more than a nominal degree of political freedom and from 1858 onwards the Crown assumed direct control of British India and became largely responsible for determining the policies of neighbouring Indian states.

The organs of government were, in India, a Viceroy and Governor-General, each with his own council, and in London an India Office presided over by a Secretary of State. This system, which by 1906 had lasted almost fifty years, was little more than benevolent despotism. An Indian Councils Act of 1861 had introduced a non-official element into the Governor-General's Council and an Act of 1892 increased this element to one-third, but there had as yet been no real progress towards the goal of representative self-government. Many observers believed, indeed, that such a goal was happily unattainable, and Morley himself, the new Secretary of State, writing to the Viceroy, Lord Minto, in May 1906 commented that it was "not one whit . . . desirable or possible, or even conceivable, to adapt English political institutions to the nations who inhabit India."[22] By the end of the century, however, the latter felt that the time had come for a definite recognition of their ability to look after themselves. The Indian National Congress, founded in 1885, was gaining strength in all parts of the country, and in 1908 would reaffirm its aims as the attainment of "a system of government similar to that enjoyed by the self-governing members of the British Empire and a participation by them in the rights and responsibilities of the Empire on equal terms with those members. These objects are to be achieved by constitutional means." Others, however, were convinced that violence was the only answer. It was thus against a terrible backcloth of secret societies, riots, bomb-outrages and murders that Morley and Minto laboured, with painful slowness, to carry through a modest programme of constitutional reforms.

Minto, like Morley, was a newcomer to the Indian scene, having succeeded Curzon only a few months previously. The latter, unfortunately, had done much to bring British rule into additional dispute by his autocratic behaviour and open contempt for Indian sensibilities. Bengal had been partitioned, against the wishes of all those directly affected, and great emphasis had been placed upon the rights of central government, much to the indignation of provincial legislative councils.* "Official persons of high station and responsibility," writes Morley in his memoirs, "assured the new Viceroy that the political change within the last dozen years was enormous and, though the mass of the people remained ignorant and un-moved, it would be a fatal mistake to suppose that the change was con-fined to the preachings of political agitators. The fairly educated Indians were thoroughly dissatisfied with the old order of things."[24] Minto sym-pathised with their grievances, as did Morley himself, but they were both men of infinite caution and neither was prepared to venture beyond the limits of what were, to them, reasonable concessions. The maintenance of law and order was always their chief concern, and they would not act under anything approaching duress.

It had been promised in 1833, and again in 1858, that neither race nor creed would be a barrier to public service in India. In 1861, as we have noted, there had been added a non-official element to the Governor-General's Council but the Indianisation of the civil service was a very slow business and the Act of 1892 had not greatly improved matters. "I wonder," wrote Morley to Minto on June 15th, 1906, "whether we could not now make a good start in the way of reform in the popular direction. . . . Why should you not now consider as practical and immediate things —the extension of the native element in your Legislative Council; ditto in local councils. . . . (Of course officials would remain a majority.) . . . I suppose the notion of a native in your Executive Council would not do at all. Is that certain?"[25] Minto, replying on July 5th, declared that he had "very nearly, on several occasions, suggested to you the possibility of a native gentleman on my Council, but thought it would be premature to say anything about it. . . . One must remember that such a colleague would necessarily become acquainted with all our State secrets, both interior and foreign, and that in this country it is difficult to dissociate any native, how-ever able, from the influences of religion. . . . I believe we should effect the most solid reforms by beginning at the bottom."[26] He added, six days later, that "popular representation in our sense of the word is, of course, out of the question and all we can at present aim at is the selection of cer-tain bodies [i.e., universities] to whom the power of nominating a member can be given."[27]

Ten months later, having overcome his own qualms and those of his

---

* "I think I should be wrong," he wrote to Morley on December 20th, 1905, "if I did not let you know how intensely Curzon's egotism (I can call it nothing else) and ambitions have shed their influence over public life in India. . . . It is only right that you should know the bitter native feeling he has aroused against him by the partition of Bengal."[23]

advisers, the Viceroy was at least able to put forward a formal proposal to the effect that a "native gentleman" be allowed to join his Executive Council. Morley strongly supported the idea but encountered opposition from Ripon, Elgin and Fowler, who argued that the security risk was too great. At length, however, the Cabinet agreed and in March 1909 the King reluctantly approved the proposal. Two Indian members had meanwhile been appointed (August 1907) to Morley's own Council.

In October 1908 (as a result of constant prodding by Morley) the Viceroy submitted specific proposals for improving the degree of popular representation on the country's governing bodies. Morley's Council, after many long discussions, approved these recommendations on November 27th. "The Cabinet," noted Morley later that day, "took the thing on trust, having rather urgent business of much domestic moment on their hands."[28]

On November 2nd, 1908, fifty years after the Crown's assumption of the administration of British India, the King-Emperor had issued a special proclamation. It declared, in lofty and not particularly graceful tones, that the principle of representative institutions would be "prudently extended" and that satisfaction would eventually be given to those who claimed equality of citizenship. Reforms, in short, were on the way but no hint was given of what they were or when they would arrive. The anger aroused by the partition of Bengal was ignored and although the "responsible elements" in Bombay and Madras welcomed the King's announcements the general feeling was that they had proved sadly unworthy of the occasion. This feeling was shared by several members of the House of Commons.

The Cabinet therefore decided, after approving Minto's recommendations towards the end of November, that the Lower House should be informed of them without delay. Morley, who had entered the Upper House seven months earlier, came very near to resignation at this stage of the proceedings. "What zanies do politics make of men!" he wrote to Minto on December 4th. "The Indian group in the H. of C. waxes more wrath every day that the arrogant, privileged, hereditary, abominable H. of L. should have the early Indian asparagus and first dish of my green peas and all the other delicious 'primeurs' from my oratorical garden, hothouses and forcing-pits. Asquith, to my astonishment, pressed me very hard to let Buchanan expound our projects first in the H. of C. The feeling is so strong against the H. of L., he said. I was utterly inexorable. It would have been to give an intolerably wrong notion of the dimensions of what is intended for a reform of the first order, wise or otherwise, not to let the S.S. have the first innings."*[29] Asquith, for the sake of a quiet life, gave way and it was Morley who therefore announced, on December 17th, the Government's plans for India. What they wanted to do, he explained, was to give both the Governor-General's Legislative Council and the provincial councils a more representative character, first by increasing their membership, secondly by substituting election for nomination and, finally, by allowing greater freedom of discussion.† These proposals were favourably received and an Indian Councils Bill to put them into effect made its first appearance in the Lords two months later. Curzon and Lansdowne, both of them ex-Viceroys, opposed it on the grounds that the Government was pandering to extremist pressure but the main body of Unionist peers was not unduly alarmed (nor even interested) and the Bill became law at the end of May 1909.

It is argued by certain writers that the scheme had one very grave defect in so far as it established the principle of separate representation for Muslims and Hindus. This resulted from the anxious pleadings of a Muslim deputation, led by the Aga Khan, which had called upon Minto shortly after the King's proclamation. The Aga Khan pointed out that the reforms of 1892 had resulted in Hindu supremacy in every sphere of local government. Muslim representation was virtually non-existent. He urged that a certain number of seats should be set aside for the exclusive use of Muslims in any scheme of constitutional reform which Britain intended to introduce. Minto was impressed by the Muslim claims and in a speech which he delivered a few weeks later drew attention to the possible plight of minorities if the Hindus were to have a monopoly of that political power allotted to the natives. "The Muslims in India," Professor R. P. Masani

---

* Minto, however, probably sympathised with Asquith. "There is much that is charming about him [Morley]," he wrote to his wife on April 10th, 1907, "but [he is] so sensitive that one wastes hours over letters and telegrams so as not to hurt him." Writing to Sir Arthur Bigge on July 5th, 1910 he declared that "if I had been going to stay [here] longer I should have felt bound to ask that the position of the S. of S. towards the G. of I. should be considered. No one except those who have been behind the scenes here knows what the interference has been about every little thing. . . . As a matter of fact, I believe I have gained my point in everything since I have been here, but it has generally been by not losing my temper when I should have been thoroughly justified in doing so . . . and often by humouring the peculiar personality with whom I had to deal."[30]

† Wilfred Blunt, for one, was not very impressed. "Morley's much expected Indian reform speech," he noted the following day, "has at last been made in the House of Lords, amid much Tory applause, great care having been taken that there should be no hostile criticism here or in India. Here the speech was put off till the last working day of the Session and in India the leaders of the opposition, including the chief newspaper editors, had been clapped into prison. These reforms, if they had been introduced three years ago when Morley first came into office, or if they had been introduced now as an avowed first step towards Home Rule . . . [together with] a release of the political prisoners, might have affected a reconciliation with the extremists, but now I feel it is too late. In themselves the reforms are poor things."[31]

has argued, "were mainly Hindus converted to Islam: they were descendants of parents born and bred in India and had lived peacefully with Hindus for centuries, having the same cultural traditions, customs and way of life."[32] There was no real reason, in short, why they should be afforded special treatment, but the Indian Councils Act of 1909 nevertheless set aside a specific number of seats for them.* "Hindu–Muslim tensions," Masani concludes, "only developed as a result of the Morley–Minto reforms."[34]

The Act represented, for the moment, the most that Britain could concede in the way of constitutional reform. India remained in a state of ferment and the general dissatisfaction with British rule showed no signs of lessening. Bomb-throwing continued and Minto himself, a little while later, only narrowly escaped assassination. A considerable number of political agitators were deported without trial, which produced some lively debates in the Commons, and it was with feelings of relief that Morley, in November 1910, surrendered the India Office to Crewe. Minto's retirement, at approximately the same time, brought to an end a disappointing phase in India's history. The tolerant but cautious Viceroy and the elderly, well-meaning but querulous Liberal Minister had left their mark on the scene, but it had come too late, and was too insubstantial, to be of much significance.

(5)

This chapter must now come full circle, concluding as it began with the subject of South Africa.

It was, perhaps, inevitable that the Transvaal and Orange River Colony should now fuse with Natal and the Cape into one autonomous unit, although the motives for unification were mixed. It was easy to argue its desirability on practical grounds and to declare that only a central government could make the best use of native labour and natural resources, but the most important, if the least emphasised objective, was the creation of a white-dominated South African state. The idea of federation on the Australian pattern had certainly been under consideration for several years

---

* Morley nevertheless congratulated himself and Minto (although principally himself), in a letter to the Viceroy dated November 18th, 1909, on having made this provision. "I am very sure of one thing," he wrote, "and this is that if we had not satisfied the Mahometans we should have had opinion here—which is now with us—dead against us." Minto, however, was by this time by no means so certain that they had done the right thing and ventured to say so in his reply. Morley, always quick to take offence, wrote to him on December 6th, declaring that he would not continue the argument, "only I respectfully remind you once more that it was *your* early speech about their extra claims that first started the M. hare. I am convinced my decision was best."[33]

and Smuts, writing in August 1906, declared "that unless the power of the magnates in the Transvaal is broken by our entry into a unified or federal South Africa, the danger of their capturing supreme power . . . will continue to exist."[35] The remaining members of the "kindergarten" were equally attracted by the idea and Lionel Curtis, in particular, did much to interest Selborne and various South African politicians in its potentialities. In May 1908 it was discussed at an inter-colonial conference which was followed in October by a National Convention attended by representatives of each colony. By February 1909, after some lengthy and contentious debates, a draft constitution for a united South Africa had been drawn up. In May the leading figures of the Convention, including Botha and Smuts, set sail for England. If the mother-country gave the scheme her blessing, all would be well.

The Asquith administration was, in fact, sympathetic to the idea and Unionist politicians had no real objections. It was felt that Britain ought to do everything she could to retain the friendship of the Boers, since a united South Africa could do more to keep the Cape route open in time of war for British shipping than four states pursuing independent policies. The only objection in Parliament came from those Liberal and Labour members who objected to the introduction of a colour-bar. In the Cape, for example, no such bar existed and both the Gold Coast and Fiji natives had possessed political rights for several years. Asquith himself agreed that racial discrimination was "invidious", but the trouble was that the mother-country had no real power to intervene on this issue. "If the Imperial Parliament amended the colour-bar provisions of the draft South Africa Act," writes Mr L. M. Thompson, "the official delegates of the South African colonies, bound as they were by instructions to accept no amendments of principle, would take their stand on the high ground of colonial liberty and unanimously declare that the amendments were unacceptable; their parliaments would agree with them by overwhelming majorities; the governments of Canada, Australia and New Zealand would very likely rally to their support; and Britain would almost certainly be obliged to yield. Nothing would have been gained."[36]

In 1909, as we shall see, Britain was much preoccupied with her own domestic affairs. If the South African states wanted unification, the Asquith administration would not stand in their way. So it was that Dilke and other members had no official support for their opposition to the colour-bar provisions. Crewe, on July 20th, told the delegates that the Government were "prepared to see the Bill through as it stands both as to franchise and to representation" and ten days later could add that it was "in quite smooth water . . . and the demonstration which the very well-intentioned, but on this occasion unwise, advocates of native claims may make in the House of Commons will not in any way endanger it."[37] His confident forecast proved only too true: the South Africa Bill was passed by the Lords on August 4th and secured an easy passage through the Commons. Dilke, Keir Hardie and others battled gamely but unavailingly against the great majority of Liberal members and the whole of the Unionist Party. Balfour dismissed their arguments with the contemptuous remark that "to suppose that the races of Africa are in any sense the equals of men of European descent, so far as government, as society, as the higher interests of civilisation are concerned, is really, I think, an absurdity." Asquith, though sympathetic to criticism, made it plain that the Government had no intention of impeding the Bill's progress. Several amendments tabled by would-be reformers were either withdrawn or defeated. The Prime Minister, moving the Third Reading on August 9th, emphasised Britain's regret at the provisions for natives and trusted that they would be revised "sooner rather than later." There was no division and the Bill became law on September 20th.

The South Africa Act of 1909 provided a Senate and House of Assembly for the whole Union. Each province would have its own council, while the general care and treatment of the natives (who formed more than four-fifths of the total population) would be the concern of the central authority. The protectorates of Basutoland, Bechuanaland and Swaziland were to remain, for the time being, under the control of the British Government. The Cape would retain its native franchise but in the Transvaal, Orange River Colony and Natal electoral rights would be restricted to men and women of European descent. Herbert Gladstone (whose departure from the Cabinet was no great loss) was created a viscount the following February and became the first Governor-General.

The Union of South Africa came into existence on May 31st, 1910 and Britain, with an almost audible sigh of relief, was free to concentrate on her own domestic affairs. It is a debatable point whether the mother-country had really done all in her power to secure an equitable settlement, but clear anough, unfortunately, that by 1909 her actual influence on South African politicians was extremely limited. To have rejected the Bill might well have precipitated an imperial crisis of the first magnitude and, engrossed in the battle of the "People's Budget" and with the possibility of a general election in the near future, the Government had no desire to bite off more than it could chew. It is easy to criticise the Liberals from the safe distance of more than half a century, but it should be remembered that a genuine peace had been made with the Boers and that South Africa would now become a prominent member of the British Empire. Two world wars would show that Campbell-Bannerman's confidence had not been misplaced. As for the native problem, South Africa would have to find her own salvation, in her own time and by her own means: Britain, from now onwards, could do no more than point the way.

CHAPTER EIGHT

DOMESTIC AFFAIRS,
JANUARY–DECEMBER 1907

(1)

"There is no prospect, I hear," wrote Crewe to Ripon on January 22nd, "of an early Cabinet, i.e. before the first week in February. The Prime Minister remains in Scotland and Asquith has gone off to Italy, etc. I must say that this seems to me unfortunate, and likely to lead to a repetition of last year's hurry and confusion. The Licensing Bill is literally the only one which the Cabinet has so far decided to introduce; and I have no conception of the effect which the change of Chief Secretaries is to have on the Irish proposals. . . . Isn't this postponement of all discussions rather unusual?* Particularly bearing in mind that the autumn Cabinets, with one exception I think, all dealt with transient matters arising out of the autumn Session."[1]

Crewe's perplexity was a measure, to some extent, of the strange mood of apathy which had now descended upon the Government. Twelve months before, with their enemies in disarray and a spectacular victory at the polls behind them, it had seemed inconceivable that anything could halt them in their march from triumph to triumph: the promised land, after ten years in the wilderness, had finally been reached and the fruits thereof were theirs for the taking. By January 1907, however, they were beginning to realise that office did not necessarily mean power and the prospect of another long Session as frustrating as the last was enough to daunt the keenest of their number.† Free Trade, admittedly, had been given a fresh lease of life, "Chinese slavery" brought to an end and a relatively satisfactory measure of self-government conferred upon the Trans-

---

* The last meeting of the Cabinet had been on December 21st; the next did not take place until February 6th.

† Three months of the new Session proved, in fact, more than enough for the Cabinet, and Campbell-Bannerman informed the King on April 22nd that they had "agreed that an autumn session could not be contemplated this year and therefore that the programme of legislation will have to be curtailed."[2]

vaal, but the Education Bill had failed to reach the Statute Book and it seemed only too probable that the Licensing Bill which they now hoped to introduce would also run into difficulties in the Second Chamber. Apart from the Licensing Bill, moreover, there was a notable absence of anything important in the Ministerial pipeline and many members of the Liberal Party were beginning to wonder if the Government really did intend to introduce a programme of "progressive reforms", an assumption which had not been seriously questioned hitherto.* Morale could, of course, be raised by an attack on the peers, and Lloyd George and Churchill (supported, rather unexpectedly, by the Attorney-General), were brimming over with proposals for limiting the powers of the Upper House, but the Government as a whole had no zest for such a battle. One swallow does not make a summer and one defeated Education Bill did not mean a constitutional revolution.

The Ministry underwent a minor reshuffle at this time. Bryce had been appointed Ambassador to the United States and was succeeded by Birrell as Chief Secretary for Ireland, a position which Harcourt had declined. There was much conjecture as to who would succeed Birrell at the Board of Education, Morley favouring Harcourt† and Ripon suggesting Crewe, while Churchill allowed it to be known, as tactfully as he could, that he would not be averse to promotion.‡ In the event, however, Campbell-Bannerman chose McKenna. Walter Runciman stepped into McKenna's shoes at the Treasury and Thomas Mcnamara took the latter's place as

* The repeal of the Aliens Act of 1905, for instance, was one reform which it was believed the Government could undertake without much difficulty. The Manchester *Evening Courier* reported on February 4th, 1907 that "during 1906, 49,017 immigrants came to us, and of these 489 (less than one per cent) were rejected. And it cost £24,000 or £50 each to keep them out. No fewer than 792 appealed against their ejection, and 442 appeals were successful. . . . The Act calls for amendment, because it is useless and vexatious." Churchill sent a cutting of this passage and others to Gladstone on February 8th. "I was concerned to find the other day," he wrote, "how very bitter and disappointed the Jewish community [in Manchester] have become in consequence of the continuance of this very harsh and quite indefensible measure. I am sorry to trouble you on such a matter, but . . . I am sure the Liberal Party would support the repeal of such a foolish piece of legislation." Nothing, however, was done.[3]

† Sinclair (January 8th) reported to Campbell-Bannerman that Morley was "very emphatic" with regard to Harcourt: "Says that you should insist on his taking the Education Office. Is strongly against any man loafing into the Cabinet. Lou-lou ought to put on the collar and do some H. of C. and administrative grind like every other man, and earn his position in a respectable place. Thinks McK. comes next, so far as can yet be seen."[4]

‡ See Morley's letter of January 3rd, 1907 to Campbell-Bannerman, quoted on page 351. "The P.M.," wrote Esher on January 9th, "won't hear of Winston being in the Cabinet at present. He is, like Mr G., old-fashioned and disapproves of young men in a hurry." Campbell-Bannerman seems, however, to have written reassuringly to Churchill at this time. The latter, on January 24th, expressed gratitude "for the kindness of your letter" and declared that he was "quite ready to serve your Government wherever I am thought to be most useful." (He went on to urge that a place be found for Colonel Seely—another ex-Unionist—in the administration, a plea which he had also made in December 1905, but Sir Henry showed no enthusiasm for this suggestion.) Another complimentary exchange of letters took place nine months later.[5]

Secretary to the Local Government Board. It almost seemed as though the India Office would become vacant too, since Morley had suggested to Campbell-Bannerman on December 22nd that on the grounds of advancing years, etc., his resignation should not be too long delayed and he returned to this theme in a letter dated January 23rd. "J. M.," wrote the Prime Minister to Sinclair on January 30th, "is bent on retiring. . . . Can we afford to let him go out of the Cabinet? Whitely says he is no use in H. of C. or on platform. But his name is an asset and he is sound in the Cabinet. I am to see him before Cabinet on Friday, and I am writing to ask him would it ease matters if he went to the Lords."[6] Morley was duly seen and duly allowed himself to be persuaded to remain at his post for the time being.* This was, as it transpired, the first of many such episodes.

(2)

The Liberal Party remained united, but the Unionists were still seeking that harmony which the publication of the "Valentine letters" was officially supposed to have achieved. Joseph Chamberlain, it is true, had vanished from the scene, but his absence only served to intensify and continue the split between the Tariff Reformers and their would-be converts. Balfour had touched upon the subject of Imperial Preference as little as possible in his speeches while the Chamberlainites, led by the painstaking yet prosaic Austen, were redoubling their efforts to make it the party's sole *raison d'être*.† Bereft of the prophet's leadership, growing steadily less sure of their purpose, they pinned their dwindling hopes upon a spectacular *coup d'etat* which would make the Conservative Party the vehicle of fiscal reform in practice as well as in theory.‡ "Between ourselves," wrote Austen Chamberlain to Lord Ridley on January 16th, "I believe there is no ex-

---

* Morley hinted at his impending resignation to Lady Minto on April 3rd: "Though I do not suppose I shall hold on very long, my colleagues say I must not go just yet."[7]

† Sandars, writing to Balfour on April 2nd, complained that Tariff Reformers, posing as Liberal Unionists, "are, with the encouragement of Austen & Co., trying to squeeze out or else to capture our local Conservative Association. . . . It is the *same* movement below as that which is going on above." Later in the year (October 23rd) Balfour remonstrated with Austen Chamberlain at the activities of a mysterious band of Tariff Reformers known as "the Confederates"."Whoever they may be," he wrote, "if they are acting in other constituencies, and towards other important members of the party, as they are acting in Nottingham towards Portland, they seem to me to be doing a very ill service to the cause of fiscal reform." Chamberlain, replying the following day, declared that "whoever the Confederates are, they are *not* the Tariff Reform League. . . . I have heard that Leo Maxse is one of them, but I have never been able to learn their names, nor can I find that they have any organisation or headquarters."[8]

‡ Milner was looked upon in some quarters as a possible successor to Chamberlain, having delivered two speeches in December on the subject of Imperialism and social reform. His lordship, notwithstanding an oft-proclaimed dislike of "party politics", was anxious to obtain control of the Tariff Reform League but unable to secure the guarantee of £20,000 which he felt would be necessary for launching a fresh campaign.

Cabinet Minister on whose assistance I can confidently count in an *uphill* fight except Arnold Foster. Akers-Douglas is always sympathetic, but of course he is a party man before all things and never takes the lead. Walter Long is with us, but he is more and more engrossed, as is only natural, by the Irish question, which for him as an Irish member overshadows all others.* Balfour seems to me very impracticable, and Alfred Lyttelton besides being impracticable will not move at all unless it is agreeable to Balfour."[10]

The rumour that the Tariff Reform League had been guaranteed an annual income of £10,000 for five years did not, on the other hand, bring much comfort to the Balfourites. "There has," wrote Sandars to Balfour on January 23rd, "been a general weakening of your authority throughout the country. To this weakening, Austen and Long and Bonar Law, Maxse and Amery and others are contributing. . . . George Curzon has designs of some kind—he is manoeuvring for a seat in the House of Commons—but Hood cannot fix him with any responsibility beyond opposition to yourself. . . . If you do not speak on the fiscal question, then the malcontents will declare that their contention is well founded and that you are indifferent. . . . The bulk of the party do not for a moment desire that you should commit yourself to details . . . but they do want a statement on broad lines touching fiscal reform in its relation to finance both Imperial and local; they would like a sympathetic reference to closer commercial union with the colonies; they would like a point made of the fact that schemes of social reform cannot be accomplished without the elasticity of revenue which alone can be obtained from a wider basis of taxation." Acland-Hood felt that if such a speech was not made in the near future the great bulk of the party would drift away from Balfour's leadership, "very likely not all at once, but by degrees, until anarchy is succeeded by a new authority."[11]

On February 1st, when speaking at Hull, Balfour made the speech for which his impatient colleagues had long been waiting. "I cannot quite understand," he declared, "why a monthly bulletin is required of my opinions upon the fiscal question. . . . My opinions upon great matters are not subject to monthly variations and when I have spoken as much and, I venture to say, as clearly and consistently as I have done upon the fiscal question for many years past, I might have been credited with still retaining the views to which I had so often given public utterance." Austen

---

* Long himself, writing to his brother on January 26th, felt that "the method most likely to succeed is for the leaders to put the case [for Tariff Reform] before the country from time to time . . . upon broad and general lines. . . . The most important and effective work, however, can in my judgment only be done by quiet and persistent labour in the constituencies."[9]

E

Chamberlain, speaking at Stirchley on February 4th, professed himself much impressed with this latest declaration and, in private, urged Balfour to open the new Session with a motion regretting the absence of fiscal reform from the Government's legislative programme. The Unionist leader was, however, very cool towards this proposal and, after ascertaining the views of Long, replied to the effect that they would be better advised to concentrate on the forthcoming Colonial Conference and press the Ministry to state its intentions concerning the Empire.

This did not satisfy the Chamberlainites. Austen discussed the matter with Bonar Law, Ridley, Gilbert Parker and Goulding and they agreed that, if Balfour did not move a Tariff Reform amendment, then they would do so themselves. In deference to Balfour, the amendment might be moved from the back benches but the front bench would have to give its official support and blessing. Long suggested a motion pressing for "more intimate relations with the colonies" but this did not meet with their approval and Austen drafted one urging "freer trade within the Empire and closer commercial union with the colonies on a preferential basis." Balfour, with time running out, gave way at the last moment and the Tariff Reformers were able to chalk up another tactical victory.*[12]

(3)

Parliament was opened on February 12th. King Edward VII had made it plain beforehand that he would not be prepared to bewail the fate of the Education Bill and the speech from the Throne, while noting that "unfortunate differences" had arisen between the two Houses, merely observed that Ministers were endeavouring to find a solution to the problem. The Speech then listed a modest series of reforms which the Government hoped would become law before the end of the Session, namely the Licensing Bill (which took pride of place), proposals for the reorganisation of the regular and auxiliary forces, bills dealing with the holding and valuation of land in Scotland, "measures for further associating the people of Ireland with the management of their domestic affairs," reform of university education in Ireland and "proposals for the establishment of a Court of Criminal Appeal, for regulating the hours of labour in mines, for the amendment of the Patent Laws, for improving the law relating to the valuation of property in England and Wales, for enabling women to serve on local bodies, for amending the law affecting smallholdings in England and Wales and for the better housing of the people."

* Esher saw Balfour on February 16th and found him "depressed at the dead set made against him in his party."[13]

No reference had been made to the thorny subject of education, but on February 26th McKenna took advantage of the ten-minute rule to introduce a one-clause bill into the Commons. It was designed to relieve local authorities of the cost of special religious instruction in non-provided schools, which was estimated to be one-fifteenth of the education rate, and passed its First Reading by 264 to 109. The Nonconformists, however, were far from impressed and the usual objections poured in from Churchmen. After a few weeks' hesitation the Government decided to withdraw the bill and introduce a more ambitious scheme the following year.

On March 8th a Liberal backbencher moved the Second Reading of a Women's Enfranchisement Bill. There was nothing new in the idea of votes for women—during the 1870s, in fact, nine female suffrage bills had actually passed through the Commons—but the issue was now coming to the fore of Britain's political life, due mainly to the establishment in 1903 of the Women's Social and Political Union under the militant leadership of Mrs Emily Pankhurst. Female suffrage had already been granted in Australia and there seemed no logical reason why it should not also be conceded in the United Kingdom. The Government, however, was curiously divided on this issue. Campbell-Bannerman himself was more or less in favour of votes for women,[*] as were Haldane, Grey and Churchill, but strong opposition came from Asquith and others. A free vote was therefore allowed and the measure was eventually talked out.[†] What did become law this Session, however, was the Qualifications of Women Act referred to in the King's Speech. Since 1894 women had been entitled to sit on district and parish councils and this right was now extended to county and borough councils.

The first important piece of Government legislation, excluding Haldane's schemes of army reform, entered the House on March 19th, namely the Patents and Designs Bill, which had Lloyd George as its exuberant

[*] Campbell-Bannerman, on December 29th, 1905, had confessed that he was being driven to the belief that women ought to be allowed to express their views on the great social questions of the day, but this was as far as he dared to go. Incidents throughout 1906 helped to keep the issue alive, however, and a suffragette demonstration in October had resulted in some of the women being imprisoned. On February 9th a procession of almost 4,000 women marched through the West End and at the opening of Parliament there occurred the first of those unpleasant clashes between the suffragettes and the mounted police.

[†] Another private member's bill reintroduced at this time was one for the promotion of a Channel tunnel. On February 20th Campbell-Bannerman informed the King that the Cabinet were against the measure but would allow a free vote. King Edward, who had been "disgusted", as he told Knollys on March 12th, at Sir Henry's "backing up" the Women's Enfranchisement Bill, received this information somewhat sceptically, but on March 21st it was stated in both Houses that the Government were formally opposed to the Bill and it was withdrawn a few weeks later. "I rejoice to see," wrote the King to Campbell-Bannerman on March 29th, "that you 'put your foot down' regarding the Channel tunnel.... I only wish you could have done the same regarding female suffrage."[14]

custodian. It was a measure designed to prevent inventions patented in England from being used exclusively abroad. Tariff Reformers observed, somewhat sourly, that this marked a departure from the creed of Free Trade, but Lloyd George had an easy time steering the Bill through the Commons.

March 19th also witnessed the introduction of the Small Landholders (Scotland) Bill. This was a scheme which had been drawn up in a hurry, under the impetus of John Sinclair, the Secretary for Scotland, and the Cabinet as a whole were not greatly impressed with it.* It had the firm backing of the Prime Minister, however, and useful precedents in the Crofters' Act of 1886 and the Congested Districts Act of 1897. Its purpose was the relief of overcrowding in the towns of southern Scotland, it being argued that half the population lived in conditions of severe discomfort, 493,000 people in one-room dwellings and more than two million in two-room dwellings, while the amount of cultivable land set aside for sport, which had been 1,800,000 acres in 1892, had now risen to 3,000,000. The Government proposed the appointment of Land Commissioners, who would have the power of compelling landowners to set aside certain portions of their estates for the creation of smallholdings. Rents would be fixed by the Commissioners and the tenants, like the crofters of the Highlands, would be protected against unjust eviction. The Bill passed its First and Second Readings without a division and its Third on August 9th by 167 to 48.

Asquith's second Budget, which he introduced on April 18th, was as unexciting as his first. A surplus of £5,399,000 which had accrued from the previous year was deposited in the Sinking Fund while it was estimated that there would be, for the year 1907–8, a surplus of £3,433,000: £1,500,000 of this was earmarked for the Sinking Fund while another £1,500,000 would be set aside for old age pensions. The Labour members, while gratified at this latter announcement, expressed their indignation at the retention of duties on sugar, tea and coffee and subsequently voted against the Second Reading.

(4)

The Lords were meanwhile making a half-hearted attempt to set their House in order, in an effort to forestall Government proposals, and a Bill introduced by Newton was debated on May 6th. These proposals, which

* "The Bill," wrote Sinclair to Campbell-Bannerman on December 12th, 1907, "has not—bar Bob Reid—one single friend in the Lords: nor has any single member of the Cabinet, except him and yourself and Asquith, said one word in its favour. Tweedmouth has entirely cancelled his qualified support in the Lords."[15]

provided for a reduction of the hereditary element in the Upper House, were supported by the Duke of Devonshire and the Archbishop of Canterbury but opposed by Lord Halsbury, of whom we shall hear more later, while Lansdowne and Cawdor thought that the whole issue should be referred to a select committee. Newton agreed to withdraw his proposals and a committee which had Rosebery as its chairman was appointed to examine the subject of reform in general terms. Crewe, for the Government, stated that the debate was "shadowy and unreal" and advised the House to wait until the Government had produced proposals of its own.

These were still evolving. A Cabinet Committee had reported in March advocating that, in the event of a deadlock between the two Houses, a hundred peers (including all members of the administration) should sit with the Commons in a single-chamber assembly and that they should debate and vote together until agreement had been reached. Crewe, a member of the Committee, told Ripon that "we were practically unanimous . . . that this plan offers the best path out of the thicket."[16] Ripon himself thought that it was the best that could have been prepared in the circumstances and "greatly preferable to the restriction of the Lords' veto to one Session, to which I see great objections the more I think of it."[17] The Prime Minister, however, was not particularly impressed, and in a memorandum dated May 31st dealt with the Committee's proposals in scathing terms.

Campbell-Bannerman objected first of all to the arbitrary choice of a hundred peers and pointed out that an assembly of seven hundred-and-seventy persons would be far too large for a conference. "Is the so-called joint vote," he asked, "more than a device—and a rather transparent device—for disguising the proposition that, in case of difference between the two Houses, the opinion of the elective House must eventually prevail? And, if so, is it not open to the same objections and will it not encounter the same opposition as the suspensory veto?" He went on to put forward a plan of his own which he thought would meet the situation.* "Like the plan of the Cabinet Committee," he wrote, "it would invite legislation. The terms of the bill would be somewhat as follows:

"(1)   If in any session a bill sent from the House of Commons to the House of Lords fails to become law, by reason of the House of Lords having rejected the bill, or postponed its consideration, or made amendments to which the House of Commons does not agree, a conference shall,

* Campbell-Bannerman's proposals are usually described as based on a plan put forward by Bright in 1884. A similar scheme, however, had been canvassed (but with no great success) by Roebuck in 1835.

unless the Government otherwise determine, be held between members appointed by the House of Lords and the House of Commons respectively, with a view of arriving at a settlement of the difference between the two Houses. (Or the conference might, if preferred, be held at an earlier date.)

"(2)   If, after the conference, the bill is reintroduced into the House of Commons, with or without modifications, and is again sent to the House of Lords, and again fails to become law, it may, in the next subsequent session, be again introduced in the form which it was last agreed to by the House of Commons, and if passed by the House of Commons in that form, and again sent to the House of Lords, it shall, in default of agreement between the two Houses, have effect as if passed by both Houses and shall be enacted in the customary words accordingly."

In the case of the Education Bill of the previous Session, therefore, a few months would elapse after its rejection by the Upper House during which public opinion would be "sounded, tested and organised" and the situation reviewed. At the beginning of the next Session there would be an informal discussion between small delegations from each House, after which the Government would reintroduce the Bill with or without modifications. Discussion of the Bill would be largely confined to any alterations that might have been made and it would then be rushed through the Commons and sent to the Lords at an early stage in the Session. If it were rejected for a second time, then Parliament would be prorogued and there would be a new Session later in the year in which the Bill would be introduced for a third time in the form last agreed to, "passed swiftly through the Commons, and sent to the Lords with an intimation that, unless passed in that form by the House of Lords, it would be passed over their heads." Even now, however, the Commons might make concessions if they saw fit to do so and the Bill would be passed by both Houses in the usual way.

"It may be said," concluded Campbell-Bannerman, "that this procedure, occupying much of the time of three sessions, would involve intolerable delay. But, in the first place, delay is desirable and necessary before resorting to the extreme course of overriding the House of Lords. What is necessary is to avoid the risk of hasty or arbitrary action. As a bill has, for this reason, to be read three times by one House before it can be passed by either House, so a bill would have to be passed three times by one House before that House is allowed to override the other House. In the next place, the procedure would not be adopted except in the case of measures of first-class importance. And, lastly, the necessity for adopting the procedure would not often arise. What is essential is that the power of overriding the Lords should be available as a last resort. If such a power existed the Lords would, except when dealing with a shaky Government or towards the close of a Parliament, practically always give way at an earlier stage."*18

Campbell-Bannerman sent a copy of this memorandum to each member of the Cabinet and it was agreed, at length, to put his scheme forward for consideration by the Commons. June 24th was the day selected for the debate and it was opened by the Prime Minister moving "That, in order to give effect to the will of the people as expressed by their elected representatives, it is necessary that the power of the other House to alter or reject bills passed by this House should be so restricted by law as to secure that within the limits of a single Parliament the final decision of the Commons shall prevail."† "It is a singular thing," he commented, "when you come to reflect upon it, that the representative system should only hold good when one party is in office and should break down to such an extent as that the non-elective House must be called in to express the mind of the country whenever the country relapses into Liberalism." Next, he turned his attention to Balfour. "I cannot conceive," he said, "of Sir Robert Peel or Mr Disraeli treating the House of Commons as the right hon. gentleman has treated it. Nor do I think there is any instance in which, as leaders of the Opposition, they committed what I can only call the treachery of openly calling in the other House to override this House." Having thus disposed of the leader of the Opposition, Campbell-Bannerman devoted the rest of his speech to outlining the scheme which he had put forward in his memorandum. It would eventually, be informed the House, be drafted into statutory form but he did not say when this might be.

Balfour, in reply, defended the recent actions of the House of Lords and went on to explain the principles which determined its conduct. It was, he said, "absolutely bound to see that no hasty decision should upset in one reckless hour interests which have been slowly and painfully built up by our predecessors." When the people decided on a change it would have to be after the most mature consideration. The House of Lords, in other words, prevented the passage of legislation which did not represent the

---

* The Prime Minister's blueprint for constitutional reform was far from revolutionary in appearance and was, in fact, designed to depart as little as possible from the pattern of established procedure. That little, notwithstanding, would prove more than enough so far as the members of the Upper House were concerned.

† "The King," wrote Knollys to Campbell-Bannerman on June 16th, "desires me to say he thinks the expression 'to give effect to the will of the People' savours more of a republican than a monarchical form of government, but that no doubt you had to consider the feelings of the left wing of your party. He also directs me to mention that he is sorry no Liberal peer . . . has been nominated by the Government to the House of Lords Committee."19

real wishes of the people. He pointed out, in a passage which might well have attracted the attention of Lloyd George, that the power of the Upper House was in any case "limited by the fact that it cannot touch money bills," and in conclusion he chided the Government for its attempt to pull down a portion of the constitution simply because it found itself unable to frame constructive legislation. "Why," he demanded, "are we wasting a week of parliamentary time over an abstract resolution when the Government could have brought in a bill or could have prepared a bill to bring in early next year and could have allowed us to proceed with their legislative programme contrived for this year? Sir, the whole thing is insincere from beginning to end. The right hon. gentleman is treating the constitution, of which he ought to be the guardian, as a plaything of the moment, as a mere political expedient, as a means of electrifying and revivifying, if he can, the waning popularity of himself and his colleagues."

The first day of the debate, as Mr Roy Jenkins has noted, was thus "chiefly notable for Balfour's wonderfully arrogant charge that the Prime Minister, who was in fact at his wits' end to show the country a few worthwhile Acts, framed his legislative proposals for the express purpose of getting them rejected."[20] On the second day, June 25th, Churchill was among the principal speakers and delighted both his colleagues and the Opposition by his wrath against the Upper House. "Has the House of Lords ever been right?" he demanded. "Has it ever been right in any of the great settled controversies which are now beyond the reach of party argument? Was it right in delaying Catholic Emancipation and the removal of Jewish disabilities? Was it right in driving this country to the verge of revolution in its efforts to defeat the passage of reform? Was it right in passing the Ballot Bill? Was it right in the almost innumerable efforts it made to prevent this House dealing with the purity of its own electoral machinery? Was it right in endeavouring to prevent the abolition of purchase in the army? Was it right in 1880 when it rejected the Compensation for Disturbance Bill? I defy the party opposite to produce a single instance of a settled controversy in which the House of Lords was right."

Lloyd George's contribution, on the third day, was below his usual standard but he made one good hit by ridiculing the notion of the House of Lords as the watchdog of the constitution. It was, rather, Mr Balfour's poodle: "it fetches and carries for him and barks and bites anybody he sets it on to." Asquith, who wound up the debate for the Government, admitted that he had been a slow and reluctant convert to Campbell-Bannerman's schemes of constitutional reform but stated that he was now convinced that no *modus vivendi* could be found to solve the problem. "What the people see," he commented, "is a partisan assembly worked in a partisan spirit and yet assuming to hold the position and to exercise the functions of an unprejudiced umpire."

The resolution was carried by 432 against 147 and there, for the moment, the matter rested: the Government had shown that it was prepared, if need be, to launch an attack upon the powers of the House of Lords but its resolution was more in the nature of a threat than a positive proposal to change the structure of the constitution. It was now up to the House of Lords, if it wished to avoid a crisis, to adopt a more moderate and conciliatory attitude towards the legislation of the Lower House. The trouble was, however, that many members of the Lords did not take the Government's declaration seriously and those who did were determined that they would not yield their position without a fight. The Government, they thought, was not yet in a position where it could claim widespread support from the general public, since the measures with which the Lords had dealt most drastically had so far been of a partisan rather than a popular nature: they overlooked the fact that continual mutilation or rejection of bills from the Lower House would eventually goad the Government into taking decisive steps to alter the situation.

(5)

On July 13 the Tariff Reformers, much to Balfour's annoyance, brought the subject of Protection to the attention of the Commons when Lyttelton proposed a resolution regretting that the Government had declined the unanimous invitation of the Colonial premiers to consider favourably any measure of Imperial Preference. The debate which followed resulted, of course, in an easy victory for the Government, the resolution being rejected by 404 to 111 amidst cheers and laughter. It was, for Balfour, an unpleasant afternoon: quite apart from a spirited drubbing from Lloyd George the debate had emphasised, once again, the widening gulf between himself and an important section of his party. His reluctance, indeed his positive unwillingness, to take an active part in the crusade for Tariff Reform had now become only too apparent, even to those who had hitherto clung faithfully to the idea that A. J. B. had undergone a thorough immersion in the waters of Imperial Preference. There was, admittedly, no Joseph Chamberlain to challenge his leadership, but what of Austen Chamberlain or Walter Long? The situation demanded a man with the wisdom and the cunning to lead the Conservatives from triumph to triumph and back into office. The great bulk of the party were not particularly interested in examining the merits or pitfalls of Tariff Reform:

what they wanted was to regain that power which had been lost so igno-
miniously eighteen months before, and if that power could only be obtained by sacrificing the present leadership, then so be it: Balfour would
have to go.

The reader might, at this point, be pardoned for wondering precisely
why such a curious split between Balfour and the majority of the Unionist
Party's members should have been allowed to continue. Surely no great
issues were at stake? Balfour had, after all, publicly accepted Chamberlain's
doctrines as the new basis of party policy: he had undergone a rapid but,
on the whole, fairly conclusive conversion to the advantages of Tariff
Reform: he had several times spoken in its favour and several times loftily
rebuked those who had dared to suggest that his conversion had not been
all that it should have been. What more could be needed? Why, then,
should there still be this rift? The truth of the matter was, as we have seen,
that the Tariff Reformers did not trust their normal leader: they suspected
that he was not only wholly devoted to the cause to which they had dedi-
cated themselves, that he looked back with longing to the days when Mr
Chamberlain was still in South Africa and that fateful speech had not yet
been made, and that he did not altogether relish the prospect of being
bound to the Birmingham caucus for the rest of his public life. These misgivings were not entirely without substance, but they were in some respects several degrees removed from the truth. Balfour's unwillingness to
parade the streets banging the drum of Imperial Preference arose, in fact,
not so much from reluctance as from sheer repugnance. He had no desire
to transform himself into a crusader. He did not like the idea of having to
fill the space left vacant by Chamberlain. He did not wish to soil his hands
by endulging in the rough and tumble of party warfare, which was a very
different thing from the niceties of parliamentary debate. It was not that
he had any particular aversion to the cause of Tariff Reform—that point,
at any rate, he had made clear over and over again throughout 1906 and
1907—but simply that he had a deep aversion to the means by which the
cause was propagated. The Chamberlainites, to his way of thinking, represented a crude and vociferous element in the party. Their political campaigns were no doubt effective but, at the same time, not very dignified;
he tolerated their methods (indeed, he had no choice) but would not,
under any circumstances, resort to them himself. Better, far better, to concentrate one's attention on the task of bringing down the Government
than to constantly proclaim the attractions of one particular policy which
might or might not prove an effective vote-winner and which was, in any
case, only one issue among many. Rather than put all his eggs in one

basket, in other words, he would distribute them among baskets galore. "As regards the attacks on myself," he wrote to a friend at this time, "I quite understand your point of view that they do harm to the party and therefore ought, if possible, to be put an end to. But you will admit, I think, that I can do nothing to put an end to them. I am certainly not going to go about the country complaining that I am 'honest and industrious' like a second coachman out of place! If people cannot find it out for themselves they must, so far as I can see, remain in ignorance."[21] This, unfortunately, was not what the Tariff Reformers desired and the debate of July 13th thus marked indirectly another stage in the story of Balfour's decline and fall from the leadership of the Conservative Party.

(6)

"The last month of the Session," noted a disapproving Mr Harcourt Kitchin in the *Annual Register*, "was occupied mainly by hasty legislation after hurried debates." The use of the closure was much extended, especially in regard to the Evicted Tenants Bill. The Government argued that this was the only way in which the House could get through the great amount of business that had to be tackled, the Opposition condemned it as a means whereby measures of a contentious nature could be rushed through the Commons with the minimum of debate while the Labour Party, anxious to have the best of both worlds, demanded that Parliament should reassemble later in the year. There was, however, a general disinclination for an autumn session. The new Parliament had sat for almost fourteen months out of the eighteen in which it had been in existence, the first wave of reforming zeal had exhausted itself, there was no important programme of legislation waiting to be dealt with and there seemed little point in wasting further time, energy and enthusiasm in devising measures which would either be mutilated or rejected by the Upper House. Most of the members, in fact, felt that they deserved a good long holiday before returning to the parliamentary grindstone.

The Small Landholders (Scotland) Bill had, as we have noted, passed its Third Reading in the Commons on August 9th. The Government's representatives in the Upper House, however, awaited its arrival with feelings of trepidation. Elgin told Ripon on August 10th that, although he did not dislike the Bill as much as other members of the Liberal Party, he did not wish to defend it. "I think it is very doubtful," he wrote, "if the demand for it, which the P.M. and Sinclair believe, is genuine, in the sense that many people will take land under the Bill, though it may be that many of our supporters in Scotland desire that they should do so. . . . It is true I was a member of the Cabinet Committee on this Bill, but the Committee only met once."[22] Ripon (two days later) replied that he did not like the Bill much either "and I do not think that the Cabinet were very well treated about it. However, as it has come up to our House we must make the best we can of it."[23] In the event, the Bill as such was not debated: Lansdowne, on August 21st, said that he was quite willing that time should be found to discuss the Bill but he made it clear that the Unionists had no intention of allowing it to reach the Statute Book in its existing form and the measure was promptly withdrawn by the Government.*

"On the whole," wrote Morley to Minto on August 23rd, "Ministers are not at all dissatisfied with the position."[25] This was, in the circumstances, a somewhat staggering pronouncement, since the Government's legislative programme for the Session had been cut to shreds. Of the nine major measures which it had hoped to carry, only the Patents Act, the Small Holdings and Allotments Act and the Territorial Army Act had come into existence. The Education Bill, an Irish Devolution Bill and a Special Religious Instruction Bill had had to be abandoned before reaching their Second Readings; the Small Landholders (Scotland) Bill had been defeated in the Lords, while an Evicted Tenants Bill for Ireland, although allowed to pass, had been drastically amended. The Licensing Bill had been a non-starter while nothing more had been heard of university education in Ireland or of an Eight Hours Bill for miners, which the Prime Minister had promised on June 3rd would be introduced before the end of the Session. In all, fifty-six bills had found their way on to the Statute Book by the time Parliament was prorogued on August 28th, including one for the establishment of the Court of Criminal Appeal and another allowing marriage with a deceased wife's sister, but these were, for the most part, insignificant measures to which the staunchest of Unionists could scarcely object. No one, least of all the members of the Government itself, could pretend that this was an imposing record of achievements, and the Session drifted to an end in an atmosphere of frustration, exhaustion and boredom.†

Lloyd George, speaking at Manchester on October 15th, warned his colleagues that this was a state of affairs which could not be allowed to

---

* The Unionists had intended to chop the Bill into two sections and remodel the larger of these on the lines of the Government's Small Holdings and Allotments (England) Bill. "This is a proceeding entirely without warrant," wrote Campbell-Bannerman to the King on August 21st, "and so far as this Government are concerned they deem it equivalent to the rejection of the Bill . . . and will take no more responsibility in the matter."[24]

† Of the 16 contested by-elections which the Liberals fought in 1907, they lost 3 seats (1 to a Unionist, 1 to the Labour Party and 1 to Victor Grayson, a Socialist), retained 7 and failed to capture the remaining six from the Unionists.

continue. "If," he declared, "at the end of an average term of office it is found that Parliament has done nothing to cope seriously with the social condition of the people, to remove the national degradation of slums and widespread destitution in a land glittering with wealth; if they do not arrest the waste of our national resources in armaments; if they do not save up, so as to be able to provide honourable sustenance for deserving old age; if they tamely allow the House of Lords to extract all the virtue out of their bills, so that when the Liberal Statute Book is produced it is simply a bundle of sapless legislative faggots fit only for the fire, then a real cry will arise in this land for a new party. And many of us here in this room will join in the cry."

It was a timely warning. Whether his colleagues were prepared, at this time, to take note of it is another matter.

(7)

The Labour members had also been disappointed at the Government's lack of reforming zeal during this Session. None of the measures introduced held much attraction for them and their attendance at debates had dwindled. On several occasions the party had been unable to muster a strength of more than eight in support of its own motions and Keir Hardie was dismayed at the extent to which its fortunes were becoming linked with those of the Government. Taking this factor into consideration with the notable lack of enthusiasm with which his election to the chairmanship had been accepted in February 1906, he felt that the time had come to assume a position of greater independence. "My strongest reason for desiring to get out of the chair," he wrote to Snowden towards the end of 1907, "is that I may be free to speak out occasionally. In the last Session the party practically dropped out of public notice. The comic papers and the cartoonists are ignoring us. A fatal sign! The tendency is evidently to work in close and cordial harmony with the Government and if this policy be persisted in we shall lose our identity and be wiped out along with the Liberals and we should richly deserve our fate. By another Session, those of us in the party who are Socialists and who believe in fighting will have to get together occasionally on our own account."[26] He was succeeded as Chairman by Henderson.

An additional cause for bitterness was the fact that Victor Grayson, a young man who professed to be a Socialist of the fieriest hue, had succeeded in defeating both the Liberal and Conservative candidates at a by-election in the Colne Valley division of Yorkshire. He refused to join the Labour Party, regarding it rather as Hardie had regarded the Liberal Party in 1892, and devoted his time to making a long series of polemical speeches outside rather than inside the walls of Parliament. The I.L.P. rapidly came to the conclusion that this valiant young crusader was the one man capable of leading it to victory and two years later Hardie, MacDonald, Snowden and Bruce Glasier would resign from the National Council of the I.L.P. in protest at its evident approval of Grayson's activities. So began a parting of the ways which, exacerbated by Grayson's I.L.P. pamphlet of 1910 entitled "Let us reform the Labour Party", has lasted ever since.

One consolation, however, had been the arrival of Peter Curran in the House of Commons. Curran was a well-known figure in the trade union world and was also a member of the I.L.P. The death of the Liberal member for Jarrow had led to a by-election in July, the unusual feature of this contest being that all four parties put forward candidates. The Nationalists, not surprisingly, came bottom of the poll with 2,122 votes, the Liberal came next with 3,474 (less than half the previous Liberal vote, only eighteen months before), then the Unionist with 3,930 and, finally, Curran with 4,698. This was, on the face of it, very much a feather in Labour's cap, surpassing even the triumph of Barnard Castle four years before, but Hardie no doubt noted that while the total poll had increased by 9% Labour's share had actually decreased by 8%.

(8)

There occurred, during the remaining months of 1907, an episode which, while important in its own right, was destined to be of special significance to the political history of Great Britain in the years that lay ahead. This was Lloyd George's settlement of the dispute between the railway companies and the Amalgamated Society of Railway Servants, a settlement which succeeded in warding off a national crisis on an unprecedented scale.

In 1900 the Taff Vale Railway Company of South Wales claimed damages from the Amalgamated Society of Railway Servants, which it refused to recognise as a union, for having fermented a strike among its employees. The House of Lords declared in favour of the Company and the latter was awarded £23,000 plus costs. The Taff Vale judgment resulted, as we have seen, in the Trade Disputes Act of 1906, which was designed to protect trade unions against such actions in the future. The Society, however, was still not accorded union status by the railway companies (with the exception of the North-Eastern, which had done so in 1897) and its members became increasingly restless at this unsatisfactory state of affairs. In January 1907, under the leadership of Richard Bell, the

Society demanded better wages and shorter hours for all railwaymen, and above all, recognition of their union by the employers. These demands were ignored by the companies. During the ten months which followed, despite strenuous efforts by the Society, the situation remained unchanged. Finally, a vote was taken. On Sunday, November 3rd, at a mass meeting of railwaymen in the Albert Hall, Bell announced that the members of the Society had declared overwhelmingly for strike action.

A railway strike meant that the industrial activity of the country would be brought to a standstill. Road haulage was still in its infancy. Canals had ceased to be of much importance. The transportation of raw materials and manufactured goods would come to a stop. Large towns and small villages alike would be cut off from the needs and essentials of everyday existence. People would be unable to travel long distances except at great cost and much inconvenience. Struggling businesses and thriving concerns would suffer heavy set-backs. Goods from abroad would pile up at the docks, unattended and unheeded. Coal, iron and wool would be unable to reach the ports. Great Britain's overseas trade would undergo grave diminution. Widespread unemployment might well result. Everything depended upon the railroad and a railway strike would paralyse the economic life of the country. It would not be merely a crisis in a particular concern. It would be a crisis on a national scale.

Lloyd George was instructed by Campbell-Bannerman to do whatever he thought necessary to avert disaster. Here was the golden opportunity for the "people's David" to show his ability in time of crisis and he seized it with both hands. "A strike at this juncture," he wrote to the Prime Minister in mid-October, "would be disastrous to our trade. It is doing well just now—extraordinarily well—but it is just on the turn here, in the United States and in Germany, and a strike would have the effect of pre-cipitating the slump here and postponing it in the United States and Ger-many. . . . It can only be obviated if the directors accept conciliation—the only way. We must, when Parliament meets, at once introduce such a measure making arbitration in railway disputes compulsory in all cases where the Board of Trade considers the nature and magnitude of the dis-pute warrants such a course being adopted."[27] The following week he saw representatives of both the union and the companies and he scored his first triumph on October 25th by persuading the directors to consider a plan of arbitration which he had put forward. "An excellent beginning." he wrote jubilantly to his uncle Lloyd, ". . . I have won their confidence and that is almost everything."

Further snippets were despatched to Criccieth during the week that followed. Thus, on October 31st: "All day with the directors. In the morning I had to threaten them. Told them that there must not be a strike on any account." On the following day he believed that the strike was all but settled. By November 4th he had presented the Prime Minister with the terms of a settlement: "He is delighted with them. Thinks it a feather in my cap and, indeed, in the cap of the Government if I can pull it off."[28] An agreement was finally reached on November 7th ("I had great difficulty in getting the directors to sign but they behaved well.") whereby the employers conceded most of the men's demands without actually recognising the union. Bell and his supporters were moderately satisfied and the directors themselves, in private letters to Lloyd George, expressed their sense of relief at having been deftly extricated from an embarrassing position. Campbell-Bannerman lost no time in informing the King of the "happy results of the negotiations" and was also careful to emphasise that the country was "largely indebted for so blessed a conclusion of a time of great anxiety and danger to the knowledge, skill, astuteness and tact of the President of the Board of Trade and those around him in his department."[29]

The details of the railway settlement do not concern us at this juncture. What does concern us, however, is that the skill shown by Lloyd George in arranging it sent his reputation soaring. He had become, in a twinkling, the man of the moment. It must be remembered that his record had so far been of a rather dubious nature. The public knew him as the man who had delivered colourful and outrageous attacks upon the five most cherished institutions of late Victorian and early Edwardian England—the Church, the House of Lords, the royal family, the South African War and Mr Joseph Chamberlain. He had been generally regarded as a demagogue, a trouble-maker and someone who did not play the game. Now, in a flash, all this was changed. His prestige, admittedly, had waxed steadily but slowly throughout the first two sessions of the new Parliament, but with the settlement of the railway crisis it rose to a point which it would not reach again before 1918. He suddenly found himself, if we might be pardoned for adopting Macaulay's famous phrase, the rising hope of the stern, unbending Liberals. Praise flooded in from all quarters. King Edward, the Press, senior members of the Government—all of them suddenly realised just how capable an administrator and how wise a legislator Mr Lloyd George actually was. They vied with one another in showering compliments upon him. The King sent his warm congratulations. The Prime Minister, at the Lord Mayor's banquet on November 9th, spoke of "his great gifts of unconquerable hopefulness, of unfailing courage and of alert diplomacy." The *British Weekly*, when summing up the events of the year, noted that "observers who, last Christmas, said he might win the second place but would never reach the first are now less disposed to set limits to his career."* Sir William Holland and Lord Glantawe even wrote to *The Times* suggesting that the annual salary of the President of the Board of Trade be raised from £2,000 to £5,000, a proposal very gratifying to Lloyd George but not so pleasing to other members of the Government.

On November 12th Lloyd George and Campbell-Bannerman attended a reception at Windsor where they were presented to the German Emperor, then on a state visit to England. The Kaiser, much to the delight of the hero of the railway settlement, devoted three times as much of his attention to Lloyd George as he did to the Prime Minister. "He said," wrote the former to his brother the following day, "that whenever I came to Germany I would receive a great reception. . . . He laughed and talked at such length that the King came up and fetched me away. . . . The King was against the working man in the matter of the railway strike. Thought it was madness on their part to threaten a strike—didn't know what they wanted to strike about—might lose their pension, etc. He is a Tory at heart.† God help the people with such rulers. The Emperor was just as bad. I came away hating all kings."[31]

What conclusions are we entitled to draw from all the fuss, fêting and hullabaloo which surrounded Lloyd George in the November of 1907? The delights of being a public hero are, it must be admitted, of a very transitory nature, but in this instance something permanent remained. Lloyd George's reputation had definitely been enhanced. The House of Commons would henceforth look upon him with a kind of affection. It is, indeed, not too much to assert that it had not been for his handling of the railway dispute he would never have become Chancellor of the Exchequer in Asquith's administration. Had the latter been called upon to form a Government in September 1907 it is more than probable that Lloyd George would have been passed over, assuming that Asquith did not wish to retain the post for himself, in favour of Morley, Haldane, Birrell or Gladstone. Asquith, quite apart from the personal distaste he felt for the President of the Board of Trade, would have had no desire to fill one of the most important vacancies in his Ministry by appointing a man who was unpopular with his sovereign, his colleagues and the public at large. By

---

* The editor of the *British Weekly*, Sir William Robertson Nicoll, has been described by Mr A. J. P. Taylor as "the man who first, by supporting Lloyd George, raised him up; and then, by withdrawing his support, cast him down."[30]

† This sentence, and the one which followed it, were in Welsh, presumably as a safeguard against interception.

April 1908, however, he had been made to realise that Lloyd George would be the most acceptable choice for this key position. The *enfant terrible*, it seemed, was blossoming into an elder statesman: the responsibilities of high office would no doubt complete the process.

(9)

While Lloyd George marched from triumph to triumph the Unionist Party was plunged into an ever-deepening mood of despondency. There was, on all sides, irritation at Balfour's lethargy and a strong desire for a more dynamic leader if only one could be found. Even Balfour's closest supporters, as the following letters make plain, were fast losing patience.

Wyndham to Akers-Douglas, November 2nd, 1907

It is very desirable that A.J.B. should . . . lead an attack. He ought to speak in Edinburgh on the Scotch Bills and the House of Lords. And I wish he would speak in the Free Trade Hall, Manchester and the Albert Hall before the Session. He is our leader and the only person, besides Rosebery and C.B., who is reported. Anything we say is without authority to our audience and rarely gets beyond that audience except in fragments selected by our opponents' Press.[32]

Long to Sandars, November 7th, 1907

I am not afraid of the extreme Tariff people—they are contemptible! What I am much more afraid of is that A.J.B. will not assert himself enough and that the trouble will go on steadily increasing and be really more serious in two years' time than it is now. There is a general feeling amongst good fellows of *all* classes that he is not strong enough and does not enforce discipline and you and I know there is some ground for this. The party is certainly in better heart and condition, but wherever I go I have found the same feeling about the Chief, in Scotland worse than anywhere! It is too horrible and surely there must be some way of remedying it? To lose him would be the greatest disaster which could happen to our party. But I am honestly afraid that unless he changes his methods somewhat he will never regain his hold upon the party. . . .

What do you think about Bonar Law? I am not sure. Tell me but keep this to yourself.[33]

Lord Robert Cecil to Long, December, 1907

For four years Balfour has devoted a vast amount of the highest intellectual effort to discovering a fiscal policy which should be acceptable to protectionists and not objectionable to Free Traders.

What has been the result? Sometimes both wings have claimed him as an adherent. At others both have rejected him. Meanwhile the body of the electors regard his utterances as either intentionally ambiguous or else marked by culpable levity. I cannot believe that this is due to any clumsiness on Balfour's part. If anyone could reconcile the irreconcilable it would be he. But it cannot be done. And the attempt to do it merely taints the party with a suspicion of dishonesty, the most fatal of all accusations in English politics.[34]

The crux of the matter was, of course, that with Joseph Chamberlain's disappearance from the scene there was no obvious alternative leader near at hand. "What we really suffer from," wrote Carson to Lady Londonderry on December 23rd, "is a want of first-class men,"[35] and the dearth of talent on the Unionist benches was painful evidence of the truth of this remark. There were, on the face of it, only two possible contenders for the leadership, Austen Chamberlain and Walter Long, but neither of them were regarded with much enthusiasm by the bulk of the Unionist Party. The former had done much to alienate potential supporters by the arrogance and officiousness of his manner, evidently believing that the deference which had been paid to his father was also due to himself,* while the latter, albeit a worthy and forthright individual, did not possess either the initiative or the drive that was required in a potential leader. For the moment, therefore, the impasse continued, but it will have been noted that a third possible contender was coming to the fore. This was the man whom Milner, earlier in the year, had recommended to Sandars as a possible lieutenant for Balfour and the man to whom Long had referred in the last sentence of the letter quoted above: Andrew Bonar Law, the middle-aged ironmaster from Glasgow.

* It was at this time that he offended Long himself by rebuking him, albeit in friendly tones, for arranging to speak on behalf of a member of the Unionist Party who was not a fiscal reformer. Long was incensed and promptly complained to Balfour. The member in question had once been Long's private secretary, but quite apart from this he objected most strongly to Chamberlain's venturing to dictate his actions. A lofty reply was agreed with Akers-Douglas and sent to Chamberlain on or about November 17th, the latter (in a reply dated November 20th) being apologetic but unrepentant.[36]

CHAPTER NINE

PRELUDE TO HOME RULE, 1906-8

(1)

It had become increasingly clear to the leaders of the Nationalist Party, as the election results flowed in, that the cause of Irish independence would not necessarily benefit from the Liberals' landslide victory. Dillon saw Bryce on February 6th and found that although the position was "entirely satisfactory" with regard to administrative reforms it was not so good when it came to the question of repealing the Crimes Act or improving the Land Act of 1903. "So far as positive legislation goes," he wrote to Redmond the following day, "we have . . . got nothing beyond the hope of a satisfactory Labourers' Bill, and even as regards that there is no definite promise. . . . In the event of there being no amending Land Bill in the King's Speech, it will be necessary for us to make a very strong protest."[1]

The references to Ireland in the Speech proved, however, tantalisingly vague. It transpired that plans were under consideration for improving the machinery of government and for "associating the people with the conduct of Irish affairs": this was in accordance with previous assurances and was satisfactory so far as it went but it left the Nationalists with no alternative but to sit back and wait for the promised reforms to materialise. Their patience was rewarded, three months later, with the arrival in the Commons of the Town Tenants (Ireland) Bill and the Labourers' (Ireland) Bill. The first of these measures stipulated that the lessees of residential or business premises in towns should receive compensation for improvements made to the property if they were obliged to move. The Lords eventually approved it, but made it slightly less favourable to the tenant. The second measure was designed to promote the erection of 25,000 labourers' cottages, most of which would be furnished with plots of land. Loans to the extent of £4,500,000 would be made to the rural district councils at $3\frac{1}{4}\%$ interest for this purpose and there would also be an annual grant of £50,000 from the Imperial Exchequer. This Bill received a smooth passage through the Lower House but the Lords made several alterations, one of which would have resulted in a substantial increase in Irish rates. The Commons protested and on August 1st the peers gave way, although Lansdowne emphasised that they did not accept the Commons' claim to exclusive privilege in the sphere of financial legislation.

The Nationalists, however gratified they may have been at the introduction of these two measures, were embarrassed by the Government's Education Bill. The Catholic clergy, like the Anglican, were strongly opposed to the idea of undenominational teaching in local elementary schools and the party was allowed little or no freedom of opinion where the Irish Church was concerned.* Birrell tried to reassure Redmond by telling him that "there would be a clause in our favour which he hoped would satisfy our view,"[3] but the Nationalists voted against the Second Reading. Redmond, however, did his best to prevent the extremists of his party from antagonising the Liberals unnecessarily. "Our attitude," he wrote, "is not one of opposition to the majority in carrying out their views in their own schools. It is a protest against the minority . . . being compelled to have a form of teaching from which they profoundly dissent forced upon their children."[4] The Government realised, of course, that Redmond was obliged to take this line, but it needed all the support it could muster in its battle with the Unionists. On November 1st Lloyd George warned him that consideration of Home Rule would be indefinitely postponed if the Irish continued to oppose the Education Bill. Redmond stood firm, however, with the result that on November 20th, when the Lords were engaged in hacking the Bill to pieces, the Cabinet intimated that it would be prepared to make several important concessions in return for Irish support. Redmond agreed to give this support if the concessions materialised and the Nationalists voted for the Government's motion of December 12th to reject the Lords' amendments.

Relations were also strained over the issue of a Catholic university in Ireland.† In March 1906 Bryce told Redmond that he intended to appoint a Royal Commission to investigate the workings of Dublin University and Trinity College. It would not be charged directly with enquiring into the possible establishment of a Catholic university but this might well be something that it would recommend in its report. Redmond, however, viewed the proposal with considerable distrust, and suggested to Bryce

* "The bishops," wrote Redmond to Dillon on April 26th, "have not yet considered what course of action to advise in the event of the Second Reading of the Bill being carried, but the Archbishop's view remains unchanged that in that event we ought to concentrate ourselves upon the work of endeavouring to obtain certain amendments in Committee."[2]

† Trinity College, Dublin, was open to Catholics but it was overwhelmingly Protestant in character and very few Catholics had allowed their sons to be educated there. Gladstone, in 1873, had been defeated in his efforts to establish a new Irish university and the issue had since lain dormant, despite constant agitation by Catholics.

(March 26th) that the Commission should confine its activities to examining the revenues, constitution and administration of Dublin University and Trinity College, together with their relationship to the general state of education in Ireland. Bryce replied (April 13th) that, while it had not been his intention to open up the whole university question at this stage, he did not want to prevent the Commission from advocating, if it thought fit, "ideas which might tend to advance the solution of the general question." Redmond felt that there was no further point in discussing the matter. He wrote to Bryce in this sense on May 3rd and the Commission was thus appointed without the Nationalists' blessing.*5

Campbell-Bannerman had told Redmond and O'Connor in November 1905 that the Liberal Party (if returned to power) would introduce an interim measure which would serve as a half-way house to complete Home Rule. The Nationalist leaders had been satisfied with this and later intimated to Bryce that they would raise no objection if such a scheme was not brought forward until the Government's third year of office. Bryce, however, set to work on devising a scheme as soon as the general election was over, and before Parliament rose for the summer recess the Cabinet had approved his proposals for an Irish Council with limited administrative and legislative powers, the members of which would, in the main, be nominated by the county councils. Redmond, who had not been consulted in any way, only heard of this scheme in August and was understandably annoyed at having been kept in the dark. He complained of this in a speech delivered in Limerick on September 23rd and Bryce eventually showed him the proposals on October 8th. The Irish leader, so Bryce then reported to Campbell-Bannerman, declared himself "profoundly disappointed", arguing that they would not bring him any nearer his ultimate goal and that "the creation of a new body in Ireland, created irrespective of the existing Irish members, would fatally reduce the importance of the latter and practically deprive him of the power of criticising most branches of Irish administration."†7 Redmond agreed, however, to consult

---

* The Catholic university cause made good progress, however. "The statement of our Irish university policy and plan was very favourably received by the representative five R.C. laymen to whom it was made on Friday," wrote Bryce to Campbell-Bannerman on January 27th, 1907, "and by the Presbyterian deputation not unfavourably. . . . No pledge whatever was given as to the time when we would introduce a bill and freedom as to details was reserved. It will of course be necessary to consider these most carefully, and possibly to resist some prelactical demands. . . . Never was there a country in which the game of bluff was so consistently played as it is in Ireland, by all parties alike, against the Government."6

† Redmond himself, writing to Birrell in January 1907, declared that the moment he had read the scheme, "without consultation with anyone, I told Bryce he had better put it in the wastepaper-basket; and I sent a message to Campbell-Bannerman that I was shocked beyond measure at what I considered a gross breach of all their pledges and promises."8

Dillon before giving his final verdict, and Bryce meanwhile showed the
scheme to James Sexton, editor of *The Freeman's Journal*. Sexton objected
to it for the same reasons as Redmond, and a crestfallen Bryce complained
to Campbell-Bannerman that the Irish cared "more for a showy bird (very
much) in the bush than a plump little bird in the hand."[9]

Dillon, like Redmond, condemned the scheme as totally inadequate.
The Irish leader then proposed a host of changes in the constitution of the
Council, but Lloyd George informed him on November 1st that these
were unacceptable. He then, so Redmond recorded,

asked my views as to following plan:

(1) Next year King's Speech to contain promise of Irish Land Bill, and *also* Bill
for better government of Ireland.

(2) The Government to concentrate themselves upon an English Land Bill and
take it *first*.

(3) If the Lords cause *hanging up* of Education Bill, and *reject* Plural Voting Bill
this year and *reject* English Land Bill next year, *then* dissolve and go to country on
House of Lords. N.B. This would mean Irish Bills not being reached next year.

He thinks if in new election the country gives Liberals a majority on the question
of modification of power of House of Lords that they could reform it, or curtail it
powers.

I expressed no opinion. We arranged to meet again soon.[10]

This was, in one sense, an invitation to the Irish to join forces with the
Liberals against the Upper House; it was also a warning that Home Rule
would be shelved if the Nationalists refused to co-operate with the Government.

In January 1907 Bryce's place at the Irish Office was taken by Birrell.
This was a change for the better, so far as the Nationalists were concerned,
but their confidence in the Government's good intentions had waned
considerably and Redmond and Dillon now insisted that a bill for improving the government of Ireland be brought forward without delay. Morley
urged upon Dillon and O'Connor that the change of Chief Secretaries
made this impracticable, since Birrell would wish to consider the subject
afresh, but the Nationalist leaders refused to give way. They pointed out
that Sir Antony MacDonnell, the Permanent Under-Secretary at the Irish
Office, had publicly promised such a bill and it was now "notorious" that
one was ready. Any delay would be fatal to the credit of the parliamentary
party in Ireland and "throw the game into the hands of the extremists,
who are raising their heads." If the Government's proposals were acceptable they would no doubt be rejected by the Upper House, but this would
ensure the Liberals the strong support of the Irish vote in Britain when the

time came to appeal to the country against the House of Lords. If the scheme put forward were as weak as Bryce's, however, the Irish vote in Britain would be alienated and there would be a rupture between their two parties.[11]

Morley reported to Campbell-Bannerman, on January 20th, 1907, that there was much bitter feeling in the Nationalist camp against both Bryce and MacDonnell. "The situation for Birrell will be mighty difficult," he concluded, "for he will have to bear all the odium of Sir A. M. on his back, and that's a heavy load."[12]

(2)

Coercion of any kind was anathema to the Liberal Party and the Cabinet were anxious to conciliate the Irish by repealing the emergency measures which had been introduced in the 1880s. Agrarian outrages still flickered here and there, as a sign that the storms of those days were not yet over, but by and large the Ireland of 1906 was in a much more settled state than the Ireland of 1886 or even 1896. It seemed that the time had come for a return to normalcy.* The only member of the Cabinet who did not share this view was Bryce himself, who argued that coercive measures on the Statute Book, even if dead-letters for nine-tenths of the time, were essential safeguards against lawlessness. "Our policy so far," he wrote to Ripon on July 8th, "has been to take notice only of overt acts. We check all seditions or intimidating meetings, we protect all persons who need protection: we 'maintain law and order.' But we don't feel bound to prosecute everybody for a foolish or even an unbecoming speech where there is nothing to show that it is likely to provoke breaches of the law. . . . The country as a whole (Clanricarde's estate is the one conspicuous exception) has been quiet and no person of any consequence has talked 'disloyalty.' "[14] Bryce's protests, however, were overruled. The Government suspended the Crimes Act of 1887 in the few districts in which it had still been in force and later in the year the Peace Preservation Act of 1881, which had suspended habeas corpus on anyone found in possession of firearms, was omitted from the Expiring Laws Continuing Act in which it had figured since 1892. "I advised the Cabinet against it," wrote Bryce to Lord Fitzmaurice on November 30th, 1908. "But I had not a single supporter: all were for dropping: and it is no doubt probable that we could not have

---

* "The Liberal Party," Dilke had written in December 1905, "will not face the fact that they cannot avoid dealing with the Irish question without the certainty of the Irish moderates, of whom Redmond is the most, being forced to say:'We can no longer keep Ireland quiet for you.' The Liberal Party will not have coercion, and, that being so, they have no alternative except to do what they ought to do. It would be wiser to do it before they are compelled."[13]

carried its retention against the Irish, the Labour men and our own Radicals except by beating up the Tories to support us."[15]

In retrospect the Government's decisions certainly appeared unfortunate, for there opened in 1907 a new and bitter phase in the troubled history of Ireland. All the old agrarian outrages of cattle-driving and maiming and boycotting reappeared, accompanied by murders and bomb-explosions, and there were riots in Belfast in the summer which had to be put down by troops. The discontent was partly due to disappointment with the Government's Irish Devolution Bill, which will be discussed in a moment, and partly to increasing economic hardship.* That it was able to find such strident means of expressing itself was automatically ascribed to the withdrawal of the emergency regulations. The scale of these new outrages has very probably been exaggerated, but the Unionist leaders, their darkest forebodings justified and their gloomiest prognostications vindicated, were in a bitterly triumphant frame of mind. To make matters worse, two of Carson's relatives were murdered. "Only three or four weeks ago," he declared on December 8th 1907, "my own kinsmen were shot as they were leaving their place of worship on Sunday in the presence of a jeering and cheering crowd. This is a disgrace to civilisation under the British flag. I warn the Government and Mr Birrell that no man ever made a greater mistake than to play with crime in Ireland. I speak vehemently as an Irishman to English people, and say that if you are not prepared to govern Ireland according to the ordinary conditions of civilisation that prevail in every country, then go out of Ireland and leave us to govern ourselves."

Birrell, however, stood firm against strong pressure from many quarters to reintroduce coercion. In doing so he did, to some degree, succeed in regaining for the Government that confidence of the Nationalist leaders which Bryce had so deservedly forfeited.

(3)

The Speech from the Throne, inaugurating the second Session, announced that "measures for further associating the people of Ireland with the management of their domestic affairs" would form part of the

---

* "In certain congested districts," wrote Campbell-Bannerman to the King on January 23rd, 1908, "especially in Galway and Duncannon, mobs of peasants have driven the cattle from land let for grazing, their excuse being that it was understood . . . that this grazing land should be purchased by the Commissioners and divided among the landless neighbours. . . . The result is a disorderly condition with which it is almost impossible for the police to cope: and this disorder spreads by contagion into other counties where there is not even alleged to be the same excuse. There is not much serious crime, but a considerable extension of the lighter offences."[16]

Government's programme and on May 7th Birrell introduced his Irish Devolution Bill, sometimes referred to as the Irish Council Bill, into the Commons. This measure proposed the creation of a central Council consisting of 82 elected and 24 nominated members (together with the Chief Secretary, who would have no vote) which would take over the administration of existing organs of local government. It would be presided over by the Lord-Lieutenant, who would have the authority to defer action on any resolution pending reference to the King, and would possess no legislative power. A special Irish Fund would receive annual grants of £650,000 from the Imperial Exchequer. "I dare say," commented Birrell, "we shall be told that this Bill paves the way to Home Rule. If the proposals contained in this Bill become law and obtain a fair trial, if the new Council after some years is a success, why, then, it *may* pave the way to Home Rule. If, on the other hand, it is failure, it appears to me that it would present a very considerable obstacle to persuading the electors in this country who have been called the predominant partners to accept Home Rule."

It goes without saying that the Unionists opposed the measure. The Irish Nationalists, on the other hand, were bitterly disappointed, their feelings having been aggravated by the well-founded suspicion that Birrell's original scheme, before being submitted to the Cabinet, had been far more generous than the version now put forward. They did not, at this early stage, reject the proposals as they stood out of hand, but they allowed it to be seen that they did not embrace them with any great enthusiasm.* Redmond said that the scheme would be submitted to his countrymen at a National Convention and that its future would depend upon their acquiescence or disapproval. This in itself was ominous: the events which followed were decisive.

The Irish National Convention, composed of some 2,000 delegates, met at the Mansion House, Dublin, on May 21st. Redmond moved a resolution declaring that the Irish Devolution Bill was totally inadequate in its scope, unsatisfactory in its details and deserving of rejection by the

---

* "The explosion of disappointment and anger in the country," wrote Dillon to Redmond on May 11th from Dublin, "will have some very wholesome results. It will let Birrell and Co. see how much they can rely on Sir Antony's information as to Irish feeling, and make them realise what would have been the result of producing Antony's original Bill. And I think if we make full use of it, and of the reception of the Bill by the Liberal Party, we may be able to secure some necessary amendments." He added (May 13th) that it would "be a great tactical misfortune if we are compelled by the force of public feeling against the Bill to take such an attitude at the Convention as will coerce the Government to abandon the Bill, and so relieve the Lords of the odium and embarrassment of dealing with it." Dillon's wife fell seriously ill and died the following week; his absence from the Convention thus removed a restraining influence from Redmond.[17]

Irish nation. The Liberal Party, he declared, must abandon the Roseberyite idea of settling the Irish question (a reference to the "predominant part- ners" theme) and return to the standard set by Gladstone. This resolution was carried unanimously.

One is inclined to feel, at first glance, that the Nationalists acted too hastily in refusing to consider the Irish Devolution Bill.* It was, admit- tedly, a far from perfect measure, but it was certainly better than nothing. The main objection to it seems to have been, quite simply, that it was not a Home Rule Bill, and since the Government had never claimed that it was anything more than a half-way house to ultimate self-government this objection was quite irrelevant. The second objection had been that the scheme was unworkable, but the only proof of this would have been to put it to the test. Whether it could or could not be worked, in fact, is any- one's guess, and the Irish were simply too prejudiced to admit this.

One must, on the other hand, consider the delicate position in which the leaders of the parliamentary party found themselves. If they had accepted the Bill and not pressed for complete self-government they would have been deluged with criticism from their supporters. If, however, they had rejected the Bill out of hand on their own responsibility they would probably have been accused by these self-same supporters of withholding some great and unknown boon from Ireland. They were forced to safe- guard themselves by calling upon the National Convention to advise them, and since the Convention had agreed, admittedly on their own recom- mendation, to reject the Bill, there was an end of the matter.† Their posi- tion was appreciated by Birrell, and Redmond, writing to Dillon on June 2nd, observed that the Chief Secretary did "not seem at all bitter about our action and told me he did not think we could be expected to risk a break up of our party and movement for such a Bill."[20] What the National Convention had done, however, was to make it quite clear— despite the agreement between Redmond and Campbell-Bannerman in November 1905—that the Nationalists were not prepared to accept any- thing short of an Irish Parliament and an Irish Exchequer. "Another Councils Bill is a sheer impossibility," wrote Birrell to MacDonnell on

* "Already," wrote MacDonnell to Ripon on May 23rd, "reaction and remorse have set in after the foolish and hasty rejection of the Irish Councils Bill. The Convention's decision is now recognised by a rapidly growing number of people as having been too hasty and based on a great misconception of the scope and advantages of the Bill."[18]

† It is interesting to note, however, that the Nationalist leaders had apparently told certain members of the Government that the Convention *would* accept the Bill. Thus Crewe, writing to Ripon on May 25th, declared that he thought it "evident that Redmond & Co. entirely miscalculated the force of the varied opposition to the Bill—by their extreme supporters on the one hand, and I suppose by the hierarchy on the education proposals. Birrell, therefore, seems to have been rather scurvily treated."[19]

September 12th, "unless it goes much further than the late one. . . . The next Bill must be Home Rule of some sort."[21]

Campbell-Bannerman, on June 3rd, reluctantly announced that the Irish Devolution Bill would have to be withdrawn.* In its place the Government introduced an Evicted Tenants Bill, which gave the Estates Commissioners the power of purchasing land, compulsorily if need be, upon which tenants who had previously been evicted from it could be reinstated. Any occupying tenants dispossessed to replace a previous holder would be provided with holdings elsewhere or financial compensation. This Bill passed its Third Reading on August 2nd by 228 to 49 and was then referred to the Upper House, which proceeded to maul it beyond recognition. The Lords decided that the Estates Commissioners should have no compulsory powers of any kind, that the number of tenants to be reinstated should not exceed 2,000 and that the sporting rights of landowners would have to be punctiliously observed. The Commons formally disagreed with these amendments but the Lords insisted upon them and on August 26th, rather than abandon the Bill altogether, Birrell advised the House to let the amendments stand. The Nationalists, their fury aroused to a degree hardly equalled in recent years, bitterly denounced the actions of the peers and Redmond declared that if Ireland desired useful legislation she must, henceforth, make her movement sufficiently strong and menacing to overcome opposition.†

(4)

By the end of 1907 it was clear that no easy solution to the problems of Ireland would be found, at any rate not in the immediate future, and the prospects of a settlement now seemed much further off than they had in 1905. "If the Session of 1906 had aroused the impatience of the Irish leaders," writes Mr F. S. L. Lyons, "that of 1907 had been sufficient to cause them active alarm, for the Liberal Government had shown itself at its worst in the handling of Irish affairs. An inadequate offer of an Irish Council and a mutilated Evicted Tenants Act were the only fruits of that second Session, and it is not surprising that the party returned to Westminster for the Session of 1908 in the least conciliatory temper it had yet displayed in this Parliament."[23]

* "It was," Campbell-Bannerman had written to the King on May 27th, "an honest attempt to improve the system of administration by enlarging the powers and enlisting the direct help of the Irish people and if it did not please them the Government have no desire to proceed with it."[22]

† The Act nevertheless produced some beneficial results. During the nine months which followed 562 evicted tenants were reinstated, 429 by landlords and 133 by the Commissioners, on land specially purchased for them.

Redmond was, moreover, finding it difficult to restrain those members of his party who advocated a stronger line, namely that they should go into opposition unless the Government undertook to introduce a Home Rule Bill as soon as possible. The new Sinn Fein organisation had increased in importance since the episode of the rejected Irish Council and the Senior Whip of the Nationalist Party, Sir Thomas Esmonde, resigned his post in protest at what he considered the futility of Redmond's methods. The Irish leader needed, therefore, some trophy whereby he could reassure his followers of the Government's desire to conciliate him. In May 1907 he had urged Birrell to introduce a University Bill, arguing that while there would be no time to carry it Trinity College would realise that the Government meant business and his own followers would be satisfied. Birrell sympathised but there was no time in which to draw up a scheme for the 1907 Session. Redmond's next hope, therefore, was that the Government would assent to a Home Rule resolution at the opening of the 1908 Session. Birrell agreed to this proposal and Redmond and Dillon accordingly drafted a resolution which, they hoped, Campbell-Bannerman himself would introduce.

Sir Henry, who was by this time far from well, was favourably inclined towards the resolution but wanted certain alterations made. "As you may guess," wrote Birrell to Redmond on January 26th, "it is not easy in C.B.'s state of health and circumstances to thrash anything out with him, and I am nearly worn out with the attempts I have made. . . . He thinks it would be *disastrous* to use words which would give force to the contention that 'he and his' were in favour of an *independent* Irish Parliament. . . . Before he could ask his friends to support any resolution this must be made plain."[24]

The details were at length agreed but in the event neither the Chief Secretary nor the Prime Minister was able to introduce the resolution, the former because of a heavy cold and the latter for reasons of a more serious nature. It was carried on March 30th, though in a rather lukewarm manner, and the following day Birrell introduced his Irish University Bill. The Commission set up by Bryce had recommended that Dublin University, hitherto synonomous with Trinity College, should be enlarged to embrace five teaching colleges, but Birrell decided that it would be best to leave Trinity undisturbed and create two new universities. One, for Catholics, would have three colleges, in Dublin, Cork and Galway; the other, for Presbyterians, would be established in Belfast. The Royal University, a purely examining body, would be dissolved. University staff would not be subjected to religious tests. The Bill met with general approval and passed speedily through both Houses, becoming law on July 31st.

Campbell-Bannerman had meanwhile been succeeded by Asquith, who was known to be less sympathetic towards Home Rule. The Nationalists accepted his accession with no great delight and lost no time in putting his professions of good faith to the test. The occasion was Churchill's by-election contest at Manchester.* Redmond declared, on April 15th, that Asquith had displayed a distinct lack of ardour for the motion of March 30th and there was, as yet, no evidence of his Government's desire to aid the Nationalists in their struggle for freedom. He could not, therefore, recommend the Irish electors of Manchester, who formed a considerable element of that city's population, to vote for the new President of the Board of Trade.

Churchill promptly announced that the Government would take up the cudgels on behalf of Home Rule in the next Parliament. This declaration was, however, greeted with ironic cheers and a few days later Churchill found himself without a constituency. Asquith, on April 30th and again on May 4th, emphasised that the self-denying ordinance as regards Home Rule only applied to the present Parliament and the Liberals would, in the next, claim a free hand to deal with Irish affairs as they thought fit. The Nationalists remained deeply suspicious of the new premier and Asquith's subsequent behaviour did not really help matters. Redmond tried, without success to discover the form that a Home Rule Bill would take. "I have been trying to arrange a conference with Lloyd George and the Prime Minister until I have given up the attempt in utter disgust," he wrote to Dillon on July 22nd. "It is quite clear these men do not want a conference, do not see any importance in it and are trying to let the whole question drift. I feel really humiliated in having run after them the way I have done and I will ask them for no more interviews."[25]

In November Birrell introduced an Irish Land Bill, a complicated measure designed to facilitate land purchase by tenants, which passed its Second Reading on December 8th but had to be abandoned for lack of time. A Housing of the Working Classes (Ireland) Bill did succeed, however, in reaching the Statute Book and a supplementary grant of £114,000 for Irish education was also agreed upon.

The situation in December 1908 was therefore marginally better than it had been at the close of the previous Session. Asquith had been obliged, however reluctantly, to resume the Liberal Party's Irish crusade from the point where it had been suspended on Gladstone's retirement and it was

* See p. 154.

very probable that the Nationalists would, in the next Parliament, be able to exercise a greater influence on Government legislation. In their battle with the House of Lords the Liberals would obviously need all the support they could muster and would presumably make substantial concessions to obtain that support. Whatever happened, barring a Unionist victory at the polls, the future seemed reasonably bright for Ireland.

CHAPTER TEN

DOMESTIC AFFAIRS,
JANUARY–DECEMBER 1908

(1)

"One question in all our minds," wrote Morley on January 6th, "though not so much upon our lips, is the likelihood or otherwise of the Prime Minister being strong enough in health to accompany us through the year or beyond it. What is certain is that he will not desert the bridge until the doctor or Nature . . . orders him off."[1] Two heart attacks which Campbell-Bannerman had experienced in November had made it clear that his days as premier were numbered, but he was determined not to resign until actually forced to do so, which meant that his disappearance might come at an awkward moment.* The new Session, moreover, would clearly be a difficult one: the Ministry, after taking things easy in 1907, had at last made up its mind to introduce some Radical measures, foremost among which would be the long-awaited Licensing Bill. It would obviously need careful management and a firm hand to steer them on their way. The one compensating factor, as Morley remarked in the letter already quoted, was "the weakness of the other side in personnel, and their incoherence in policy."† As for the constitutional conflict with the House of Lords, that would have to be postponed until the new Session had run its course and the position

---

* It is pleasant to note that before Campbell-Bannerman died Grey did much to make amends for his attitude in December 1905. "I have felt from the early days of this Parliament," he wrote to Sir Henry on December 31st, 1907, "that all my forecast before the election was wrong, and that your presence in the House of Commons has been not only desirable but essential to manage this party and keep it together; and so it continues to be; and I most sincerely wish you health and strength for the coming year."[2]

† The Unionists, as usual, were more concerned with their own problems than those of the Government. The Tariff Reformers had discovered that a rival organisation, a group of Free Traders led by Cromer and known as "the Centre Party", was taking shape and rumour had it that Lansdowne was encouraging them. Crewe, writing to Campbell-Bannerman on December 16th, 1907, remarked that "the opposition leaders seem hard put to it to maintain even an appearance of unity when Tariff Reform is mentioned." Gladstone, writing the same day, described the other side of the coin when he declared that "our people are in excellent heart, and excepting Ireland and one or two F. O. questions things seem pretty smooth—always excepting naval expenditure."[3]

had been considered afresh at the end of the year. The Liberals were not yet strategically well-placed for such a conflict: the rejection of the Education and Plural Voting Bills thirteen months before, together with the defeat of measures of secondary importance in 1907, did not in themselves merit a full-blooded attack upon the bastions of the peerage. If, however, the Lords continued their policy to the extent of rejecting or mutilating the Licensing Bill and other measures especially dear to Liberal hearts, then the Government would be prepared to take steps of a more positive nature to secure the supremacy of the House of Commons in the field of legislation. The new Session was thus, in every respect, a crucial one: much would depend upon the events of the next few months.

It was generally assumed that Asquith was the person best fitted to succeed Campbell-Bannerman, this being due as much to the absence of any serious rivals as to his own capabilities.* Morley was the only other person who might have been in the running, but the truth of the matter seems to have been that he was never even considered (except by himself) as an eligible candidate.† There was no real alternative to Asquith, but apart, presumably, from Grey and Haldane, no one was particularly eager to see him ensconced at No. 10 and the feelings of the Liberal Party at the prospect of having him as their leader can best be described as lukewarm. It would be untrue to say that there was any positive opposition: there was simply an absence of enthusiasm. Campbell-Bannerman's return to England from Biarritz on January 20th, however, put an end, for the moment, to speculation about his successor. To all outward appearances he seemed to have recovered his old buoyancy and zest, being in high spirits and anxious to get down to work.

Parliament was opened on January 29th.‡ The Licensing Bill, as in 1907, occupied pride of place in the Government's programme, and it was supported by an Education Bill, an Old Age Pensions Bill, an Eight Hours

---

* Knollys remarked to Austen Chamberlain on January 4th "that C.B. had a difficult task before him this Session, and said that he was told by Liberals that if anything happened to C.B. the party would go smash in six months." Knollys himself thought that Grey ought to be the next Prime Minister, since Asquith was not "quite the right stamp of man", but Harcourt told Esher on January 28th that Asquith was the only possible choice. "Grey, according to him, has little influence in the H. of C., and none in the country."[4]

† He told Esher on November 16th, 1907 that he would not accept office under Asquith, although he might do so under Grey, and repeated this statement on February 11th, intimating that he would like to be premier himself.[5]

‡ The opening was not without incident. The suffragettes, ever hopeful of winning notable converts to their cause, mobbed the royal coach as it approached Westminster and almost succeeded in pitching a petition of their grievances into the King's lap. In the House of Lords a gentleman claiming to be a candidate for the dormant peerage of De Morley had meanwhile presented himself and had to be removed shortly before the monarch arrived, doubts having been expressed as to the validity of his credentials.

F

(Coal Mines) Bill and a plan for reforming university education in Ireland. The Small Landholders (Scotland) Bill again appeared on the agenda, despite a noticeable lack of enthusiasm for it in the Cabinet and grumbles from the King.*

The Land Values (Scotland) Bill and the Small Landholders (Scotland) Bill, the two chief casualties of the previous Session, were reintroduced into the Commons on February 6th. Campbell-Bannerman, on February 12th, moved that the time allowed for discussion of them should be limited, since they had aleady been passed once by the same House. The motion was carried the following day by 331 to 84. This was Sir Henry's last public appearance. He returned to No. 10 Downing Street that evening and never left it again during his lifetime. A sudden heart seizure a few hours later was followed by a heavy attack of influenza. At first the full gravity of the situation was not realised. Campbell-Bannerman himself was certain that he would be resuming his normal duties once the bout of illness had passed and the members of the Ministry did not concern themselves unduly at his absence. Asquith, with very limited powers at his disposal, assumed control of the Government and his first Cabinet letter to the King was written on February 17th.

On February 24th McKenna introduced the Government's latest Education Bill. It resembled, in some respects, the one-clause bill which had met such a sorry fate the previous year. It envisaged only one type of public elementary school, controlled by the local authorities, with no religious tests for teachers and religious instruction identical with that given in board and council schools since 1870. It passed its First Reading without a division.

On February 27th the much-heralded Licensing Bill made its entry into the Commons, with Asquith as its stern-faced custodian. This measure, intended to supersede the 1904 Act, was destined to be the most controversial of the whole Session and soon came to occupy, in fact, the place filled by the Education Bill in 1906. It provided for the compulsory reduction of licensed premises throughout the country during the next fourteen years so that, by 1922, the number remaining in any one area would not exceed a fixed ratio to the population. This meant the suppression of at

* Vaughan Nash, writing to Knollys on January 24th, explained that while Campbell-Bannerman was "aware that the measure has been much criticised in some quarters he believes that many of the objections are due to a misunderstanding . . . and he has been much impressed by the favourable way in which the Bill has been received in Scotland." Knollys replied, next day, that the King was unable to share this view: "He happens to know a great number of Scotsmen, both Liberals and Conservatives. He believes they understand the provisions perfectly, and from what they say it is evident to him that in Scotland people are not so immeasurably satisfied with the Bill as Sir Henry believes to be the case."[6]

least 32,000 licences, about a third of the whole number then in existence, and though compensation would be paid by a levy on the trade these payments would cease at the end of the fourteen years. New licensing hours would also be drawn up. The First Reading was carried without a division, but the initial Unionist reactions indicated that stormy scenes lay ahead.*

On March 2nd Campbell-Bannerman felt well enough to send Asquith a cheerful letter of thanks for all that he and the rest of his colleagues were doing. "I can," he wrote, "get nothing whatever out of the doctors as to how long I am to expect to be in quarantine. The only thing they say is that nothing must be hurried."[8] Asquith replied the following day, assuring him that the Cabinet were "not only content but eager that you should be relieved of all worry and avoidable responsibility for as long a time as may be needed for your complete restoration to health."[9] In reality, however, the situation was far from satisfactory. The work of the Session had, of course, been drafted well beforehand, but it is one thing to draw up a plan of attack and another to put it into execution when the commander-in-chief is indisposed. "I am afraid that C.B. makes very little real progress," wrote Asquith to Ripon on March 4th. "The party here is in good heart, but has some stiff work before it and must face the prospect of losing by-elections."[10]

King Edward VII was about to depart for his annual sojourn at Biarritz. First, however, he was anxious to make sure that the domestic situation was in a satisfactory state. On March 3rd he had an important interview with Asquith. The latter was already aware that he occupied the position of heir-apparent to Campbell-Bannerman but the conversation which followed made it quite clear, if any doubts still lingered, that he was destined to be the next Prime Minister of Great Britain.

Asquith to his wife, March 4th, 1908

I had quite a pleasant interview with the King after the Privy Council yesterday. He talked sensibly about the Licensing Bill and other such matters, and said generally that he thought the offices in the present Government were very well filled, and that he should be sorry to see anything in the nature of a general shuffling of the cards. The only exception he made was Portsmouth, whom he is anxious to get rid

---

* The new Bill, if it becomes law, did not mean that men would drink less but simply that they would have less places in which to drink. The Liberals regarded the reduction of licences as an essential feature of any programme of temperance reform, while the Unionists argued that licences were a form of property. The truth of the matter seems to have been that the Government, while anxious to satisfy the bulk of its supporters with a colourful piece of legislation, was equally anxious to strike a blow at a group of men forming one of the staunchest pillars of the Conservative Party. "The brewers are the enemy," wrote Morley to Minto on April 9th, "and they will pay us out at the next election."[7]

of, and to see Brun [Lord Lucas], of whom he spoke highly, in his place.* He had heard gossip that Winston was anxious to get into the Cabinet keeping his present office of Under-Secretary. He was opposed to this and said that Queen Victoria had vetoed a similar proposal by Rosebery in favour of E. Grey when he was Under-Secretary for Foreign Affairs. I said that Winston had every claim to Cabinet rank and that he had behaved very well when twice passed over for Loulou and McKenna, both of whom had inferior claims. The King agreed and was quite warm in his praise of Winston, but thought he must wait till some real Cabinet office fell vacant.

He said that he had quite made up his mind to send for me at once in the event of anything happening to C.B., or of his sending in his resignation. He thought it a pity C.B. would not go to the Lords and said there was no inconsistency in his doing so with his House of Lords policy. I told him I was sure C.B. would never do it. He said he thought C.B. very useful so long as he was equal to the job, at making things smooth and keeping people together. But it was evident that he was breaking-up and we must provide for the future: what were my plans? I told him I should do as little as possible—probably nothing—to alter the composition of the Cabinet or shift the men, at any rate until the Session was over, and that in the meantime I should keep the Exchequer. . . . He said that if a change became necessary he hoped I would come out to him at Biarritz. . . . Altogether it was quite a satisfactory interview.[12]

Quite apart from establishing good relations with the man who would most probably be his next Prime Minister, King Edward was anxious to keep in touch with the present occupant of the post. On March 3rd Knollys wrote to Vaughan Nash, Sir Henry's private secretary, stating that the King had asked "whether it would be possible for him to see the Prime Minister for a minute (merely to take him by the hand) to-morrow."[13] A reply was speedily forthcoming to the effect that Campbell-Bannerman would be deeply honoured by a visit. Late on the afternoon of March 4th, therefore, King Edward VII arrived at No. 10 Downing Street to "shake Sir Henry by the hand," as Knollys described it. "The King," Crewe reported to Ripon the following day "thought better of the patient than he expected, especially as to spirits,"[14] and it was, presumably, the apparent improvement in Campbell-Bannerman's condition that led the King to ask Sir Henry if he would, as a special favour, delay his resignation until after Easter, when he himself would have returned from Biarritz. Sir Henry was a good-natured man and, whatever his private feelings

* The King was in good company with regard to Portsmouth. Ripon, writing to Campbell-Bannerman on February 13th, had complained that he was "no use at the War Office and he gives us no help in general debates in the House of Lords. He could be easily replaced in his present office and we might get some help in debates. At present we are very weak and the front opposition bench has just been strengthened by the arrival of Curzon."[11]

may have been, agreed to retain office for at least another five weeks. No more would be said of resignation until the King was back in England. King Edward was satisfied with this assurance and took his departure in a contented frame of mind. Steps were taken, moreover, as the following letter indicates, to ensure that Campbell-Bannerman did not go back on his promise.

Sir Arthur Davidson to Vaughan Nash, March 14th, 1908

The King wishes you to impress on Sir Henry, should he have suggested anything of the kind, his earnest hope that he will not think of resigning before Easter. Apart from any political considerations, the King feels sure that it would react injuriously on Sir Henry's health and might retard his recovery.

Of course this intimation of the King's wishes is only intended in the event of the Prime Minister stating the idea, but the King knows that very often invalids resolve an idea in their minds and unless it is checked authoritatively "ab initio" it is apt to become an "idée fixe."[15]

On March 16th Sir Henry's illness took a turn for the worse and tentative representations were made to Biarritz to the effect that it might be better for all concerned if the resignation was not unduly delayed. These representations were, however, brusquely dismissed. "So far as one can gather from the Press and from private letters," wrote Davidson to Vaughan Nash on March 20th, "there appears no suggestion whatever that the Prime Minister is hanging on to office and I think the feeling is generally recognised that while he remains Prime Minister his leadership is unquestioned and the party is more or less united. With his resignation a split, or at all events differences, appear inevitable, a state of affairs to which no one looks forward with pleasure."*[16]

(2)

The Ministry struggled along as best it could, beset on the one side by cries that it was doing nothing to halt the rise in unemployment and on the other by accusations that it was trying to take away the working man's beer. In the midst of all these trials and tribulations Rosebery, like an accusing spirit, once again rose up in the political arena. His lordship, it seemed, was suddenly alive to the dreadful dangers of Socialism and, at a meeting of the Liberal League on March 12th, described it as the "end of all things—Empire, religious faith, freedom and property." It was, he declared, the duty of the present Government to protect the country from

---

* This fear of "differences" was echoed in a letter of Grey's dated April 7th to Campbell-Bannerman: "We all feel now that troubles, which your presence at the head of the Government kept in abeyance, will have to be faced."[17]

this horrid fate and not to waste the said country's time by devising such measures as the Small Landholders (Scotland) Bill, which had been rejected by the Lords the previous day. It was becoming difficult to believe that Rosebery had, fourteen years before, been a Liberal Prime Minister.

On March 13th an Unemployed Workman's Bill, introduced by a Labour member, received its Second Reading. It envisaged the creation of unemployment committees throughout the country which would either provide work or relief. Burns, in a typical broadside, ridiculed the whole idea on the grounds that such a system would attract wastrels. The Bill was defeated by 265 to 116, although 74 Liberals voted in its favour and another 136 abstained. "Of course," wrote Austen Chamberlain to his father that evening, "we supported the Government, but it was a pretty sight for us onlookers. Henderson, sessional chairman of the Labour Party, wound up with a clever and damaging little speech against the Government and many of their people were uncomfortable, hating the Bill and yet awfully afraid of voting against it."[18]

The external fortunes of the Government, partly as a result of the Prime Minister's continued absence, were going from bad to worse.* It had lost several by-elections during the past few months but a defeat at Peckham on March 24th, when a Liberal majority of 2,339 was transformed into a Unionist majority of 2,494, was one of the heaviest blows that it had yet sustained. "I do not believe there has ever been such a political situation before," wrote Knollys to Crewe. "Lord Chatham's case when he was Prime Minister one hundred and fifty years ago is the nearest approach to it. . . . Vaughan Nash is too sensible not to realise that it would be impossible to carry on the present state of affairs much longer. The country, the Government and the party would all suffer from it, and the machinery connected with the office of a Prime Minister has come to a complete standstill. The position of a Prime Minister will moreover be weakened if Asquith is not soon appointed. I quite understand Nash shrinking from saying anything to C.B. on the subject and it is hardly his business to do so, but either the Dr or C.B.'s sister ought to speak as soon as possible."[20]

Knollys, presumably, was not aware that the only reason Campbell-Bannerman clung to office was the promise which he had made to King Edward three weeks before. Even the King, however, was now beginning to realise that Sir Henry's resignation could not be postponed much longer, for on March 19th he instructed Knollys that "in the event of

* Campbell-Bannerman could, on his best days, do no more than sit in his chair and reminisce or gaze out of the window at Horse Guards Parade. "Of politics," writes his biographer, "he spoke little, but he brooded over the question of resignation, the chief consideration in his mind being the King's desire that it should be postponed till his return."[19]

Prime Minister's resignation or fatal crisis in illness, the King would like the authoritative announcement made that before he left England it was settled that Mr Asquith should at once come out to see His Majesty at Biarritz."[21]

Asquith was growing impatient. Towards the end of March he told Knollys that Campbell-Bannerman's return to public life was not possible and that the present situation was "demoralising".[22] On April 1st, therefore, Knollys wired to Biarritz that Campbell-Bannerman would probably resign at the end of the week but King Edward, who was still obsessed with the idea that nothing should be done until his return, telegraphed in reply that he was "most anxious that he should not resign till Easter vacation."[23] Fortunately, however, this telegram arrived too late to influence the course of events, for a letter was sent from Campbell-Bannerman to the King that same day signifying that he was no longer able to continue in office. The King had no option but to give way before a situation which could not, in fact, be altered. He telegraphed a regretful acceptance of his Prime Minister's resignation on April 3rd and at five o'clock that afternoon Campbell-Bannerman signed his formal submission. "There's the last kick," he remarked to his secretary, and then—noting the latter's disconsolate expression—"My dear fellow, I don't mind! I've been Prime Minister for longer than I deserve."*[24]

On April 22nd the "person of an easy-going disposition" passed peacefully away, esconced to the last in his room at No. 10 Downing Street. His premiership had lasted less than two and a half years, but during that time he had succeeded in proving that the Liberal Party, coalition of diverse elements though it might be, was capable not only of governing but of governing well. "Starting as the subject of some prejudice," wrote Crewe many years later, "and with only a few ardent supporters, he finished with unchallenged authority and in an atmosphere of universal affection."[26]

(3)

The coming man had finally arrived. It was twenty-one years, almost to the day, since Herbert Henry Asquith had delivered his maiden speech in the House of Commons and sixteen since he had, without previous administrative experience of any kind, been presented by Gladstone with the Home Office and a seat in the Cabinet. This was undeniably an impressive ascent which appears, in retrospect, to have been smoothly inevitable, yet

---

* "I have just got the news that my old chief C.B. is going," wrote Haldane to his mother. "I fear that he will not be alive much longer. We shall miss him. Whatever the wisdom or otherwise of the line he took in the South African War seven years ago, he had brought his party together out of the wilderness. He was a loyal leader and I owe a great deal to him."[25]

to the great mass of the British people he was something of an enigma. He had never, in public life, put a foot wrong, but he had never been unduly venturesome. He had spoken often, and he spoke with great lucidity, but his elegant prose and calmly reasoned expositions had left little more impression on his audience than the reassuring utterances of a company secretary. He was a model of efficiency and a capable administrator, but these were not necessarily qualities which betokened great powers of leadership. It does not follow that a tactician, however brilliant, is automatically an expert strategist and Asquith had shown, on many occasions, that he was more attracted by established practice than innovations. Originality of thought and decisiveness of deed, however much he admired them in others, were not qualities to which he himself aspired. The epitome of caution, he had argued against granting independence to the Transvaal and Orange River Colony, against the Trade Disputes Bill, against female suffrage and against Home Rule as an immediate objective. It was only with extreme reluctance that he acquiesced in the cause of constitutional reform. Lip-service was paid to social reform, but this was not a field which really interested him. Fortunately for the Liberal Party, his opposition to Imperial Preference was the one thing which distinguished him from the typical Unionist of his day: to Free Trade he did, indeed, cling with the limpet tenacity of the true Conservative.

The great offices of State, however, are rarely filled by those who have not struggled hard to reach them and Asquith, affable, mild and courteous as he undoubtedly was, could also be cold, calculating and ruthless. He had entered public life, it seemed, more from a sense of duty than personal inclination, but his desire for power was as real as that of Lloyd George and all the more deadly for being less obvious. Having secured the premiership he would not let it go in a hurry. Finally, he had the one tremendous advantage of being virtually unrivalled. Morley might still gaze longingly at the goal which he would never reach, Lloyd George might rub his hands in gleeful anticipation of future events, but from the start of Campbell-Bannerman's illness Asquith's succession had been a foregone conclusion. The Liberal Party as a whole were prepared to welcome their new Messiah with relief.* If nothing else, the period of suspense was at last coming to an end and they would soon be able to resume the normal conduct of parliamentary affairs.

Asquith was informed by Vaughan Nash on April 5th that Campbell-

---

* Morley, writing to Minto on April 9th, remarked that Asquith had "not yet attracted the popular imagination, but he has made an enormous advance in the H. of C. since he has been the acting leader."[27]

Bannerman had tendered his resignation and next day the expected summons arrived from the King, calling upon Asquith to form a Government and inviting him to Biarritz "in order to hear from him what proposals he has to make."[28] Asquith left England without delay and reached the Hotel du Palais on April 8th.* Here it was that he received his appointment as First Lord of the Treasury, the glad tidings being speedily relayed to Margot—"Have just kissed hands; back Friday, ask Grey to dinner. Bless you. H."[29] A more detailed account was also despatched. "This morning," he wrote, "I put on a frock coat and escorted by Fritz and old Stanley Clarke went to the King, who was similarly attired. I presented him with a written resignation of the office of Chr. of the Exr., and he then said 'I appoint you P.M. and 1st Lord of the Treasury,' whereupon I knelt down and kissed his hand. Voila tout! He then asked me to come into the next room and breakfast with him. We were quite alone for an hour and I went over all the appointments with him. He made no objection to any of them and discussed the various men very freely and with a good deal of shrewdness."[30]

The new Prime Minister arrived back in England on April 10th, being met at Charing Cross by his wife, and together they drove to Downing Street to enquire after Campbell-Bannerman. It was not until the latter's last illness had reached its close that the Asquiths were able, at the end of the month, to move from Cavendish Square to No. 10. They were, unfortunately, not particularly impressed with their new residence.† Violet, the Prime Minister's daughter, found it "pitch dark, with highly official, wholly influenceable furniture (different Prime Ministers having lived and died in every chair) and not a bathroom or a bookshelf anywhere (how *can* they have never washed nor read?)";[32] Mrs Asquith thought it "an inconvenient house with three poor staircases" and decided that she "could only entertain my Liberal friends at dinner or at garden parties."[33]

Asquith's original intention had been to keep changes in the Government to a bare minimum, but in the event there proved to be a considerable number. He mentioned to Churchill, at this time, Gladstone's dictum that "the first essential for a Prime Minister is to be a good butcher," and added that there were several "who must be pole-axed now."[34] Heading this list of victims came Elgin and Tweedmouth.

Elgin's tenure of the Colonial Office had not been distinguished. His

---

* *The Times* expressed concern at Asquith's departure to kiss hands on foreign soil. It would have been still more perturbed by the arrangement first suggested by King Edward, namely that all the Cabinet should meet him in Paris and receive their seals of office in the Hôtel Crillon. This idea was shot down by Knollys.

† Campbell-Bannerman had once described it as "this rotten old barrack of a house."[31]

fear of change made decisions of any kind a painful business and his speeches in the House of Lords had been sadly ineffective. He rarely spoke at conferences on colonial matters, preferring to tug at his beard in silence, and on one memorable occasion when he was expected to sum up astonished his colleagues by carefully putting the end of it into his mouth. He laboured under the additional disadvantage of being constantly overshadowed by Churchill and relations between them had been strained. It was hardly surprising that Asquith could find no room for Elgin in the reconstituted Government, but his lordship accepted dismissal with a very bad grace and made it clear that he went unwillingly. A casual offer of a marquisate was refused and he complained bitterly to Crewe (his successor) at the injustice of the treatment meted out to him. "Why cannot I continue my work?" he demanded, evidently convinced that his dismissal was the result of some Churchillian intrigue. "I have no answer to that question and I do not ask for one."[35]

Tweedmouth's shortcomings were rather more serious. In addition to the curious episode of his correspondence with the Kaiser, which is noted elsewhere,* it was now common knowledge that he owned half the ordinary shares in a firm which supplied the navy with most of its beer. This latter disclosure would have been enough in itself to seal his fate and Campbell-Bannerman's resignation provided the ideal opportunity for his own. He was anxious, indeed, to disappear from the public scene completely, but Asquith persuaded him to take Crewe's place as Lord President of the Council.

The most important of the new appointments was that of Lloyd George. On March 4th Asquith had told the King that he intended to continue as Chancellor of the Exchequer, but by the end of the month he had changed his mind, evidently realising the desirability of preserving an equilibrium between the right and left wings of the Government. On April 3rd he saw Lloyd George and it was agreed that the latter should succeed him but that Asquith should introduce the Budget for the current financial year.† The post was formally offered to Lloyd George in a letter dated April 10th and the latter accepted it the following day, declaring that "I shall be proud to serve under your premiership and no member of the Government will render more loyal service and support to his chief."‡ The new Chancellor's

---

* See page 194.

† In a letter to his relations dated April 11th, announcing his appointment as "second-in-command in the Liberal host", Lloyd George stated that "we had settled everything last Friday week"—i.e., April 3rd. "The world," his letter continued, "says that it is a much more dazzling promotion than Asquith's."[36]

‡ Morley told Esher on April 9th that Lloyd George had threatened to resign if he were not made Chancellor. This was probably nothing more than spite on Morley's part but even if he

letter concluded, however, with an angry fulmination against the un-known member of the Cabinet who made the "amiable suggestion" that he was responsible for informing the *Daily Chronicle* of the composition of the new Ministry.* "Men whose promotion is not sustained by birth or other favouring conditions," he declared, "are always liable to be assailed with unkind suspicions of this sort. I would ask it therefore as a favour that you should not entertain them without satisfying yourself that they have some basis of truth."[39]

Churchill's admission to the Cabinet was generally recognised as being long overdue† and early in March Asquith had discussed his prospects with him. Churchill subsequently wrote to him on March 14th stating that he would willingly accept the Colonial Office or, failing that, the Admiralty. Failing either of these he would content himself with the presidency of the Local Government Board, although this was a post which he did not par-ticularly covet. Asquith's decision to surrender the Exchequer to Lloyd George, however, created a new opening, and on April 8th he offered Churchill the presidency of the Board of Trade, declaring that "I shall hail with much gratification your accession to the Cabinet, both on public and on personal grounds."[41] Churchill accepted this post on April 10th, but he was none too pleased with it. "I've got this job too late," he grumbled, "Lloyd George has pulled out all the plums!"[42] Young Harold Nicolson, who met him at this time, was applauded for his decision to follow in his father's wake and enter the diplomatic service. "The thing you must never do," said Churchill, "is to go into politics. It's a most ungrateful profession."[43]

McKenna took Tweedmouth's post at the Admiralty, being succeeded by Walter Runciman at the Board of Education, while Colonel Seely suc-ceeded Churchill as Under-Secretary for the Colonies and Lord Lucas

were right it can also be argued that Lloyd George, by 1908, had earned the right to be con-sidered as next in line to Asquith himself. His settlement of the railway dispute five months before had sent his stock soaring and to have been passed over in a major Cabinet reshuffle would have been nothing less than a calculated insult. Asquith, whatever his personal opinion of Lloyd George, was too astute not to realise that they needed to work in harmony if the Government were to survive.[37]

* It was actually Vaughan Nash, who had been asked by the editor of the *Daily Chronicle* whether the new Prime Minister could add anything to the details of the Cabinet changes which had already been given to him by Lloyd George.[38]

† One has the impression that Campbell-Bannerman, for all the kind words which he had written in 1907 (see footnote on page 109), had not relished the prospect of Churchill as a member of his Cabinet. It is also noticeable (like the dog that did nothing in the night) that Churchill in his subsequent writings, while devoting much space to Rosebery, Asquith, Lloyd George, Balfour and Chamberlain, studiously avoided any but the most formal of references to Sir Henry. He told Riddell in 1912 that "Campbell-Bannerman's was a kindly manner which caused [an] applicant to go away feeling that his request would if possible be granted, and that if it was refused the premier would regret the refusal more than anyone else."[40]

succeeded Portsmouth as Under-Secretary for War. Morley, while retaining the India Office, went to the House of Lords.* Despite these
changes, Asquith's premiership did not entail any immediate break with
the past. The three Roseberyites were in powerful positions, but Lloyd
George at the Exchequer and Churchill at the Board of Trade were sufficient guarantees that the Liberal Imperialists would not have it all their
own way.

(4)

Several by-elections took place during the Easter recess, the one which
attracted the most attention being that fought by Churchill at Manchester.
Before 1919 it was necessary for members of the Commons appointed to
ministerial posts to submit themselves to their constituencies for re-election, and since his victory in north-west Manchester had been a highlight
of the 1906 triumph there was considerable speculation as to whether the
achievement could be repeated. On this occasion, it could not. The Irish
Nationalists, feeling that their problems were not receiving the attention
they deserved and anxious to remind Asquith that the Liberal Party could
not yet do without their support, campaigned vigorously against the new
President of the Board of Trade. Churchill obligingly underwent fresh
baptism in the troubled waters of Home Rule, pledging the Government
to definite action in the next Parliament, but failed to retain the allegiance
of his Catholic constituents: polling took place on April 24th and the
Unionist candidate, Joynson-Hicks, won by twenty-nine votes. "The belief among competent voters in the place," wrote Morley on April 30th,
"is that the resounding defeat of Winston at Manchester was due to wrath
at rather too naked tactics of making deals with this, that and the other
group, without too severe a scrutiny in his own political conscience of the
terms that they were exacting from him. It is believed that he lost 300 or
400 of these honourably fastidious electors."†[45] Churchill, however, was

---

* He had originally resolved not to serve under Asquith, but as the moment for departure
approached his resolution wavered. "I suppose," he told Asquith at the end of March, "that I
have a certain claim from seniority of service for your place at the Exchequer, but I don't
know that I have any aptitude for it under present prospects; and I am engaged on an extremely important and interesting piece of work. . . . So, if you approve, I will stay on at the India
Office and go to the House of Lords." Asquith was quite content with this arrangement and
Morley's dignity was thus preserved, although he made a great show of reluctance at having to
depart for the Elysium Fields. Lady Minto, for instance, found him in a particularly bad mood
on May 3rd—"I am unhappy at having to leave the House of Commons," he told her, "which
has been the scene of all my parliamentary tussles, and I have no wish to go to the Lords."[44]

† He also, it seems, endeavoured to woo his Jewish constituents by promising that the
Aliens Act of 1905 would be repealed as soon as possible. Cf. the letter by his secretary, Edward Marsh, to Gladstone on April 15th:"Winston is careering about the city and has not a
moment to write himself, so he asks me to tell you that he had an interview with the leading
Jews yesterday and that they were perfectly satisfied with the statement which he was able to

not without a constituency for long: within minutes of the result of the poll he had received a telegram asking him to stand as candidate for Dundee, where another vacancy had been created. Away to the north he sped, therefore, and in the ensuing election, which took place on May 9th, secured a comfortable majority over his Unionist and Labour opponents, as well as an ardent Prohibitionist by the name of Scrymgeour.*

On May 6th Asquith introduced his Budget for 1908–9. An estimated surplus for the following year of £4,901,000, together with a realised surplus of £4,726,000 for the current financial year, meant, he explained, that it would now be possible to finance a scheme of old age pensions. The surplus which remained would be partially utilised to reduce the sugar duty, at a cost of £3,400,000 to the Exchequer, leaving a final balance of £3,988,000. These announcements were, on the whole, favourably received; that provision would be made for old age pensions had been expected, but the reduction of the sugar duty came as a welcome surprise. The latter was, in fact, meant partly as a sop to the Labour Party, who had complained bitterly the previous year at its retention, and partly as a means of boosting the Government's popularity in the country at large. Lloyd George was none too pleased at liberality on so grand a scale, since it left him with very little room in which to manoeuvre, and leaving the Commons with Austen Chamberlain on May 25th, after a debate on the Budget, remarked that he had "wanted to keep the sugar duty on and use it for pensions."[47] His immediate reaction, however, seems to have been one of approval.

Lloyd George to his brother, May 6th, 1908

Budget over. Asquith spoke for over two hours—a very fine performance. Old Age Pensions at 70. Five shillings a week and half the sugar tax off. Very great satisfaction to our side and it leaves the coast clear for me to initiate my own schemes. It is time that we did something that appealed straight to the people—it will, I think, help to stop the electoral rot, and that is most necessary.† If it failed it might react in the House and bring us down. prematurely.

Asquith, who drove me from the Levee this morning, put the Old Age Pensions in my charge. Dundee excellent. I am told we will win Stirling and probably Forfar and that we have quite a good chance of pulling off Newport. If we do, the Government is set up.[48]

make after seeing you on Monday, and that he thinks he will have almost the entire Jewish vote."[46]

* When Churchill was defeated at Dundee in 1922, however, the victor was Mr Scrymgeour.

† Of the 20 contested by-elections which the Liberals fought in 1908, they retained 8 seats, lost 7 to the Unionists and failed to capture the other 5, which remained in Unionist hands. In almost every instance there was a sharp decrease in the Liberal turnout and a corresponding increase in the Unionist vote.

A Housing and Town Planning Bill, a rather vague measure introduced into the Commons by Burns on March 26th, received its Second Reading on May 12th. Slum clearance and a greater degree of town planning were its twin objectives: the Housing Act of 1890 was to be amended, so that local authorities might build new houses without having to apply to their County Councils for permission, while the Public Works Loan Commissioners would make grants to rural authorities and the Local Government Board would itself decide the merits of town planning schemes put forward by borough or urban district councils.

On June 10th a two-day debate began on the Second Reading of the Government's Old Age Pensions Bill.* Asquith, in his Budget speech, had envisaged that as from January 1st 1909 all persons over the age of 70 (with certain specified exceptions) would receive pensions of 5s. a week: married couples living together would receive 7s. 6d. The number of pensioners was estimated at 572,000 and the cost of the scheme as £2,240,000 for the current financial year and an annual average of £6,000,000 thereafter. The Bill as published on June 2nd, however, did not altogether tally with this description: the new Chancellor of the Exchequer, who had not been a member of the Cabinet Committee on the subject, had some ideas of his own. These included a qualified character test and the extension of the limitation on the pensions of married persons to relatives other than a husband or wife living in the same house. Lloyd George also announced that the Government was willing to consider a sliding scale as long as this involved no extra expense.

The Labour members were not greatly impressed with the Bill and pressed for the lowering of the age limit to 65 and the removal of the restrictions on married couples, etc., while the Unionists argued that it was a pity not to have waited until the Poor Law Commission's Report had thrown fresh light on the matter.† An Opposition amendment, commending State insurance against the principal risks of life but condemning the expenditure of taxpayer's money in subsiding persons selected by arbi-

---

* Old age pensions had been introduced in Germany in 1889. A Royal Commission concluded in 1895 that they were undesirable, but a parliamentary committee (with Lloyd George as one of its members) advocated in 1899 that pensions of 5s. a week should be given to the needy and deserving poor over the age of 65. A departmental committee calculated in 1900 that the cost of such a scheme in 1901 would be £10 million, rising to £12 million in 1911. In March 1906 the Commons passed a motion in favour of old age pensions and Asquith promised, when introducing his Budget for 1907, that a scheme would be put forward the following year.

† On December 4th 1905, the day Balfour resigned, a Commission had been appointed to study the workings of the Poor Law, which had remained virtually unchanged since 1834, and the methods used for alleviating distress caused by unemployment. Its 18 members included Beatrice Webb.

trary standards of age, income and character, was defeated by 417 to 29 the following day and the Second Reading was then carried without a division.

Almost two hundred amendments had been tabled when the Committee Stage opened on June 23rd and the Government was obliged to make extensive use of the guillotine.* The Unionists, hoping to win Labour support, now denounced the Bill on the grounds of inadequacy and Lloyd George, cast in the unusual role of an opponent of progressive reform, declared that it was their policy to move wild, illogical amendments, regardless of cost, in order that they might later say to every class in turn "We voted for you and those wicked Radicals voted against you."† Two important alterations were made. The first of these was that married couples should receive individual and not joint pensions, while the second was the acceptance of Lloyd George's sliding scale and the abandonment of a fixed standard rate.‡ The Labour members, especially Snowden, were far from satisfied with this but voted in favour of the scheme for want of anything better. "We were so severely guillotined that much of the Bill went undiscussed," wrote Austen Chamberlain to his father, "but the Government were in very considerable argumentative difficulties on several occasions and we had the satisfaction of at least seeing the Labour Party chafing under the operation of the closure for which they had so

---

* Shortage of parliamentary time meant that a private member's Woman's Enfranchisement Bill had to be abandoned. This measure had passed its Second Reading on February 28th, its supporters consisting of 218 Liberals, 32 Unionists and 21 Nationalists and its opponents of 53 Liberals, 27 Unionists and 12 Nationalists. Asquith told a deputation of Liberal M.P.s on May 20th that the Government would introduce a bill before the present Parliament ended to reform the male franchise. Those who wished to extend the vote to women would be able to propose amendments to the Government's bill. This half-hearted announcement was too much for the King, who informed Asquith via Knollys on June 15th that he deplored "the attitude taken up by Mr Asquith on the Women's Suffrage Bill." On December 3rd he returned to the subject, declaring that he was "rather disgusted at seeing in today's *Times* that Lloyd George is to preside at the Albert Hall meeting 'pro' women's suffrage. . . . I shall have no more to do with him than what is absolutely necessary." At the meeting in question (December 5th) Lloyd George stated that he was in favour of votes for women but that the suffragettes were ruining their own cause. Asquith told the King on December 7th that Lloyd George had not presided and had not committed the Government in any way: the question was an open one in the Cabinet, Haldane and Grey favouring the idea and he himself opposing it. See also the correspondence between Gladstone and Mrs Richmond in 1909, quoted on pages 353–4.[49]

† Sir Alfred Watson, Chief Actuary to the National Health Insurance Joint Committee (1912–19) "was astonished", according to W. J. Braithwaite, "to find that the Act was passed without any actuarial consideration of changes of the age distribution in the population. . . . This he regarded as nearly incredible! But it was nothing to what Ll. G. had had to face in Committee whilst the Bill was going through. He was constantly referring to this in conversation in 1911. . . . The cost of the amendments which he had had to consider . . . came to £62,000,000—the Government's income then being about £200,000,000. This had taught him what the cost of free grants could be."[50]

‡ "My capture of the party yesterday over Married Couples was quite the best thing I have ever done in the House," wrote Lloyd George to his brother on June 25th. "I was prepared to give away £400,000, but . . . the Married Couples cost £334,00 only and I have rallied all the party with that concession to resist further pecuniary demands."[51]

cheerfully voted."[52] The Bill eventually passed its Third Reading on July 9th by 315 to 10.

The final reading of the Old Age Pensions Bill was carried in the House of Lords on July 30th without a division. Lansdowne took the opportunity of asserting, in answer to the Government's claim that this measure formed part of the Budget, that precedents of 1833, 1849, 1891 and 1906 showed the Upper House had the right to amend those bills which were only partially financial in character. Several alterations had been made in Committee, however, to which the Commons, when the Bill was returned to them on the morning of July 31st, took strong exception: the Speaker ruled that some were a breach of privilege while others were simply condemned as unacceptable. The Bill was returned to the Upper House later that day and the Lords, albeit with reluctance, decided not to insist upon their amendments.

(5)

The debate on the Second Reading of the Coal Mines (Eight Hours) Bill began on June 22nd. This measure, piloted through the House by Gladstone, was one which had aroused much controversy when discussed in previous years, although it had been approved in principle by the Commons as long ago as 1893. On purely humanitarian grounds there was obviously much to be said for reducing the working day of the miner to eight hours, but it was argued by the Bill's opponents that this would lead to a fall in output of more than 10% and that the price of coal would rise by anything up to 9d. a ton. The Government had hesitated to introduce such a measure in 1906 and had appointed a Committee of Enquiry, which reported in May 1907. The Committee had not been altogether in favour of the idea and had, indeed, gone to great lengths to enumerate the difficulties which would arise if it was adopted, but by 1908 the need to conciliate the Labour members carried rather more weight in the Cabinet than the possibility of a slight rise in the price of coal. It could be anticipated, moreover, that the Unionists, as with the Trade Disputes Bill in 1906, would hesitate before challenging the combined strengths of the Liberal Party and the trade unions. Even so, within three weeks of the King's speech having given notice of the Government's intention to introduce such a measure, there had come into existence a Coal Consumer's Defence League, the product of big business interests. "Under this Bill," the League declared in one of its pamphlets, "the miners would not work eight hours, but only some six-and-a-half hours. The other hour-and-a-half represents the time it takes them to go down to their work and return, and also their meal time. Does your employer count the time it takes *you* to get to work? . . . The miner has a sliding scale. If coal is dear his wages rise. If he works six-and-a-half hours he will get less coal, and the price of coal will rise because there is not enough. So the miner will get the same pay for less work!" The Home Secretary, who already had to contend with the suffragette problem, was deluged by angry correspondence on the subject and, as the following exchange indicates, he did not bear up any too well under the strain.

Ripon to Asquith, March 19th, 1908

I hope you will endeavour to infuse a little firmness into Herbert Gladstone about the Miners' 8 Hours Bill. He *seems* from what he said yesterday and from the two memoranda which he has circulated to be full of doubts about the effect of the measure on the price of coal. Now this is a question which ought to have been fully considered before we pledged ourselves to bring in a bill and put it in the King's Speech. It is too late now to draw back. The coal owners are obviously trying to alarm the consumers. This is a game which has been played by employers ever since the earliest days of the Factory Acts and such prophecies have never been fulfilled. If the object of the Bill can be attained and greater securities given to the consumers well and good, but it can only be done *now* with the consent of the men, whose case we promised to take up. But I strongly deprecate any signs of weakness on the Second Reading.[53]

Asquith agreed with these comments and the Second Reading was carried by 390 to 120 on July 6th. Churchill, whose crusading fervour had known no bounds since his arrival at the Board of Trade, wound up for the Government with a lusty peroration which, as Halévy has noted, "was the only speech by a member of the Cabinet which aroused the enthusiasm of the House and of the Labour members in particular."[54] One of the Labour members, David Shackleton, was so impressed with Churchill's new found Radicalism at this time that, as the following letter shows, he approached him with a suggestion that the Government should sponsor an International Labour Congress. (Such Congresses had been held intermittently since 1883.)

Churchill to Gladstone, July 8th, 1908

Shackleton told me some little time ago that the trade unions think the time has come for another International Labour Congress, and I have also heard that it has been suggested to Mr Roosevelt that he should propose such a Congress next year, and that there is much probability of the United States Government issuing invitations unless some other Power should forestall them.

I have been considering whether it might not be worth our while to endeavour to arrange for a Congress of the kind in London next year. Undoubtedly Labour in this country would warmly welcome any initiative taken by the Government in this direction. On the other hand, some embarrassment would certainly arise, if a Labour Congress were being held, or were about to be held, in this country, and the Government were at the same time bringing in bills on the subjects which were being discussed, or were about to be discussed, by the Congress. We cannot afford to neglect this consideration as the reform of the Poor Law, questions connected with unemployment, etc., have to be dealt with during the next two years, and it would unquestionably be inconvenient to have a new Labour programme thrust upon us by the Congress at a time when it would be difficult to carry it through. And after ourselves summoning the Conference, it might involve some loss of prestige if we were unable to give effect to, at any rate, some of the more important resolutions passed by the delegates.

I should much like to know what you think about this.[55]

Gladstone was quite attracted by the idea, but in the event, nothing came of it and the Government was thus spared any embarrassment.

The Coal Mines (Eight Hours) Bill eventually passed its Third Reading on December 14th by 264 to 69. The Lords made several alterations, some of which were accepted by the Government, and it became law on December 21st, being known as the Coal Mines Regulation Act. It was not a particularly satisfactory measure, albeit the first that had ever restricted the working day for men as well as for women and children. In its original form the Bill had stipulated that only one of the journeys between the surface and the pit should be counted as part of the eight hours, but this was later amended to read that neither of the journeys would be so counted. It was also stipulated that the Government could suspend the Act, if the need to do so arose, and that the employers could demand an additional hour's work from each man on sixty days in the year. In many ways, therefore, the miners were not much better off than before.

(6)

The Second Reading of the Licensing Bill had been carried by 394 to 148 on May 4th and on May 16th the Liberals held a great demonstration in its favour at the Albert Hall: the Unionists retaliated with an equally colourful demonstration of their own on June 24th. By-election results suggested that the Government was getting the worst of the conflict— at Peckham, Manchester, Pudsey, Shoreditch and Newcastle-on-Tyne the Liberals suffered grievous defeats—but it could also be argued that these were simply marginal constituencies returning to their pre-1906 allegiance. The Committee Stage of the Bill began on July 20th and the guillotine procedure once again came into use: 980 amendments filled 52 pages of orders, but the remaining parliamentary time simply did not allow for thorough discussion of each and every provision. Nineteen days were allotted for the Committee Stage, five for Report and one for the Third Reading, but the first half of the 1908 Session was almost at an end and only two days could be spared for debate: further discussion was consequently postponed until October 14th. Parliament was adjourned on August 1st but agitation over the Bill continued unabated. The Liberals held a monster meeting in Hyde Park at which Churchill warned the Lords not to assume, if they rejected the measure, that the resources of the constitution were exhausted. On September 27th a rally of the "Trade" also took place in Hyde Park, but this probably did more to strengthen the Government's case than anything they themselves might have devised.★

On October 12th, when Parliament reassembled, the King discussed the Bill with Lansdowne. The House of Lords, he pointed out, would suffer seriously in popularity if it appeared to be obstructing the cause of temperance reform. He hoped that they would amend rather than reject the measure since he knew that the Government were willing to make concessions if forced to do so. The time limit, for example, might be extended from fourteen to twenty-one years. Lansdowne replied that there was no truth in the rumour that the Lords had already decided upon rejection: this point had not even been discussed and they could, in any case, reach no decision until it had been seen how the Bill fared in the House of Commons. He protested, however, that it was an extremely unjust measure and cited the Old Age Pensions Act as "a bitter experience of the manner in which His Majesty's Government treated amendments inserted by the House of Lords."[56]

Discussion of the Bill was resumed two days later, the Committee Stage continuing until November 10th. "It is very difficult to say what may happen," wrote Crewe to Ripon on November 12th. "Balfour's demeanour on the latter half of the Bill has been encouraging."[57] The Report Stage began the following day and on November 21st the Third Reading was carried by 350 to 113. Events were now bubbling up to a crisis. On

---

★ Seventy trains brought up supporters from all parts of the country, and a crowd of 200,000 assembled in the park in a jovial mood. They were addressed by several Unionist M.P.s, none of them particularly well known, and then regaled their spirits by revelry in the streets. Since it was a Sunday, this behaviour can scarcely have met with much approval from local inhabitants and *The Westminster Gazette* felt that the demonstrators had been "especially chosen to illustrate the ravages of drink on the human frame." Balfour, on October 6th, adopted a loftier note when he denounced the Bill as the greatest injury ever done to public morality and went on to claim that the Unionists were the only party who cared about genuine social reform.

November 19th, at the annual conference of the Conservative and Constitutional Associations held at Cardiff, each delegate had received a card printed in scarlet stating that, if Lansdowne yielded to the pressure of certain peers and allowed the Bill to become law, thousands of Unionists would never vote for the party again.* On November 25th the measure came up for its Second Reading but the result of the debate was a foregone conclusion.† Lansdowne declared that the Government's refusal to accept any amendments left them with no alternative but rejection. The Archbishop of Canterbury, the Bishop of London and Rosebery (for a wonder) spoke in the Bill's favour but it was defeated on November 27th by 272 to 96.

(7)

Several ministerial changes had taken place during the summer recess. Tweedmouth, now a very sick man, resigned the Presidency of the Council, being replaced by Fowler (now Lord Wolverhampton); Fitzmaurice succeeded the latter as Chancellor of the Duchy of Lancaster while McKinnon-Wood took Fitzmaurice's place as Under-Secretary for Foreign Affairs. Ripon resigned and Crewe, while remaining Colonial Secretary, assumed in addition the duties (such as they were) of Lord Privy Seal. Later in the year an indignant John Morley, taking offence at the decision to inform the Commons of his proposals for reform in India at the same time that he was announcing them in the Lords, also threatened to leave the Government.‡ He was partially appeased by Asquith's declaration that "your resignation at such a moment and on such a ground is a thing I cannot bring myself to think of,"[60] but a few months later he repeated his threat with less satisfactory consequences.

Ripon's resignation was the outcome of a rather unfortunate chain of events. He had relinquished the leadership in the Lords to Crewe when Asquith succeeded Campbell-Bannerman but had remained Lord Privy Seal and had played a useful part in Cabinet discussions. This arrangement

---

* The "certain peers" were Lytton, Carlisle, St Aldwyn, James of Hereford, Milner and Balfour of Burleigh. Undeterred by the mysterious cards, they continued to urge upon Lansdowne the inadvisability of rejecting so important a measure as the Licensing Bill. "My strongest feeling in the matter," Milner wrote to him on November 22nd, "is a great fear that the out-and-out rejection of the Bill should give a great check to the tide which is steadily settling against the Government." Rejection was decided upon, however, at a meeting of 250 Unionist peers at Lansdowne House on November 24th.[58]

† George Riddell, who had breakfasted with Lloyd George the previous day, had found him not "at all disturbed at the fate of the Licensing Bill. He said that a thanksgiving service would take place in the Treasury at 10.30, as he was looking forward to taxing the trade. He ridiculed the rumour that the peers would or could interfere with or reject the Budget."[59]

‡ See page 102.

might well have continued indefinitely had it not been for the fact that the Archbishop of Westminster, acting as chairman at a Eucharistic Congress which met in London from mid-August to mid-September, felt that the Congress could best mark the conclusion of its labours on Sunday, September 13th by a lengthy procession through London in which the Host would be carried amidst great pomp and ceremony. Small processions of Catholic clergy (but not the public elevation of the Host) had been allowed in 1898 and 1901 and the Archbishop saw no reason why this one should not take place. At the end of July he approached the Commissioner of the Metropolitan Police (Sir Edward Henry, himself a Catholic) and ascertained that a procession would be in order. During the month which followed, however, various bodies made their feelings known in no uncertain manner, angry letters of protest were despatched to Asquith and the King, and it was pointed out that under the Catholic Emancipation Act of 1829 a ceremonial procession of the type now proposed was clearly illegal. The King was alarmed and sent urgent telegrams to the Home Secretary (on holiday in Scotland) asking him to take action. Gladstone did nothing and the King, in exasperation, turned to Asquith and urged him to enlist the aid of Ripon, the only Catholic member of the Cabinet. Asquith himself had no strong views on the subject but on September 9th, in response to the royal pressure, he telegraphed to Ripon asking him to use his influence with the Archbishop "to secure abandonment of public procession which is contrary to letter of law and provocative to Protestant sentiment."*61

Gladstone, aware at last that a storm was brewing, sent Ripon a rather pathetically worded appeal for assistance at the same time. "The Protestant Alliance," he wrote, "threatens mischief. The police will have to be out in large numbers. I am asked to stop action which is illegal . . . [but] I could only do so if there was sufficient reason to anticipate a breach of the peace. But I do think a very serious responsibility rest on Archbishop and his advisers. Cannot something be done at the last moment to simplify the procession and to avoid the danger of serious trouble?"63 Ripon replied to Gladstone the following day, rebuking him, with some justice, for not having acted sooner. The intention of holding the procession, and its character, had been known to the public for at least six weeks, but no warning had been given by the Home Office to the Archbishop that it

* "I should not have been disposed myself to interefere," he wrote to Ripon on September 10th, "as I hoped it would pass without exciting much notice, and I hate anything in the nature of intolerance. It is now, however, pointed out that the proceeding is clearly contrary to an unrepealed Statute, and Protestant sentiment, much of it bigoted, but some of it quite respectable, is being aroused."62

might lead to a breach of the peace.[64] "It is clear to me," he wrote to Asquith, "that Gladstone paid no attention to the matter till he was stirred up by the King, and that the position of the Govt., when the subject comes to be discussed in Parliament, will be of the most unpleasant kind. You may rely upon it that the anger of the Roman Catholics, and consequently of the Irish M.P.s, will be very great. . . . It is sad to think that departmental neglect should have landed us in such a mess."[65] He agreed, but only with great reluctance, to use his influence with the Archbishop to ensure that the ceremonial aspect of the procession was abandoned, and this action and its consequent success drew forth many grateful thanks from Asquith. "We have got as well as we could out of the difficulty," wrote the latter to Ripon on September 12th. "The Archbishop has agreed to abandon the ceremonial side of the procession (vestments and Host) as a result of an interchange of messages with me. He will of course make a grievance of it— quite legitimately, so far as the law is concerned. But I do not think I could have acted differently. The King has been in a very excited state, firing off long cipher telegrams, wanting to know why the procession was not at once proclaimed and prohibited, etc etc."[66]

Ripon, however, could not view the results of his intervention with equanimity, and on September 14th tendered his resignation to Asquith. "I can't totally desert my own people and be responsible for such treatment as they have received," he wrote," . . . I don't blame you for what has happened, but I do blame Gladstone."[67] Asquith subsequently offered what he hoped would be a satisfactory explanation; namely that the Home Office was not seriously to blame since the Catholic authorities, when they approached the police at the end of July, had not made it clear that the procession would include the elevation of the Host. This fact had not become known until the beginning of September. If Ripon was still determined to resign, however, a decision which he very much regretted, he hoped that he would do so on grounds of ill health.[68] The old man agreed to this request and they parted on friendly terms.*

Gladstone, who had been only too plainly responsible for the mismanagement of this episode, was also very anxious, for a while, to depart from the political scene, especially after receiving a rather curt letter from the King with strong hints to this effect† He had not proved a notable suc-

* Loreburn wrote to Ripon on October 30th to express his regrets at his old friend's decision. "I was very downcast about it," he wrote, "for C.B. and Bryce and you were, on the formation of the Government, the men I most agreed with and relied upon. . . . It is a different Government today from what it was three years ago. But I will not dwell on these things and will hope for the best and recall how much there still is in the Cabinet that inspires hope."[69]

† "You will find H.M. very bitter about Herbert," wrote Crewe to Asquith on September 16th, "and longing to get rid of him."[70]

cess as Home Secretary and earlier that year (on January 22nd, before the new Session began) had been so unbelievably careless as to leave a draft of the Licensing Bill on a train, where it passed into the dubious hands of a Tory M.P. who may or may not have perused it.[71] On September 24th, therefore, Gladstone offered himself up to Asquith for sacrifice, but the latter's suggestion that he become Lord President of the Council was indignantly rejected and, for the moment, no more was said about his departure.

(8)

In February, it will be recalled, McKenna had introduced a new Education Bill into the Commons. It had passed its First Reading, but had not been taken any further through the House. Behind the scenes, however, important negotiations were in progress between the Board of Education and the Church authorities and towards the end of the year it seemed that there was a real chance of a compromise solution to the dispute which had raged since 1902. "I think the Archbishop had been finally brought to the point of breaking with his extremists," wrote Crewe to Ripon on November 12th, "and he is supported by the Bishops of Southwark and Stepney. Only some six of the Nonconformist M.P.s object."[72]

A new Education Bill, designed to satisfy both sides, was introduced into the Commons on November 20th. Rate aid, on the one hand, would be restricted to "provided" schools, but non-provided schools—if they met certain conditions—would be eligible for parliamentary grants. No sooner had this measure entered the Commons, however, than the Archbishop of Canterbury was apparently struck for the first time by what he felt was the inadequacy of its financial proposals. He immediately wrote to Runciman, McKenna's successor, protesting that the sums allotted to the non-provided schools were far from generous. His protest did not elicit any satisfactory reply and from this point onwards the prospects of a settlement melted rapidly away. On November 27th, admittedly, the Bill passed its Second Reading by 323 to 157,* but much bitterness had now been aroused over the financial provisions and extreme Churchmen and Catholics attacked the whole scheme with the ardour of 1906. The Archbishop

---

* The Labour members voted against the Government. The Old Age Pensions Act had disappointed them and the defeat of the Licensing Bill left them despondent. One cause for rejoicing, so it was argued, had been the decision of the Miners' Federation in June to seek affiliation to the L.R.C., which would bring the total strength of the parliamentary party up to 42, but Hardie regarded this as a dubious blessing and remained very disgruntled about the general situation. "I suppose," he wrote to Glasier on December 27th, "we are in for another year of Henderson's chairmanship, which means that reaction and timidity will be in the ascendency. . . . The annual conferences will be controlled by Coal and Cotton, and . . . that means more reaction. There are times when I confess to feeling sore at seeing the fruits of our toil being garnered by men who were never of us and who even now would trick us out."[73]

still hoped for a compromise, but a vote taken at a special meeting of the Representative Church Council on December 3rd showed that only 18 bishops, 35 clerics and 46 lay members supported the Bill as opposed to 3 bishops, 73 clerics and 113 lay members. This vote changed the whole situation and Asquith informed the King the following day that "it was hopeless at this moment to force through as a settlement a measure which so many of the responsible leaders of the Church find unacceptable."[74] On December 7th, therefore, the Bill was withdrawn. Thus ended the Government's last attempt to settle the education problem.

(9)

On December 22nd the third Session of the 1906 Parliament came to an end. It had, like its predecessors, proved disappointing, although its achievements should not be underestimated. On the credit side were the Old Age Pensions Act, the Coal Mines Regulation Act, a Children Act, a Prevention of Crimes Act,* an Act setting up the Port of London Authority, an Education (Scotland) Act, the Irish University Act and an Evicted Tenants (Ireland) Act. Ministerial casualties were the Licensing Bill, the Education Bill, the Housing and Town Planning Bill, the Small Landholders (Scotland) Bill and the Land Values (Scotland) Bill.† To Government supporters it was obviously intolerable that so much time and effort should have resulted in so meagre a list of achievements. "Practically everything that could be done with the consent of the House of Lords had now been accomplished," wrote J. A. Spender twenty years later, "and on all the major measures of Liberal policy—education, temperance reform, land reform, Welsh Disestablishment, Irish Home Rule—the road seemed to be hopelessly blocked."[76] At this point, therefore, the question arises as to whether the Government ought not to have asked for a dissolution of Parliament, fighting the election solely on the issue of whether or not the House of Lords should be allowed to reject or drastically amend important legislation put forward by a party which, enjoying an overwhelming majority in the House of Commons, presumably represented the wishes and desires of the great mass of the British people.

Perhaps this was, in certain respects, the ideal moment to raise the issue

---

* The Children Act, piloted through the Commons by Herbert Samuel, established a completely new system of juvenile courts throughout the country and abolished the imprisonment of children. "Bulky as it was," wrote Samuel later, "it passed through both Houses on oiled wheels—without a single division in either, except on points of detail." The Prevention of Crimes Act, which ran in harness with it, extended the Borstal system throughout the country by establishing reformatories for offenders between the ages of 16 and 21.[75]

† The Small Landholders (Scotland) Bill was rejected outright by the Lords, while the Land Values (Scotland) Bill was drastically amended and sent back to the Commons.

of Lords versus Commons, but from other viewpoints the time was far from propitious. It was difficult to pretend, for instance, that either the two Education Bills or the Licensing Bill had really been popular measures, while the steady stream of by-election defeats throughout the year indicated that the Government's prestige had decreased to an alarming extent. The Unionist tide seemed to be on the turn and unemployment had given the advocates of Tariff Reform a golden opportunity to extoll the virtues of Protection and the need to implement measures of fiscal reform as soon as possible. Asquith, moreover, was painfully aware that Cobdenite doctrines of finance had been almost played out. "I have realised from the first," he wrote to St Loe Strachey, the editor of the *Spectator*, on May 9th, 1908, "that if it could not be proved that social reform (not Socialism) could be financed on Free Trade lines, a return to Protection is a moral certainty. This has been one of the mainsprings of my policy at the Exchequer."[77] A general election before the Finance Bill of 1909 had been introduced, quite apart from other considerations which will be discussed below, would be strategically unwise: it would also be acknowledging that the peers could choose the moment for dissolution. Such an election would have been fought on the lines of Free Trade versus Protection rather than Commons versus the Lords.

Any appeal to the country in January 1909 would have been a tacit admission of impotence, an admission which, in view of the enormous majority which the Liberals had secured three years before, would have been humiliating in the extreme. The Unionists would argue, as Balfour had already done, that they had raised the issue of the Upper House as a means of cloaking their own shortcomings and that they had abandoned the task of steering the country through a difficult economic period before the woeful inadequacy of Free Trade doctrines could stand properly revealed.* There is no doubt that a general election at this time, if it did not result in a Liberal defeat, would at any rate have slashed the Government's majority to a bare minimum. The Government was therefore impelled towards the conclusion, as the Session of 1908 ran its melancholy course, that it would have to stand or fall by the Finance Bill of 1909, a measure which would, so it was hoped, revive its fortunes in the country at large and reach by indirect means goals which would otherwise have been unattainable. On May 6th, as we have already noted, Lloyd George had told his brother that "it is time that we did something that appealed straight to

---

* "My main concern,"Wyndham had written to his father on October 30th, "is that I fear this wretched Government will collapse next March and let us in, before we are ready to face national bankruptcy."[78]

the people," and he had thereafter plunged into a determined but unsuccessful battle to secure a reduction in the expenditure on armaments. On June 29th he had been obliged to confess to the Commons that he had no nest-eggs: "I am looking for someone's hen roost to raid next year." Unless new nest-eggs materialised there was the likelihood, hateful to every member of the Liberal Party and even more so to those of the Labour Party, that expenditure on the army and navy would have to take precedence over expenditure on schemes of social reform. Asquith, however, having supported both the Admiralty and the War Office against the demands for economy made by the new Chancellor of the Exchequer, was left with no alternative but to give Lloyd George complete freedom in drawing up his Budget proposals for 1909. The Liberal Imperialists, in any case, were largely in sympathy with Lloyd George's objectives (although not with Lloyd George himself) and Haldane, in the course of a long letter of advice and exhortation to Asquith dated August 9th, declared that "we should boldly take our stand on the facts and proclaim a policy of taking, mainly by direct taxation, such toll from the increase and growth of this [national] wealth as will enable us to provide for (1) the increasing cost of social reform: (2) National Defence; and also (3) to have a margin in aid of the Sinking Fund." He could not resist adding that "the condition of success is that you should direct operations yourself. No one else is competent to do it."[79]

Lucy Masterman, the wife of the Parliamentary Secretary to the Local Government Board, had sat next to Churchill in the dining-room of the House of Commons on the evening of November 26th. "He was," she noted, "perfectly *furious* at the rejection of the Licensing Bill by the Lords, stabbed at his bread, would hardly speak; murmured peroration about 'the heart of every Band of Hope in this country sinking within them.' 'We shall send them up such a Budget in June as shall terrify them, they have started the class war, they had better be careful.' I asked him how long he thought the Government had to live. 'If they thurvive the next Budget, two or three years. That'll be the teth'."[80] There was, however, no intention of "sending up such a Budget" as would tempt the Lords into the extreme course of rejection. Lloyd George told his brother on November 25th, for instance, that "I am thinking out some exquisite plans for outwitting the Lords on Licensing,"[81] and he was probably remembering Gladstone's inclusion of the rejected Paper Bill of 1860 in the Finance Bill of 1861 and, more especially, the "revolutionary" death duties included in Harcourt's Budget for 1894. A fortnight later on December 9th, he wrote that there would be no dissolution—"at least not before the Budget is over.

Cabinet meeting today unanimously agree in putting the Budget through all its stages in the Houses. The Prime Minister has approved of my plans."[82]

On December 11th, at the National Liberal Club, Asquith delivered a speech which did much to revive the flagging spirits of his supporters. He made it plain that he did not yet consider the time ripe to ask for a dissolution but that the Liberal Party would treat the veto of the House of Lords as the dominating issue of the day. "Finance," he declared, "is an instrument of great potency and also of great flexibility . . . and it may be found to be, in some directions at any rate, a partial solvent of what, under our existing constitutional conditions, would otherwise be insoluble problems. . . . The Budget of next year will stand at the very centre of our work." This was a clear enough hint to the Unionists that the strategy of 1894 would be repeated and it was followed up by Lloyd George's declaration, on December 21st, that the "House of Lords is purely a tool of the Tory chief agent. . . . We are not going to stand any longer the usurpation of King Lansdowne." The decks were finally being cleared for action: all now depended upon the events of the next Session.

CHAPTER ELEVEN

FOREIGN AFFAIRS AND DEFENCE,
1905–8

(1)

Sir Edward Grey gloomily but dutifully acquiesced in his appointment as Foreign Secretary. He knew that he was the only senior member of the Liberal Party properly qualified to undertake the task of managing Britain's affairs abroad, and it was also his duty as a Liberal Imperialist to ensure that control of the Foreign Office did not fall into Radical hands, but he did not approach his duties in any spirit of enthusiasm. Once at the helm, however, he became absorbed in his work to a remarkable degree and the death of his wife transformed it into what was, in those bleak days, practically the sole reason for his existence. No man could have been more conscientious in the execution of his duties, and if an infinite capacity for taking pains be regarded as a hallmark of greatness Sir Edward would surely be hailed as one of the greatest Foreign Secretaries Britain has ever had.

It was his misfortune, however, to be cast by fate as the perpetual victim of circumstances. He was a man who liked a quiet life and we shall see him, in the course of the next few years, being buffeted from crisis to crisis, seeking always to exercise a moderating influence, trying hard to ensure that the claims of common sense should prevail and constantly wringing his hands at the discovery that he was more deeply embroiled than ever in a situation from which he had struggled desperately to escape. Just as he had never understood, in December 1905, how it was that he came to occupy the position of opponent-in-chief to Sir Henry Campbell-Bannerman, so it was that he was never too clear in his own mind why there should, from January 1906 onwards, be a steady deterioration in Anglo-German relations. He had taken up the reins of his new office with the best of intentions towards everybody, the Kaiser included, and yet, despite all his efforts, things steadily went from bad to worse so far as Britian's Teutonic neighbour was concerned. He never realised, it seems, that he was surrounded at the Foreign Office by men who had, perhaps unconsciously in some instances, accustomed themselves to thinking of Germany as Britain's opponent in nearly every sphere. Lord Sanderson, the Permanent Under-Secretary and one of the few officials to have remained untouched by this trend, retired in February 1906. Sir Charles Hardinge, his successor, and Sir Francis Bertie, the Ambassador to Paris, were henceforth able to rule the roost unchallenged and they had, moreover, attracted to themselves a host of followers in the Foreign Office, including Sir Arthur Nicolson, Sir Louis Mallet, Eyre Crowe and Sir George Spicer.* This does not mean, of course, that they did not necessarily have good reason for their opinions, but it does mean that the new Foreign Secretary, who was a weak man and easily affected by the atmosphere in which he worked, had little opportunity of asserting himself in his own right. Balfour's description of Campbell-Bannerman as "a mere cork, dancing on a torrent which he cannot control" could more appropriately have been applied to Sir Edward Grey at any time between December 1905 and August 1914.

It was especially unfortunate, moreover, that Grey's arrival at the Foreign Office should have coincided with the final and most critical stage of what has since become known as the Algeciras crisis. Scarcely had he seated himself at his new desk, and barely had he become acquainted with the permanent officials of the Department, let alone the intricacies of policy, than he was called upon to decide the extent to which Britain would support France if the latter should be forced into war with Germany. A less tranquil beginning to his term of office could hardly be imagined.

(2)

The Algeciras crisis was an indirect result of the *entente cordiale*, an agreement concluded between Britain and France in April 1904 whereby the former recognised that Morocco should be largely under French control and the latter acknowledged British suzerainty in Egypt. It was a pact which owed more to events in the Far East than it did to fear of Germany: in February of that year Japan, the ally of Britain, had declared war on Russia, the ally of France, and neither of the two western Powers wanted to be involved in the conflict. Little or no consideration had been given to the effect which such an agreement might have upon Germany, but the inhabitants of the Wilhelmstrasse were, in fact, much affronted. "If we let ourselves be trampled on in Morocco," wrote Holstein, the grim old tyrant of the German Foreign Office to Prince Bülow, the Chancellor,

---

* Nicolson had served as Ambassador at Madrid since the beginning of 1905 and would now be representing Britain at the Algeciras Conference before becoming Ambassador at St Petersburg; Mallet was Grey's private secretary (until appointed Assistant Under-Secretary in 1907); Crowe was Senior Clerk and Spicer was Assistant Clerk.

"we invite similar treatment elsewhere." The conclusion of a treaty between France and Spain in October 1904, which defined their respective
spheres of influence in Morocco, and the despatch of a French mission to
Fez at the end of the year with a programme of domestic reforms for the
Sultan's implementation, were all that was needed to fan smouldering
resentment into open fury. Holstein persuaded a reluctant Wilhelm II to
intervene personally in the situation and the Kaiser led an expedition to the
scene of operations, landing at Tangier on March 31st, 1905 and treating
Morocco as an independent country. "The German Empire," he declared,
"has great and growing interests in Morocco. Commerce can only prosper
if all the Powers are considered to have equal rights under the sovereignty
of the Sultan and respect the independence of the country. My visit is the
recognition of that independence." Germany demanded an international
conference to determine Morocco's status and the Sultan, thus encouraged,
rejected the French programme of reforms and placed himslf under the
all-embracing protection of the Kaiser.

The demand met with a mixed reception in France. The Foreign Secretary, Delcassé, was all for ignoring it and calling Germany's bluff.
Rouvier, the Prime Minister, recommended appeasement: France had
called Germany's bluff in 1870 and look at the consequences! On June 6th
Delcassé resigned: the way was now clear for Rouvier to secure, as he
hoped, some sort of Franco-German understanding, but Bülow and Holstein, having demanded a conference, had to go through with the business. From the legal viewpoint, moreover, their case was a good one.

The Russo-Japanese war came to an end in September 1905, with Russia soundly defeated and engulfed in revolution, which left Rouvier with
no space in which to manoeuvre. On September 30th, after meditation by
President Roosevelt, the French Government agreed to an international
conference being held at Algeciras in Spain the following January. In the
winter of 1905-6 France was thus on the search for allies to sustain her
cause at the conference table and, moreover, for some means of answering
force by force if the need arose. It was plain that no help could be expected
from Russia, but what of Britain? Would it be possible for the *entente* to
be transformed into some kind of military alliance, with Britain coming
to the aid of France if German obstinacy rendered war between the
countries unavoidable? This, it seemed, was the only hope for France, and
Sir Edward Grey's arrival at the Foreign Office could not have taken place
at a more crucial moment.

In a letter dated December 29th, from Major Repington, the military
correspondent of *The Times*, Grey was informed that the French Military

Attaché in London, Major Huguet, "felt anxious. . . . It was not a question of sympathies, but rather of acts, and of what the British Government were prepared to do in a situation which presented dangerous aspects."[1] Grey, for the moment, was not prepared to do anything out of the ordinary. He certainly sympathised with the predicament of France but saw no reason why his sympathy should extend beyond the limits already agreed upon, namely diplomatic support at the Conference. On January 3rd, however, he warned the German Ambassador, Count Metternich, that "feeling in England and sympathy with France, if she got into trouble over the document which originated our friendship with her, would be so strong that it would be impossible for any government to remain neutral." This, he noted, was simply repeating what Lansdowne had told Metternich on a previous occasion.*[2]

A week later the French Ambassador, Paul Cambon, paid a visit to the Foreign Office. He explained that he was not seeking a formal alliance, but his Government wanted to know whether, if Germany declared war upon France, Britain would intervene. Grey replied that, with the elections in progress, the Prime Minister out of town and the Cabinet dispersed, it was impossible for him to answer this question: the most he could promise was benevolent neutrality, although he felt that public opinion would favour France. Cambon, of course, was far from satisfied with this assurance and said that he would repeat his question once the elections were over. He suggested, in the meantime, that unofficial discussions should take place between the French Naval and Military Attachés and the Admiralty and the War Office. Such conversations, he thought, had already been held and they did not pledge either Government to take action in the event of an emergency.† Grey raised no objection to this proposal.

Two days later Haldane spoke on Grey's behalf at an election meeting, after which they went for a long carriage drive. Grey asked him how far detailed Anglo-French military discussions had gone. Haldane replied, somewhat vaguely, that the exchange of ideas had not taken place to anything like the extent which modern standards of preparedness required and it was agreed that further conversations should be organised on a more regular basis. Grey also learned, as he wrote to Bertie on January 15th, "that 80,000 men with good guns is all we can put into the field in Europe to meet first-class troops."[3]

The Foreign Secretary was by this time under the impression that un-

* On June 28th, 1905.
† Fisher had seen the Naval Attaché on January 2nd but had told him nothing of any importance: this seems to have been the limit of Anglo-French naval co-operation at this time.

official military and naval discussions had been in progress for several months, and he evidently did not enquire too closely into their origins. In fact, however, there had been no such discussions before December 1905: it was, if anything, the arrival in office of a Liberal Government which had precipitated them. Georges Clemenceau, lunching with Lord Esher on December 13th, had spoken of the need "to arrange very secretly what military and naval action should be taken in the *first weeks*" if Germany declared war on France, and Esher and Sir George Clarke, the Secretary of the Committee of Imperial Defence, feared that the new Ministry would be less inclined to support France than its predecessor.[4] It was decided, therefore, to present Grey and Campbell-Bannerman with a *fait accompli*. An informal discussion between Clarke, Esher, Sir John French and Sir Charles Ottley, the Director of Naval Intelligence, as to how Britain could best assist France in the event of a German attack, resulted in Repington handing Huguet a questionnaire to be answered by the French General Staff. Huguet left London on January 7th and returned four days later, bringing with him the reply that direct military assistance would be the best form of aid.

Campbell-Bannerman and other Ministers were fully engaged in electioneering. Ripon, however, was less preoccupied with the domestic situation and surveyed the international scene with deepening anxiety. "Our engagements with France," he wrote on January 11th to Fitzmaurice, "are, as I understand it, confined to the promise of full *diplomatic* support and I have no doubt that the French Government understands that we are bound to nothing beyond that. But there are indications . . . which seem to show that the French people and many of their public men are expecting support of another kind, if the Conference breaks down and serious trouble with Germany arises. If that occurs and we decline, as I think we ought to decline, to go further than diplomacy will reach, I cannot but fear a cry of 'perfide Albion' and a destruction of the present friendship between the two nations."*[5]

On January 15th Cambon called again at the Foreign Office. Grey told him that a reply to his question could not be given until the end of the month. Now that the elections were almost over there was, of course, no reason why the whole issue of Anglo-French relations should not be placed before the Cabinet and in a letter dated January 21st Campbell-Bannerman asked Sir Edward when he would like such a Cabinet to be

---

* This letter was passed to Campbell-Bannerman for attention. "Sanderson and I," ran Fitzmaurice's covering note, ". . . decided this afternoon in regard to the above matter, the fewer communications there are the better, and that I should ask *you* to write to Lord Ripon."[6]

held and whether the answer to the French would be confirmed or decided by that body.[7] "I think," Grey replied the following day, "the date
of any Cabinet apropos of the French question had better not be fixed till
I have talked the matter over with you. I can do this on Monday the 29th,
if not before, and if need be there could be a Cabinet afterwards on the
1st."[8] In the event, however, the Cabinet met on the 31st but nothing was
said about the military conversations. Campbell-Bannerman's report to
the King that day referred merely to "the progress of affairs at Algeciras
and the little difficulty with Turkey at the head of the Red Sea."[9] The
reason for this change of course may, perhaps, have been that Bertie had
been impressing upon the Foreign Office the need to give France all possible support. He did so partly from his own convictions and partly because Mallet had asked him (January 11th) "to write a very strong personal
letter" to Grey and to urge Hardinge "to buck up these miserable creatures."[10] Bertie warned his chief on January 13th that there was "serious
danger of a complete revulsion of feeling on the part of the French
Government and of public opinion in France." If Britain could promise
no more than diplomatic support at the Conference and neutrality in the
event of a German attack, the Government "would consider that they had
been deserted and might, in order to avoid the risk of war without an ally,
deem it advisable to make great concessions to Germany outside Morocco
in order to obtain liberty of action in that country." Such concessions
could very well prove "detrimental to the interests of the British Empire."[11] Grey was unable to withstand pressure of this nature, despite the
fact that Bertie was placing an interpretation upon the *entente* which it had
never been meant to bear. He discussed the situation with Ripon on January 22nd, finding him strongly opposed to giving any guarantees, and
spent the weekend with the King and Campbell-Bannerman at Windsor.
Ripon's reactions, it was realised, would probably be those of Loreburn,
Bryce, Lloyd George and other Radical Ministers, and the Liberal Party
could not yet risk another split within its ranks. If Cambon's question
came before the Cabinet it would be necessary to refer to the military discussions and "certain Ministers", so the French Ambassador later recorded
Grey as saying ,"would be astonished at the opening of such talks."[12]

On January 31st Cambon once again asked whether France could rely
on Britain's assistance if she were forced into war with Germany. Grey
replied that while he did not see the need for a specific assurance much
progress had been made with the military talks and if a crisis arose no time
would be lost through lack of a formal alliance. He had, moreover, informed Metternich of the impossibility of any British Government re-

maining neutral if Germany used the *entente* as a pretext for declaring war on France and believed that this warning had been effective. Thirdly, the transformation of the *entente* into an alliance would mean that Britain must thenceforward be consulted on French policy in Morocco, whereas France had a free hand under the present arrangement. The Cabinet, he felt, would not be opposed to a formal alliance but this was a very serious step and the need for it was not yet apparent. There, for the moment, the matter rested. It was presumably thought that, once the immediate crisis had passed and the tension had relaxed, it would be possible to wind up the military conversations without the full Cabinet knowing that they had been held.

Personal tragedy now intervened. On February 1st, the day following his third conversation with Cambon, Grey was informed that his wife, still at Fallodon, had been thrown from her carriage and was critically ill. He hurried home immediately but Lady Grey died two days later and her husband did not resume his duties until February 7th.

During Grey's absence Campbell-Bannerman himself took charge of foreign affairs, and was plainly not very happy about the arrangement that had been reached with France. "I do not like the stress laid upon joint preparations," he wrote to Ripon on February 2nd. "It comes very close to an honourable undertaking and will be known on both sides of the Rhine." [13] This was, however, the furthest he went in questioning their wisdom.*

(3)

The Algeciras Conference had begun on January 16th. It was attended by representatives of all the leading Powers and those with trade interests in Morocco, namely France, Great Britain, Germany, Italy, Austria-Hungary, Russia, the United States, Spain, Belgium, Holland, Portugal, Sweden and Morocco herself. Britain was represented by Nicolson, one of her ablest diplomats.

There were two points at issue: control of the State Bank and control of the police at the eight ports. Germany claimed that the *entente* and the Franco-Spanish treaty had denied to her and other countries the right to trade with Morocco except on terms acceptable to France: she felt that the police should be under international, or at any rate impartial, control, and she also felt entitled to a port of her own. France, on the other hand, proposed that the police should be under the control of herself and Spain, with Italy exercising a theoretical supervision over them both. She saw no reason why Germany should be accorded special privileges. "As far as I

---

* He was, in fact, doing no more than echo Ripon's own misgivings.

can discover," Grey wrote to Nicolson on December 21st, "the Germans will refuse altogether to concede to France the special position in Morocco which we have promised France not only to concede to her but to help her by diplomatic methods to obtain. If she can succeed in getting this with our help it will be a great success for the Anglo-French entente. If she fails the prestige of the entente will suffer and its vitality will be diminished."[14] He was not at first opposed, however, to the idea of concessions, and told Campbell-Bannerman on January 9th that it might prove "that a port for Germany on the west Atlantic coast of Morocco would solve all the difficulties of the Morocco conference."[15]

Deadlock was soon reached. Grey, in a letter dated February 15th, told Nicolson that, although he could not exercise any pressure on the French, he thought that they might be prepared to accept a modified version of the latest German proposal, which would involve control of the police by a minor Power.[16] A memorandum which he wrote five days later is a useful summary of his views at this time.

Memorandum by Grey, February 20th, 1906

If there is war between France and Germany it will be very difficult for us to keep out of it. The entente and still more the constant and emphatic demonstrations of affection (official, naval, political, commercial, municipal and in the Press) have created in France a belief that we should support her in war. . . . If this expectation is disappointed the French will never forgive us.

There would also, I think, be a general feeling in every country that we had behaved meanly and left France in the lurch. The United States would despise us, Russia would not think it worth while to make a friendly arrangement with us about Asia, Japan would prepare to reinsure herself elsewhere, we should be left without a friend and Germany would take some pleasure, after what has passed, in exploiting the whole situation to our disadvantage, very likely by stirring up trouble through the Sultan of Turkey in Egypt.

On the other hand, the prospect of a European war and of our being involved in it is horrible. I propose therefore, if unpleasant symptoms develop after the Conference is over, to tell the French Ambassador that a great effort and if need be some sacrifice should in our opinion be made to avoid war . . . I should myself be in favour of allowing Germany a port or a coaling station, if that would ensure peace.[17]

Neither Tweedmouth nor Fisher saw any reason why Germany should not be given a port on the west coast of Morocco, but rumours of this "weakening" soon reached the ears of the French Ambassador, and Hardinge was obliged to deny that such an idea had ever been considered. The Foreign Office staff, moreover, speedily discovered reasons why such a concession would be detrimental to British interests, and Grey had to give way.

On March 3rd a vote at Algeciras on the following day's agenda, a minor point in itself, revealed the startling fact that Austria-Hungary and Morocco were the only countries which supported Germany. Even Italy, her other partner in the Triple Alliance, voted against her. The German representatives therefore abandoned their hope of a diplomatic triumph and thankfully agreed to a compromise solution put forward by Austria-Hungary on March 8th whereby the Moroccan police would be under French or Spanish control in every port except Casablanca, where they would be under the control of a Swiss or Dutch official. The latter would also have general powers of inspection throughout Morocco. Nicolson welcomed this proposal, as did all the other delegates except those of France and Spain, and he urged Revoil, the French representative, to give way. "The Germans," he wrote, "have been wonderfully conciliatory," and Grey told Campbell-Bannerman on March 10th that "the Germans have in effect climbed down and declared for peace."[18]

The French, however, believed that better terms could be exacted. The Rouvier Ministry had fallen on March 7th and that of M. Sarrien, which took its place, was less friendly towards Britain. Bertie warned Grey on March 12th that it would create an "unfortunate impression" in France if the willingness of the Foreign Office to accept the latest proposal became known and Grey was obliged, once again, to give way. "As the French take Casablanca so seriously we must take it so too," he wrote on March 14th and he instructed Nicolson to support Revoil whatever the outcome.[19] The following day Clemenceau, the new Minister of the Interior, paid a visit to the British Embassy in Paris. He and his colleagues, he told Bertie, were disturbed to learn of Nicolson's earlier advice to Revoil about Casablanca: it seemed to confirm their suspicions that Britain had reached some secret agreement with Germany. Grey reacted indignantly when told of this visit and instructed Bertie to state that Nicolson would continue to support his French colleague at the Conference, pointing out that "cordial co-operation with France in all parts of the world remains a cardinal point of British policy and in some respects we have carried it further than the late Government here were required to do."[20] Clemenceau and his colleagues professed to be duly reassured but the whole episode illustrated the alarming extent to which, in the space of three months, the *entente* of 1904 had been twisted into something very close to an alliance, with Britain dancing to whatever tune France might happen to call.

Fortunately, the crisis was nearly at an end. On March 18th the German delegate announced that his Government would yield on the police question if assured of compensations elsewhere and by April 1st agreement had been reached. The Pact of Algeciras was signed the following day. At Tangiers and Casablanca the police would be under the control of both French and Spanish officers, at two more ports they would be solely under Spanish control and at the remaining four they would be solely under French control. The State Bank would, however, be controlled by all the Powers.

(4)

Russia's defeat at the hands of Japan, together with her domestic upheavals, had temporarily removed her from the ranks of the great Powers. Grey was "impatient to see Russia re-established as a factor in European politics,"[21] since he felt that an *entente* between Britain, Russia and France would be the one really effective way of keeping Germany in check. Friendship with France had resulted from the settlement of outstanding differences over Egypt and Morocco: friendship with Russia, therefore, would presumably result if agreement could be reached over Tibet, Persia and Afghanistan, subjects which had been sore points for many years. Such an agreement had previously been sought in vain by the Foreign Office, but Russia might now be more amenable in view of her weakened status.

Talks between Nicolson, who had succeeded Hardinge as British Ambassador, and the new Russian Foreign Minister, Alexander Isvolsky, began on June 7th, the first subject for discussion being Tibet. Nicolson had been instructed to put forward the following requests: first, that Russia would recognise, as Britain had done, China's suzerainty over Tibet and pledge herself not to interefere in its internal administration; secondly, that she would recognise Britain's right to uphold Tibet's integrity; thirdly, that in common with Britain she would not attempt to secure for herself any concessions for railways, roads, telegraphs, mining or other rights in Tibet; and fourthly that she would refrain, again in common with Britain, from allowing Tibetan revenues, whether in kind or cash, to be pledged or assigned to her.

These discussions went off fairly well, Isvolsky acquiescing in the British proposals. Next, however, came the subject of Persia, on which it was less easy to reach agreement. Nicolson had been instructed to obtain Russia's recognition of an area in south-east Persia, on the north-west border of India, as one which she would abandon entirely to British influence. Britain, in return, would be prepared to recognise Russia's predominance in other provinces. Also in the wind was the question of an Anglo-Russian joint loan to the Sultan for railway construction.*

Isvolsky trod very cautiously. His greatest fear was that, by entering into partnership with Britain in the administration of Persia, Russia would arouse German hostility. Russia's domestic affairs, moreover, were once again in a sorry state and on July 22nd the Duma, the parliamentary institution which had been brought into being by the recent revolution, was dissolved. The following day Campbell-Bannerman received a delegation from twenty-two European parliaments who were present in London for a Congress, among them representatives from the now defunct Duma, and created a minor sensation by exclaiming "La Duma est morte, vive la Duma!" The Russian Ambassador, Count Benckendorff, was annoyed at this incident and Grey had the delicate task of convincing him that Sir Henry was merely repeating sentiments expressed by the Czar himself. Nicolson was extremely indignant at what he considered a clumsy intervention. "The attitude of our Press is most unfortunate," he wrote on August 6th, "and they have completely misunderstood the picture. On top of this comes the speech of the P.M. Isvolsky's former eagerness has been replaced by silence and bitter indifference. The Emperor is wounded. Two months ago there was every hope, and now very little. When I mentioned to Isvolsky that I should like to have some outline of his views on Persia, he looked blankly at me and said that he had no views at all."[23]

Nicolson at length submitted a draft convention on spheres of influence to Isvolsky in November and the Russian Foreign Minister presented him with counter-proposals in February 1907. The chunk of Persia which Russia claimed was, as Grey observed to Benckendorff on March 7th, "a very large one", and included Tehran, the seat of the central government. Benckendorff was politely apologetic but it was obvious that Russia was not going to give way on this point.[24] Grey, in a letter to Nicolson dated March 8th, accepted the Russian claim to Tehran but stipulated that the Russian zone should not touch the boundary of Afghanistan. Isvolsky, on April 2nd, agreed to this condition and the Persian Convention was, to all intents and purposes, complete. Another point, however, now arose. What of Britain's interests in the Persian Gulf? Would Russia agree to acknowledge these? Russia did agree, though somewhat grudgingly, and a separate declaration to this effect was drafted.

The subject of Afghanistan at last came up for discussion. Britain's proposals on this topic had been presented to Isvolsky on February 23rd: the

* Grey had been warned by one of his advisers on April 24th that "if Great Britain and Russia do not very soon come to an agreement with regard to their respective interests in Persia they may find themselves confronted there with Germany very much as did France in Morocco."[22]

main point was that Russia should acknowledge Afghanistan to be "outside the sphere of Russian influence." On May 15th Isvolsky put forward counter-proposals, concerned with trading concessions, and these were passed on to the Foreign Office. By June 17th Britain had drawn up another set of proposals, designed to go half-way to meeting Russian demands, but Isvolsky explained on July 8th that his colleagues would "demur strongly to . . . unconditional engagement on the part of Russia not to annex or occupy any portion of Afghanistan and . . . they would probably wish to insert a saving clause—something to the effect that their engagement held good provided that no change occurred in actual state of things in Afghanistan."[25] This caused much alarm in the Foreign Office but Grey agreed, at length, to the insertion of the following sentence in the Convention: "Should any change occur in the political status of Afghanistan the two Governments will enter into a friendly interchange of views on the subject." This, fortunately, did the trick and the Conventions were signed on August 31st, 1907.

(5)

Anglo-German relations had never been really satisfactory since 1896. The "Kruger telegram" came, indeed, as something of a revelation to the British people, since it had been unhesitatingly accepted until then that the "natural alliance" between the Saxon races transcended all the usual petty feuds of nation states. The Kaiser, after all, was the grandson of Queen Victoria, and in many of his pursuits had seemed more English than the English; that his admiration for the British way of life should be mixed with jealousy was something which had simply not occurred to the British.

Once the thought *had* occurred, however, it was one which proved very difficult to erase. Talk of a formal alliance in 1898 did something to paper over the cracks, but the talk came to nothing and Britain remained in isolation. By 1900, however, she was forced to realise, amidst the vicissitudes of the South African War, that with interests in all parts of the globe in need of defence, and with her military and naval resources stretched to their utmost, she could no longer steer a wholly independent course. It was then inconceivable that she should come to terms with either France or Russia, and Chamberlain made a final effort to bring about an Anglo-German alliance. Bülow and Holstein were not satisfied with the terms offered and decided to play a waiting game, but no better terms were forthcoming, and by the end of 1901 the prospect of an alliance had vanished altogether. Britain, intent upon preventing Russian domination in the Far East, looked elsewhere for allies, and in 1902, the year in which she formed an alliance with Japan, relations with Germany touched a new low. Bülow referred to Chamberlain in contemptuous terms when speaking in the Reichstag and the insult was returned with interest by the Colonial Secretary. This episode set the seal on all hopes of an understanding between the two countries.* The Admiralty, moreover, suddenly became aware that the German Navy Acts of 1898 and 1900, which provided for the creation of a splendid new fleet of battleships, were a potential threat to Britain's naval supremacy.† "I am convinced," wrote Selborne, the First Lord of the Admiralty, in a memorandum dated October 17th, 1902, "that the new German navy is being carefully built up from the point of view of a war with us," and two years later the new First Sea Lord, Sir John Fisher, cheerfully advocated the "Copenhagening" of the German fleet.[28]

It had been hoped by the new Government that Anglo-German relations would improve if Germany behaved gracefully over Morocco, and Grey, writing to Sir Frank Lascelles, the British Ambassador at Berlin, on January 1st, 1906, declared that "if we were only quite sure that Germany did not regard our public engagements as incompatible with German interests, and if she would only believe that we do not mean badly to her, recent frictions would disappear."[29] Germany's acceptance of her defeat at Algeciras with a relatively good grace and the dismissal of Holstein on April 4th did not, however, lead to an immediate improvement: Abdul Hamid, the Sultan of Turkey, was proving unexpectedly obstinate in a dispute over certain territory on the Egypto–Turkish frontier and it was generally believed in the Foreign Office that he was being encouraged by Germany. By the end of the year Grey was telling President Roosevelt that "it is in German diplomacy alone that one now meets with deliberate attempts to make mischief between other countries by saying poisoned things to one about the other."[30]

The Foreign Secretary took, on the face of it, a more pessimistic view of Anglo-German relations than events seemed to warrant. A party of German journalists which visited London in June was welcomed by Bryce and Loreburn and a royal visit to Cronberg in August passed off success-

---

* "You would be interested to see the effect created in England by the German treatment of us," wrote Cecil Spring-Rice to a friend on April 17th, 1902. "The change is extraordinary. Everyone, in the [Foreign] Office and out, talks as if we had but one enemy in the world, and that Germany."[26]

† The programme laid down by the Acts was, as Mr Arthur J. Marder notes, "executed silently, rapidly and systematically, without the shipbuilding delays which were occurring in England. Between 1900 and 1905 twelve battleships were laid down and proceeded with swiftly. Fourteen battleships were launched in these years, only two fewer than the British (omitting the two purchased by the Admiralty from Chile in 1903). The consensus of British expert opinion was that in 1906 Germany would be the second naval power in the world."[27]

fully, while Haldane and Churchill were both the guests of the Emperor at the army manoeuvres a few weeks later.* Sir Edward, however, grew ever more convinced, as the year wore on, that Germany was not to be trusted, and his anxiety for the preservation of the *entente cordiale* became, indeed, something of an obsession. On June 20th, for example, we find him assuring Cambon that "if anything arose which made it necessary to choose between France and Germany, public opinion here would be as decided on the French side as ever," and in September he noted, with regret, that "the difficulty of making an alliance with France now is that Germany might attack France at once, while Russia is helpless, fearing lest when Russia recovered she (Germany) should be crushed by a new Triple Alliance against her."†[32] Nowhere does Grey's desire to placate the French emerge more clearly than in the correspondence evoked by Haldane's acceptance of the Emperor's invitation to attend the German army manoeuvres at the end of August. The French pointed out that a commemoration of Sedan formed part of these manoeuvres and Grey urged Haldane not to attend this particular review and even to give up the visit altogether. Haldane, after consulting with the King and Campbell-Bannerman, refused to give way, and Grey warned him on September 3rd that "serious consequences" might follow. "I want to preserve the entente with France," he wrote, "but it isn't easy, and if it is broken up I must go."[33] In the event the trip passed off without any undue incident, although Cambon told Grey on November 8th that his Government feared that there was a pro-German element influencing English policy. Sir Edward promptly repeated the assurance that he had given June 20th, namely that in the event of anything like another Moroccan crisis "France might depend upon it that our support would be just as strong and our attitude as firm as it had been before."[34]

The importance of the *entente cordiale* as the basis for maintaining peace in Europe was emphasised in the letter which Grey wrote to President Roosevelt in December 1906. It meant, he explained, good relations for both Britain and France with Italy and Spain, and the conclusion of an

---

* Haldane, very much in his element, told the Kaiser that he was looked upon with pride in Britain "as being an Englishman as well as a German", and in his spare time compiled a nice gossipy diary for the private perusal of King Edward. Churchill, who regarded himself as a connoisseur of military technique, studied the manoeuvres with a more critical eye and concluded that the German army, for all its splendour, was not yet as efficient or as terrible a machine as had sometimes been depicted. These visits were regarded with satisfaction by Fitzmaurice, who told Lascelles on September 21st that "things are certainly better than they were—nevertheless the anti-German current in the Office still flows, though it has been checked."[31]

† He was commenting on an article which had appeared in a German newspaper entitled "An Anglo-French Military Convention?"

arrangement with Russia would help to complete the foundation. Nothing would be done to provoke Germany, so long as she accepted the situation and did not try to make mischief. If the *entente* were broken up, however, Germany would become the dominating Power in Europe, and sooner or later Britain would be obliged to go to war with her.

President Roosevelt's comments on this letter are not recorded.

(6)

On February 10th, 1906, a date of decisive importance in British naval history, there was launched at Portsmouth the biggest, fastest, most formidable battleship in the world. This was the *Dreadnought*, an ironclad monster of 17,900 tons which had cost £1,800,000 to construct. It possessed four special features: a top speed of 21 knots, two faster than any other battleship; a main battery of ten 12 inch guns, as opposed to the four 12 inch and ten 9·2 inch guns of the Lord Nelson type; an absence of secondary features and, finally, a turbine engine. Its design was revolutionary and its construction meant that all existing battleships, including those of Britain herself, were automatically rendered obsolete.

The decision to begin Dreadnought construction had been taken at a meeting of the Committee of Imperial Defence in March 1905, the reason being, quite simply, the desire to keep safely ahead in the race for naval supremacy. In theory, at any rate, that supremacy had never been in doubt, but from 1900 onwards the Admiralty had been painfully aware that the increased rate of shipbuilding in Russia, Germany, Japan and the United States meant that the two-Power standard (i.e., that the British navy should always exceed the combined strength of the two next largest navies in the world) could only be maintained with the utmost difficulty. The appointment of Fisher as First Sea Lord in October 1904, however, had resulted in a host of whirlwind reforms in nearly every sphere,* and the Cawdor–Fisher programme of 1905, drawn up with the German Navy Acts of 1898 and 1900 in mind, provided for the annual construction of "four large armoured ships" so that, by the end of 1907, Britain would have a dozen actually in commission and the keels of another four laid down. The Navy Estimates for 1905–6 provided for the construction of one Dreadnought and three Invincibles, a new type of battle-cruiser, and

---

* This ebullient, pugnacious and dynamic (if sometimes malevolent) personality was sixty-three years old at the time of his appointment. He was an old man in a hurry, and his determination to overhaul the navy from top to bottom led to much bitter controversy. Apart from intensifying the dissolution of class barriers in the service, he introduced the nucleus-crew-system, whereby fighting ships in reserve were to be manned by two-fifths of the normal crew and maintained in a much greater state of efficiency; the scrapping of obsolete ships, and the redistribution of the fleet so that Great Britain herself came to be more adequately protected.

on December 4th, 1905, the day Balfour resigned, the Admiralty announced that, while "the output of four large ships a year should suffice to meet our requirements, there would be no difficulty whatever in increasing the output to whatever may be necessary in consequence of any increase of naval power abroad."

These were threatening words and, taken in conjunction with the launching of the *Dreadnought*, the immediate effect on Germany was more than gratifying: her shipbuilders flew into a panic and no new construction began in their yards for almost a year. It was not, however, fully appreciated at this time that Britain was handicapping herself as well as her nearest rival: the race for ordinary battleships, in which she had a respectable numerical superiority, would now be succeeded by a race for Dreadnoughts, in which she had a majority of no more than one.

The new Government accepted the Cawdor–Fisher programme without question at first, but the rank and file of the Liberal Party, all good Gladstonians to a man, were greatly alarmed at the prospect of heavy expenditure on armaments in peacetime. They saw no reason why Britain should embark upon a large and expensive programme of shipbuilding, especially when money was needed for schemes of social reform, and on June 21st a deputation of 120 Liberal M.P.s urged Campbell-Bannerman to reduce the programme for the current year. Sir Henry consulted with Clarke, who assured him (July 3rd) that, from the viewpoint of security, one ship alone would suffice for the 1906–7 programme: they could afford to mark time a little and would be in a better position, twelve months hence, to see what was coming in foreign armaments and build accordingly.[35] This view, however, was not shared by Tweedmouth, who was reluctant enough to cut the programme by one ship, let alone two or three. When the Cabinet met on July 10th Asquith urged that the programme be reduced from four armoured ships to two: Russia, he argued, was out of the running as a naval Power, while it was in the highest degree unlikely that France and Germany would ever combine against Britain. Tweedmouth refused to give way initially, but it was eventually agreed on July 18th that while the programme would be cut from four ships to three work would not begin on the third ship until the second Hague Conference on the humanisation of war had been held in 1907.† The Conference

---

* A report issued by the C.I.D. later that month stated that "the Franco-Russian Alliance as a factor in determining our standard of naval strength has disappeared, and years must elapse before the Russian navy can again be a formidable force. Our present relations with France are and should remain satisfactory, while in certain conditions the Japanese Alliance would add to our potential strength."[36]

† See pages 348–9 for Campbell-Bannerman's reports to the King on the Cabinets of July 10th and 18th. Tweedmouth, admittedly, returned to the attack later in the year. "All

would result, it was hoped, in a general agreement to cut down on the construction of battleships and it might obviate the need to construct the third ship altogether.*

The other European Powers were not particularly impressed with these revisions. The German Emperor, on August 15th, told Lascelles that each state must decide for itself the degree of military and naval strength which it needed: if the Hague Conference were to raise the question of disarmament, then Germany would refuse to be represented. The Radicals were mollified, however, and expenditure on the navy for 1906-7 eventually showed a saving of £1,866,000. The Chancellor of the Exchequer, as the following letter shows, meanwhile remained far from happy at the attendant difficulties of Dreadnought construction.

Asquith to Campbell-Bannerman, December 30th, 1906

I am much disquieted by Tweedmouth's memorandum on Navy Estimates. The total reduction shown, as compared with last year's, is only £450,000: although it is no doubt true that, if we had continued the system of borrowing for Land Works, this would have come to about £1,200,000. But, on either view, this is very poor and inadequate fulfilment of our pledges in regard to reduction of expenditure on fighting services.

The enclosed article from today's *Spectator* ... suggests that we are going ahead in the matter of construction far beyond any real necessity. Moreover, the Admiralty now propose to commit us to an expenditure of £2,000,000 on Rosyth (in addition to nearly a million at Portsmouth) which, as they admit, can only be justified because the new big ships require big docks. Tweedmouth, in a few words I had with him after the last Cabinet, intimated that from this point of view Chatham would become absolutely useless. They want a new east coast dockyard entirely to meet the requirements of what is admittedly up to now a purely experimental type of new ship, of which no other Power—except perhaps Japan—possesses or effectively contemplates a single specimen.

Surely the time has come for a complete review of the whole naval situation (before we accept these estimates) either by the Cabinet or a Cabinet Committee.

I confess that, after a year's experience, I have very little confidence in the

governments for the last twenty-one years," he wrote to Campbell-Bannerman on November 21st, "have accepted and acted up to the two-power standard and it is not to be lightly abandoned now." The First Lord's views were not altogether consistent, however, with an Admiralty memorandum of the previous month, which had concluded that "the outlying fleets no longer require to be maintained at the strength which was admittedly necessary a year ago when France and Russia were our most probable opponents."[37]

* The second Hague Conference (June–October 1907) proved a disappointment to Britain. She found herself the only major European Power embracing the cause of limitations upon shipbuilding with any enthusiasm. Lord Reay, a member of the British delegation, concluded that instead of encouraging disarmament the Conference had "increased the existing feeling on the Continent of Europe that no Power can afford to neglect its means of offence and defence. . . . It has not given a greater sense of security, but rather the reverse." Crowe, perhaps characteristically, felt that "the dominating influence . . . clearly has been *fear* of Germany."[38]

present lot of Sea Lords, who chop and change as the whim which suits them. Our naval supremacy is so completely assured—having regard to the sketchy paper programmes and inferior shipbuilding resources of the other Powers—that there is no possible reason for allowing ourselves to be hastily rushed into these nebulous and ambitious developments.[39]

In the event, the Hague Conference disappointed British expectations and work then commenced on the third battleship of the 1906–7 programme. The Navy Estimates for 1907–8, however, did not mark a return to the original Cawdor–Fisher programme: while they showed (as Asquith complained) a saving of no more than £450,000, they too provided for the construction of only three Dreadnoughts. To this extent, therefore, the Liberal Government struggled to reconcile Radical theory with the exigencies of practical politics.

(7)

Haldane was meanwhile finding the War Office a surprisingly satisfactory substitute for the Woolsack. "I am enjoying myself simply hugely," he wrote towards the end of December 1905. "The dear generals are angels, no other name is good enough for these simple honourable souls. I have already made changes which might have tried them and they gulp them down."[40] Unencumbered with preconceived notions or dogma, he tackled the problems that faced him—chief of which was the woeful inadequacy of the army, which the South African War had done so much to reveal—in a manner which was self-confessedly amateurish but, at the time, one that returned to first principles, explained itself as it went along and concentrated upon reaching certain fixed objectives. Leisurely contemplation of the situation was, for the moment, Haldane's chief pastime, but a few days later the War Office was suddenly jolted into activity by the realisation that the emergency for which it was in the midst of preparing might be nearer than anyone had anticipated.

The negotiations leading up to the military conversations between France and Britain have already been described. The first of these took place on January 16th between General Grierson and Major Huguet, a Belgian representative also being present. Grierson stated that, if Britain were to join France in war against Germany, it would take thirty-two days to transport 105,000 men across the Channel: mobilisation, moreover, would take two months. Small wonder that the French did not view the prospects of British aid with much delight after being supplied with this information! "Hardly a brigade," wrote Haldane later, "could have been sent to the Continent without being recast. As they stood, the brigades were generally incomplete and in a form that was inconvenient in peace-time but wholly inadequate for mobilisation. . . . In order to put even 80,000 men on the Continent preliminary preparations requiring at the very least two months would be required. But that was far from all. The Continental Powers fought, not with brigades, but with great divisions and corps, each containing two divisions. We had not in 1906 a single division that was a reality. Moreover the brigades, such as they were, wholly lacked accessories. . . . Their transport was deficient and so were their medical organisations. The field artilleries consisted for peace purposes of ninety-nine batteries. But these batteries were seriously short, not only of men in the ranks but of reserves. Only forty-two batteries could be put in the field, a number which a proper General Staff would have pronounced to be ludicrously inadequate for the Expeditionary Force required."[41]

The crisis passed, but the lesson had been learnt. The army must be reorganised and transformed into a hyper-efficient machine. At the same time, however, in order to satisfy the conscience of the Liberal Party, it must be run on as small a budget as possible. Efficiency and economy must therefore go arm-in-arm. On March 8th Haldane set the scene for the reforms to follow. "Our army," he declared in the Commons, "is wanted for purposes abroad and overseas. It is necessarily a professional army; we could not get such an army by conscription. . . . It does not exist merely for our own insular interests. . . . We have to protect the distant shores of the Empire from the attack of the invader. We want, therefore, an army which is very mobile and capable of rapid transport. For fighting which has to be done at a distance and cannot be against large masses of men it ought to be on a strictly limited scale and perfect rather in quality than expanded in quantity." This was one of Haldane's best speeches and Campbell-Bannerman congratulated him on it warmly. "I had no idea," he said later, "that Schopenhauer would cut such a figure in the barrack yard."* Sandars reported to Balfour that the speech was "very moderate in tone, pleased our boys but was sulkily received by his own side."[43]

On July 12th Haldane announced his plans for the creation of an expeditionary force. It would consist of six "great divisions", each of twelve infantry battalions, together with sixty-six batteries of field artillery and complements of the Royal Engineers, divisional cavalry and various

---

* Only a few days before, in fact, he made it plain in a letter to a friend dated February 27th that he had seen no reason to change his low opinion of Haldane's capabilities. "I never discuss things with him," he wrote, "but I have warned him against talking and speaking in public too much, and above all against dogmatism and swagger; and have advised him whatever he does to give the credit of it to the soldiers, and never to seem to be making capital for himself. In short, to be as unlike his two predecessors as he can."[42]

specialised groups, including the new Air Corps. In all, 150,000 men were needed, as opposed to the previous maximum of 100,000: 50,000 to serve permanently, 30,000 on a non-regular basis and 70,000 in reserve. There would also be 5,550 officers. To balance this, the regular army would be reduced by 20,000 men. The colonial establishment was to be reduced by three battalions (two from Malta and one from Gibraltar) and six battalions were to be recalled from South Africa. The Third Scots Guards were to be abolished and the Third Coldstream Guards sent to Egypt, where a permanent battalion would remain. These proposals met with general approval, and came into effect on January 1st, 1907.

The creation of the expeditionary force was the first of Haldane's achievements: the next was the establishment of a strong second-line army for home defence and possible service overseas. The idea of such an army had long been favoured, but what was to be the fate of the Militia and the Volunteers?* In May 1906 a committee under Esher's chairmanship grappled with this question but broke up without reaching a decision. The Militia refused to be amalgamated with the Volunteers or used as an appendage to the expeditionary force. Another committee, again with Esher as chairman, proved equally inconclusive. Haldane therefore resolved to go ahead without the Militia's approval. A scheme was devised whereby the latter would be transformed into a special reserve and the Yeomanry and Volunteers into a territorial army, consisting of brigades and divisions, which would be administered by county organisations. Conscription was considered at this time, and intermittently during the next few years, but it was generally agreed that such a measure in peacetime was undesirable and would lead to a lowering of standards. Another committee meanwhile drafted a scheme by which public schools and universities could be used as training-centres for officers and by the end of 1906 a new Bill was ready for the consideration of a Cabinet Committee.

"We had a full two hours this afternoon on the army scheme," wrote Sinclair to Campbell-Bannerman on January 8th, 1907,"—Asquith asking questions, Grey rather silent, J. B[urns] usefully loquacious and suspicious, Haldane overflowing and assertive, but absolutely vague and his figures in the air, J. M[orley] critical."[44] Haldane himself, writing to the Prime Minister the following day, declared that there was "now a spirit of frugality, and it is bearing fruit. The estimated cost of the Territorial Army, plus the new Special Reserve, is no greater than the four and a half millions that is

---

* The Militia (numbering 90,000) were a body of men on call in case of emergency. The Volunteers (numbering 25,000) had come into existence in 1858. Like the Militia, they were intended purely for home defence.

spent on the auxiliary forces, and may be—and for some years probably will be—less. . . . The whole question rests with our own people, and I think that if I can present this very temperately . . . we may be able to carry our own people with us. . . . If, by steering carefully, I can reduce the consumption of parliamentary time to a moderate amount, and at the same time succeed in making our people feel that the Liberal Government is the one government that can produce a business-like and economical army, then all should go well."[45]

Campbell-Bannerman was evidently rather sceptical about the proposals,* but the scheme was approved by the Cabinet and introduced into Parliament as the Territorial and Reserve Forces Bill on March 4th. It had been designed, Haldane explained, primarily for home defence. The War Office would command and train the forces, but the county associations (headed, in most instances, by the Lord-Lieutenant) would be responsible for their organisation and would be represented at military councils. The maximum size of the force, which would be divided into fifty-six cavalry regiments, fourteen divisions and various auxiliary corps, would not exceed 300,000. In the event of general mobilisation, it would receive war training for six months. The Bill received a smooth passage through both Houses. Haldane, there is no doubt, had scored a triumph at a time when the Government's prestige had sunk sadly low, and he can scarcely be blamed for making the most of the praise which his efforts attracted.†

The Territorial Army came into existence on April 1st, 1908, but it experienced some teething difficulties. Recruitment was not so brisk as it might have been, only 50% of the Volunteers re-engaging and 70% of those only for the period of one year in the first instance. By 1910 the number of officers and men had increased to 276,000, but it was evident that this level would only be maintained with difficulty. Even so, the fact that this army had been brought into existence at all was a considerable achievement: taken in conjunction with the creation of the expeditionary force and Fisher's labours at the Admiralty it meant that Great Britain, for the first time in almost a century, was equipping herself for the rigours of genuine warfare as opposed to maintaining the traditions of a bygone age.

* "R.B.H.," he wrote to Sinclair on February 3rd, "left all the papers on the army with [me]. . . . He dwelt on the fact of the Cardwell system being maintained, a committee of experts . . . having examined and approved the whole thing. . . . All is therefore for the best— the soldiers delighted; the Volunteers everywhere enthusiastic; Grey and Asquith very warm for it; Burns and J. M. most appreciative. Every bolt-hole was thus stopped! I could only congratulate him, and hope it would turn out a success. He can be cross-examined at the Cabinet. . . . He thus rides the storm and directs the whirlwind."[46]

† "Haldane is here," wrote Crewe to Campbell-Bannerman from Dalmeny House on October 10th, "quite in his element, being compassed about by a great cloud of Lord-Lieutenants to whom he is explaining the Army Act. I have not joined the symposium."[47]

(8)

On January 1st, 1907 the Senior Clerk at the Foreign Office, Eyre Crowe, circulated a lengthy memorandum dealing with Anglo-German relations. "From 1884 onward," he wrote, "when Bismarck first launched his country into colonial and maritime enterprise, numerous quarrels arose between the two countries. They all have in common this feature—that they were opened by acts of direct and unmistakable hostility to England on the part of the German Government, and that this hostility was displayed with a disregard of the elementary rules of straightforward and honourable dealing, which was deeply resented by successive British Secretaries of State for Foreign Affairs." The events connected with the Algeciras Conference, however, appeared "to have had on the German Government the effect of an unexpected revelation, clearly showing indications of a new spirit in which England proposed to regulate her own conduct towards France on the one hand and to Germany on the other."

Since then "our relations with Germany, if not exactly cordial, have at least been practically free from all symptom of direct friction, and there is an impression that Germany will think twice before she now gives rise to any fresh disagreement. In this attitude she will be encouraged if she meets on England's part with unvarying courtesy and consideration in all matters of common concern, but also with a prompt and firm refusal to enter into any one-sided bargain or arrangements, and the most unbending determination to uphold British rights and interests in every part of the globe. There will be no surer or quicker way to win the respect of the German Government and of the German nation."[48]

This memorandum was presumably designed to ensure that Grey did not deviate from the path laid down for him by his permanent officials at the time of the Algeciras Conference. There was, however, little danger of this: Sir Edward accepted the conclusions of the memorandum without question and passed it on to Campbell-Bannerman. The only criticisms came from Sanderson, who had left the Foreign Office the previous year and wrote only as a private individual.*

Outwardly, at any rate, Anglo-German relations continued to be fairly

---

* "The history of German policy towards this country," he declared, "is not the unchequered record of black deeds which this memorandum seems to portray. . . . A great and growing nation cannot be repressed. . . . It would be a misfortune that she [Germany] should be led to believe that in whatever direction she seeks to expand she will find the British lion in her path." Elsewhere he remarked that "it has sometimes seemed to me that to a foreigner reading our Press the British Empire must appear in the light of some huge giant sprawling all over the globe, with gouty fingers and toes stretching in every direction, which cannot be approached without eliciting a scream."[49]

harmonious. France, indeed, took alarm at this and on April 9th the new French premier, Clemenceau, had a conversation with Campbell-Bannerman in which he emphasised anew the menacing nature of Germany's European policy. Once again the French asked if they could rely on Britain's support if war were to break out between themselves and their neighbour on the other side of the Rhine. Sir Henry, however, replied that he did not think that public opinion would allow British troops to be used on the continent of Europe. Consternation in the Quai d'Orsay! Despatches flew back and forth. Was Sir Henry not aware, demanded one of them, that military conversations were being held between France and Britain in preparation for just such an eventuality as a Franco-German war? The matter was hastily smoothed over by the British, Grey pointing out that Sir Henry had merely intended to lay stress on the point that Britain could not regard herself as having entered into formal obligations. "What Sir Henry Campbell-Bannerman said to Clemenceau," wrote Bertie to Grey on April 17th, "was, I suppose, intended as a douche to cool any martial ardour that he might feel in reliance on military support from us. The French Government are, however, anything but bellicose. They are terribly afraid lest Germany should place France in a position in which war would become unavoidable."*[50]

King Edward VII paid a State visit to Berlin in August, where he was received by both the Kaiser and the aged Franz Josef, the Emperor of Austria-Hungary, and in November the Kaiser paid a visit to Windsor, which he appeared to enjoy. Anglo-German relations, however, were not improved by the announcement, towards the end of the year, of a further increase in Germany's shipbuilding programme. Henceforth the life of a battleship would be reckoned at twenty instead of twenty-five years and a Dreadnought would replace each vessel as it became obsolete. Construction for the next six years would be increased by five Dreadnoughts, and the Admiralty, now in a state of alarm, estimated that by April 1912 Germany would have thirteen modern (i.e., post 1905) battleships in com-

---

* The desire to maintain Anglo-French relations on a satisfactory basis was responsible, later that year, for an extraordinary episode concerning the band of the Coldstream Guards. The Army Council had agreed that the band should visit Germany, although it had previously withheld permission for a similar visit to France. The Foreign Office was angry, and Grey (October 4th) protested in no uncertain terms to Haldane. "It is really important," he wrote, "that the Coldstream band should not go to Germany. The Germans must be content with the Emperor's visit; there has been so much embracing already this year and there is so much still to come that our foreign policy will not stand any more." Both the King and Haldane were angry at Grey's insistence but were forced to give way, since Grey hinted at his resignation if they did not. Knollys told Sir Edward (October 8th) that the Kaiser would think it extraordinary that "the sovereign of this country, supported by the Secretary of State for War, cannot even send a military band abroad without the approval of the Foreign Office."[51]

mission or nearing completion as opposed to Britain's eighteen. Fisher now resolved that the limit of concession had been reached so far as the new Government's views were concerned: henceforth there must be no further reduction in naval expenditure.

The Cabinet had decided in November that the Navy Estimates for 1908–9 ought not to exceed those for 1907–8 (£31,419,500), but Tweedmouth informed Campbell-Bannerman on December 16th that the Board of Admiralty were unable to agree to this. When the matter came up for discussion in the Cabinet on January 21st, 1908, however, Harcourt, Lloyd George, Burns, McKenna and Morley made it plain that they were firmly opposed to any increase, and it was calculated that they had the support of at least a third of the parliamentary party and probably the whole of the Labour Party. The matter had not been resolved when Parliament assembled for the new Session and the Government was placed in an awkward position by a private member who tabled an amendment to the Address regretting that the Government's promise to reduce expenditure on armaments was not being fulfilled. It was agreed that discussion of this amendment should be postponed until the Estimates had been introduced, but the position was critical: if the Liberal dissentients voted in its favour, together with the Labour Party and the Unionists, the Government would be defeated by a majority of a hundred. On February 4th the Cabinet therefore agreed that the Estimates should be reduced by £1,340,000 and that a committee consisting of Lloyd George, Harcourt and McKenna should be appointed to implement this decision.

Harcourt saw Fisher later that day but the latter refused to consider fresh reductions of any kind, declaring that the Admiralty's figure was an "irreducible minimum."[*] Harcourt then said that he and other members of the Cabinet would resign if Fisher did not give way and, when Fisher threatened his own resignation, remarked that Lord Charles Beresford, the Commander-in-Chief of the Channel Fleet and a persistent critic of Admiralty policies, would be only too willing to take his place. Harcourt's efforts having failed, Lloyd George and Churchill dined with Fisher in the evening and endeavoured, with equal lack of success, to win him over. Lloyd George also tried again the following morning, but all to no avail. The old Admiral stood his ground and that afternoon Edmund Robertson, the Secretary to the Admiralty and a friend of the Prime Minister, explained to Campbell-Bannerman in great detail the Board's reasons for not agreeing to further reductions. Sir Henry was, at this time, sinking into

---

[*] The increase was due to a number of reasons, but the most important of them seems to have been the shortage of stores. See Campbell-Bannerman's letter of January 29th, 1908 to the King, quoted on page 353.

that lethargy which was to characterise his final weeks in office,* but he listened patiently to Robertson's arguments and after considering the matter sent for Asquith and told him that the Admiralty's figure was to stand. Haldane, instead, would be asked to cut the Army Estimates by £300,000.[53]

The dispute ended with the Radical members of the Cabinet reluctantly agreeing on February 10th to an increase in the Navy Estimates of £900,000, which meant a final figure of £32,319,000, and only seventy-three members voted against the Government when the amendment to the Address came up for debate on March 2nd. Paradoxically, however, the actual construction for this year included only two large armoured ships—i.e., one less than in either 1906–7 or 1907–8—although there was, by this time, considerable agitation in the Press over the rapid growth of the German navy and a widespread belief that Britain was falling behind in her overall supremacy.

An organisation known as the Imperial Maritime League was formed in Britain at this time, one of its objectives being the dismissal of Fisher, and an invitation to join its council was sent to Esher. The latter declined, however, and declared in his letter of refusal that there was "not a man in Germany, from the Emperor downwards, who would not welcome the fall of Sir John Fisher." He sent a copy of this letter to *The Times*, which printed it on February 6th, and the Kaiser was so incensed that, acting in his capacity as "a British Admiral of the Fleet", he wrote to Tweedmouth to assure him that the German navy was purely for peaceful and defensive purposes. Each nation, he declared, had a right to build as many ships as it thought fit and the German programme of construction from 1900 to 1918 had been known to the British public for seven years. Why, then, these mischievous Press attacks—Esher's comments, in particular, were "unmitigated balderdash"—and why should the German fleet be regarded as a menace to the Royal Navy? If Britain wanted to build a hundred, a hundred-and-fifty or even two hundred battleships within the next twelve years, no one would object. It was surely unreasonable for exception to be taken to Germany's modest goal of thirty to forty battleships by 1920.†

Tweedmouth received this "astounding communication" on February 18th and promptly informed Grey. The latter agreed that he should acknowledge its receipt but should not reply to it directly at this stage. He was given permission, however, to send the Kaiser details of the Navy Esti-

---

* King Edward, the previous day, had found him "very languid and feeble", unable to "bring his mind to bear upon any large questions of policy."[52]

† The accelerated obsolescence of pre-1888 battleships was evidently not regarded as a modification of the 1900 programme. At any rate, the Kaiser made no reference to it.

mates, which had not yet been presented to Parliament for approval, together with the text of the speech which he intended to make explaining why the Estimates had been increased. This gesture, it was thought, would demonstrate both the Government's desire for cordial relations and their determination to maintain the two-Power standard.* If the matter had ended there, all would have been well. Tweedmouth, however, was immensely flattered at having been approached by no less a personage than the German Emperor and could not resist the temptation of displaying the Kaiser's letter to his friends and associates. Colonel Repington soon came to hear of it and, sensing that here was "a matter of grave importance," promptly wrote to *The Times*, declaring that the letter was said to be "an attempt to influence, in German interests, the Minister responsible for our Navy Estimates."

The Times published Repington's letter on March 6th and supported his demand that the correspondence be made public. Asquith defended Tweedmouth in the Commons later that day by arguing that this was a private correspondence and that the Estimates for 1908–9 had already been decided. In order that there should not be too much probing, however, he was obliged to explain the situation to Balfour and Lansdowne, who agreed not to press for an enquiry. It would, of course, have placed the Government in an awkward predicament if the nature of Tweedmouth's reply had become known. They were embarrassed enough, even so, and the King was far from pleased at the manner in which this episode had been handled. Even the obsequious Lord Esher found himself out of favour for a few days.

(9)

One of the first things that Asquith did, when he became Prime Minister in April 1908, was to appoint a Cabinet Committee to consider further military economies. This was a move to compensate the Radicals for their defeat over the Navy Estimates and the members of the Committee were, in fact, the three most ardent Gladstonian economists in the Cabinet at this time: Lloyd George, Harcourt and Churchill.† Lloyd George, in particular, was determined not to be thwarted. "I meant to cut down army expenditure," he wrote to his brother on May 12th. ". . . I am not going to increase taxation to pay old age pensions until I have exhausted all means of reducing expenditure. I have told the P.M. he must help me.

* A direct answer to the Kaiser's letter took the form of a memorandum on naval construction which Lascelles presented to Bülow a few weeks later.

† McKenna's appointment as First Lord of the Admiralty was also a move to pacify the Radicals and King Edward only agreed to it on condition that Fisher remained First Sea Lord.[54]

He promises to do so, and my difficulties over old age pensions are now much less than they seemed a week ago."[55]

The reformers had not anticipated, however, the tenacity with which the Secretary of State for War would resist their proposals*, but a speech delivered by Lloyd George on May 25th hinting at economies to come soon showed the way the wind was blowing. Haldane took strong exception to it and, in the words of Esher (in a letter to Knollys written the following day), "put on his hat, went straight over to Asquith, plumped himself down in an armchair and tendered his resignation then and there. Asquith gave him an assurance that the Cabinet Committee . . . should not touch the question of army *policy*. With this Haldane is satisfied for the present, but his back is against the wall."[57] Lloyd George's next move was to persuade Churchill to lead a frontal attack upon Haldane in the Cabinet. Churchill plunged happily into the conflict, spending several long days at the War Office accumulating facts and figures to substantiate his case, and on June 18th circulated a lengthy memorandum in which he argued that the British army had become too large and too costly and that drastic reductions were needed in the Estimates for 1909–10.† This memorandum was discussed by the Cabinet on June 22nd and was followed a few days later by an equally detailed reply from Haldane. The latter dealt with Churchill's arguments point by point and mentioned, in addition, "certain Treaty obligations which might compel us to intervene on the Continent."[59] What brought matters to a head, however, was a report in *The Times* on June 25th that Haldane might soon be made Lord Chancellor and his place at the War Office given to Churchill. An enraged Haldane decided that this was the final indignity. He stormed into Asquith's room, declaring that he had no desire to vacate his present position and that he was determined not to accept further cuts in military expenditure. Asquith pacified his friend as best he could and asked Esher, the following day, to persuade Churchill not to press his attack any further. Esher did as requested, noting in his journal that Churchill, with whom he had two hours' conversation, "was clever and ingenious, but wild and unpractical. I

---

* Halévy claims that Haldane wanted the Exchequer for himself, but there does not appear to be any basis for this story. He told his mother, when Campbell-Bannerman resigned, that he had "firmly decided to stay at the War Office", and it was tacitly understood at this time that only a vacancy on the Woolsack would tempt him into leaving. An offer of the Indian Office, in October 1910, was declined, although he put himself forward as a candidate for the Admiralty some twelve months later.[56]

† On Sunday, June 21st, he found himself in Balfour's company at a house-party, and "did not attempt to conceal that they were in an awful mess about next year's finances and at their wits' end how to provide for their expenditure. He said he must leave by an eight o'clock train on Monday morning in order to be in time for a Cabinet Committee . . . 'where', he added, 'I intend to make myself damned disagreeable!' "[58]

think, however, he realises the difficulty of forcing Haldane's hand and the undesirability of breaking up the Government."⁶⁰ By the end of June, therefore, the dispute was at an end, with Haldane triumphantly holding the ring against all comers. A rueful Lloyd George confessed to the Commons on June 29th that he had no nest-eggs: "I am looking for someone's hen roost to raid next year."

The summer recess afforded Lloyd George and Churchill the opportunity of renewing, from another angle, their efforts to reduce Britain's military expenditure. The root of the trouble lay, it seemed, in the Government's suspicion of German intentions. Very well, then! They would make it clear to all concerned that neither side had anything to fear from the activities of the other. Lloyd George, on August 12th, told a reporter from the *Neue Freie Presse* that he would welcome an Anglo-German understanding; Churchill, three days later, made a vigorous speech in which he dismissed the idea of war between the two countries and emphasised the mutual desire for good relations.* These pronouncements aroused comment in the Press and it was suggested that the two *enfant terribles* were endeavouring to undermine Grey's position. Both hotly denied this accusation and Churchill pointed out that he was only echoing—though in a more colourful fashion—sentiments expressed by Grey himself. King Edward VII, however, was indignant at these amateurish excursions into foreign affairs and ordered Grey to reprimand the Ministers concerned.† Grey, indeed, was equally cross—on February 4th he had dismissed Churchill as someone who knew "nothing about the F.O. work, and thinks that because a Parliamentary Under-Secretary can travel and pick and choose and gallop about the field and toss his head and sniff what breeze he pleases, therefore a Foreign Secretary can do the same."⁶³ Asquith was summoned back to town and strong rebukes were dealt out to the offenders.‡

* He evidently had ambitious schemes at this time for improving trade relations with France and Germany. "I hope you will look very carefully at the memorandum circulated by Winston Churchill," wrote Ripon to Morley on July 18th, "of which I enclose a copy. It shows clearly that he desires to adopt a policy of Commercial Treaties wherever possible, in France first and then (see last paragraph) in Portugal and to some extent in Germany. Now the Cabinet cannot be committed to this without the fullest and most careful consideration. I am not very confident in the result of the Committee appointed at the last Cabinet. I am rather afraid of Lloyd George. I wish you would speak quietly to the Prime Minister and urge him [Churchill] not to embark on these wild schemes."⁶¹

† "It is a mercy that we have you as Under-Secretary at the Foreign Office," he wrote to Hardinge on August 25th, "and that Lloyd George and Winston Churchill do not occupy that position! I cannot conceive how the Prime Minister allows them ever to make speeches on foreign policy, concerning which they know nothing."⁶²

‡ Grey himself, however, had aroused Lloyd George's interest in foreign affairs by bringing him into contact with Metternich the previous month.

Lloyd George and Churchill were, at this time, in closer association than at any other point in their lives. They had been friends ever since the latter crossed to the Liberal benches, but from the spring of 1908 onwards they formed a virtually inseparable combination. That there was much to unite them cannot be denied: both were ambitious; both had arrogant confidence in their own abilities; both were brilliant orators and lively conversationalists; both were capable of arousing passions, whether of admiration or hatred, wherever they went, and both possessed the wonderful gift of leadership in time of crisis. Dynamic, flamboyant and electrifying are epithets that can be easily applied to each, but when all is said and done there were important basic differences that need to be noted. Lloyd George was a politician in the fullest meaning of the word: Churchill, on the other hand, always remained something of an amateur. Where Lloyd George intrigued, charmed and compromised in order to get his own way Churchill would bulldoze majestically forward, oblivious of obstacles and concerned only with reaching his destination as swiftly as possible. Where the one bent with the wind the other remained a rock of obstinacy; where the one darted this way and that with the dazzling rapidity of a jumping cracker the other would trundle stolidly along, colourful and impressive, but letting off his fireworks in a predictable manner. While Lloyd George was, admittedly, a dextrous improviser and opportunist, it must be said of him that he always had a pretty shrewd idea of what he was doing and why he was doing it. Churchill, however, was never too sure of his ultimate objectives and frequently changed course without realising it. Ideas, for Lloyd George, had to be pulled this way and that, embroidered upon or rejected, according to how they fitted his needs of the moment; for Churchill, they were something to be clung to tenaciously and stubbornly, defended by vivid phraseology and moralisings of a sententious nature, but in the right hands he could easily be persuaded into taking up cudgels on behalf of a very different viewpoint.

Churchill admired and envied Lloyd George, while the latter had a soft spot for his companion that was occasionally tinged with irritation. "Sometimes when I see Winston making these speeches," he told Masterman in 1909, "I get a flash of jealousy and I have to say to myself, 'Don't be a fool. What's the use of getting jealous of Winston?' "*64 By and large, however, the bonds between the two men were of an enduring nature: they were companions in arms, united by respect, affection and a strong

---

* Writing to his brother on March 13th, 1916 Lloyd George would describe Churchill as "a brilliant fellow without judgment which is equal to his fiery impulse. His steering gear is too weak for his horse-power."65

sense of humour. Such a partnership was not without its hazardous moments: very often, and especially after 1911, they clashed in acute disagreement. The element of rivalry was never far from the surface and, as the years slipped by, became steadily more apparent, but in the stormy years of 1908, 1909 and 1910 we see Lloyd George and Churchill joined together in what can only be described as a truly formidable combination.

(10)

In 1906 Baron Aloys von Aehrenthal had succeeded Goluchowski as Foreign Minister of the Austro-Hungarian Empire. An arrogant, ambitious and cunning man, intent upon re-establishing the authority of the Habsburgs in European affairs, he had observed with satisfaction the setback to German ambitions at the Algeciras Conference and felt that Austria-Hungary, hitherto regarded as a satellite of Germany, was now in a position to pursue a programme of her own. He was very anxious, at first, for improved relations with Russia, but was disappointed to find Isvolsky more intent on securing the friendship of Britain than that of Austria-Hungary. The Anglo-Russian agreements set the seal upon his dissatisfactions and, throwing caution to the winds, he resolved to use the discontents of the Near East to his own advantage.

Towards the end of 1907 Aehrenthal told the Sultan of Turkey, Abdul Hamid II, that the Mürzsteg programme—proposals for improving conditions in Macedonia which Russia and Austria-Hungary had been urging on the Sultan since 1903—need not be implemented if Austria-Hungary were allowed to build a railway through the Sandjak of Novi-Bazar (a part of the Ottoman Empire which had been under the military control of the Habsburgs since 1878) into Macedonia. The Sultan agreed to this proposal. Isvolsky, when he learned of it in February 1908, was extremely angry. Austria-Hungary, he felt, had broken an agreement made with Russia ten years previously whereby both Powers had pledged themselves not to disturb the *status quo* in the Balkans.

In order to understand the story which follows it is necessary to remember that the Ottoman Empire, extending from the Adriatic in the west to the Persian Gulf in the east, was generally regarded as tottering on its last legs. Neither Russia nor Austria-Hungary was anxious to see it actually collapse, but each of them was interested in obtaining whatever might be available in the way of choice pickings. Now that Aehrenthal had stolen a march on him Isvolsky gave serious consideration to the question of whether the balance might not be redressed by securing a revision of the Treaty of Berlin (concluded thirty years previously) so far as it related to the Straits of the Dardanelles and the Bosphorus which were closed to vessels of war. This meant that Russian warships had no access to the Mediterranean.* The Power chiefly responsible for this provision had been Britain, although it was one which had been readily supported by France, Germany and Austria-Hungary. Since 1905, however, the Russian fleet had been virtually non-existent, and Grey had seen no harm in telling Benckendorff on March 19th, 1907 that, in the event of an improvement in Anglo-Russian relations, "England must no longer make it a settled object of her policy to maintain the existing arrangement with regard to the passage of the Dardanelles."[66] Isvolsky was "highly gratified", and when King Edward VII, with Hardinge and Nicolson in attendance, met Nicolas II and Isvolsky at Reval in June 1908 he noted that Hardinge was also guardedly sympathetic to the idea of the Straits question being reviewed.

The Russian Foreign Minister had now got the bit between his teeth. Britain, the one Power which had consistently opposed Russia's attempts to secure control of the Straits throughout the nineteenth century, was at last ready to enter into fresh discussions on the subject. This was too good an opportunity to miss! He wrote, somewhat unwisely, to Aehrenthal on July 2nd suggesting that if Austria-Hungary supported Russia in her efforts to open the Straits Russia would agree to Austria-Hungary annexing the provinces of Bosnia and Herzegovina. The Austrian Foreign Minister was naturally very interested in this proposal: 1908 was the golden jubilee year of Franz Josef's reign and, in view of the set-backs which the Habsburg Empire had suffered during the past sixty years, it would be nice to commemorate it with at least one sparkling success. Bosnia and Herzegovina, while nominally part of the Turkish Empire, had been under Austro-Hungarian administration for thirty years and annexation would simply legalise a *de facto* situation. It would, moreover, be an opportunity for effectively crushing the organs of Serbian propaganda in these provinces.

The situation in the Near East was abruptly transformed by an unexpected event—the Young Turk revolution. This began on July 22nd at Resna and two days later the Sultan agreed to restore the "liberal" constitution of 1876. The forces of enlightened democracy, it seemed, had triumphed over those of benighted despotism and the Foreign Office in London was more or less jubilant. Grey thought it "marvellous" news and, while noting that "we must be careful not to give Russia the impression that we are reverting to the old policy of supporting Turkey as a barrier

---

* This stipulation had also formed part of the Treaty of Paris (1856) and the Treaty of London (1871).

against her," was anxious that nothing should be done to impede the reformers in their enormous task of liberalising the Ottoman Empire.

Isvolsky meanwhile decided that the best way of securing a revision of the 1878 treaty would be to pay personal visits to Rome, Paris, London and Berlin in order to ascertain the feelings of each of the chief Powers. It might even, perhaps, be possible to by-pass Austria-Hungary altogether and have the Straits opened without reference to the question of Bosnia and Herzegovina. At any rate, presumably regretting his letter of July 2nd, he did not intend to contact Aehrenthal until his tour was over. The Austro-Hungarian Foreign Minister, however, persuaded Isvolsky to meet him at the castle of Buchlau in Moravia at the outset of his journey. This meeting took place on September 15th, but what transpired has never been clearly established. The *quid pro quo* of the Straits and the annexations was certainly discussed and Aehrenthal later asserted that Isvolsky had agreed to Austria-Hungary going ahead with the annexations and had promised Russia's support. Isvolsky's story was that he had agreed in principle to the annexations but only as part of an overall revision of the Treaty of Berlin. It seems probable that Isvolsky made some very indiscreet statements and committed himself generally to a degree which he never afterwards dared to admit.

On October 3rd the Austro-Hungarian Ambassador in London, Count Mensdorff, presented Hardinge with a letter from Aehrenthal in which the latter announced that his Government intended to proclaim, very shortly, the annexations of Bosnia and Herzegovina. To compensate for this act, however, the Austro-Hungarians would withdraw altogether from the Sandjak of Novi-Bazar. Isvolsky, by this time, had reached Paris. He was apparently startled to learn of Aehrenthal's intentions and in a conversation with Bertie denied that there was any concerted agreement between himself and the Austro-Hungarian Foreign Minister. "From my interview with M. Isvolsky," reported Bertie, "I have the impression, I may say the conviction, that he did not quite tell me the truth, the whole truth and nothing but the truth. ... The probability is that Monsieur Isvolsky obtained promises from Baron d'Aehrenthal and M. Tittoni on the subject of the Straits and that he intended on his visit to Paris and London to prepare the ground for the acquiescence of France and England in Russia's desires in that question. He did not imagine that the Austro-Hungarian Government would proceed to carry out their projects without further consultation with the Russian Government. In this he was mistaken and deceived."[67]

Grey's initial reaction was one of anger. This was not lessened by

Bulgaria's formal renunciation, on October 5th, of her allegiance to the Sultan. The Ottoman Empire, it seemed, was being dismantled in theory as well as in fact: hitherto the fiction of its impregnability and independence had served to keep Balkan discontent at a minimum. Once it was acknowledged, however, that Turkish authority was nothing more than a sham, there was no telling what forces of chaos, anarchy and destruction would be let loose in the Near East. If Austria-Hungary and Bulgaria were to take advantage of Turkey's misfortunes, who could deny an equal right to Serbia, Montenegro, Albania or Greece? Who, moreover, could deny such a right to Russia? Angry protests were thus despatched to Vienna and Sofia, making it plain that Britain could not be a party to the violation of international treaties.

Isvolsky, striving in vain to secure French support for a revision of the Straits agreement, now found himself in an embarrassing position. The general belief that he had made some private arrangment with Aehrenthal about the annexations and that Austria-Hungary had simply jumped the gun did not improve the atmosphere at the Quai d'Orsay. His own Government, moreover, was furious, suspecting that he had sacrificed the interests of Serbia and other Balkan states in return for vague promises of support on the Straits question. Stolypin, the Russian Prime Minister, and his colleagues were not interested in the Straits, the opening of which could be of no practical use to them, but were very anxious indeed not to offend Slav susceptibilities. To save his face, therefore, Isvolsky proposed a conference of the signatories to the Treaty of Berlin. The agenda would include both the annexations and Bulgaria's declaration of independence: it might also include the question of the Straits.

The annexations came into effect on October 7th. By this time passions were running high and Austria-Hungary discovered, apparently to her surprise, that her actions had been none too well received by her neighbours. Opposition from France, Russia and Britain had no doubt been expected, but Germany was equally furious and Italy was far from pleased. The Young Turks themselves, however, had no desire for war and while expressing their formal indignation were chiefly concerned with securing adequate financial compensation. They were agreeable to the idea of an international conference, but did not want the question of the Straits to form part of the agenda.

To Isvolsky, who arrived in London on October 8th, Grey explained that Britain was not opposed in principle to the opening of the Straits but did not feel that this was the right time to seek a revision of the Treaty of Berlin. He also made it clear, moreover, that there was a vital distinction between the British and Russian interpretations of this subject: the Foreign Office would want the Straits opened to *all* warships and not simply to those of Russia.* Isvolsky, realising at last that he had misinterpreted Hardinge's vague comments at Reval, was very upset at this news and spoke of resigning at the earliest opportunity. His mission had been a failure. He had been duped by Aehrenthal. He was in disgrace with his colleagues at home and had no means of satisfying Russian public opinion. What point was there in going on? Grey and Hardinge made haste to rally the failing spirits of their visitor. They would, it was explained, do their best to support Russia over the question of the annexations and suggested that an agenda should be drawn up for the proposed conference. Isvolsky, heartened by this support, succeeded in drafting a programme which met with their approval. The Foreign Office had now reconciled itself to the new situation and Grey felt, as he wrote on October 16th, "that the wise course is for Turkey to give up what are purely points of form in return for a settlement which would give her some substantial pecuniary compensation."[69]

The policy of the Russian Government towards the annexations, it should be emphasised at this point, was largely determined by the attitude of Serbia. This tiny Slav state, now virtually surrounded by potential enemies, felt that she had the most to lose by the actions of Austria-Hungary and Bulgaria. She demanded territorial compensation and called up her reserves. Austria-Hungary, after complaining to the other Powers at this warlike activity, began to mobilise her own forces. Isvolsky urged moderation upon the Serbian Government but was obliged, at the same time, to ensure that their complaints received adequate attention. Had it not been for this Serbian activity it is probable that Russia would have accepted the annexations with no more than a token protest: she was in neither the mood nor the position to undertake a major war. Grey did not have much sympathy with Serbia, feeling that she was a trouble-maker and that her best policy, if she feared Austria-Hungary, was alliance with Turkey, but he kept these views to himself for the moment.

The Isvolsky who now made his way home to St Petersburg was scarcely recognisable as the man who had set forth so blithely on his travels only five weeks before. His hopes of securing the opening of the Straits to

---

* Grey had made this point clear at the outset, in both the conversation he had with Benckendorff on March 19th, 1907 and a memorandum which he had handed to the Russian Ambassador on May 1st, 1907. Sir Edward had pointed out, in the latter, that a memorandum which Isvolsky had presented to Nicolson on April 14th "makes no definite mention of the fact that the [British] proposal [of March 19th] contemplated the passage of the Dardanelles and the rest of the Straits being made available for other Powers as far as the entrance to the Black Sea on the same terms for all, although it is certainly implied."[68]

Russian warships had been shattered and he had allowed himself to be duped, not for the first time, by a man whom he henceforth regarded as his arch-enemy. At Berlin, moreover, a fresh shock awaited him: the Germans were "very stiff", telling him "practically nothing except that they were going to support Austria" and he received the general impression that they "were in distinctly ill-humour with regard to Russia and very much changed in their feelings towards her". The idea of an international conference, while not dismissed altogether, was not received with any great favour.[70]

(11)

Isvolsky's icy reception in Berlin owed something, at least, to the lingering resentment at the state visit which Edward VII had paid to the Czar at Reval five months before. That visit, together with one which the French President made to London at the end of May and another which he made to St Petersburg a few weeks later, formed for "thinking Germans", so Grey was informed by one of his correspondents on June 1st, 1908, "part and parcel of the same diplomatic drama,"[71] and Germany and Austria-Hungary were convinced from this time onwards that they were encircled by a "Triple Entente", Anglo-German relations underwent a further deterioration when it was learnt that Krupps had more than doubled their labour force since 1902 and had increased the size of their shipyards at Essen and Kiel by 30%. It was estimated that a German Dreadnought could now be completed in two-and-a-half years as opposed to the previous time of three-and-a-quarter, and the Admiralty calculated that the German naval strength could be two-thirds that of Great Britain by 1915.* "If the Germans continue to execute their naval programme at a rapid speed," wrote Grey on July 31st, "we shall certainly have to ask Parliament to vote a considerable increase to our expenditure: no Government of either party could avoid doing so. The justification and necessity for this increase, which would have to be openly avowed, would be the German expenditure. We have to take into account not only the German navy but also the German army. If the German fleet ever becomes superior to ours, the German army can conquer this country. There is no corresponding risk of this kind to Germany, for however superior our fleet was no naval victory would bring us any nearer to Berlin."[72]

On October 29th the *Daily Telegraph* intrigued its readers by an account

---

* There was also a growing suspicion that the collection of the necessary materials for the construction of Germany's capital ships, a formidable task in itself, was being carried out well in advance of the Reichstag's formal authorisation.

of an interview between the German Emperor and a certain Colonel Stuart Wortley which had taken place the previous November.* The purpose of its publications at this time was the desire to improve Anglo-German relations, but the means adopted to reach this goal were rather strange. The Kaiser declared that Germany was Britain's only true friend in Europe and in proof of this claimed that during the South African War he had not only refused to join France and Russia in going to the rescue of the Boer Republic but had actually sent Queen Victoria a plan of campaign for England to follow. There was also the usual pained denial of any sinister designs upon the supremacy of the Royal Navy: the German fleet was being enlarged in order to cope with any possible trouble in the Far East. These revelations, however, did not produce the anticipated effect: the initial astonishment of the British public soon gave way to mirth, and it speedily became apparent that the Kaiser had committed a personal blunder of the first magnitude. Bülow and his colleagues were far from amused, despite the fact that the text of the interview had been sent to the Wilhelmstrasse for approval before publication. "The German Emperor," wrote Grey on November 8th, "is ageing me; he is like a battleship with steam up and screws going but no rudder and he will run into something one day and cause a catastrophe. He has made a fool of Germany."73

As though to distract attention from this unfortunate episode, the Germans suddenly turned their spotlight upon France. Morocco, once again, provided the occasion for a crisis and there seemed, at one point, a strong likelihood (to British eyes, at any rate) of war. This latest incident had begun on September 25th when the French authorities in Casablanca, perturbed by the fact that there had been more than two hundred desertions from the Foreign Legion in the course of a few months, espied a group of men making their way towards a German tanker tied up in the harbour. Closer inspection revealed that six of the men, three of whom were German, were listed among those two hundred. A short skirmish then ensued, in the course of which the deserters were captured but at least one member of the escorting party, all of whom came from the German Consulate, was punched on the nose. This involved, as Hardinge remarked, "a somewhat complicated question of international law"74 and the German Government took a serious view of the matter. Schön, the new Foreign Minister, agreed with Jules Cambon on October 14th that the affair should be referred to international arbitration but Prince Radolin, the German Ambassador in Paris, informed the Quai d'Orsay two days later

* The Colonel had acted as host to the Kaiser at Highcliffe Castle near Bournemouth after the State visit to Windsor came to an end.

that his Government required an apology for the assault on the members of the consulate. This apology, however, was not forthcoming. Nothing happened for a couple of weeks then on November 1st, two days after the *Daily Telegraph* interview, Radolin presented a formal request for the release of the prisoners and again demanded an apology. Cambon refused to give way and pointed out that the dispute had already been referred to the Permanent Court of Arbitration at The Hague. France would do nothing until judgment had been given.

Tension mounted, especially in London. Another attempt was being made, it seemed, to test the strength of the *entente cordiale* and Grey warned McKenna on November 5th to keep the fleet ready in case things came to a head. The possibility of war between France and Germany was so real that, as the following letter shows, the Prime Minister felt obliged to take the leader of the Opposition into his confidence.

Balfour to Lansdowne, November 6th, 1908

Asquith asked me to speak to him last night after the House rose. He was evidently extremely perturbed about the European situation, which in his view was the gravest of which we have had any experience since 1870.

He said that, incredible as it might seem, the Government could form no theory of the German policy which fitted all the known facts except that they wanted war, and war at the present time clearly means much more than it did in 1870, as it would certainly involve Russia, Austria and the Near East—to say nothing of ourselves.

I observed that the almost incredible frivolity of the excuse for hostilities which the Germans had devised would shock the civilised world beyond expression and that it was difficult to see what Germany expected to gain by a war in which she must lose so much morally and was by no means certain to gain anything materially. Asquith's only answer to this objection was that the internal conditions of Germany were so unsatisfactory that they might be driven to the wildest adventures in order to divert national sentiment into a new channel. I said that, quite apart from the Entente, we should, as I understood it, be involved under treaty obligations if Germany violated Belgian territory. Asquith assented, and said that (as we all know) the Franco-German frontier is now so strong that the temptation to invade Belgium might prove irresistible.

He gave me no information and I believe had no information which is not in the newspapers, but I was very much struck by the pessimistic tone with which he spoke of the position. I told him he might count upon the Opposition in case of national difficulty—an attitude of which, I am confident, you and all my colleagues will approve.[75]

A Guildhall speech by Asquith on November 9th made it plain that, in the event of European upheaval, Britain would stand by her friends. It is doubtful whether this declaration did much to influence the course of events but the following day Germany agreed that the whole dispute, including the treatment of the members of the consulate, should go to arbitration.* One crisis, at any rate, was over, and the judgment of the court, given six months later, was so innocuous as to more or less satisfy both sides: the French were right to apprehend the deserters but the German Consulate was not altogether wrong to connive at their escape.

There were two interesting sequels, the first of which is best described in a letter from Grey to the British Ambassador in Paris.

Grey to Bertie, November 24th, 1908

Cambon came to see me today about nothing in particular and I took the opportunity of telling him what a favourable impression the French attitude during the Casablanca crisis had made here; I added that I thought it must also have made an impression in Germany. Cambon told me that the Germans were now saying that they had never asked for apologies from France. This was, of course, untrue, for the French had the German demand in writing. . . .

He then went on to say that he had heard from his Naval Attaché that we should be prepared for an informal discussion as to the form which naval co-operation should take if war broke out, just as there had been a discussion about military co-operation in 1905. I told him this was the first I had heard of any such idea. I had always assumed that our Admiralty had considered the matter and might even have spoken informally to the French Naval Attaché; but certainly no proposal had originated with me, the idea had not even been mentioned to me before.

Cambon then told me that Haldane, in the course of a conversation with some one connected with the French Embassy, had dropped a remark to the effect that what had been done as regards military matters in 1905 should be done now in regard to naval matters. Cambon explained to me that in the event of military co-operation it was well understood that the chief command should be with the French general; but on the sea the chief command would be ours and the French would like to know what we should ask of them in case of war.

I said I would speak to McKenna on the subject.[77]

In a footnote to this letter, evidently written a few hours later, Grey added that Haldane had been pressed by Repington, or some other unauthorised person, to raise the question of Anglo-French naval co-operation in the Cabinet. Haldane had replied that such matters were for the French Ambassador and the Foreign Secretary to discuss. In the event, no

---

* "The Franco-German row settled," wrote Lloyd George to his brother on November 10th. "So glad. A war now would be horrible and inevitably it would upset my Budget plans."[76]

H

more was said at this time about naval conversations but it is important to note that while the French had raised the question after, and not during, the Casablanca crisis and had, indeed, not made any requests at all for promises of assistance, Asquith and Grey had already reached the conclusion that they *would* come to the aid of France if events took a turn for the worse. The transformation of the *entente* into a military alliance was, in short, virtually complete.

The other sequel was the realisation by Britain, referred to in Balfour's letter to Lansdowne, that if Germany declared war on France her troops would probably march through Belgium in order to launch an attack from the best possible vantage point. This meant that the terms of the London Treaty of 1839, which guaranteed Belgium's neutrality, would have to be reconsidered and reinterpreted in the light of current conditions. Grey therefore posed the following question and passed it to Eyre Crowe for comment: "How far would England's liability under the Treaty guaranteeing the neutrality of Belgium be affected if (1) Belgium acquiesced in a violation of her neutrality; (2) if the other guaranteeing Powers or some of them acquiesced?"

Crowe replied in a memorandum dated November 15th. So far as the first part of the question was concerned, he ruled that the neutrality of Belgium was not simply a Belgian interest. If, say, Belgium allowed German troops to cross her territory during a Franco-German war, France and Holland would both be entitled to call upon Britain to make good her guarantee that Belgium should remain perpetually neutral. "It seems to me," he concluded, "that only on the assumption that all the other guaranteeing Powers, and also Belgium herself, acquiesced in the violation of neutrality, would Great Britain be absolved from her liability. Even then, of course, she would retain her *right* to oppose the violation." On the second part of the question, Crowe reached the not unreasonable conclusion that "the acquiescence of one or more of the guaranteeing Powers in a violation of the neutrality of Belgium, protested against by Belgium herself, does not absolve the other guaranteeing Powers from the obligation to make good their guarantee."[78]

Hardinge, after reading this memorandum, agreed that Britain was still liable for the maintenance of Belgian neutrality but argued that much would depend upon Britain's policy at the time and the character of the violation. "Supposing," he wrote, "that France violated the neutrality of Belgium in a war against Germany, it is in present circumstances doubtful whether England or Russia would move a finger to maintain Belgian neutrality, while if the neutrality were violated by Germany it is probable that the converse would be the case." Grey contented himself with noting that Crowe's memorandum and Hardinge's comment summed up the situation very well.[79]

(12)

Another result of the Casablanca affair was a decision as to the actual manner in which Britain would intervene on the Continent in the event of a Franco-German war. That such a decision had not been formally reached before this date is little short of fantastic, and is only to be explained by the fact that an astonishing lack of co-ordination had been allowed to develop between the army and the navy.* The task of bridging this gap ought, in theory, to have been carried out by the Committee of Imperial Defence, a body set up by Balfour in 1904, but under Campbell-Bannerman it had lapsed into relative obscurity and was not restored to its former key position until the latter's departure from office.†

On January 6th 1906 a group of senior officers at the War Office had agreed that "any military co-operation on the part of the British army, if taken at the outset of war, must take the form either of an expedition to Belgium [assuming that Belgian neutrality had been violated] or of direct participation in the defence of the French frontier."[81] Huguet, when consulted, confirmed that "direct participation" would be preferred, and after the first military discussions had taken place the British told their French counterparts on January 22nd that, if called upon to intervene, Britain would mobilise an army of 105,000 men in fifteen days and despatch it to France.‡[82]

Clemenceau, who became Prime Minister of France in October 1906, was none too happy about Britain's ability to carry out such an undertaking. He paid a visit to England the following April and urged upon Grey the need for the British army to be in a state of readiness and, if possible, enlarged: Germany might declare war at any time and the failure of Britain to intervene at the outset could be a decisive factor. Haldane, whom he also saw, did his best to convince him that Britain's strategical position as the island centre of a scattered Empire was quite different from that of France. Clemenceau, however, was not impressed. "As things are

---

* Personal animosity between Haldane and Fisher had not helped matters: Fisher regarded Haldane as a "soapy Jesuit" while Haldane, rather unwisely, made no secret of his support for Beresford and other critics of the First Sea Lord.

† Sinclair, writing to the Prime Minister on January 8th, 1907, had described it as "a dangerous weapon, which is in the hands of the services to bully the Cabinet."[80]

‡ This did not accord with Grierson's earlier calculations (see page 187) that mobilisation would take two months and the actual transportation of the troops a further thirty-two days.

today," he told H. W. Steed in August, "you are hopelessly unprepared. Even if you could find the men you would have neither the arms nor the ammunition for them to use. You could smash the German fleet, which would make a great hole in the water, but in 1870 the fleet did not exist—and that did not prevent the Prussians from entering Paris."[83]

Fisher was meanwhile pursuing schemes of his own. At the time of the Algeciras Conference he had sturdily refused to take the French naval attaché into his confidence, beyond giving him a general assurance that the British fleet would be ready if the worst came to the worst, and he also refused to co-operate in the formulation of any War Office plans for transporting an expeditionary force to France. The Royal Navy, he felt, had something better to do than act as a mere ferry service, and he devoted his odd moments to elaborating a plan of campaign which he had favoured since the autumn of 1905. This was, briefly, that the navy would land small detachments of troops at points on the Baltic coast (an idea which had already been considered but firmly rejected by the War Office) but would otherwise be engaged in action on the high seas.

On October 22nd 1908 the Committee of Imperial Defence rejected Fisher's scheme and accepted the proposals put forward by the War Office. "Their conclusion," Asquith informed the King, "was that the idea of a diversion in the Baltic did not appear to have anything to commend it from a military point of view; and that the direct support of the French army offered a better prospect of useful result. In their view the presence in the field, side by side with French troops, of a British army would infuse into the former that moral confidence which they so suddenly and completely lost in 1870."[84]

Fisher accepted his defeat with a bad grace. At a joint meeting of the C.I.D. and the Cabinet on December 3rd he reluctantly agreed that the navy would be able to ferry 120,000 British troops to France, but on being pressed for further comments broke into a violent diatribe against the whole idea of an expeditionary force fighting in the field. Beyond the garrisoning of Antwerp, he declared, Britain should confine her military activity to lightning raids on the German coast and the recovery of Heligoland. He worked himself up into a wholesale condemnation of the War Office and of Haldane in particular, at which point Asquith remarked that they had better adjourn.[85] The relative merits of the two schemes were not discussed again by the Committee of Imperial Defence until August 1911, by which time some measure of co-ordination between the Admiralty and the War Office on the question of transporting troops to France had finally been achieved.

(13)

On November 10th, 1908 the Russian Ambassador called on Grey and, after describing the cool reception which Isvolsky had received in Berlin, announced that he was going to be "very indiscreet", a warning which may have reminded Sir Edward of the conversation he had had with Cambon in January 1906. What action, Benckendorff asked, would Britain take if a crisis arose in the Balkans and Germany supported Austria-Hungary? Grey replied that he could say nothing on this matter without the authorisation of the Cabinet, and "in all these questions it was impossible to come to a decision beforehand; so much depended upon how the quarrel came and who was the aggressor."[86] He did not, in fact, believe that war in the Balkans was imminent, but this was not a view shared by other observers. Both Serbia and Montenegro were mobilising and were simply awaiting, it seemed, a convenient moment to force the issue. Austria-Hungary was also making military preparations and Aehrenthal, on November 18th, rejected Isvolsky's proposals for a conference and declared that he could not agree to discussion of the annexations or to territorial compensation for other Balkan states at the expense of the Habsburg Empire. The prospects of an early settlement of the dispute rapidly receded from this time onwards: Bülow told Sir Edward Goschen, the new British Ambassador in Berlin, that it was a matter of indifference to the German Government whether a conference took place or not and suggested that Britain should persuade Turkey (who still wanted financial compensation for the loss of her provinces) to adopt a more reasonable attitude.

Sir Fairfax Cartwright, Goschen's successor in Vienna, saw Aehrenthal on December 11th and urged him to come to terms with Turkey as soon as possible. Aehrenthal replied that he was willing to do so but jibbed at the idea of financial compensation. As for Serbia, his patience was fast reaching its limits: Britain and Russia had encouraged the pretensions of this tiny Slav state and the British Press had been especially culpable in this respect. Cartwright suggested that war with Serbia would surely lead to conflict with Russia, at which Aehrenthal replied that he knew Russia like his pocket and felt sure that she was not in a position to go to war. The Austrian Foreign Minister was, of course, on firm ground, since it was now certain that Bülow would support him, whatever the consequences. For the moment, therefore, Isvolsky could do nothing more than restrain Serbia, curb the indignation of his colleagues and continue to press Austria-Hungary to agree to a conference. Russia had, in fact, lost the initiative and Britain, though in favour of a conference and anxious to secure an equitable settlement for Turkey's sake, was not prepared to play a leading role in this drama.

(14)

1908 ended as it had begun, with alarm in the Admiralty and Foreign Office at the rate of Germany's shipbulding. McKenna, in response to a request from Grey, carried out a detailed investigation into the subject and found that the money so far allocated for the construction of the four ships of the 1908–9 programme was much greater than the sums allocated to the vessels of the 1906–7 programme over a corresponding period. This must mean, he concluded, one of two things or possibly both of them: first, that German battleships were being constructed in a much shorter time; secondly, that they were going to be bigger than originally announced. This information, taken in conjunction with the increase of Krupps' capacity and labour force and rumours of acceleration, drove him to the conclusion that Britain's own naval construction must be speeded up, regardless of cries of protest from the Liberal rank and file. "I have no doubt whatever," he wrote to Grey on December 30th, 1908, "that Germany means to build up to the full extent of her capacity. The business firms must be expecting this or they would never have laid out the enormous sums they must have done this year in plant. Moreover, the gain to Germany in building up to approximate equality with us, if she can, is obviously great in the event either of war or future negotiations for the limitation of armaments. . . . If by any spurt Germany can once catch us up we have no longer any such superior building capacity as would ensure our supremacy."[87]

These conclusions were destined, as we shall see, to have a profound effect upon British politics in 1909.

CHAPTER TWELVE

DOMESTIC AFFAIRS, JANUARY–DECEMBER 1909

(1)

The year 1909 must be regarded as a turning-point in the history of the last Liberal Governments. In 1906, after a radiant beginning, the new Ministry had stumbled into a quagmire of difficulties from which it could find no easy escape: the Session of 1907 had marked time, while that of 1908 had witnessed a growing sense of frustration, impatience and bewilderment among the Liberal Party and its supporters. By the end of its third year of office the Government's popularity was at a very low ebb, with mounting unemployment, a decline in overseas trade, unrest in Ireland, impotence in domestic legislation and the unrelenting pressure of Anglo-German naval rivalry as the problems with which it had to grapple. The conflict with the House of Lords overshadowed everything and Asquith's speech of December 11th, 1908, for all its warlike spirit, was generally recognised as having been little more than whistling in the dark.* For the next few months the Ministry's only policy could be "to wait and see", since its plans for the future depended upon the success or failure of the Budget.† Granting, therefore, that the Session of 1909 produced a decisive change in the Government's fortunes, it must be recognised that this was as much by luck as judgment: splendid improvisation was the keynote of the proceedings, and what the Ministry hoped to accomplish in January 1909 was very different from what had actually been achieved by the time it went to the country in January 1910.

Parliament was opened on February 15th. From the outset it was clear that the Budget would be the most important measure of the Session and

* It did not appear, from other speeches made by Ministers at this time, that there was any clear-cut policy for the future. Churchill (January 13th) declared that reform of the Lords would be the issue at the next general election, while Crewe, five days later, contented himself with echoing Asquith's statement. Masterman (February 1st) argued that no future Liberal Government could take office unless limitations were imposed on the Second Chamber.

† Asquith informed the King (January 26th) that "the main business of the year must . . . be of necessity the Budget" but that it was hoped to avoid an autumn session.[1]

the King's Speech dwelt upon the unavoidable increase in national expenditure resulting from the old age pensions scheme and the forthcoming Navy Estimates.* The year's programme included an Irish Land Bill, the Housing and Town Planning Bill held over from the previous Session and (as a sop to the little band of Welsh Nationalists) the disestablishment of the Church in Wales. Other measures would deal with labour exchanges, wage boards for "sweated" industries, parliamentary elections and registration in London and inequalities in old age pensions. The Report of the Poor Law Commission, which had appeared a few days before, was stated to be under consideration.

Nothing was said about the conflict with the House of Lords. Asquith, when asked why he was not following up his speech of December 11th with a bill embodying the resolutions of 1907, replied that this was not the appropriate time to introduce such a measure. The Government was committed to specific tasks in the present Session and he was not prepared to let the peers choose the time of dissolution. MacDonald supported Asquith on this point and the Liberals reconciled themselves to a further postponement of constitutional reform. The Irish, however, were far from satisfied: Redmond told Lloyd George on February 17th that they were prepared to go into opposition unless the Government gave some clear indication of its desire to press ahead with Home Rule. Lloyd George returned a noncommittal reply but on February 26th Redmond noted, with reference to a forthcoming by-election, that the Liberal candidate had been authorised to say that he was "strongly of the opinion that Home Rule should be a leading issue at the next general election."[2] With this assurance they were forced, for the moment, to be content.

Churchill was responsible for piloting two measures of major importance through the Commons during this Session. The first of these was the Trade Boards Bill, introduced on March 24th, which proposed that trade boards, concerned with fixing and enforcing a minimum wage rate, should be established in those industries (such as tailoring and lace-making) where the workers were not sufficiently organised for their own protection. The second was the Labour Exchanges Bill, introduced on May 20th, which proposed that exchanges should be established in all parts of the country. Both schemes, which owed much to the Webbs, received a smooth passage through the two Houses.†

The most controversial measure of the whole Session, apart from the

* For the dispute in the Cabinet at this time over the Navy Estimates for 1909–10 see page 251 et seq.

† W. H. Beveridge, a protégé of the Webbs, was appointed the first director of the labour exchanges.

Budget itself, was the Irish Land Bill. This was designed to broaden the Act of 1903, which enabled labourers to purchase their holdings with the assistance of Government subsidies, by proposing that the subsidies should be enlarged and that landlords should be compelled to accept Government stock at 92 as well as cash. The Unionists reacted predictably at the idea of compulsion and alarm was displayed at the thought of an all-powerful peasantry. The Bill's passage through the Commons was far from smooth and it was not until August 27th that the Committee Stage came to an end, much time having been wasted by the discussion of minor points and useless divisions. The Third Reading was carried on September 17th, but drastic amendments were made by the Upper House. Leaving aside the financial and non-controversial clauses, twenty-four of the remaining thirty-seven were struck out, nine altered beyond recognition and twelve new ones added. In this mangled state the Irish Land Bill was returned to the Lower House and the Government decided, albeit with reluctance, that half a loaf was no doubt better than none.

On April 21st Asquith re-enacted his rôle of 1894 by introducing a Welsh Disestablishment Bill into the Commons. The main purpose of this measure, which no one expected the Upper House to pass, was to satisfy the Welsh Nonconformists of the Government's sympathy with their plight. There was no Second Reading owing to lack of time: the Government abandoned the Bill while stating that it would receive pride of place in their legislation for 1910.

On the afternoon of Thursday, April 29th, in a speech lasting more than four hours, Lloyd George introduced his first Budget into the House of Commons. It was not one of his better parliamentary performances: he was noticeably ill at ease and his voice, after he had spoken for two hours, became so hoarse that at Balfour's suggestion the House adjourned for thirty minutes in order that he might recover. Members listened in mounting bewilderment to an interminable mass of calculations, arguments and conclusions until, at length, their exhaustion almost matched that of the speaker himself. Only the most perfunctory criticisms could be made by the time he had finished and, the sitting over, they dispersed in relief. No one quite understood the significance of what had been said: only in retrospect did it become a great parliamentary occasion.

(2)

There are three points about the "People's Budget" of 1909 that need to be emphasised: first, in a very real sense it was unavoidable; secondly, its provisions were not so revolutionary as its opponents maintained and, thirdly, it was not deliberately designed to invite rejection by the Upper House. Once these points are fully appreciated the events which follow can be seen in their true perspective.

To begin with, therefore, we must remember that it had long been evident that the Finance Bill of 1909–10 would mark a new departure in the sphere of Free Trade economics. The increased naval expenditure, more than any other single item, was responsible for this, but an inaccurate estimate of the national income for 1908–9 had produced a deficit of £714,000, while the provision for old age pensions had been so inadequate that a supplementary grant of £910,000 had to be voted in March. It was calculated that, if the existing structure of taxation remained unchanged, a further deficit of £15,762,000 would result in the year that lay ahead. The estimated expenditure for 1909–10 was £164,152,000 and, in addition to the sums allocated for old age pensions and the navy, £170,000 would be required for the establishment of labour exchanges, £20,000 for national development in respect of roads, railways, docks and agriculture, and £50,000 for other purposes. All in all, assuming that recourse was not made to new sources of revenue, the estimated deficit would be at least £16,102,000.

Despite Lloyd George's repudiation, on January 30th, of his "bad jest" concerning henroosts, the Government had been almost at its wits' end to discover the means whereby fresh revenue might be obtained. Protective duties were unthinkable and even the most reluctant members of the Cabinet were at length convinced that the only answer to their problem was to launch an attack upon those sections of the community, principally represented by the peers, landlords and brewers, who could best afford to contribute something extra towards the national income. In this sense, therefore, the provisions of the 1909 Budget were unavoidable, although it is doubtful whether Lloyd George ever suffered loss of sleep from what Cromwell, in vaguely similar circumstances, is said to have described as "cruel necessity". Two birds could be killed with one stone, since the re-establishment of the country's finances on a sound basis would serve as a pretext for securing some of the Liberal Party's most cherished objectives in regard to licensing and land. Yet it must be admitted that the proposals which finally evolved as a result of this strategy were not so ruthless as they could have been: *The Times* of April 30th actually described them as "unadventurous" in the sense that no fresh ground had been broken.

The proposals fell into five categories, the first dealing with taxes on cars, petrol, spirits and tobacco, the second with income taxes, the third with death duties, the fourth with licensing duties and the fifth with the land.

The provisions of the first category were comparatively uncontroversial: the tax on cars throughout the United Kingdom would be on an increased scale of annual gradation, and the yield from this source, together with a uniform tax of £1 on motor cycles, was estimated at £410,000. A tax of 3*d*. per gallon was imposed upon petrol, which would produce £340,000 during the current year and an additional £35,000 thereafter. The existing duty on spirits would be raised by 3*s*. 9*d*. a gallon, yielding £1,600,000 for the first year, while the duty on unmanufactured tobacco, together with an equivalent duty on cigarettes and cigars, would be increased from 3*s*. to 3*s*. 8*d*. a pound, giving £1,900,000 for the first year and £2,250,000 for the next.

We now come to the second category. For earned annual incomes below £2,000 the tax would remain at 9*d*. in the pound; for those between £2,000 and £3,000 it would be 1*s*. and for those at present liable to 1*s*. the new rate would be 1*s*. 2*d*. On incomes less than £500 there would be a special rebate of £10 on every child below the age of sixteen. The additional yield was calculated at £3,000,000. A new super-tax of 6*d*. would be imposed on incomes exceeding £5,000, taking effect from the level of £3,000: £90 million became liable to this charge, which would yield £500,000 during the current year and £2,300,000 thereafter.

Death duties, which constituted the third category, were readjusted on a new scale, ranging from 4% on estates valued at £5,000 to 15% on those worth more than £1 million: this would raise £2,550,000 in the current year, £4,200,000 in the next and £4,400,000 thereafter. The settled estates duty would be raised from 1% to 2% amounting to £50,000 in the current year and an annual £375,000 from then onwards. The legacy and succession duty of 3% would be increased to 5% in some cases and 10% in others: this would eventually produce £2,150,000 but only £1,300,000 at first. Gifts of property would come within the scope of death duties if the donor died within five years of the transaction. An increase in the stamp duty on conveyances of sale, together with similar impositions in the same field, would raise £650,000 during the current financial year and £1,450,000 thereafter.

The most provocative of Lloyd George's proposals were those concerned with licensing and the land. The licensing duties that he contemplated would amount to 50% of the annual value of licensed premises, the latter to be determined by reference to the size of the local population. They would range from £5 in areas where the population did not exceed

5,000 to £35 in the metropolis. A new scale of charges for public house licences, starting at a minimum of £3. 10s. 0d. where the population was less than 2,000 and ending at a maximum of £23. 10s. 0d. when it went beyond 100,000, would also come into operation, although hotels and restaurants need not pay the full rates. A duty of 3d. in the pound was to be imposed on liquor sold in clubs. All in all, the extra revenue derived from licensing duties would be £2,600,000.

The land taxes were few but comprehensive. There was to be one of 20% on unearned increments, payable when land was sold and when it changed hands at death. Secondly, there would be a levy of one-halfpenny in the pound on the capital value of undeveloped land and undeveloped minerals, and thirdly a 10% reversion duty on any benefit accruing to a lessor at the termination of a lease. Finally, there was a mineral rights duty of 1s. in the pound. These would, it was calculated, produce £500,000 during the current year and a much greater yield thereafter.*

There was also to be a reduction of £3 million in the sum annually paid to the Sinking Fund. The total estimated revenue thus amounted to £162,590,000 while the total estimated expenditure was £162,102,000, leaving a balance of £488,000.

Seen in retrospect, the provisions of the 1909 Budget do not appear particularly startling. The land taxes, for example, were a logical step forward from Gladstone's succession duty of 1853 and Harcourt's death duties of 1894. Income tax did not exceed 1s. 8d. in the pound, although super-tax was certainly an innovation. The taxes on cars, petrol, spirits and tobacco were irksome but straightforward, while the land duties were destined to produce so little that they would later be repealed by Lloyd George's own administration in 1919. The licensing duties naturally enough enraged the brewers, but their fury owed more to the partisan spirit in which the duties had been conceived than to grounds of hardship. From a financial viewpoint, in short, the proposals were neither outrageous nor revolutionary.

It is in the realm of constitutional history that the 1909 Budget makes its greatest impact, although it can be argued that it merely accelerated a change in the balance of political power which was, in any case, inevitable. This brings us to our third and final point, namely that it was not designed with the deliberate intention of inviting rejection by the Upper House.

Asquith's speech of December 11th, 1908, in which he had suggested

---

* "I knew the land taxes would not produce much," Lloyd George told Riddell in May 1912. "I only put them in the Budget because I could not get a valuation without them." They were intended, therefore, as a necessary preliminary to his scheme for land reform.[3]

that the forthcoming Finance Bill might prove "a partial solvent of what, under our existing constitutional conditions, would otherwise be insoluble problems," had led several newspapers to the conclusion that the Government hoped the Lords would refuse to pass it. The Ministry would then be able to dissolve Parliament and appeal to the country for a mandate with which to reform the Second Chamber. It is probable, of course, that some such consideration had arisen at Cabinet discussions, but in the highest degree unlikely that policy would be fashioned on such a conjecture. All available evidence points to the conclusion that rejection was neither expected nor, perhaps, desired.*

The Government assumed that the convention prevailing since the seventeenth century, namely that the contents of money bills were the sole concern of the Commons, would deter the peers from tampering with the Budget and thus secure the unimpeded passage of legislation that would otherwise have been waylaid en route by their lordships. To suggest that the Liberals laid a trap for the Unionist peers is to credit the members of Asquith's administration with a remarkable degree of prescience and the Lords with a remarkable degree of stupidity. Not until the Budget had been introduced into the Commons and the idea of rejection had become more than a faint and fantastic possibility did the Government seriously reconsider its tactics.

It has sometimes been argued that if Asquith, and not Lloyd George, had been entrusted with piloting the Finance Bill through the Commons the course of events might have been very different. There is, perhaps, a smattering of truth in this assertion, but it must be remembered that the actual contents of the Bill could not have varied to any great extent from those now put forward. Moreover, the notion of a demagogic Chancellor of the Exchequer deliberately inciting the House of Lords to commit political suicide is one that needs to be dismissed at the outset: if Lloyd George's conduct during 1909 is carefully studied it will be seen that for the first six months of the year he behaved in a curiously subdued and moderate manner. He had, of course, made his reputation as a political firebrand and in private he was still happily elated at the pretty kettle of fish the Lords would soon receive, but in public he went out of his way to disclaim any vindictive spirit and showed, in the Commons, a conciliatory and sympathetic disposition towards those who disagreed with his plans. He tried hard not to give unnecessary offence and it can be reasonably concluded that he was, until the summer, acting under instructions to do

---

* "I learn that Lansdowne in private utterly scouts the suggestion that the Lords will reject the Budget Bill," Churchill had written to Asquith on December 26th, 1908.[4]

nothing which might jeopardise the safe passage of the Budget through the Upper House. Only when it became certain that the Lords were seriously considering rejection did Asquith release the brake on his activities: from then onwards, as will be seen, he became the dominating figure in British politics.

Some consideration must also be given to the question of how great a part the Chancellor of the Exchequer actually played in drafting the provisions of the Finance Bill. It can certainly be agreed that he was responsible for the general outline of the measure, but when it came to details his grasp was not so sure. Austen Chamberlain informed his father, in a letter dated May 9th, that on the night of the Bill's introduction into the Commons a Unionist member told Haldane that the Chancellor read his speech like one who did not understand what it meant. "Of course he doesn't," exclaimed Haldane. "Why, for months we've been trying to make him understand clause X and he can't!"[5] Lucy Masterman, on May 31st, noted that her husband had been "helping Ll. G. with the land clauses of the Budget and has got very fond of him in the process though he finds him very erratic and unmethodical as a colleague. His weakness is inattention to detail. Very soon it came about that the officials and C made the land clauses without consulting him at all."[6] Masterman himself, writing to Gladstone on July 8th, remarked that "it seems that I am some use to Ll.G. in these mazes of technicalities, the details of which he does not greatly concern himself with."[*7] These comments can, no doubt, be accepted as substantially correct, but they do not really amount to much. Lloyd George did not, after all, claim to be a great financial expert: he was content to plan the main strategy and leave the details to others, which is just as it should have been. It is doubtful, in any case, whether more than a very few members of Parliament, among whom Haldane himself cannot be included, understood all the intricacies of the Finance Bill, nor is this surprising. Among the Unionists, Sir Frederick Banbury appears to have been alone in his comprehension of the various provisions. The general character of the measure, in short, was determined by Lloyd George,

---

* Masterman was even more forthcoming in a letter to Gladstone written in February 1910. "[Your] warning against Lloyd George's domination," it runs, "is a silent reproach against neglect of H[ome] O[ffice] duties. When I came here [i.e., the Home Office] in July H.H.A. specially asked me to go on with the Budget work. It was the hardest bit of work I have ever done in my life (and I've worked pretty hard!) and all for nought and nothing of reward. I would have 'chucked' it a dozen times if I could: but I was in the toils: and I really believed that the thing would have been even more chaotic if I had withdrawn. . . . It was all drudgery over the Finance Bill and the Development Bill: only those who have worked intimately with our gallant [?] friend can know how much it means to be in possession of detail when dealing with a man who never reads an official paper and allows his mind to revolve round big questions, to disregard of details altogether."[8]

except where naval and military expenditure were concerned, and the Cabinet allowed him a free hand to do what he thought best.*

(3)

Several days elapsed before the Opposition and the Press were able to see the Budget in perspective and the early attacks upon it were somewhat cursory. The only immediate objection which Austen Chamberlain could raise, during the short debate that followed Lloyd George's speech, related to the establishment of the new Development Grant at the expense of the Sinking Fund. "It is certainly a 'great' budget", he wrote to his father the following day, ". . . but I do not profess to have got its cumulative effect or even its separate provisions clearly in my mind as yet."[10] Redmond denounced the increased taxes on whisky and tobacco which would, he argued, fall more heavily on Ireland than the rest of the United Kingdom: he divided the House on this issue, being defeated by 281 to 120. From the outset, therefore, the Nationalists were forced into reluctant opposition to the Finance Bill. The Labour Party welcomed the measure as a whole, claiming that it contained several ideas which Snowden had put forward the previous year, but was not altogether uncritical. "Budget going strong—overwhelmed with congratulations," wrote Lloyd George to his brother on May 1st. "Prime Minister delighted with its reception. The most extraordinary thing is the way the City have taken it. F. E. Smith told me the Lords are not such fools as to throw it out. 'Do you think they are mad?' he said to me."[11] This, however, was the calm before the storm.

The change came on May 3rd. Lansdowne, in the Upper House, denounced the Budget as a monument of reckless finance, while Unionist speakers in the Commons condemned it as a socialistic measure. The licensing taxes were declared to be both vindictive and unnecessary and the property taxes were criticised on the grounds that they would encourage evasion and force capital to flee the country.

The Committee and Report stages of the Budget Resolutions lasted from May 10th until May 26th. The Finance Bill was then introduced into the Commons and the House adjourned the following day for the Whitsun recess, which lasted six days. The Second Reading of the Bill was carried on June 8th, a motion for rejection having been defeated by 366 to 209, and on June 21st the Committee Stage began. It soon became clear

---

* The only occasion when he was overruled in the Cabinet seems to have been on March 19th. Asquith, reporting the day's proceedings to the King, stated that the Cabinet had "rejected a proposal submitted by the Chancellor of the Exchequer to tax the ground rents of land built upon [because] . . . it would involve an interference with existing contracts."[9]

that the Government had no ordinary battle on its hands. The Unionists, remembering the Irish debates of the early 1880s, seized every opportunity to obstruct, disrupt and force divisions, opposing the various proposals down to the last minute detail and extending the debates into the early hours of the morning. The Government had no alternative but to use the closure with increasing frequency. Even with this weapon at its command progress was unbelievably slow. Clause One was not carried until June 29th; Clause Two not until July 13th. After this there was a slight acceleration: Clause Ten had been reached by July 20th. In the space of five weeks there were eleven sittings which lasted well into the following day. "As I foresaw from the beginning," wrote Lloyd George to his brother on July 12th, "we must guillotine the Bill to get it through. We cannot keep up these all night sittings. . . . Guillotine means going to bed regularly and getting your Bill through. The Prime Minister is for it, but I shall have trouble with the rest of my colleagues who hate the Budget and would very much like to see it killed by time, but they won't, as the party is behind me."[12]

The battle was not confined within the walls of Westminster. The Unionists, now in crusading mood, were gratified to find both Rosebery and Rothschild entering the lists against the Government, and towards the end of June they launched a Budget Protest League under Long's presidency. Tariff Reformers, however, were disconcerted to find that Long, presumably acting on Balfour's instructions, had advised members of the League to curb their enthusiasm for Imperial Preference and to concentrate on denouncing the land taxes. The attack was thus delivered from what was, in effect, little more than a narrow class basis. Neither Lansdowne nor Balfour seem to have felt, at this time, that the Upper House should reject the measure and on July 16th, at the annual dinner of the National Union of Conservative and Constitutional Associations, Lansdowne declared that the House of Lords would "do its duty" (i.e., accept the Budget) but not "without wincing".

The Liberals established a Budget League, with Churchill as its president, since it was by no means certain that the Budget had yet captured the imagination of the people.* The cries of protest which rang out from so many quarters rather suggested that it had not, yet vested interests were inevitably in a position to make more noise than anyone else and Churchill, speaking in Edinburgh on July 17th, was able to cite the "silence and dignity" of the working classes in accepting the new taxes as opposed to

---

* Of the 14 contested by-elections which the Liberals fought in 1909, they retained 8 seats, lost 3 to the Unionists and 1 to Labour and failed to capture 2 from the Unionists.

the behaviour of the nobility. He also, however, announced that Parliament would be promptly dissolved for a general election if the Lords were so foolish to reject the Budget, an indiscretion for which he was severely reprimanded by Asquith when the Cabinet met four days later.

(4)

The Chancellor of the Exchequer, it should be remembered, had so far played a very minor part in public controversy over the Budget. In the Commons his conduct in debate had been firm, dignified and restrained. Apart from a speech at a luncheon on June 24th and another at the Banker's Dinner on July 16th, where he spoke solely on technical details of the Finance Bill, he had made no public orations. The popular demagogue, it seemed, had at last been tamed. King Edward VII, endulging in a long talk with his Chancellor on March 3rd, had found him to be an unexpectedly courteous and good-humoured individual. The royal notes of expostulation during the past three years had evidently not been in vain: yet another would-be revolutionary had been transformed into a responsible Minister of the Crown.* On the evening of July 30th, however, addressing an audience of 4,000 Londoners at The Edinburgh Castle in Limehouse, Lloyd George did more than anyone else to raise the temperature of the Unionists to fever pitch: henceforth it was war to the bitter end, with no holds barred.

The term 'Limehouse' has, with the passage of more than half a century, hardened into political currency as denoting a particular kind of invective: savage, colourful, virulent and prophetic, appealing to the best and worst instincts of an audience. Not since the cry of "Wilkes and liberty!" had popular passion been aroused to such an extent, or so the story goes, and it was admittedly somewhat unusual to find a member of His Majesty's Government endeavouring to publicise ultra-revolutionary doctrines. Yet, when one studies the text of this seemingly outrageous speech, the first reaction is one of disappointment. Instead of the ravings of a Danton or a Trotsky there is simply a carefully reasoned defence of the Budget, based on straightforward principles of equity, together with some mischievous digs at the landlord, brewer and peer. It is only when one considers the effect such a speech must have had in the Britain of 1909, together with the atmosphere in which it was delivered, that some idea emerges of just how great a bombshell it actually was. It is certainly not too much to conclude

* Towards the end of the year the King again discussed the Budget with his Chancellor. He suggested abandoning the land taxes and replacing them with a tax on sugar or tea, a suggestion which the Chancellor politely explained would not be acceptable to the Government or its supporters.[13]

that it was, from this time onwards, that feeling in the Unionist camp hardened to such an extent that rejection of the Budget ceased to be a faint possibility and became a course of action from which there could be no escape.

The gentlemen of England, he began, had demanded an enormous increase in naval expenditure. The Government had obliged by commencing the construction of eight Dreadnoughts, each costing two million pounds, and had then sent the hat round. "We sent it round amongst workmen, and the miners and weavers of Derbyshire and Yorkshire, and the Scotchmen of Dumfries who, like all their countrymen, know the value of money. They all dropped in their coppers. Then we went to Belgravia—and there has been such a howl ever since that it has wellnigh deafened us!" He mentioned old age pensions and outlined the Government's plans for national insurance, but the greater part of his speech was devoted to the new land taxes and valuation proposals. "Not far from here," he continued, "not so many years ago, between the Lea and the Thames, you had hundreds of acres of land which was not very useful, even for agricultural purposes. In the main it was a sodden marsh. The commerce and the trade of London increased under Free Trade, the tonnage of your shipping went up by hundreds of thousands of tons and by millions; labour was attracted from all parts of the country to cope with all the trade and business which was done here. What happened? There was no housing accommodation. This port of London became overcrowded and the population overflowed. This was the opportunity of the owners of the marsh. All that land became valuable building land, and land which used to be rented at £2 or £3 an acre has been selling within the last few years at £2,000 an acre, £3,000 an acre, £6,000 an acre, £8,000 an acre. Who created that increment? Who made that golden swamp? Was it the landlord? Was it his energy? Was it his brains? . . . It was purely the combined efforts of all the people engaged in the trade and commerce of the port of London—trader, merchant, shipowner, dock labourer, workman—everybody except the landlord. . . . In future, those landlords will have to contribute to the taxation of the country on the basis of the real value—only one halfpenny in the pound! Only one halfpenny! And that is what all the howling is about.

"There is another little tax called the increment tax. If land goes up in the future by hundreds of thousands an acre through the efforts of the community, the community will get 20% of that increment. . . . Take the well-known case of the Duke of Northumberland, when a County Council wanted to buy a small plot of land as a site for a school. . . . What did he demand? . . . Nine hundred pounds an acre! All we say is this—if it is worth nine hundred pounds, let him pay taxes on nine hundred pounds!"

The Unionist Press, the following morning, fell upon Lloyd George in fury and there can be little doubt that from now onwards the tide began to run in the Government's direction. The *Daily Mail* actually admitted that the Budget had gained in popularity, a blunder which drew upon it the wrathful rebukes of Northcliffe's other papers. "I see," Lloyd George wrote to his brother on August 3rd, "that reports are coming in to the Tory headquarters from all parts of the country that the Budget is popular. . . . General feeling here is that they will make a show of fight and then collapse. They are raging over Limehouse, but our fellows most enthusiastic. Prime Minister going to Birmingham to address a great Budget meeting."[14] The dukes, the landlords, the bankers and the capitalists were henceforth held up to constant ridicule by Liberal speakers and efforts by indignant noblemen to retaliate in a similar vein only served to strengthen the Government's case. The Duke of Beaufort, for example, declared that he would "like to see Winston Churchill and Lloyd George in the middle of twenty couples of dog hounds"; the Duke of Portland announced his intention of reducing expenditure on his estate and cancelling all gifts to charity, while the Duke of Buccleuch refused a guinea to a local football club on the grounds of impending impoverishment.

The King, needless to say, was far from pleased at this repetition of Lloyd George's earlier misdemeanours.

Knollys to Crewe, August 2nd, 1909

I think I had better mention that the King is so seriously annoyed with Ll. George's Limehouse speech, that when he sees Asquith tomorrow he intends to speak very strongly to him on the subject and will probably say that if he does not receive an assurance from him (Asquith) that he will do his utmost to prevent Ll. George from using such language again, he shall have to consider whether it will not be his duty to write a letter to be read at the Cabinet.

The King thinks he ought to protest in the most vigorous terms against one of his principal Ministers making such a speech and putting himself almost on a level with Grayson; one full of false statements, of socialism in its worst and most insidious form and of virulent abuse against one particular class, which can only have the effect of setting "class" against "class" and of stirring up the worst passions of his audience. It is hardly necessary perhaps to allude to its gross vulgarity.*[15]

---

* A conciliatory reply from Crewe did not, unfortunately, prove sufficiently soothing. "I have submitted to the King your letter of yesterday," wrote Knollys on August 4th, "and he desires me to express his disappointment with it. His Majesty directs me to add that he regrets that his relations with some of the members of the present Cabinet should be increasingly the reverse of harmonious." Lloyd George himself wrote to the King the following day, venturing to submit that "he was justified in retorting upon his opponents in language which fell

The ultimate effect of Lloyd George's speech upon the Unionist leaders, and one which may very well have been intended, was to make them throw caution to the winds. Yet it is important to note that there had, up till now, been little or no incentive for them to do so: the Budget Protest League was proving a dismal failure, its resolutions against the Finance Bill actually being defeated at its own meetings, and the party was still miserably divided over the question of Imperial Preference. The Lime-house episode, however, started a process of re-thinking and under the pressure of J. L. Garvin, editor of the *Observer*, Balfour finally agreed to make Tariff Reform the platform from which to fight. It is probable that he himself, at this time, resolved that the Budget should not pass the House of Lords. "What will happen if they throw it out," wrote Lloyd George to his brother on August 17th, "I can conjecture and I rejoice at the prospect. . . . I wonder whether they will be such fools." [17]

(5)

The Committee Stage of the Finance Bill continued to occupy the House of Commons throughout the summer. By August 18th, after lengthy debates and another all-night sitting, Clause Twenty-seven had been reached, which meant that most of the land clauses were now behind them.*

There was, in September, an unfortunate worsening of relations between the Government and the Irish Nationalists, caused, it seems, by over-hasty promises on the part of Lloyd George. Sixty-two Nationalists had voted against the Second Reading of the Finance Bill because of the proposed whisky tax, and with the licensing clauses now coming up for debate accommodation on this issue was obviously desirable. On August 26th Lloyd George told Redmond that, subject to the Cabinet's approval, he was willing to accept the Irish proposals on the question of valuation and, in addition, to abolish the minimum limit for licence duty. The latter concession had not been sought but the Nationalists naturally welcomed it with delight. A few days later Redmond was given to understand that the

---

short of much that has been said and repeated on the other side." The King replied two days later, noting with regret that Mr Lloyd George had been attacked with much violence by members of the Opposition but reminding him that those members did not hold high office under the Crown.[16]

* Lloyd George's uncle was rather concerned to note that the Chancellor's glory was being shared by others, which produced (September 2nd) the following explanation: "Uncle Lloyd must not get uneasy about my not being in charge of Licences. I simply could not do it without suffering not only physical breakdown, but a complete breakdown of all my arrangements for the rest of the Bill and for the Development Bill." The latter, which in effect was a sub-section of the Budget, was concerned with the general promotion of national concerns such as forestry, agriculture, rural industries, canals and roads.[18]

Cabinet, though willing to make concessions, could not take the initiative: Redmond himself must table the necessary amendments which, when they came up for discussion, would not be opposed by the Government. This was a reasonable request but on April 30th Lloyd George informed Redmond that the Cabinet had now decided not to abolish the minimum but merely to reduce it. The Irish leader was furious at this change of front and promptly sent a letter of protest to the Chancellor of the Exchequer which he demanded be shown to Asquith. No acknowledgment was received and Redmond's temper did not improve. On September 1st, when the debate on the licensing clauses began, he unsuccessfully moved that Ireland be excluded from their operation. Asquith promised that the minimum for Ireland would be reduced but the Nationalists abstained from voting on Clause Twenty-nine, which was a crucial one.* On September 17th Lloyd George told Redmond that he could make no more concessions. Redmond, suspecting that Asquith was not fully aware of the exchanges which had taken place, asked Lloyd George to inform the Prime Minister of their discussions. Receiving no satisfactory reply, he himself wrote direct to Asquith and saw him on September 30th. The premier, however, refused to admit that anything untoward had occurred and it is scarcely surprising that this episode did nothing to improve a situation which was already far from satisfactory.†[19]

There was now a deepening conviction among members of both parties that the Upper House would not pass the Budget. On September 8th the Cabinet agreed, so Asquith informed the King, that rejection "ought to be followed by an acceleration of the Register, so as to secure at the earliest possible moment an appeal to the country."[21] The leaders of the Liberal Party were, however, coming to realise that rejection might very well prove a blessing in disguise. If the Lords allowed the Finance Bill to reach the Statute Book it would, as Churchill told Wilfred Blunt on October 2nd, "be immensely unpopular and everybody would be against it." If, on the other hand, the Lords threw caution to the winds and rejected it without further ado, the Liberals would be provided with a heaven-sent opportunity to revive their party's fortunes. They would be able, at long

---

* It was passed by 155 to 96 the following day. Redmond later claimed that the Government would have been defeated if his party had gone into the Opposition Lobby.

† "The Chancellor of the Exchequer," wrote Asquith to Redmond on October 1st, "informed me that, having used (somewhat casually) language to you from which you might infer that the Government were prepared to accede to your wishes in regard not only to valuation but to the minimum, and finding on reflection and after consultation with his colleagues that such a concession on the latter point was impossible, he at once—within twenty-four or forty-eight hours of his original statement—took steps to have you informed how the matter stood. . . . I am extremely sorry that there should have been any misunderstanding."[20]

last, to launch a full-scale attack upon the Second Chamber and to claim that they alone cared for true social reform.* Certain defeat at the polls might very well be transformed into another sweeping victory and the way should be clear not only for the "People's Budget" but also for the abolition of the Lords' veto.[23] An exultant Lloyd George could tell his brother that, while it was "very doubtful" what the Lords would do, he hoped that they would "throw it out", a hope which other members of the Government were soon to be echoing in private conversation.[24] Morley, in a letter dated August 31st, declared that "the Tory whips do not in their [most] sanguine moments expect to come back after a general election more than 300 strong."[25]

The change of heart in the Ministry did not go unnoticed. "The Government," wrote Austen Chamberlain to his father on September 10th, "are now persuaded that the Lords will reject the Bill. . . . They have altered their tactics in the House accordingly, and instead of hurrying they are now dawdling. The object is to tide over till January, so as to get an appeal on the new register."[26] Many Unionists were far from happy at the prospect of the Budget being rejected: "they seem haunted by the *knowledge* that the Radicals want a dissolution", Esher wrote on September 17th, "and the *fear* that they may be trapped into one."[27] It could, admittedly, be argued that if the Upper House did not assert itself on this occasion then its utility as a Second Chamber would vanish for ever and that Home Rule and Socialism would eventually prevail, but any election fought on the issue of a "social reform" Budget could scarcely result in a Unionist victory.

Attack is always the best means of defence and Tariff Reform now came into its own. Austen Chamberlain, Bonar Law, Garvin and Goulding were convinced that Protection was the one sure way, indeed the only way, whereby the Unionist Party could regain the votes which it had lost in 1906. If the Budget were to be presented to the electorate as Socialism in all its evil trappings, then Tariff Reform must stand forth in a blaze of glory as the inevitable alternative. The discreet silence hitherto maintained by the Budget Protest League on the subject of Protection had not pro-

---

* "For the first time," wrote Garvin to Sandars on September 20th, "Kennedy Jones told me of his weekend with Lloyd George on Lipton's yacht. He said Lloyd George talked with a frankness not merely demented but useful. He went out from the Port of London transaction, and talked like a man hypnotised by the facility with which things could be nationalised. He not only spoke of the railways, first to be cheapened by motor competition practically subsidised on the new State roads and then bought, but he went on to say that he meant to nationalise public houses, and to cheapen them also by repeated increases of taxation before taking them over. There has been no such demagogue as this. It is far meaner as well as more dangerous than a campaign for open confiscation."[22]

duced the dividends expected, and by September the fiscal reformers were at last in a position to make their views prevail. It is interesting to note, in this connection, that those Conservative members of the Upper House most strongly opposed to the rejection of the Budget, namely James of Hereford, Balfour of Burleigh, Cromer, Lytton and St Aldwyn, were also well-known for their adherence to Free Trade and dislike of Joseph Chamberlain. The following letter illustrates the type of argument which they put forward.

St Aldwyn to Lansdowne, September 8th, 1909

It occurs to me that if the Licensing Clauses came to us in such a form as to be really unfair and unpopular, we might avoid the entire rejection of the Budget, and the charge of only caring for our interests as landowners, by cutting both them and the Land Tax Clauses out and passing the rest of the Bill. It would throw the onus of the loss of the Budget on the Commons, and I think they would probably avoid the loss and save their own dignity by sending up a new Bill without the obnoxious clauses which, of course, we should pass; while the cup of our iniquity might be declared full, an "Abolition of the Lords' Veto" form the first business of the next Session, and a dissolution follow—as soon as may be convenient to the Government—on our rejection of it.

If we are to do anything, this seems to me a reasonable course; but I own that my House of Commons feeling on finance is against it, and I think both the right and the wise course is to pass the Budget as it comes to us.[28]

By the time this letter was received, however, Lansdowne had already decided upon rejection. "I was much attracted at first," he wrote to Balfour of Burleigh on October 2nd, "with the idea of endeavouring to amend the Bill, but . . . if the Lords were to deal only with Land and Licensing they would be accused of deserting their fellow sufferers and thinking of their own skins only. . . . We should lose ourselves in unprofitable discussions, and the real issue would be obscured. I am therefore clear that it is a case of rejection or acceptance. . . . I am in favour of rejection, upon the broad grounds that the Finance Bill is a new departure of the most dangerous kind, to which the House of Lords has no right to assent until it is sure that H.M.G. have the support of the country. . . . We must, I think, assume that if there is a general election we may be beaten at the polls; but . . . I am much less afraid than you are of this result. The Radicals will no doubt do their best to confuse the issue and make out that a verdict in favour of the Finance Bill carries with it a *carte blanche* to deal with the H. of L. But the destruction or reform of the House of Lords is not to be accomplished in a few weeks or months; and when the heat and fury of the general election has spent itself, the country will, I believe, be quite able to discriminate between the two issues—and I do not believe the country desires a Single Chamber system. By the time the H. of L. is ripe for treatment, the popularity of the Budget will, unless I am mistaken, have greatly diminished. We shall not, in my opinion, get through the present crisis without two general elections."[29]

The Unionist leaders were thus impelled towards the conclusions that the House of Lords must reject the Budget and that Tariff Reform must be adopted as the main plank in their programme. Their chances of victory at the polls would still be dubious, even with Imperial Preference as their banner, but total victory was not desired at this stage. It would be enough if the Government majority in the Commons were slashed to so great an extent that the Liberals would become dependant upon the Nationalists and Labour members. The Unionists could then declare that the country had not shown the degree of confidence in Liberal finance which Asquith had requested and at the same time escape the burden of assuming office at a critical moment in the nation's affairs. The consequences of victory, in fact, were more to be feared than the consequences of defeat.

At Birmingham, on September 24th, Balfour and Austen Chamberlain presided at an enthusiastic rally. Neither of them ventured to speculate on the fate of the Bill, but a message from Joseph Chamberlain, hoping that the peers "would see their way to force a general election," left no doubt as to the view of the stricken Imperialist on this subject. Sir George Doughty, the Unionist member for Grimsby, declared that the peers would not be worthy of their seats if they did not decide in favour of rejection. This was the closest Balfour could come to publicly urging the Lords to reject the Budget: until the last moment he was able, with characteristic dexterity, to conceal his views from his colleagues and closest kinsmen. The significance of this meeting however, was that it marked his positive acceptance of Tariff Reform as the only alternative to the Government's proposals.

Rosebery had delivered his second attack upon the Budget on September 10th. He described it, to a Glasgow audience, as animated by the "deep, subtle, insidious" danger of Socialism, "a revolution without a mandate", and concentrated his criticism on the death duties and land taxes. The audience were also informed that his lordship had "ceased to be in communication with the Liberal Party."* These announcements marked the final breaking of old ties.

"I need not tell you," wrote Asquith to Rosebery on September 11th,

* The previous week he had actually complained to Morley that since becoming Prime Minister Asquith no longer discussed politics with him.[30]

"that I have read your Glasgow speech with the most profound regret. . . . It may be that we are all wrong, and that you alone are right. . . . Time alone will decide between these alternatives. But in the meanwhile anything in the nature of political co-operation becomes (by your own showing) the hollowest of pretences, and it is quite impossible for myself and my colleagues to continue to serve under your presidency as Vice-Presidents of the Liberal League."[31] Rosebery replied three days later. "I think you have left me," he wrote, "rather than that I have left you, but were it otherwise I hope we shall give each other the credit of acting conscientiously. All my old political friendship is locked up in your Cabinet. I doubt if any of you realise the painful struggle I had to face before speaking, but I think you must recognise by the dates that I was in no hurry to speak. As I wrote to you last year, I am a cross-bench man for life, and as I spoke for your Licensing Bill in November, so now I speak against your Budget; the balance is not unequal."[32]

With the exchange of these letters the Liberal League thus passed out of existence, being formally dissolved on May 31st, 1910, and Rosebery's last vague connections with the party were at an end. It was simply a formal acknowledgment of what had long been the case in practice: since 1906 the League had been no more than a mouthpiece for Rosebery's own sentiments and its disappearance from the scene was greeted with feelings of relief rather than regret by Asquith, Grey and Haldane. Rosebery himself now ceased to play any really important part in contemporary politics and gradually melted into the background of parliamentary life.

Rosebery, though certainly the most prominent, was not the only member of the Liberal Party who felt unable to support the Budget. Harold Cox, Sir Arthur Pease and Sir Alfred Perks were among those who opposed the measure and Carlyon Bellairs, a young Liberal Imperialist, reversed Churchill's example of 1904 by crossing the floor of the House to the Unionist benches. By and large, however, abstentions of this nature were few and not particularly damaging to the Government.

Asquith had, by this time, succeeded in establishing a genuine control over his party. His support for McKenna's Navy Estimates meant that he must also support Lloyd George's Budget and he was fulfilling this rôle to the best of his ability. "You drop in a fact," Lloyd George had told the Mastermans on August 14th, "he is very unemotional, but eventually it works like a penny in the slot."[33] According to Churchill, talking to Blunt on October 3rd, Asquith's addiction to "the polite frivolities of society" had been damaging his influence with the Radicals, "but Lloyd George and I have re-established his credit with our Budget: it has put a stop to his social career." Apart from this, however, Asquith's sheer capacity for hard work, as opposed to Campbell-Bannerman's more easy-going approach, ensured his ascendancy over his colleagues. "He will sit up playing bridge and drinking late at night," said Churchill, "and yet in the morning he will come to his office or the House and enter into the most complicated business with his head entirely clear and work on for six or seven hours. He will attend committees and give full attention to every point of discussion and draft amendments in his perfectly clear handwriting without altering a word, clause after clause, and he is far and away the best speaker in the House. That is what gives him his power." [34]

(6)

The Finance Bill emerged from the Committee on October 1st with several modifications, the most important of which related to the tax of 5% on undeveloped minerals: by a remarkable volte face the Government had abandoned its argument that such a tax would serve to drive mineral wealth on to the market and now declared that it would be imposed on mineral deposits that *were* being worked, evidently a more satisfactory device from the viewpoint of revenue but one that could hardly be reconciled with earlier ministerial reasoning. A tax concession had been made to landlords whereby, if they could prove that a certain proportion of their income had been spent upon their property, they would be entitled to relief. In essentials, however, the general character of the Bill remained unchanged: the land and licensing clauses were as obnoxious as ever to Unionist eyes and on September 26th Sandars told Esher "that it was practically decided to throw out the Budget." [35]

Many Unionists, after Balfour's appearance at Birmingham, were in an optimistic mood. An election in January, they felt, was something to be welcomed rather than dreaded: unemployment would have grown worse, the Budget would have lost much of its popular appeal, Tariff Reform would have made headway among all sections of the community and the new electoral register might well redound to their favour. "Six weeks ago," wrote Long to Garvin on October 26th, "things looked bad, but the gilt is off the gingerbread and now we have only got to keep ramming things home and I believe we shall get the country with us." [36] There were still, however, those who counselled moderation. Lord Lytton, writing to Lansdowne on October 8th, argued that if the Budget were allowed to pass "its burdens would soon prove odious in practice, and the comforting theory on which it is now founded would be exploded. By the end of another year the Government would have to go to the country and would,

I believe, suffer defeat. A Unionist Government would then be in a position to amend the Budget, strengthen the House of Lords against further attack, and save the country from the Socialism and class warfare which are being fostered today."[37]

Asquith reported to King Edward VII on October 5th that the Cabinet had "agreed that until the course of events shapes itself more clearly it would be premature to decide upon any definite course of action."[38] The following day he paid a visit to Balmoral. The King, despite his disapproval of Lloyd George's speech, was largely in favour of the Budget and suggested that he himself should advise Lansdowne and Balfour to persuade the Lords to pass it on condition that an election be held in January. Asquith did not show much enthusiasm for this suggestion. He pointed out that the Tory leaders would not welcome an election at such a time, since a surrender by the Lords would be a tacit admission that their opposition to the Budget had been wrong, and that the Unionists would have more to gain by a contest towards the end of 1910, by which time the Finance Bill would have lost much of its glamour. January was, moreover, a bad month for an election and the Government would only be justified in holding one if a constitutional crisis were to arise, which he hoped would not be the case. If the worst came to the worst, however, "the outcome of an election fought under such conditions was not unlikely to be a very small majority either way between the British parties, with the decisive vote in critical matters left to the Irish; a very undesirable state of things."[39] The King was evidently impressed with these factors, but persisted in seeing Lansdowne and Balfour. They told him, on October 12th, that the Lords had not yet decided what action to take: technically this was correct, but in fact there was hardly any doubt as to their decision.[40]

(7)

Hundreds of meetings were meanwhile being held throughout the country. Public interest, it appears, was at last aroused, though at the distance of sixty years it is difficult to determine just how genuine this interest was. Leading City financiers urged rejection, as did Unionist M.P.s and the Unionist Press, and it was rumoured that the Cabinet were considering the idea of a referendum. The Commons adjourned on October 8th and members of the Government embarked upon a new and intensive campaign on the Budget's behalf. Birrell, that evening, stated that they were ready for a contest if the Lords wanted one, while Churchill declared (with disconcerting candour once again) that rejection would be "a constitutional outrage" but "a great tactical advantage" for the Ministry.

It was, however, once more left to Lloyd George, speaking at Newcastle-on-Tyne the following day, to put the cat among the pigeons with a vengeance.

After giving a brief résumé of the new taxes, he noted that trade and industry were apparently recovering from the great blow which the Budget was supposed to have dealt them. Investments had been steady and there had even been an improvement in brewery shares. The only stock to have gone down badly was that of the dukes. "One especially expensive duke made a speech, and all the Tory Press said: 'Well now, really, is that the sort of thing we are spending £250,000 a year upon?' Because a fully-equipped duke costs as much to keep up as two Dreadnoughts; and they are just as great a terror, and they last longer." The Government were "going to send the Bill up"—all the taxes or none. "What will the Lords do? I tell you frankly it is a matter which concerns them far more than it concerns us. The more irresponsible and feather-headed amongst them will want to throw it out. . . . But still, this is the great Constitutional Party: and if there is one thing more than another better established about the British constitution, it is this: that the Commons and the Commons alone have the complete control of supply and ways and means; and what our fathers established through centuries of struggle and of strife—even bloodshed—we are not going to be traitors to.

"Let them realise what they are doing. They are forcing a revolution. But the Lords may decree a revolution which the people will direct. If they begin, issues will be raised which they little dream of, questions will be asked which are now whispered in humble voices, and answers will be demanded then with authority. The question will be asked, 'Should five hundred men, ordinary men chosen accidentally from among the unemployed, override the judgment—the deliberate judgment—of millions of people who are engaged in the industry which makes the wealth of the country?' That is one question. Another will be, 'Who ordained that a few should have the land of Britain as a perquisite; who made ten thousand people owners of the soil, and the rest of us trespassers in the land of our birth; who is it—who is responsible for the scheme of things whereby one man is engaged through life in grinding labour . . . and another man who does not toil receives every hour of the day, every hour of the night, whilst he slumbers, more than his neighbour receives in a whole year of toil? Where did the table of that law come from? Whose finger inscribed it?' These are the questions that will be asked. The answers are charged with peril for the order of things the peers represent; but they are fraught with rare and refreshing fruit for the parched lips of the multitude who have been treading the dusty road along which the people have marched through the dark ages which are now emerging into the light."

This was real fire-raising stuff, even more so than the Limehouse speech, and the reactions produced were correspondingly more shrill: there can little doubt that this speech was deliberately intended to provoke the Lords into asserting themselves. The decision to reject the Budget had already been taken by the Unionist leaders, but those who still wavered now made up their minds. Once more the full volume of outraged fury from Tory dukes and viscounts burst about the Chancellor's ears. Curzon argued that the Upper House had only waived, not abandoned, its right to amend financial measures, and Knollys asked the Prime Minister "not to pretend to the King that he liked Mr. Lloyd George's speeches, for the King would not believe it and it only irritated him."[41] Lloyd George himself wrote to his brother on October 22nd that "opinion among the initiated is hardening in favour of the theory that the Lords mean to 'chuck' the Budget."[42]

(8)

The Commons reassembled on October 18th and the following day the Finance Bill entered its Report Stage. This lasted ten days and on November 2nd there began the debate on the Third Reading. A motion for the Bill's rejection was moved by Austen Chamberlain and defeated by 379 to 149 on November 4th: the final reading was then carried and the Lower House thankfully adjourned on November 5th. "It seems incredible," wrote Grey to Mrs Asquith, "that the Budget should be over in the House of Commons; one had come to believe unconsciously that the Session would never finish and it is a surprise to find that the end is in sight. I haven't an idea of what will follow or be the result of the elections. Lloyd George has made too much running, I fear, to carry the electors with us: in this country they move slowly and distrust rhetoric."[43]

No account can hope to do justice to the incredibly intricate, prolonged and interminable debates which had taken place in the Session of 1909. Statistics alone must suffice. Seventy parliamentary days had been devoted to discussion of the Finance Bill while the usual summer recess had been completely curtailed. Of 895 divisions throughout the year, 554 had related to the Budget.* Inevitably, despite the considerable assistance which had been given to him, the main burden of guiding the measure through the House of Commons had fallen upon Lloyd George, and it is only right

---

* Lloyd George had voted in 462, Masterman in 420, Asquith in 202 and Churchill in 198. The highest division records were held by J. A. Pease, the Chief Whip, with 518 and Sir Samuel Evans, the Solicitor-General, with 505.

that the Budget of 1909 should have come to be indissolubly linked with his name. It is true that he was not altogether responsible for drafting its provisions and even probable that he did not understand the meaning of some of them, but he succeeded in raising it to a peak of importance which could never have been reached had it been left in the hands of the practical but unimaginative Asquith. By his cunning, his charm, his invective and crusading spirit he had restored to the Government some of the prestige that it had lost since 1906 and had made himself one of the most outstanding, and certainly one of the best hated, politicians of the day.

Slowly but surely the battle was drawing to its climax and the Upper House, now imbued with an additional recklessness, would do nothing to moderate its attitude towards other measures of Liberal legislation.* On November 16th Lansdowne gave notice that when the Finance Bill came up for a Second Reading he would move "That this House is not justified in giving its assent to the Bill until it has been submitted to the judgment of the country". Balfour, speaking at Manchester the following day, declared that his lordship was "abundantly right", but there were many (including F. E. Smith) who thought otherwise. "Acceptance of the Budget," wrote Mrs Asquith on November 18th, "would look like weakness, but in the end it would be better for them to give way: the Lords would hear no more of their veto, the Bill might get less popular and, between now and the time for dissolution, we may make ourselves more disliked. If the Lords reject the Budget I will back us to get in at the next election, although by a smaller majority."[44]

A week later the crucial debate began in the Upper House. Lansdowne argued that this was not a Finance Bill in the ordinary sense since it contained extraneous matter which ought to have been dealt with separately. For this reason, therefore, the peers would be justified in refusing their assent. If they were to give way on this occasion, then they would never again be able to claim the right of restraining the financial policy of a Government, however outrageous it might be. The only solution to this deadlock was an appeal to the nation. The Unionist speakers who followed Lansdowne were more or less united in their dislike of the Budget,† but they were less unanimous when it came to deciding what should be done with it. There were those who argued that to reject a finance bill would be political suicide: the Government would immediately take steps to limit,

* On October 13th the House Letting and Rating (Scotland) Bill had been drastically mutilated and was consequently abandoned by the Government. The Irish Land Bill and the Housing and Town Planning Bill were also heavily amended by the Upper House before reaching the Statute Book.

† Balfour of Burleigh was the only Unionist of any note who actually spoke in favour of it.

or perhaps even abolish, their power of vetoing measures from the House of Commons. If, on the other hand, the Budget were accepted under protest, then the time would eventually come when a Unionist Ministry could repeal the more obnoxious clauses with the approval of a disillusioned electorate. James of Hereford, Reay and, of course, Balfour of Burleigh, argued in favour of this policy, while Lord St Aldwyn showed his disapproval of Lansdowne's resolution by absenting himself from the House altogether during this debate. Milner, at the other extreme, declared that the Lords must do their duty and "damn the consequences" and Halsbury and Curzon also pressed strongly for rejection. Crewe, speaking for the Government, made it plain that if the Budget were rejected no Liberal Government would ever again take office without first securing guarantees "fenced about and guarded by the force of statute, guarantees which will prevent that indiscriminate destruction of our legislation of which your work tonight is the climax and the crown." Rosebery attacked the Budget but characteristically announced that he would abstain from voting. The Archbishop of York, Dr Gordon Lang, argued that the proposals were not so revolutionary as they appeared, since it was "the tendency of the Celtic temperament to respond to environment . . . which makes the speaker say he knows not what, and excites the audience they know not why." The latter voted with the Government, together with three bishops, while the Bishop of Lincoln voted with the Opposition: the Archbishop of Canterbury and the remaining bishops abstained.

On November 30th the motion for the Second Reading was defeated by 350 to 75. By this action, therefore, the conflict between the Government and the House of Lords entered its penultimate phase. Rejection had been highly probable for almost two months, but until the last moment there had always been a faint chance that the peers might draw back. Prudence, however, did not prevail. Many of the Unionists genuinely believed that they had a reasonable case and the results of the first 1910 election were to show that they had not been altogether mistaken in this conviction. If it could only be proved to the nation at large that the Budget was a bad Budget and Tariff Reform the real answer to their economic problems, then disaster might still be averted. The Government's reaction to this turn of events was one of elation rather than fury. Their case against the Second Chamber was complete; they could go to the country in a mood of righteous indignation and wrath, recapturing something of the crusading spirit which had swept them into office in 1906.

Redmond, in a position of real advantage at last, now urged the Government to make Home Rule a prominent feature of its immediate programme. Individual Liberal M.P.s had been allowed, as we have seen, to pledge the Ministry to such a measure in the next Parliament, but Asquith's evident reluctance to elaborate upon this pledge had done nothing to reassure the Nationalists that he would not discover some convenient means of escaping from his commitments. The unfortunate episode of the withdrawn promise to abolish the minimum had aroused Redmond's impatience and he told Morley that if the Liberal Party were not in earnest with regard to Home Rule then the Nationalists would be obliged to go into opposition. On November 25th Morley confessed that the Cabinet had not yet reached a decision, which produced from Redmond (November 27th) the warning that political conditions in Ireland were such "that, unless an official declaration on the question of Home Rule be made, not only will it be impossible for us to support Liberal candidates in England, but we will most unquestionably have to ask our friends to vote against them."[45]

The declarations of individual candidates were, he declared, not enough. The Government must announce its intentions of granting Ireland "national self-government, subject to Imperial control, in the next Parliament" and a speech which Asquith would shortly deliver at the Albert Hall must be the occasion of such an announcement. Copies of this letter were sent to other Ministers and the Cabinet agreed on December 1st that (so Birrell delightedly informed Redmond) "Home Rule is the live policy of the party, without limitation or restriction other than the old tag about the supreme control of the Imperial Parliament."[46]

(9)

On December 2nd Asquith moved "that the action of the House of Lords in refusing to pass into law the financial provisions made by the House for the service of the year is a breach of the constitution and a usurpation of the rights of the Commons," a motion which was supported by the Irish and carried by 349 to 134. Parliament was prorogued (but not dissolved) the following day and members departed to their constituencies to prepare for the forthcoming election.

It is necessary to consider what had actually been accomplished during this turbulent last Session of the 1906 Parliament. Surprisingly enough the legislative achievements, though not considerable, were greater than might have been expected: Labour Exchanges and trade boards in "sweated" industries had been established, while the Irish Land Bill and the Housing and Town Planning Bill had been passed in modified forms. Ministerial casualties, nevertheless, were heavy: a Shops Bill, a Small Dwelling

Houses (Scotland) Bill, the Welsh Disestablishment Bill, a Hops Bill, a County Courts Bill, a London Elections Bill (to stop plural voting) and the Rating (Scotland) Bill, some squeezed out due to lack of time and others abandoned because of opposition in the Upper House. The debates on the Budget certainly overshadowed everything else but they should not be allowed to obscure the fact that the machinery of parliamentary government continued to function with what was, in the circumstances, a fair degree of normality.

The rejection of the Budget, however, dominated the scene. For the Lords to refuse their assent to a Finance Bill was an unprecedented event and, for that reason, all the more outrageous to a Liberal House of Commons, yet one should resist the temptation to see the situation in the simple terms of Peers versus People. The 1909 Budget was, after all, no ordinary Budget and its opponents cannot altogether be blamed for sensing an air of vindictiveness about some of its provisions. Lloyd George's speeches had certainly done nothing to reassure them. As for charges of acting unconstitutionally, the Upper House could remind its detractors that no law prevented them from altering or rejecting financial measures: all that existed was a convention that they left finance to the House of Commons and this was obviously not binding. On the constitutional front, therefore, they had a reasonable defence and were at pains to stress that the Budget had been rejected in order that the British people might have an opportunity of pronouncing upon it. Although this might seem, to Radical eyes, a miserable subterfuge, it did not exactly substantiate the Liberal Party's contention that the Upper House rode roughshod over the wishes of the nation. Strategically, of course, the Lords had made a blunder of the greatest magnitude but this would not become apparent for several months and, in December 1909, the contestants were thought to be evenly matched. The Budget was not so wildly popular as its supporters claimed and the Lords were far from being the villains of the piece. Only in retrospect have the greys become black and white.

I

CHAPTER THIRTEEN

THE GENERAL ELECTION, DECEMBER 1909–JANUARY 1910

(1)

The general election of January 1910 ought, in theory, to have been one of the most exciting ever fought. It was waged, to begin with, on a scale altogether unprecedented: speakers scurried from one part of the country to another at a moment's notice, employing their talents wherever they were most needed and hurling themselves into the fray with a vigour worthy of Gladstone at his best and Lord Randolph Churchill at his worst. Never before, so it seemed, had so much force, ferocity and fury been packed into so short a space of time, and since the actual writs for the election were not issued until January 10th the peers were able to indulge in the unaccustomed luxury of declaiming from Unionist platforms until that date: it was estimated that they addressed well over two hundred meetings in the space of five weeks.* All in all, therefore, a lively time was had by members of both Houses, and there was certainly no lack of interest shown by the electors: 92% voted as opposed to 89% in 1906 and 87% in December 1910.

This was, however, a far from memorable election. Apart from Asquith's fateful declaration of December 10th, to which we shall return in a moment, nothing of lasting impact was said by any of the principal campaigners. Possibly this was because the arguments employed had already been rather too well rehearsed in the Press and at public meetings, possibly because a Radical party usually makes a better job of attacking a Government than it does a Conservative Opposition. Four years of office had taken some of the zest out of the Liberals and they were hard put to it to find suitable targets on which to vent their wrath. The House of Lords was, as ever, an agreeable Aunt Sally, but it was by no means certain, as we have noted elsewhere, that the electorate was greatly dismayed by the

---

* Whether they did much to further their cause is a moot point. One Unionist candidate, Joynson-Hicks, declared with some bitterness that the dukes ought to have been locked up, every one of them, until after the election.

failure of the Government's Education and Licensing Bills to reach the Statute Book nor, for that matter, by the rejection of the Budget. The Liberals endeavoured to keep the issue of constitutional reform in the limelight but they were somewhat vague when it came to discussing what should actually be done, and there was a division between those who favoured an attack on the veto and those who wanted the Second Chamber reconstituted on a more democratic basis.

The Unionist attack was intense and quite well mounted, but defence of the *status quo* is not necessarily inspiring and Imperial Preference, though often referred to, was not advocated with anything like the force that it ought to have been if it were supposed to represent an alternative policy. Lansdowne, speaking in Plymouth on December 3rd, defined the issues at stake as Tariff Reform, single-chamber government and the advance of Socialism, and he went on to argue that the Lords were fighting for the rights of the people against the despotism of the House of Commons. Balfour's election address, issued a week later, declared that the Liberal Party's attack on the House of Lords was the climax of an ingenious but foredoomed conspiracy to secure a single-chamber legislature independent of both peers and people. Austen Chamberlain's manifesto (December 30th) concluded that the Government intended to destroy both the constitution and the Act of Union.

The Government's course seemed, at first, relatively straightforward: triumph at the polls would be followed by the reintroduction of the Budget, which would presumably receive an uninterrupted passage through both Houses, and they would then bring forward a scheme to reform the Second Chamber. It could hardly be supposed that the Upper House would quietly acquiesce in such a scheme, but steps would have to be taken to ensure that the Government's wishes prevailed. With the Upper House reformed, they would then go full steam ahead with schemes that were dear to the heart of every Liberal: new Education, Licensing and Plural Voting Bills, the disestablishment of the Church, new land valuation for Scotland, measures of social reform for the Radicals and last, but very far from least, Home Rule for Ireland. A golden prospect!

In order to reach Utopia, however, they must first be sure of success at the polls, and this could partly be brought about if they were able to let their candidates and supporters know that there would be no appreciable delay in reforming the House of Lords. If a scheme of reform were rejected by the Upper House this might very well mean a second general election within a very short space of time, a prospect to which no one could look forward with equanimity. The only way of ensuring that this did not happen would be to obtain from the King a guarantee that he would, if need be, create a substantial number of Liberal peers to secure a majority for the Government in the Upper House. The threat alone would probably be enough to deter the Unionists from taking violent action. The Cabinet discussed this question on November 30th and, as a result of their deliberations, Asquith approached King Edward VII a day or so later with the request that he should decide what his answer would be if, assuming the Government were still in office after the election, he were asked to guarantee the creation of a contingent number of peers.

The Cabinet believed that the King would be bound to agree to their request and Government spokesmen wasted no time in making their feelings known to the electorate. Lloyd George, for example, speaking at the National Liberal Club on December 3rd, declared that "for my part I would not remain a member of a Liberal Cabinet one hour unless I knew that Cabinet had determined not to hold office after the next general election unless full powers are accorded to it which will enable it to place on the Statute Book of the realm a measure which will ensure that the House of Commons in future can carry, not merely Tory bills as it does—no, but Liberal and progressive measures in the course of a single Parliament either with or without the sanction of the House of Lords." Churchill, making a whistle-stop tour of Lancashire, announced three days later that "whatever may be the result of the election be sure of this, that no Liberal Government will at any future time bear the burden of office without securing guarantees that the reform [of the Lords' veto upon finance and other legislation] should be carried out."

By the evening of December 10th all the Liberal leaders were back in London and sitting on the stage of the Albert Hall waiting to hear Asquith deliver the speech that would officially inaugurate their campaign. Vague memories of the occasion four years before, when Campbell-Bannerman had launched them on the path that led to victory at the polls, no doubt did much to encourage the belief that history was going to be repeated. By 8.0 p.m. the hall was full of an all-male audience of 10,000 described by *The Times* as "boiling over with enthusiasm" and the general excitement was not diminished by the discovery of a suffragette concealed inside the organ, ready to leap out at some crucial moment in the proceedings.*

---

* Another had been ejected from the hall earlier in the day and a third, disguised as a telegraph boy, endeavoured unsuccessfully to gain admittance during Asquith's speech. The suffragettes, in fact, played a lively part during the first half of the election campaign, Churchill being attacked with a dog whip when speaking at Bristol and Lloyd George, a day or so later, being rigorously lectured by a young woman who jumped into his car and locked the door on them both.

The Prime Minister, who received a great ovation when he arrived, declared that the nation was invited to pronounce upon "the absolute control of the Commons over finance, the maintenance of Free Trade and the effective limitation and curtailment of the legislative powers of the House of Lords." With regard to Ireland, the Liberals would pursue "a policy which, while explicitly safeguarding the supremacy and indefectible authority of the Imperial Parliament, will set up in Ireland a system of full self-government in regard to purely Irish affairs." What produced the greatest response, however, was Asquith's declaration that "the will of the people, as deliberately expressed by their elected representatives, must, within the limits of a single Parliament, be made effective. . . . I tell you quite plainly, and I tell my fellow countrymen outside, that neither I nor any other Liberal Minister supported by a majority of the House of Commons is going to submit again to the rebuffs and the humiliation of the last four years. We shall not assume office, and we shall not hold office, unless we can secure the safeguards which experience shows to be necessary for the legislative utility and honour of the party of progress."

After these words, coming in confirmation of the announcements already made by Lloyd George and Churchill, who could doubt that Utopia was already in sight? The Prime Minister's statement clearly meant that, assuming his party returned to power, he would only retain office if the King promised to create peers to carry through a scheme of constitutional reform against the wishes of the Upper House. The very fact that he could make so confident a declaration must mean that the King had, in fact, already given such a promise. So, at any rate, the great majority of the Liberal Party's supporters were led to believe.

Unfortunately, this was far from being the case. Knollys, in a letter dated November 28th, had already warned Asquith that "to create 570 new peers, which I am told is the number required, would practically be almost an impossibility, and if asked for would place the King in an awkward position."[1] This warning having been disregarded, Knollys sent for Vaughan Nash, the Prime Minister's secretary, and told him (December 15th) "that the King had come to the conclusion that he would not be justified in creating new peers (say 300) until after a second general election."*[2]

This news came as a bitter blow to the Government. Liberal leaders, during the remaining four weeks of the election campaign, could no longer imply that they would be granted "safeguards" or "guarantees". The nature of the reform, moreover, remained as uncertain as ever: Asquith's speech had hinted at limitations upon the veto, as had those of

---

* Vaughan Nash's account of his interview with Knollys is quoted on pages 354–5.

Lloyd George and Churchill, but at Leith on December 4th Grey declared that the only real reform could be the substitution of popular election for the hereditary principle. Unionist speakers were quick to point out that the Government had no clear ideas on the subject: did they mean to destroy the House of Lords, abolish its right to reject money bills or simply attack the hereditary principle? In any case, whatever ideas they did put forward could only result in single-chamber government of the most arbitrary nature.

The Liberal Party's indecision strengthened the Unionist leaders in their determination not to admit that there was anything wrong with the constitution which could not be put right by minor adjustments. Balfour, writing to Lansdowne in February 1908, had described the House of Lords as an original portion of the British constitution which worked well: "it is only bad political theory which asks for anything more."[*3] Lansdowne in turn, writing to Balfour on January 3rd, 1910, remarked that "I have received several letters pressing us for a strong declaration as to House of Lords reform, but I am convinced that we should make a great mistake if we were to pledge ourselves to changes which would, in the truest sense of the word, be a revolution. . . . The House of Lords has its admitted faults, and these can be cured by reforms based on the scheme of the Rosebery Committee."[†5]

Others refused to admit the need for even minor reforms, and Curzon, speaking at Oldham on December 16th, emerged as a vigorous defender of the hereditary principle. There were, he admitted, no working men in the House of Lords, but there were no generals or ex-Colonial Governors in the House of Commons. Political ability resided to a very large degree in the aristocracy, descending from one generation to another. Moreover, 170 members of the Upper House had served in the Commons and another 200 in the armed services, and these were surely adequate qualifications for membership of the Lords. Milner, at Huddersfield the following day,

---

[*] He had suggested, however, that in the event of Rosebery's Committee (see following footnote) admitting that hereditary right was an insufficient qualification for the exercise of legislative functions it would be as well to propose the creation of life peers and a diminution of the hereditary element by means of the present House of Lords electing representatives to the new chamber. "I believe," he concluded, "that in practice this would give you almost the same House of Lords that you would get by more elaborate methods of selection."[4]

[†] In May 1907 (see page 115) a Select Committee of the Lords had been appointed, with Rosebery as its chairman, to examine the question of reforming the Upper House. Its report (December 3rd 1908) proposed a scheme whereby the hereditary peers would elect 200 representatives to sit in the Upper House of each Parliament, together with the Archbishop of Canterbury, eight bishops and any peer who had held high office in the Dominions or who had been a Cabinet Minister. The Crown would be able to create four life peers annually, on condition that the total at any one time did not exceed forty. These proposals were greeted with interest but were not discussed in the Upper House until 1910 (see page 291).

argued that over-taxation of the rich would tend to increase unemployment, while Cawdor (at Leeds on December 18th) likened the Government to Bulgarian revolutionaries. If Home Rule were granted, how could Britain prevent the establishment of a German naval base at Belfast?

Balfour, speaking at Hanley on January 4th, followed Cawdor's example and endeavoured to revive the navy scare, which aroused much indignant comment in the German and Austro-Hungarian Press. He was rebuked for this by Lloyd George, speaking at Peckham three days later, who declared that "the believers in inevitable war are the men who make them: the Unionists, after having destroyed the constituion, are prepared to destroy the fiscal system and to risk war with a European power, and all just to avoid valuation of their land."

(2)

Parliament was dissolved on January 8th and the writs for the general election were issued two days later. The Liberals, on the whole, entered the fray as a united party: the same could hardly be said of either the Unionists or the Irish Nationalists. The Tory Free Traders, now a very small body but including among their number such personalities as Cromer and Lord Robert Cecil, had drawn together towards the end of 1907 in a group known as the "Centre Party". Lansdowne had given them cautious support but the Tariff Reformers, not surprisingly, greeted this recrudescence of Cobdenite doctrines with fury. Determined to drive out these rebels from their midst an organisation called "the Confederates", which eventually included Austen Chamberlain, Bonar Law, Jesse Collings, Sir Frederick Banbury, Henry Chaplin and Milner among its members, put forward rival candidates in their constituencies.* In the Nationalist camp, meanwhile, a dozen or so members led by O'Brien and Healy had broken away from Redmond's leadership and announced that they would henceforth be known as Independents, maintaining an implacable opposition to the Budget and rejecting anything short of complete Home Rule for the whole of Ireland.

Polling began on January 15th and continued for a week. The results of the first day were encouraging to the Unionists: they gained eighteen seats, which included three in London and three in Lancashire, and their gains continued during the days that followed. The Liberal Party's losses more or less corresponded, but it soon became clear that Asquith's Government would be able to remain in office with the support of the Irish Nationalists and the Labour Party.

* See second footnote on page 110.

"The unhappy action of the House of Lords," wrote Morley to Minto on January 19th, "has brought its authors into much discredit, for everybody now sees that if they had left us to stew in the juice of what will be the extremely ugly Budget of 1910–11, they would have been much nearer the chance of an all-round win. Whether the decision to force us to the country now was Lansdowne's or Balfour's, it was a fatal error."[6] In fact, however, the House of Lords had not fared at all badly: the Liberal Party's individual supremacy in the Commons had been destroyed and the Unionists now found themselves in a far more advantageous position. It is, moreover, extremely unlikely that the latter had any great desire to assume office at this juncture: they certainly did not wish to do so in February and it can be confidently assumed that they were far from dismayed at their failure to achieve an overall majority. In size, at any rate, they now equalled the Liberal Party in the House of Commons and it could be argued that the Government had not succeeded in securing the nation's support for either the Budget or constitutional reform.

The following table shows the final position of the parties, compared with the situation after the 1906 election.

	January 1906		*January* 1910	
Liberal Party	377	⎫	275	⎫
Labour Party	53	⎬ 513	40	⎬ 397
Nationalists	83	⎭	82	⎭
Unionists (Including Speaker)	157		273	

The distribution of seats (with the January 1906 distribution shown in brackets) was as follows:

	England	*Scotland*	*Wales*	*Ireland*	*Totals*
Liberal	191 (292)	59 (58)	24 (24)	1 (3)	275 (377)
Labour	34 (45)	2 (2)	4 (6)	– (–)	40 (53)
Nationalist	1 (1)	– (–)	– (–)	81 (82)	82 (83)
Unionist	239 (127)	11 (12)	2 (–)	21 (18)	273 (157)
Totals	465	72	30	103	670

Compared with the 1906 election, the Liberals had lost 102 seats and the Unionists had gained 116. Assuming, therefore, that the Liberals were now supported by all the Irish and Labour members, they could only command a majority of 124 as opposed to an overall majority of 293 in 1906. These figures, however, do not tell the whole of the story, since it must be remembered that the support of the Irish (in theory, at any rate) was highly conditional. Eleven of the Nationalists elected formally renounced Redmond's leadership and were prepared to go into permanent opposition unless the Government granted Home Rule in the very near future,* which brought the Liberal majority down to 102. Assuming, if the worst came to the worst, that the remaining 71 Nationalists also voted against the Government in a crucial division, then the latter could actually be defeated by a majority of 40.

The Labour Party had also suffered a set-back. Seventy-eight candidates had been put forward by the L.R.C. (26 of whom engaged in three-cornered contests), but only 40 had been successful.† On balance, they had lost eleven English and two Welsh seats, their one solitary triumph having been the capture of Wigan from the Unionists. They could console themselves, however, with the reflections that (a) taking into account their parliamentary strength at the time of the dissolution they had only lost six seats, (b) only twenty-nine of the Labour members elected in 1906 had been sponsored by the L.R.C., and (c) the decline in their parliamentary fortunes was relatively insignificant when compared with that of the Liberal Party.

The immediate reasons for the Government's declining popularity are not hard to find. Many of the seats which it had won in the exceptional circumstances of 1906, for example, had simply returned to their customary allegiance.‡ One must also take into account the reaction which usually follows when a Radical party has been in control for several years (resentment on the one hand and disillusionment on the other) and there was, by this time, a marked lack of general support for the Liberal Party. When due allowance is made for these factors, however, the problem still remains of why its appeal to the nation should have produced so lukewarm a response.

---

* Three members of this group, however, were independent rebels unattached to O'Brien's rival organisation: two of them were soon absorbed back into the official party and the third did not stand at the next general election.

† One of them was J. H. Thomas, who succeeded Bell as M.P. for Derby.

‡ It should be noted, however, that the Government won twelve seats which the Unionists had held in 1906 and that most of their by-election losses, including Churchill's old constituency of north-west Manchester (where Joynson-Hicks was defeated) now returned to the Liberal fold. The party's losses were, broadly speaking, heaviest in the south of England, occurring more in the county divisions and small boroughs than the large towns.

Perhaps the old magic of Free Trade really was losing its hold. Tariff Reformers certainly thought so. Acland Hood, reporting to Austen Chamberlain on the Unionist campaign in Lancashire and the north of England in a letter dated January 27th, declared "that the decision of the Lords as to payments of members out of trade union funds . . . did us infinite harm.* I had a stiff fight, but . . . we won purely from the support of the agricultural element, farmers and labourers alike, for Tariff Reform and a strong navy."7 Austen Chamberlain himself, writing to Balfour two days later, argued that Imperial Preference had been their trump card. "Where we won," he proclaimed, "we won on and by Tariff Reform. Even where we lost, it was the only subject in our repertoire about which people really care."8 Yet it was still very uncertain, despite these optimistic reports, just how great an impact the fiscal reformers had made. It would be surprising, in view of their hard work since 1906, if their cause had not gained in popularity, but Balfour was still none too happy about its potentialities as a vote-winner—a tax on food was an indispensable part of the Tariff Reform creed—and even Austen Chamberlain could not deny that the general results were disappointing. "Scotland," he wrote, "is very bad; Wales about as good as I hoped, though we have not made the progress in the places in which I expected it; London did not come up to my expectations, nor did Manchester."9

Tariff Reform may well have attracted an important percentage of voters but it is doubtful whether this alone can account for the steady decline in the Liberal Party's fortunes. The inescapable answer can only be that, by 1910, the Government had alienated the various forces which had swept them into power four years before and that they were left, once again, with the hard core of Nonconformist and Radical supporters who would automatically back them through thick and thin. Their success in 1906, it must be remembered, had been due more to anti-Unionist than pro-Liberal feeling. A violent reaction against Balfour and Chamberlain had hurled Campbell-Bannerman into office, but since then the Liberals had done nothing to consolidate their position and the reaction had died away. The defeat of the Education and Licensing Bills had not been enough to justify an appeal to the nation: even the Budget's rejection had produced an apathetic response. The prevailing mood of the nation was a curious mixture of boredom and impatience so far as the Liberal Party was concerned. Too hidebound for some and too progressive for

---

* This was a reference to a judgment delivered by the Lords on December 21st, 1909 on an action brought by W. V. Osborne (a staunch Liberal) against his union, the Amalgamated Society of Railway Servants. It stipulated that unions could not use their funds for political purposes, a ruling which came as a bitter blow to the Labour Party.

others,* barking loudly but reluctant (except when pressed) to actually bite, its *raison d'être* was fast ebbing away.

For the moment, however, the House of Lords provided an answer to the Liberal dilemma. It gave them, as Morley wrote, "something to swear at and swear by."[11] It kept alive the crusading spirit of Gladstone. Without the constitutional conflict, dull, prolonged and wearisome as it undoubtedly was, the party would have broken up far more quickly than it did. Its members, so far, had always cherished a mission whereby they could justify their existence to themselves and to the country. Free Trade and Italian unity had called them into being and electoral reform had held them together. Now, in 1910, reform of the House of Lords became their first objective: Home Rule for Ireland would be their next. So long as these goals remained unattainable, their existence was assured. The time to worry would be the time when they had been reached.

* "I found all over the country," wrote Harcourt to Asquith, "that all Ll. G.'s speeches and Winston's earlier ones (not the Lancs. campaign) had done us much harm, even with the advanced men of the *lower* middle-class."[10]

CHAPTER FOURTEEN

FOREIGN AFFAIRS AND DEFENCE, 1908–10

(1)

The first three months of 1909 were something of a crisis period for the Government. The reason, once again, was the question of naval expenditure. In 1906 Campbell-Bannerman had placated his critics by reducing the Cawdor–Fisher programme of Dreadnought construction for 1906–7 from four ships to three, and had repeated this reduction in 1907–8; in 1908–9 he had gone even further, reducing the total construction for that year to one Dreadnought and one battle-cruiser. The Liberal rank and file, however, were still far from happy. They noted with satisfaction that the estimates for 1906–7 showed a saving of £1,520,000 as opposed to those for 1905–6 and then, with rather less satisfaction, that the saving in 1907–8 amounted to only £450,000.* The following year they were actively alarmed, despite the still greater reduction in new construction, since the estimates for 1908–9 showed an increase of £900,000. There were, as we have noted, disputes in the Cabinet over this increase, McKenna (for once) joining forces with Lloyd George against Tweedmouth, and it was only with considerable reluctance, and on the clear understanding that economies would be made elsewhere in armaments expenditure, that the Radicals had given way. Asquith himself shared their alarm to some extent, and had appointed McKenna as Tweedmouth's successor at the Admiralty in the belief that here was the ideal man, an ex-Financial Secretary to the Treasury, a keen amateur statistician and a cool-headed administrator, to wield a new broom so far as the estimates were concerned. The failure of

---

* The reason for this was that the Treasury had decided that certain works should henceforth be met by capital expenditure rather than loan, which meant an increase of more than £1 million in the Estimates. Asquith, writing to Campbell-Bannerman on January 6th, 1907 about a "characteristic outburst" from Fisher, declared that the latter's "claim that the Admiralty has reduced the Estimates by 2 millions is based on two obvious fallacies, viz. (1) that £1,010,300 (really £903,400) has been charged to votes instead of to loans: which is true, but merely a fulfilment of our announced policy, and (2) that the 'automatic' increase of £517,000 can, or even could, for this purpose be disregarded. . . . But, of course, the most serious question is whether we are to assent in principle to a *new* expenditure of nearly 3 millions for dockyard extensions."[1]

the Radicals to secure a reduction in military expenditure, moreover, was an additional reason for seeking an assurance from the new First Lord that all would be well so far as the Navy Estimates for 1909–10 were concerned, and early in July 1908 Asquith allowed his anxiety on this point to become apparent. "As you know," he wrote to McKenna, "I have for a long time been growing sceptical (in the matter of shipbuilding) as to the whole Dreadnought policy. I don't want to press you, but as you have now surveyed the whole situation from inside I should be very glad to know if you have come to any conclusion of your own as to the lines upon which construction ought to proceed for the next few years. There is much money in it—and more than money."[2]

McKenna's initial replies were not reassuring. It soon became evident, in fact, that he was playing Becket to Asquith's Henry II, and that far from ruling the Sea Lords with a rod of iron he was now one of Fisher's most ardent supporters. By December 1908 he had been convinced by his advisers that the programme for 1909–10 would have to provide for at least six Dreadnoughts, which meant an increase of three million pounds in the Navy estimates. Lloyd George and Churchill were horrified at this news, and preliminary skirmishes in the Cabinet apparently went in their favour. "Two very important Cabinets on Navy Estimates," wrote the Chancellor to his brother on December 19th. "Winston and I fought McKenna, Morley supporting me and Grey.[*] We have won. It looked three days ago as if he would ruin my financial plans by his extravagant demands. That danger is, I believe, over."[3] The battle was, however, only just beginning, since the Admiralty was now reaching the conclusion that Germany had accelerated her shipbuilding programme and that Britain's naval supremacy would be seriously endangered unless she increased her rate of Dreadnought construction. On January 3rd McKenna supplied Asquith with a copy of the report which he had sent to Grey four days previously,[†] together with some additional information, and he claimed in a covering letter that Germany would certainly have thirteen "big ships" by May 1911 and probably twenty-one by May 1912, by which time Britain herself (if she continued her present programme of construction) would have eighteen.[‡] Germany's capacity to build Dreadnoughts was probably equal

---

* There should, presumably, be a comma after "me" in this letter, since it otherwise appears that the Foreign Secretary had joined the ranks of the economists.

† See page 212.

‡ Under the 1907 Act Germany's official programme provided for nine ships in commission by February 1911 and thirteen in commission by February 1912. The Admiralty calculated, however, that while the figure of nine ships by February 1911 still held good, four additional ships would be completed during the next two months. By February 1912, it was argued, Germany would have seventeen ships in commission, and twenty-one by May 1912.

to Britain's own, which "would give the public a rude awakening should it become known."[4]

Asquith was already aware of the gist of the Admiralty's report, since he had instructed Grey on January 1st to broach the whole subject with the German Ambassador, "on the lines that nobody here can understand why Germany should need, or how she can use, twenty-one Dreadnoughts, unless for aggressive purposes and primarily against ourselves."[5] This meeting between the Foreign Secretary and Metternich took place on January 4th. Grey emphasised that the two-Power standard had to be maintained and pointed out that if no clear indication were given of the extent to which Germany intended to build Britain would be obliged to increase her own programme in order to keep ahead of her rival. He reminded the Ambassador that Britain had always been ready to enter into discussion on this subject. Metternich queried the accuracy of the Admiralty's calculations and said that the German naval programme was fixed by law and would not be increased, no matter how many vessels Britain might build. Discussion of this subject was resumed on February 3rd, when Metternich admitted that material for four ships had been collected in advance because it was definitely known that they were to be built: "in the case of subsequent ships, which were not allocated in advance, materials would not be collected beforehand unless the shipbuilding firms cared to do so at their own risk." He agreed that Germany might have thirteen Dreadnoughts completed by March 1912 if her shipbuilding proceeded at its normal rate but denied that materials would be collected in advance to give her seventeen by that date or twenty-one by May 1912.[6]

McKenna had meanwhile returned to the attack in the Cabinet. This led, once again, to a head-on collision with Lloyd George, and on February 2nd the Chancellor wrote to Asquith asking him to give careful consideration to the views expressed by Morley, Churchill and himself. He reminded him of their election pledge "to reduce the gigantic expenditure on armaments built up by the recklessness of our predecessors" and pointed out that many Liberals throughout the country were already discontented. An increase of three million pounds in the construction of battleships would lose the Government much support and lead to a fresh split in the party. "The discussion of Naval Estimates," he declared, "threatens to reopen all the old controversies which rent the party for years and brought it to impotence and contempt. You alone can save us from this prospect of sterile and squalid disruption."[7] Churchill meanwhile circulated a Cabinet memorandum expressing scepticism about the German menace and told Esher that he would resign rather than agree to the Admiralty's demands.[8]

By February 10th the position was that the Admiralty demanded six Dreadnoughts, being supported by McKenna, Grey, Haldane, Runciman, Crewe and Buxton, while Lloyd George, Harcourt, Churchill, Morley, Loreburn and Burns would only agree to four. In the meantime, however, Fisher had gleefully decided that while six were sufficient he was going to press for eight, and he succeeded in enlisting the support of Northcliffe's *Observer* for this purpose. Crucial Cabinets were held during the next few days and the situation became explosive when it was realised that McKenna also wanted agreement that, if necessary, the construction of two more Dreadnoughts would be authorised before the end of the year. "The crisis is still on and getting more serious," wrote Lucy Masterman on February 16th. "Morley has not been 'squared' but is still firm, which makes things more formidable for the Leaguers. Winston and Ll. G. are fighting for all they are worth, certain that the party is behind them, as the Liberal Press certainly is."[9] On February 17th or 18th Lloyd George put forward some compromise proposals which were favourably received, at first, by Asquith and Crewe, and on the 19th he informed his brother, somewhat prematurely, that he had had "complete success with navy. Late last night got a letter from the Prime Minister practically accepting my alternative proposals, and saying they were better than those of the Admiralty, but Winston, Morley and myself had to threaten to resign."[*][10]

It was presumably at this time[†] that McKenna suffered defeat in the Cabinet and, according to a version of events that he wrote some twenty years later, remained behind in the Cabinet room "reflecting on the terms in which I should send in my resignation. I suppose Grey discovered that I had not left the room with the other members of the Cabinet, for after a little while he came in again and said to me, 'You look very dejected.' I replied that I was and that I was sending in my resignation. He answered, 'Do you really mean that? Are you so certain that you are right?' I answered 'absolutely certain. I have no alternative but to go.' Grey replied, 'If you go, I shall go too. I shall see Asquith.' When the Cabinet met, either Grey or Asquith opened the proceedings with the suggestion that the decision on the shipbuilding programme should be reconsidered. It was reconsidered, and the programme, with immaterial variations, was sanctioned."[‡][11]

---

* Lloyd George proposed that four Dreadnoughts be approved for the moment and that Parliament be asked to sanction the construction of two more later in the year if these were found to be necessary.

† But it may have been towards the end of March.

‡ "I fear," Grey had written to Morley at the beginning of the month, "if we say 'we lay down six this year' the party will be split. But if we do *not* promise to lay down six, I think

However much truth there may or may not be in this account it is, at any rate, certain that the tide now began to turn against the Radicals. "The economists," wrote Asquith to his wife on February 20th, "are in a state of wild alarm, and Winston and Ll. G. by their combined machinations have got the bulk of the Liberal Press into the same camp. There is no real danger in the Cabinet—both J. Morley and Lulu for various reasons being disinclined to make common cause with the other two. They [the latter] go about darkly hinting at resignation (which is bluff) and there will be a lot of steam let off, and at any rate a temporary revival of the old pro-Boer animus. I am able to keep a fairly cool head amidst it all, but there are moments when I am disposed summarily to cashier them both. E. Grey is a great stand-by always, sound, temperate and strong."[13] From the tone of this letter it does not appear that McKenna and his supporters had been fighting a losing battle and one doubts, in fact, whether there was ever much possibility of the Radicals prevailing.

Nonetheless, the situation remained critical. "This morning," wrote Masterman to his wife on February 23rd, "I attended a *Nation* lunch, where a chorus of condemnation swept the Government. Indeed, with all their majority I think they are in a tight place—all the life and spirit has gone out of them, and the uncertainty about the Naval Estimates hangs over all. Our rank and file won't listen to anything more than four Dread-noughts and if the Govt. propose six they will have to depend on Tory votes and that will mean the beginning of the end."[14] As the following letter indicates, however, an unexpected solution to the problem was already at hand.

Asquith to his wife, February 25th, 1909

We had our final Cabinet on the navy yesterday, and I was quite prepared for a row and possible disruption. A sudden curve developed itself of which I took immediate advantage, with the result that strangely enough we came to a conclusion which satisfied McKenna and Grey and also Ll. G. and Winston. The effect will be to make us stronger in 1912 than McKenna's original proposal would have done.[15]

It was agreed, in fact, that the construction of four Dreadnoughts would now be sanctioned and that Parliament's consent would, if necessary, be sought for the construction of an additional four later in the year. A foot-

with the extent of German shipbuilding disclosed the feelings of apprehension in this country will be such that the country will become ungovernable. There will not only be scare but panic." He added (February 13th) that he would resign "if there are Navy Estimates which seem to me not to provide a sufficient margin of safety against possible German strength in 1912–13."[12]

note to this effect was inserted in the Estimates. Even so, Lloyd George and Churchill did not give up without a struggle, much to the irritation of their associates. "I think we are a very forbearing Cabinet to his chatter," Birrell told the Mastermans on March 9th, in reference to Churchill, and Grey commented that "Winston, very soon, will become incapable from sheer activity of mind of being anything in a Cabinet but Prime Minister."[16] As for Lloyd George, he was already intensely disliked by the majority of his colleagues and this latest proof of his inability to co-operate served only to strengthen their jealousy and distrust. Yet he was, of course, a dangerous person to antagonise, and the uneasy coalition between the Radical and moderate sections of the Liberal Party depended to a very large extent upon this one man.

Last-minute efforts were meanwhile made to see if Britain could reach some kind of accommodation with Germany. Grey suggested to Metternich on March 5th that the only way of settling the question of whether or not acceleration was taking place would be to let the British Naval Attaché in Berlin see the number of ships actually under construction and the stages which they had reached. Britain would, of course, grant reciprocal advantages to the German Naval Attaché in London. The German Ambassador replied five days later that his country could not agree to mutual inspection or to the exchange of information. He also announced that his statement of February 3rd had been incorrect and that Germany would not have thirteen Dreadnoughts until the *end* of 1912. Grey, somewhat taken back, argued that thirteen capital ships were surely under construction in some form or other, but this was stolidly denied.*[17]

The estimates were published on March 14th and debated by the Commons two days later. They totalled £35,142,700, an increase of £2,823,000 over those for 1908-9. In order to silence the angry mutterings of the Liberal rank and file, Asquith and McKenna were obliged to show that the scale of Britain's shipbuilding programme had become dependent upon the pace set by Germany. The arguments they used were, in effect, those already referred to above, namely that Germany had accelerated her construction during 1908, although it was not known to how great an extent, and by April 1912 might have thirteen or

---

* Asquith pointed out to Metternich on March 12th that work had been in progress on three of the four German Dreadnoughts of the 1909-10 programme for several months and that the keel of one of them had actually been laid down. Britain could obviously not object to this, but she must take it into account when calculating her own programme. Metternich was eventually forced to admit (March 18th) that contracts for two ships of the 1909-10 programme had indeed been placed in advance, in order to forestall the formation of a cartel by German shipbuilders. The vessels would, however, be built at a slower pace than usual and this procedure would not be repeated.

possibly seventeen capital ships. By the end of 1912, assuming that acceleration continued, she might even have twenty-one.* This being so, Britain had no alternative but to increase her own construction at a corresponding rate. Two Dreadnoughts would be laid down in July and two more in November but, most important of all, the Government claimed the right to propose the construction of four additional capital ships during the current financial year if the international situation compelled it to do so.

The effect of these revelations upon the Press and the general public was electric.† The possibility that by 1912 Germany might very well be in a position to challenge the British navy came as a shock and a wave of panic swept through the country which was scarcely distinguishable from mass-hysteria. Popular writers of the day gave their imaginations full vent and busied themselves with depicting the dreadful consequences of a German invasion. The Government was condemned for spending too little, rather than too much, upon sea defences and Lord Charles Beresford, Fisher's leading critic, was hailed as the hero of the hour. The Radicals were silenced and the Unionists, taking full advantage of this mood, demanded the immediate construction of the four contingent Dreadnoughts. George Wyndham, on March 27th, coined the slogan "We want eight and we won't wait!" and popular songs with this refrain were very soon being chanted in the streets.

McKenna's position in the Cabinet, as the following letter indicates, was immensely strengthened by the public clamour for eight Dreadnoughts.

Asquith to Grey, March 19th, 1909

Ll. G's remarks were, I believe, resented by the whole Cabinet, with the doubtful exception of Winston. Harcourt spoke to me about them afterwards with much indignation. The fact is that Ll. G. and Winston and J. M. feel that the course of things this week has been a complete débâcle for them and their ideas, and the two former cannot help reflecting how they would have looked at this moment if they had resigned, with (as Winston predicted) "90 per cent of the Liberal Party behind them".[19]

* These "public" calculations were less alarming than those which the Admiralty had made in private. Balfour, whose sources of information were extremely reliable, did in fact claim that the situation was even worse than the Government had depicted, and argued (as McKenna himself had done in his letter of January 3rd to the Prime Minister) that Germany might very well have thirteen battleships by May 1911 and twenty-one by May 1912. Asquith, however, pooh-poohed these figures.

† "All they said in their defence against the Little Navy men," wrote Austen Chamberlain on March 18th, "only served to strengthen the real attack—the charge that they are not doing enough."[18]

An Opposition vote of censure on March 29th was defeated by 353 to 135 and the estimates then received a speedy passage through both Houses. Asquith himself, however, despite his irritation with the "economists", continued to cherish hopes that it would not be necessary to construct the four contingent Dreadnoughts,* and Lloyd George and Churchill argued that if they *were* authorised during the current financial year then the number of Dreadnoughts for 1910-11 would have to be no more than two. McKenna, so Knollys reported to the King on March 27th, was "very sore" at this latest turn of events, and Grey again threatened to re-sign.[21] In a speech at Glasgow on April 17th the Prime Minister nevertheless argued against laying down the four additional Dreadnoughts, since tech-nical innovations might result in their obsolescence at an early date, and claimed that Britain's naval supremacy would still be assured for several years by virtue of the large number of pre-Dreadnoughts which she pos-sessed. A split in the Government was only averted, it seems, by the news that Austria-Hungary and Italy were also embarking upon programmes of Dreadnought construction. Asquith suppressed his misgivings and on July 16th the Cabinet decided that the four contingent vessels would have to be built, a decision which McKenna announced to the Commons on July 26th. Their actual construction would not begin until the following April, but the material that was needed for them would be ordered now. It was also emphasised that their construction would be "without prejudice" to the 1910-11 programme. Fisher, in short, had triumphed, and by this time Lloyd George was preoccupied with other matters.

(2)

Fisher's triumph was destined to be short-lived. Nemesis was at hand in the form of Lord Charles Beresford, until recently Commander-in-Chief of the Channel Fleet, and before another six months had elapsed the old warrior's tenure of the Admiralty was at an end.

Beresford, known to the service as "Charlie B.", was a colourful and popular figure. He had been a close friend of Fisher for many years, but from 1905 onwards their relationship had deteriorated. Beresford was strongly opposed to many of Fisher's innovations and the opponents of the First Sea Lord found him a satisfactory spokesman. Beresford's appoint-ment to the command of the Channel Fleet in April 1907 failed to improve matters. He disapproved of the policy of scrapping obsolete ships and the

* A letter to McKenna on March 2nd had referred to the possibility of laying down "two or even four", thus making it plain that he personally did not yet accept that the case for eight Dreadnoughts was incontrovertible.[20]

general emphasis on economies, felt that too much attention was being given to Dreadnought construction, lamented the absence of prepared plans in the event of war and described Fisher as a "dangerous lunatic". From 1908 onwards the Fleet was virtually split into Fisherites and Beresfordites. Both sides engaged in a pamphlet war, manipulation of the Press and violent public speeches. The "silent service" found its soubriquet in sorry disrepute. To add to this, another quarrel broke out between Beresford and a Rear-Admiral of the Fleet, Sir Percy Scott, who sympathised with Fisher. Arthur Lee, the Unionist Party's chief spokesman on naval affairs, remarked in a letter to *The Times* on July 6th, 1908 that it was no secret that "the Commander-in-Chief of the Channel Fleet (who is presumably the Admiralissimo designate in the event of war) is not on speaking terms with the admiral commanding his cruiser squadron on the one hand or with the First Sea Lord on the other."

Beresford was pressing, within a few months of his appointment, for a full-scale enquiry into Admiralty policy. He had several sympathisers in high places but the Board of Admiralty argued, in a memorandum to the Cabinet dated January 25th, 1908, that "it would be simply impossible for the members of the Board to retain office if . . . the investigation of its fighting policy by its subordinates were to be sanctioned."[22] Campbell-Bannerman apparently promised Fisher in February that no enquiry would be made and Asquith repeated this promise on April 15th, 1908. On the other hand, it was difficult to get rid of Beresford, whose friends in the Cabinet included Haldane and Lloyd George. McKenna endeavoured to do so in May 1908 but failed: seven months later he succeeded. Beresford was ordered to strike his flag when the Fleet reorganised in home waters the following March.

The controversy now entered its most virulent phase. Beresford, so it was said, had been sacked because he dared to criticise Fisher's policy. Viewed as David battling against Goliath, he was accorded a tremendous reception when he hauled down his flag at Portsmouth on March 24th. Crowds cheered him on his arrival in London and the Unionist Party adopted him as its hero. After consulting Balfour he saw Asquith on March 30th and told him that he would be forced to stump the country if the Government did not investigate Admiralty administration. He alleged that the navy was starved of cruisers and destroyers, that its strategical distribution was poor and that no war plans had been made. Fisher, moreover, had done much harm to the service by encouraging young officers to write to him privately about the conduct of their superiors. These charges were repeated in writing on April 2nd and, much to Fisher's disgust and indignation, Asquith decided on April 19th that an investigation would have to be made. It was announced three days later that a sub-committee of the Committee of Imperial Defence, composed of Asquith himself, Crewe, Morley, Grey and Haldane, would hold a private enquiry.

Between April 27th and July 13th, 1909 the committee met fifteen times, listening to the evidence of a long stream of naval witnesses. It soon became clear that, although Beresford's case could not be substantiated, Fisher's high-handed methods had aroused enough resentment in the service to make his tenure at the Admiralty seem perilously akin to a reign of terror. His reforms, their value not yet fully appreciated, were off-set by the manner in which he had ridden rough-shod over his critics. It was clear that anyone who had objected to Fisher's proposals stood in dire peril of having his career permanently wrecked. On August 12th, therefore, the committee issued a report which concluded that, although the Admiralty's arrangements for war were "quite defensible in themselves, though not ideally perfect," the absence of cordial relations between the Board of Admiralty and Beresford meant that they would have been seriously hampered in practice. The committee had, moreover, "been impressed with the differences of opinion amongst officers of high rank and professional attainments regarding important principles of naval strategy and tactics, and they look forward with much confidence to the further development of a Naval War Staff."*

Both Fisher and Beresford professed to regard this report as favourable to themselves, although the First Sea Lord was shaken by the Government's lack of support. He felt that the committee had taken Beresford's allegations far too seriously and that they had, in effect, condoned insubordination. His friends and sympathisers were equally disgruntled. "I am not myself surprised at the colourless report," wrote Knollys to Esher on August 23rd, "considering the composition of the committee, which I always thought an absurd one, and that the members of it were terrified of C. Beresford . . . especially Asquith."[23] His position materially weakened, Fisher felt that resignation at the earliest moment was the only possible course. He had, after all, done all that he had set out to do: the navy had been re-vitalised and Dreadnought construction was as assured for the immediate future as he could reasonably expect. The King and the Government had expressed their gratitude but had also made it plain that he was outstaying his welcome. In November, therefore, he accepted the

* Haldane, in 1906, had created a General Staff for the army, the principal task of which was the formulation of grand strategy. The navy, however, possessed no such body, and its plans, such as they were, were known to Fisher and hardly anyone else.

title of Baron Fisher and his resignation took effect from January 25th, 1910.

There was considerable bitterness at Fisher's departure. There were also many sighs of relief. From now onwards the navy became a much happier place and the feuds, intrigues and dissensions which had been so marked a feature of his tenure of office gradually disappeared. The period of whirlwind activity was followed by one of steady consolidation. At the same time, however, it must be emphasised that it was this one man who had dragged the British navy, squalling, kicking and screaming, from the beguiling somnolence of the nineteenth century into the piercing rigours of the twentieth. This was, at the very least, something of an achievement.

(3)

The reverberations of the Balkan crisis, which had been sparked off by the Habsburg annexation of Bosnia and Herzegovina in October 1908, continued into 1909. Serbia continued to behave in a provocative manner and Aehrenthal continued to proclaim that his patience was nearing exhaustion. Austro-Turkish negotiations had not made much headway nor, for that matter, had those between Bulgaria and Turkey, and the Habsburg Foreign Minister chose to regard Britain as the chief impediment to progress.* There was a slight easing of the tension with the conclusion, on January 26th, of an agreement between Austria-Hungary and Turkey, whereby the former undertook to renounce the Sandjak and to pay an indemnity of two and a half million francs. An agreement between Bulgaria and Turkey was, however, rather more difficult to arrange. Both sides were interested in some kind of military alliance but the stumblingblock to this was Bulgaria's refusal to pay more than 82 million francs in compensation, whereas Russia and Britain felt that Turkey was entitled to at least 102 million. Isvolsky suggested to the Bulgarian agent on January 30th that Russia should make up the difference by cancelling some of Turkey's war debt to herself. The agent was very taken with this idea and so was Nicolson when he heard of it. The Sultan was not, at first, particularly responsive and the British Ambassador at Constantinople was told to use all his powers of persuasion to secure acceptance of Isvolsky's scheme.

Germany was, at this time, endeavouring to improve her relations with France and Britain, presumably in order to isolate Russia in her dispute

---

* "From all I hear," wrote the British Ambassador to Grey on January 7th, "Aehrenthal is incensed against us and his fury is fanned with all their might by the Germans. . . . He frequently alludes in a vague manner to what I may term the 'mauvais vouloir' of His Majesty's Government in not using their utmost influence to stop the boycott and so on. To others he is more outspoken."[24]

with Austria-Hungary. On February 9th she concluded an agreement with France whereby she recognised the latter's political predominance in Morocco in return for an assurance that her economic interests therein would not be injured. France was pleased with this agreement and so, for that matter, was Britain. It coincided with a State visit to Berlin which King Edward VII, accompanied by Hardinge and Crewe, paid from February 9th to the 12th, and Hardinge, discussing the Near Eastern crisis with Bülow, discovered what he felt was "a community of interests with Germany in her desire for the preservation of peace in the Balkans and the maintenance of the 'status quo' ." They also agreed, moreover, that a conference should not be held until preliminary understandings had been reached. "Bülow's disapproval of Aehrenthal's procedure was most marked," wrote Hardinge to Nicolson on February 16th, "and I left with the impression that Bülow would, under certain circumstances, act with France and ourselves in the Near East and proceed in conformity with Anglo-French and Russian views."[25]

Mobilisation orders were now issued to the Viennese reserves and the Foreign Office instructed Fairfax Cartwright, their new Ambassador, to co-operate with his French, German and Italian colleagues in asking Aehrenthal whether there was any definite action on the part of Serbia of which Austria complained or whether she had any reason to apprehend such action. Cartwright found, however, that France and Italy would not act without Germany's approval. Bülow felt that action should be taken at Belgrade rather than Vienna and on February 24th Germany suggested to France that they should secure the co-operation of Britain and Russia in persuading Serbia to come to terms. The French were favourably disposed towards this idea and approached the British. The latter, however, felt they could not reply without prior consultations with the Russians, and Isvolsky was strongly opposed to the proposal, which he said had been made simply to place Russia in an embarrassing position. He was furious with France for daring to support it. On February 26th France dropped even further in his estimation when she informed the Russian Government that she felt Serbia's demands were unjustified and that French public opinion would not agree to a declaration of war in support of them.

Grey felt that the time had come for Russia to decide just how far she intended to go in pressing Serbia's claims for territorial compensation. He was relieved to learn on March 1st that Isvolsky had persuaded Serbia to drop them, and he told the Russian Chargé d'Affaires that Britain would do all she could by diplomatic means to secure the best possible settlement for Serbia. Aehrenthal, however, was not particularly impressed by this turn of events; he was well aware that Russia was in no fit state to go to war and he had no intention of allowing international arbitration. What he wanted from Serbia was complete submission, and on March 6th he demanded her agreement to the annexations and to the new situation in the Balkans as set forth in the protocol to the Austro-Turkish agreement. He also demanded that Serbia abandon her warlike activity, adopt a more friendly attitude and agree to the conclusion of a commercial treaty.

Serbia, on March 11th, circulated a note to the other Powers in which she stated that she desired to be on friendly terms with Austria-Hungary, that she did not ask for territorial compensations and that she entrusted her case to their hands. Britain and Russia hoped that these declarations would convince Austria-Hungary of Serbia's pacific intentions and pave the way to a negotiated settlement, but Aehrenthal told Cartwright that unconditional agreement to his demands was all that he could accept. On March 14th Serbia produced her formal reply, but it was couched in such impudent language that the Foreign Office feared that it might lead directly to war. Far from being a docile submission to Austria-Hungary it amounted to nothing more than a condescending agreement to enter into negotiations for a commercial treaty which would, presumably, benefit both participants.

The situation became very tense. The Foreign Office hastily drafted a much more conciliatory answer for Serbia to make, and Aehrenthal, when sounded by Cartwright, had no initial objection to its wording. Serbia agreed to make it, but just when it seemed that the gulf had finally been bridged the Austrian Foreign Minister had second thoughts. He pointed out that, among other things, the British draft referred to a *continuance* of good relations between Austria-Hungary and Serbia, whereas past relations had been far from satisfactory. It also made Serbia's acceptance of the annexations conditional upon that of the Powers, whereas it ought to be given independently and at once. What Aehrenthal wanted, in fact, was a clear official guarantee from Serbia that she would immediately abandon all her objections to the annexations and that she would henceforth act in a friendly manner. These points were made in a revised version of the British draft with which Aehrenthal presented Cartwright on March 21st. He stated, as the one concession which he was prepared to make, that if each of the Powers informed him privately in writing that it would raise no objection to the ratification of the Austro-Turkish protocol when it came before the conference, he would be prepared to accept a declaration from Serbia that she would recognise any alteration in the Treaty of Berlin approved by the Powers.

Isvolsky was incensed at this latest example of Habsburg guile. The more concessions that were made to Austria-Hungary, he complained to Nicolson on March 21st, the more she would be encouraged to ask. This was a conclusion which Grey had also reached, but neither Britain nor Russia was in a position to call the tune. Slowly but surely they were being out-manoeuvred on every level. Another draft was put forward by the Foreign Office, but this too was deemed unacceptable by Aehrenthal.

Germany had not yet played a really important part in the Near Eastern crisis. To some extent this was, of course, understandable: Aehrenthal's ventures had not been regarded with too friendly an eye in the Wilhelmstrasse, while Bülow, although proclaiming Germany's steadfast intention of supporting Austria-Hungary through thick and thin, was known to be far from happy about the general situation. The Austrian Foreign Minister wanted, moreover, a free hand in the Balkans and did not welcome unsolicited assistance from the Kaiser. None the less, it was impossible for Germany to resist using the situation to suit her own ends and the news of Russia's decision (taken in secret) not to go to war over Serbia apparently precipitated the last act in this drama. On March 17th the German Ambassador to St Petersburg urged Isvolsky to agree to recognise the annexations if Austria-Hungary asked him to do so. The Russian Foreign Minister promised to think about it. On March 21st the German Foreign Office instructed their Ambassador to repeat the request but this time to demand a definite reply within twelve hours. The reply was to be simply yes or no: any evasive, complicated or ambiguous answer was to be regarded as a refusal, in which case Germany would "withdraw and allow matters to take their course."

The Ambassador carried out his instructions the following day and Isvolsky submitted to the German demands with little more than a momentary hesitation. He saw Nicolson on the evening of March 23rd and read him the text of Russia's reply, which was a simple acceptance of the annexations. There had been, he explained, no time to consult either the British or the French Ambassador. In any case, Britain's support could only be of a diplomatic nature, while France, sad to relate, could not be relied upon to honour the obligations of an ally. For all practical purposes Russia was isolated and defenceless, in no fit state to embark upon another war, and confronted with a powerful military combination had no option but to give way. Nicolson, though privately somewhat relieved that he had not been consulted, argued that Great Britain, France and Russia would have been more than equal to any combination. Isvolsky replied that this might be so in a sense but that there was no alliance binding them together. The British Ambassador pondered upon this lack of a positive alliance and, a few hours later, wrote the following letter to his chief.

Nicolson to Grey, March 24th, 1909

After this easy victory, I should not be surprised if greater demands were made of Russia and that she, like Serbia, will be asked to change her course of policy. . . . My firm opinion is that both Germany and Austria are carrying out a line of policy and action carefully prepared and thought out. Algeciras had to be revenged: the "ring" broken through and the Triple Entente dissipated. The Franco-German agreement was the first step; and France is a quarter of the way towards a fuller understanding with Germany. Russia is temporarily weak, with a timorous Foreign Minister. She had to be frightened out of the entente and the first step towards this has been eminently successful. The Franco-Russian alliance has not borne the test and the Anglo-Russian entente is not sufficiently strong or sufficiently deep rooted to have any appreciable influence. . . .

Our entente, I much fear, will languish and possibly die. If it were possible to extend and strengthen it by bringing it nearer to the nature of an alliance, it would then be possible to deter Russia from moving towards Berlin. The bulk of intelligent public opinion is at present in favour of working with us and is hostile to Austria and Germany, but if it be found that the entente cannot save them from humiliating concessions public feeling would, perhaps reluctantly, recognise that terms had better be made with the other parties. . . .

If we could keep France and Russia on our side it would be well; and if we could contract some kind of alliance with Russia, we should probably also steady France and prevent her from deserting to the Central Powers.[26]

The Foreign Office was angered by Russia's capitulation and on March 25th Grey indignantly rejected Metternich's proposal that Britain should now recognise the annexations. Such a recognition, he declared, would have to form part of a general Near Eastern settlement and could not be given without reference to the other issues at stake. Two days later, however, Sir Edward climbed down. He accepted the wording of a declaration which Aehrenthal had drafted for deliverance by Serbia and agreed that Britain would recognise the annexations if Serbia made the declaration. Serbia in turn had no option but to give way, which she did on March 30th, and Britian's formal recognition followed a fortnight later. The crisis was at an end, but the cost in national prides had been heavy and feelings were bitter. There had been no international conference and no compensation for Serbia, but the annexations had been recognised and Aehrenthal had been able to dictate his own terms. Britain did not, in the circumstances, suffer too great a loss of face, which was something that could not be said of her associate. "I have been assured," wrote Nicolson to Grey on March 29th, "that there has never previously been a moment when Russia has undergone such humiliation. Though Russia has had her troubles, both internal and external, and has suffered defeats in the field she has never had, for apparently no valid cause, to submit to the direction of a foreign Power."[27]

Nicolson's plea for an alliance with Russia had meanwhile been weighed in the balance and found wanting. "I do not think," Grey wrote to him on April 2nd, "that it is practicable to change our agreements into alliances: the feeling here about definite commitments to a continental war on un-foreseeable conditions would be too dubious to permit us to make an alliance. Russia too must make her internal government less reactionary—till she does, liberal sentiment here will remain very cool, and even those who are not sentimental will not believe that Russia can purge her administration sufficiently to be come a strong and reliable power. Meanwhile, let us keep an entente with Russia in the sense of keeping in touch, so that our diplomatic action may be in accord and in mutual support."[*][28]

(4)

The guiding lights of Grey's policy during his first three years at the Foreign Office had been the preservation of the *entente cordiale* and the establishment and maintenance of good relations with Russia. In theory, this was the ideal combination to keep in check the machinations of the Triple Alliance, but in practice the "Triple Entente" had proved of little value so far as real power politics were concerned. France was too slippery and Russia too weak to be relied upon.[†] Britain's foreign policy from this point onwards, therefore, would have to follow one of three courses: she could transform the agreements with France and Russia into formal alliances, she could seek to improve Anglo-German relations or, finally, she could do nothing at all for the moment and simply wait upon the course of events.

The first of these courses was not, on the whole, an attractive one. The entente with France was already, for all practical purposes, a military

---

[*] "I shall be glad of a change of Government," wrote Nicolson to his wife on May 3rd. "I am afraid we are not likely with the present people to have a well defined, firm foreign policy. We shall drift on amicably from day to day. I shall not continue to plead for an alliance with Russia, as it is clearly useless to do so."[29]

[†] On May 6th the Foreign Office instructed its staff not to use the term "Triple Entente" in official documents: "the expression is one which is no doubt convenient, but if it appeared in a Parliamentary Bluebook it would be assumed to have some special official meaning and might provoke inconvenient comment or enquiry."[30]

alliance, and the transformation of an "understanding" into a formal agreement would be difficult to achieve and, in the event, might very well do Britain more harm than good.* An alliance with Russia, moreover, was quite out of the question at this time. The Czarist regime was detested in Britain, and the agreements of 1907 and the King's subsequent trip to Reval had given rise to much angry criticism from a good many members of the Liberal and Labour Parties.

Anglo-Russian relations, following upon the settlement of the Near Eastern crisis, were in fact somewhat cool. Britain, quite apart from Isvolsky's sudden capitulation to Germany (which was regarded in many quarters as a put-up job),† was not pleased at the sudden arrival of Russian troops in northern Persia, ostensibly to protect the newly formed government at Tehran against domestic upheaval and possible attack from Turkey. Russia's assurances of good faith were dutifully accepted and the Czar's visit to Cowes in August, during which Isvolsky had several long but unimportant talks with Asquith and Grey on board the *Enchantress*, helped to improve matters, but the bonds of friendship were no longer so tight as before and during the crisis.

The second possibility was one which the Foreign Office considered worthy of investigation. The public outcry over the Dreadnought revelations had brought home to the Government the realisation that the only alternative to spending more and more money on bigger and better battleships, and possibly splitting the Liberal Party in the process, was to improve relations generally with Germany and to reach agreement on the shipbuilding question in particular. There were signs, moreover, that the Triple Alliance was not so formidable a combination as it seemed. Reports from Vienna made it clear that Aehrenthal was far from pleased at the Serbian crisis having been settled by German intervention and he allowed it to be rumoured that Isvolsky had given way as the result of a threat from Austria-Hungary to publish certain correspondence of the previous year. From Rome, meanwhile, came news of Italy's lack of

---

* The fall of Clemenceau's Government on July 24th and the appearance of a less dynamic administration under Briand was another important factor. "The French," wrote Valentine Chirol (a foreign correspondent of *The Times*) to H.W. Steed on November 13th, "do not seem to realise that there is amongst a large section of public opinion here—with which, however, I do not in the least sympathise—a growing feeling that the entente is not worth the risks in which it involves us, owing to the delicate situation in Morocco."[31]

† Goschen reported to Hardinge on June 11th that he had heard " 'on the best authority' that it was Isvolsky himself who engineered the whole of the so-called Russo-German incident." In a conversation with Cartwright in September, Isvolsky alluded to the "so-called German ultimatum" and declared that it had been nothing of the kind. Germany had acted in a friendly spirit and had merely stated that if war broke out between Russia and Austria-Hungary it would be very difficult for her to remain neutral. He claimed to be irritated at the distorted accounts of this episode which had appeared in the European Press.[32]

enthusiasm for the annexations and for any further provocative actions on the part of Germany or Austria which would compromise her own security.*

Goschen reported from Berlin that the Press and Government officials were anxious for an understanding or *rapprochement* with Britain and this was followed on May 7th by his account of a long talk with Schön, the new Foreign Minister. The latter declared that he would like an agreement with Britain on all outstanding colonial problems, which would "have an excellent effect upon public opinion both here and in England and show the Press that the two countries could work well and amicably together." Such an agreement might be the prelude to an even closer understanding. On June 22nd Schön asked the Ambassador what he could suggest as a remedy for the present uneasy situation. "The only remedy," wrote Grey, when he learned of this conversation, "can be exchange of naval information through the respective naval attachés, and that the Germans will not adopt. As regards smaller matters between us we will adopt a conciliatory attitude if they will reciprocate."[33]

On July 14th Bülow resigned. He told Goschen, in the last conversation he had with him as Chancellor, that Germany was very anxious to be on good terms with Britain and his successor, Theobald von Bethmann Hollweg, reiterated this theme. On August 21st the latter informed Goschen that Germany was ready to conclude a naval agreement. This agreement would form part of a larger understanding and each country would declare that it had no hostile designs against the other. If Russia, for instance, made an unprovoked attack on Austria-Hungary, Germany would have to assist her ally. If, on the other hand, Germany were to launch an unprovoked attack on France, Britain would be fully justified in coming to France's rescue. The fact that these statements should be made at all was regarded as heartening by the Foreign Office and, with a new Chancellor still feeling his way, Grey was anxious not to appear unco-operative. Goschen was therefore instructed to inform Bethmann Hollweg that his views had "made a most favourable impression upon H.M. Government," that Britain was ready to discuss naval expenditure at any time and that any proposal for a political understanding would be received with "the greatest sympathy", although Britain would have to take into account her friendships with other Powers.[34] Grey felt, in fact, that proposals for a naval agreement would be very welcome but that any proposals of a

* Italy had concluded a secret agreement with France in 1902 whereby she agreed to remain neutral in the event of a Franco-German war. The Foreign Office did not learn of this agreement until 1908.

wider nature would probably go far beyond anything so far concluded with France and Russia. "It strikes me at first sight," he commented, "that if any general political understanding is to be arranged it should be one not between two Powers alone but between the two great groups of Powers, ourselves, France and Russia on one side and the Triple Alliance on the other. Whether any understanding of this sort is possible it is difficult to say, but anything short of it is sure to be regarded as invidious by those who are left out."[35]

On October 15th Goschen had two long talks with Schön, at the first of which Bethmann Hollweg was present. The Chancellor agreed that a general Anglo-German understanding would exceed anything that Britain had reached with France and Russia but pointed out that the *entente cordiale* and the Anglo-Russian conventions had had an unsettling effect upon public opinion in his country. A formal assurance to the effect that neither of these agreements was directed against Germany would be a great help when it came to negotiating a naval arrangement. Without such an assurance, in fact, it was doubtful whether any real progress could be made. Both Bethmann Hollweg and Schön were very vague as to the form that a naval arrangement might take, but Goschen finally gathered that Germany, while committed to the programme of 1900 which had stipulated certain goals to be reached by 1918, would not be averse to slowing down the pace of construction for a couple of years. During 1910 and 1911, in other words, fewer ships would be built but the difference would be made up in 1916 and 1917. There was just a faint possibility that the Reichstag, satisfied with Britain's pacific assurances and the smooth working of this arrangement, would meanwhile "look twice at incurring unnecessary expenditure" and decide not to proceed with the vessels held in abeyance.[36]

These proposals took a more definite shape on November 4th, when Bethmann Hollweg presented them to Goschen as a basis for negotiations. Both Governments were to declare that they would neither attack nor entertain any hostile thoughts against the other and that each would remain neutral in the event of the other being involved in war with a third party. The naval arrangement, the details of which would be settled by their respective Admiralties, envisaged both countries binding themselves for three or four years not to build more than a stated number of capital ships. The Foreign Office, for reasons which need not be stated at too great a length, was not impressed. It seemed that Germany was more concerned with reducing her current expenditure than in improving her relations with Britain and that, contrary to Bethmann Hollweg's conciliatory remarks, she was simply playing for time in a rather obvious manner. Churchill, as President of the Board of Trade, had on November 3rd circulated among his colleagues in the Cabinet a memorandum on Germany's internal finances. They were, he concluded, in a bad way, since the Imperial debt had more than doubled since 1898 and now stood at about £220,000,000. "The overflowing expenditure of the German Empire," he wrote, "strains and threatens every dyke by which the social and political unity of Germany is maintained": the tension could only be "relieved by moderation or snapped by calculated violence."[37] Bethmann Hollweg's proposals presumably represented moderation. It was, however, difficult to take them seriously. The naval programme of 1900 was going to be slowed down only to be speeded up again in a few years' time, but Britain was expected to follow suit despite the fact that Austria-Hungary and Italy had started constructing Dreadnoughts of their own. She was also expected to avoid participation in a European war except on terms approved in advance by the Kaiser and his ministers.

Bethmann Hollweg's scheme, in short, was quite unacceptable, and since a mutual assurance of non-aggression was regarded as a necessary prelude to negotiations there seemed little point in giving the subject any further consideration. In Britain, as Grey had written to Goschen on October 28th, "a general understanding would have no beneficial effect whatever on public opinion and would indeed be an object of criticism so long as naval expenditure remains undiminished"; to Germany it was a *sine qua non*.[38] Too prompt a rejection would, however, be unwise and Grey duly informed Metternich, on November 17th, that a decision could not be taken until the forthcoming election was out of the way. A week or so later, it should be noted, the Admiralty decided to increase the number of capital ships in the estimates for 1910–11 from four to six.

It was, therefore, the third of the three possible courses of action listed above which Britain eventually followed.

(5)

Another subject which gave rise to some controversy at this time was the Baghdad railway. In 1899 Turkey had granted a German company the right of constructing a railway from the Sea of Marmora to the Persian Gulf. Russia had been rather alarmed by this concession but France and, at first, Britain had been only too pleased to see the Germans occupying themselves in spheres which seemingly had no direct bearing upon their own respective interests. Work on the railway did not commence until

1903 and it was clear from the outset that the Germans lacked the resources to carry it through to rapid completion. Foreign assistance would have to be sought, but such assistance was likely to have strings attached and the Germans trod very carefully. Grey, while interested, did not feel that Britain should pursue independent negotiations with Germany, and it was not until November 1906, when Isvolsky told Nicolson that he would be willing to initiate discussions with Germany with a view to Britain, France and Russia joining forces in offering her financial assistance, that the Government gave the matter any serious consideration. A Cabinet Committee, composed of Grey, Asquith, Morley and Lloyd George, examined the question and (with an eye on the security of India) decided, as Morley informed Minto on May 31st 1907, that British participation would have to "be on the footing of our having entire rights of construction and management from Baghdad or from Mosul."[39] A few days later the Foreign Office sent a memorandum on this subject to the French and Russian Ambassadors, arguing that the railway would displace the existing means of communication in Mesopotamia and introduce changes into the trade of the whole region. Prudence surely dictated that they should press Germany to agree not only to the establishment of international control over the railway but to the construction and maintenance of individual sections of the line by France, Russia and Britain. These proposals did not, however, meet with a very warm reception: French businessmen, by this time, had invested heavily in the railway, while Russia hesitated to incur the wrath of the Wilhelmstrasse.

In November 1907 the Kaiser told Haldane that he had no objection to consulting Britain, France and Russia over the future of the railway. The British were delighted with this declaration, but as the months slipped by with nothing more said their hopes began to fade. Metternich, at length, called at the Foreign Office on June 25th, 1908 to state that a conference between the four Powers was not, after all, regarded as a practicable proposition, but Germany would be pleased to discuss the Baghdad railway at any time with Britain herself. "This would mean," commented Grey, "a quarrel with Russia: and if we bargain alone we shall not get good terms. The Germans have now arranged for some further sections of the railway to be built: these will take some years and for the present I can see nothing for it but to get as many levers into our hands as possible with which to bring pressure to bear later on."[40]

The opportunity for obtaining a few levers came almost a year later, in the summer of 1909, when the Sultan announced his intention of increasing the customs duties by 4%. Turkey's finances were under international control and such an increase could only be effected if all the Powers agreed. Britain, in this instance, did not agree since the only reason that the Turks needed more money was their desire to guarantee, for Germany's benefit, every kilometre of the Baghdad railway against possible loss. Without such a guarantee work on the railway would be held up, but two-thirds of the additional revenue would have to come from British pockets and Britain had no desire to finance an undertaking that could only result in the crippling of her own commercial supremacy in Mesopotamia. The Foreign Office decided, therefore, to press for either a substantial share in the control of the projected railway or permission to build a rival Baghdad railway. Sir Gerard Lowther, the British Ambassador, did in fact ask the Grand Vizier in September whether a British company could be granted the concession of constructing a railway through the Tigris Valley. The Grand Vizier was reluctant to agree to this request and Germany was none too pleased when she heard of it. Grey, on October 28th, argued Britain's case with Metternich. No direct reply came from the Wilhelmstrasse but a few days later a Dr Gwinner, a director of the Deutsche Bank and an agent of the Baghdad Railway Company, intimated to a Mr Whittall, a British businessman with several interests in Constantinople, that it might be possible to grant Britain the construction, control and maintenance of the railway from Baghdad to the Gulf as long as she agreed to the increase in the customs duties.

Sir Ernest Cassel, a very well-known British financier and a close friend of King Edward VII, participated in the negotiations with Gwinner from early December onwards and it was felt, in some quarters of the Foreign Office, that genuine progress was at last being made. On December 15th, however, Schön told Goschen that, although Cassel and Gwinner might reach a provisional agreement, "it did not follow that the Imperial Government would see their way to confirming such an agreement—at all events not at once." Public opinion would be enraged if Germany gave way to Britain in too abrupt a fashion and there would certainly be a universal cry that German interests were being sacrificed if Britain made no concessions in return. "From the remark which Herr von Schön casually dropped with regard to what might happen when the discussions concerning Anglo-German future relations were resumed," commented Goschen, "it may, I think, be fairly surmised that it is in the mind of the Imperial Government that the construction and control of the Baghdad/Persian Gulf section of the Baghdad railway may be utilised as a lever to push His Majesty's Government further in the direction of a political understanding than they have yet shown any disposition to go."[41]

K

(6)

The general election of January 1910 came and went. The Liberals were returned to power but with their majority so drastically slashed that they were henceforth dependent upon the Irish Nationalists and the Labour Party for their continuance in office. A prominent feature of the Unionist campaign had been the accusation that the Government was unable to cope with the growing menace of the German navy. Lurid speeches were made by Balfour and others at which the Kaiser and his ministers were only too ready to profess themselves mortally offended. The Foreign Office, caught between two streams of fire, did its best to discount the effect of these speeches but with no great success. It was noted, towards the end of January, that the German Emperor was lavishing much attention upon the French, attending a party at their Embassy and going out of his way to praise an exhibition of French paintings which had opened in Berlin. To the Russians he was equally civil but at the British Ambassador, alas, he wagged a reproachful finger and declared that the English were "mad, all mad". Nothing was said about the proposals of November 4th.

Wilhelm II would, perhaps, have been even more offended at this time had he known the size of the Naval Estimates which McKenna was pushing through the Cabinet. The Admiralty modified some of their initial proposals but insisted that the programmes for 1910–11 and 1911–12 should each include five capital ships, namely four Dreadnoughts and one cruiser. The Cabinet gave way, the Liberal Party reluctantly acquiesced and the Opposition contented themselves with the reflection that this was the least that could be expected. "In ordinary circumstances," wrote Churchill to King Edward VII on March 11th, "these Estimates would have led to vehement debates in the House of Commons" but the times, of course, were far from normal. "The political issues between the two Houses dominate the situation. The resistance to expenditure of all kinds was never at a more feeble ebb."[42]

The negotiations between Cassell and Gwinner dragged on for another three months, the main point at issue being the sum which Turkey should set aside from her revenue for kilometric guarantees, but the Foreign Office had ceased to take them very seriously. Lowther was instructed to remind the Grand Vizier that Britain was still awaiting a reply to her request of the previous September for a Baghdad railway of her own: if the Turkish Government were unable to grant it and were equally unable to secure Britain's satisfactory participation in the German scheme, then there could be no question of her adhesion to the proposed customs increase.

Metternich, on March 22nd, reminded Grey that nothing had been said about Anglo-German negotiations since the general election. Sir Edward apologised for the delay, but explained that the Cabinet had been so preoccupied that he had not yet had an opportunity of putting Bethmann Hollweg's proposals before them. He observed, however, that there had been no indication when the negotiations were suspended that Germany was prepared to modify her naval programme in any way. Metternich replied that it had always been made quite clear that the programme could not be altered, a statement which Grey seized upon as the crux of the matter. Any agreement, he argued, would have to result, so far as Britian was concerned, in a diminution of naval expenditure, but if Germany refused to modify her programme that expenditure would have to remain unchanged.

The Wilhelmstrasse promptly played a return match. Bethmann Hollweg summoned Goschen to him on April 10th and told him that he had gathered that the naval proposals which he had made the previous November would not be acceptable to the British public. This was a pity, but he feared that any proposal to hand over the southern section of the Baghdad railway to Britain would be equally unacceptable to the German public. The railway was, after all, justly acclaimed as a great national undertaking but Britain had hampered its construction from the outset, persuading France and Russia to do the same. How, then, could the Imperial Government possibly make a present of the most valuable section of the whole line to the very Power which had most bitterly opposed her?* Some very substantial concession on Britain's part was obviously called for and he did not feel that agreement to the 4% increase in Turkey's customs duties would be enough. What would, however, go some way towards satisfying German public opinion would be an assurance that German capital and industry would be allowed a fair share in the construction of roads, railways and telegraphs in the British sphere of influence in Persia.

The Foreign Office had no difficulty in deciding that Bethmann Hollweg's latest proposals, like his earlier, were totally inadmissible, and the following letter is a fair enough indication of Grey's news at this time.

Grey to Goschen, May 5th, 1910

Crawford, of the Turkish Customs Service, tells me that 65% of the trade with Mesopotamia is British. On this trade, in the first instance, will fall the burden of

---

* One would scarcely have thought, from this tirade, that the original suggestion of such a presentation had emanated from Dr Gwinner.

the 4% increase, until it is passed on to the Turkish consumer. There will be a great outcry when the increase is made and I shall have all I can do to get public opinion here to recognise that participation in the Baghdad railway is an adequate "quid pro quo" for a new burden upon British trade, only a part of which is interested in Mesopotamia. This is my first difficulty. It would be insuperable if I had to make another set of concessions as well.

In the next place, with regard to any understanding with Germany, the attention of public opinion here is concentrated on the mutual arrest or decrease of naval expenditure as *the* test of whether an understanding is worth anything. In the first overtures of Bethmann Hollweg last year I felt that the naval question was not sufficiently prominent. Since then it has receded into the background and the perspective of his last proposals is therefore even less advantageous. This is an important point.

In the third place, there is this difficulty with regard to any general political understanding: we cannot sacrifice the friendship of Russia or France. There is no intention of using either for aggressive purposes against Germany. When Germany settled her difficulty with France about Morocco, not only was I free from jealousy but I had a sense of absolute relief. I had hated the prospect of friendship with France involving friction with Germany and I rejoiced when this prospect disappeared. My attitude is the same with regard to Germany's difficulty with Russia about Persia. Also, I am quite sure that neither France nor Russia wishes to quarrel with Germany; indeed, I know that they wish to avoid a quarrel. So on this ground I am quite easy. But I cannot enter into any agreement with Germany which would prevent me from giving to France or Russia, should Germany take up towards either of them an aggressive attitude such as she took up towards France about Morocco, the same sort of support as I gave to France at the time of the Algeciras Conference and afterwards until she settled her difficulty with Germany. Any agreement which prevented the giving of such support would obviously forfeit the friendship of France and Russia and this is what makes me apprehensive of trouble in finding a political formula.[43]

(7)

After the alarums and excursions of the previous two years, a period of unexpected peace now descended upon Europe. Schön was succeeded by Kiderlen-Waechter, who bided his time before reviving the tactics of Holstein, while Isvolsky thankfully departed to the Paris Embassy and left Sergius Sazonow in control of Russia's foreign affairs. A British mission, led by Rosebery, arrived in Vienna in September to announce to Franz Josef the death of King Edward and the accession of George V and was said to have made a very good impression. All that really happened to mar the generally tranquil atmosphere was a fresh outbreak of Turkish atrocities in Macedonia. Bulgaria appealed to the Powers to intervene, but since neither Germany nor Austria-Hungary were willing to respond Britain contented herself with advising Turkey to be more "moderate" in her administration.

Anglo-German negotiations about a possible naval agreement still continued. To clarify the situation, Grey sent Goschen a memorandum for Bethmann Hollweg's attention which summarised the position so far reached. This document, dated July 26th, referred to the two proposals already made, first that Germany should alter her existing naval law, which had been declared impossible, and secondly that she should reduce the tempo of her shipbuilding, which Britain was ready to consider. A third suggestion, not yet discussed, was that Germany should bind herself not to increase her present programme of construction but that the two Admiralties should regularly exchange information in order to reassure themselves of the actual progress of shipbuilding in their respective countries.

Bethmann Hollweg was quite impressed with this memorandum, but the Kaiser upset the apple-cart when he informed Goschen on October 16th that he would in no circumstances bind himself not to add to Germany's naval programme. The Foreign Office decided, therefore, to play for time by citing the impending general election as a reason for postponing any detailed consideration of the Chancellor's reply. Grey felt, none the less, that Germany's professed readiness to enter into an exchange of naval information was an advance on her previous position. He ascertained from the Admiralty that the minimum information required would be the dimensions of the vessels to be laid down, their protection, armament and speed and their estimated time of completion. He then asked Metternich whether the German Government insisted that the exchange of information should depend upon a general political understanding. The Ambassador was able to inform him, on December 16th, that his Government did not so insist and that they were ready to co-operate whenever Britain gave the word. Grey thanked him and explained that, now that the latest election was over and the Government once again confirmed in office, the Cabinet would discuss the whole question of a political formula and the German naval programme at the earliest possible opportunity.

The Admiralty and the Foreign Office had, by now, realised that the menace of Germany's shipbuilding activities was not so serious as it had seemed in March 1909. It could be appreciated that the forecasts made at that time were wildly inaccurate and that Germany, so far from having twenty-one capital ships completed by the end of 1912, would be lucky if she had fourteen.

(8)

The whirligig of time was, it seemed, producing some strange combinations. The Triple Alliance was no longer the formidable instrument it had once appeared: Italy had defected in everything but name, making private defence agreements with France and Russia, while Germany and Austria-Hungary were, for the moment, rivals rather than partners. The "Triple Entente", on the other hand was now even less of a reality than it had been in 1907: the Bosnian crisis had shown that international commitments were only worth what those committed chose to make of them. France was content, for the most part, to ignore anything which did not concern Morocco, although she had not approached Britain for assistance during the Casablanca episode, and Anglo-Russian relations had undergone something of a deterioration.*

None the less, the events of the past five years could not be easily forgotten. There had been three occasions on which war in Europe had been spoken of as a real possibility, and there was no guarantee that the impossible might not actually happen on a fourth occasion. Grey's arrival at the Foreign Office had coincided with the first of these crises, and it seems that his outlook was henceforth coloured, to an alarming extent, by the events of December 1905 and January 1906. He developed, as we have noted, something of an obsession about preserving the *entente cordiale* and was correspondingly disinclined to make peaceful overtures to Germany, which he came to regard with increasing (and often unjustified) distrust. It was, admittedly, argued by the Foreign Office that Britain had a moral obligation to support France in any dispute with a third party arising from the terms of the 1904 agreement, but it does not follow that this was an adequate reason for secret Anglo–French military discussions, based on the supposition that Germany would one day attack France, nor does the presence of a Belgian representative at these discussions justify them in retrospect. The plain fact of the matter was that Sir Edward had gone as far as he could in transforming the *entente* into an alliance, and had concealed his activities in this respect, like many other aspects of his foreign policy, from all but a few members of the Cabinet.†

* It was with some indignation, indeed, that the Foreign Office eventually learned that Russia had acknowledged Germany's right to a free hand over the Baghdad railway in return for an assurance that Austrian adventures in the Balkans would not be encouraged. Sazonow had neither consulted Britain about this decision nor informed her of it once it had been taken.

† Mr G. W. Monger, on pages 307–9 of *The End of Isolation: British Foreign Policy, 1900–1907,* lists some of the many important Foreign Office documents which were not shown to the Cabinet. Grey, it seems, regarded the conduct of foreign affairs as a "mistery", the details of which were to be kept from as many people as possible. He even resented the fact that

A study of Britain's diplomacy during both the Algeciras Conference and the Bosnian crisis suggests that she could have contributed to the maintenance of peace in Europe by being, in the first instance, crystal-clear in her own mind as to what it was that she wanted to do and, in the second, making sure that other Powers realised the exact extent to which she was prepared to act. Secret military discussions of any kind should have been ruled out, since it was only by a truly independent policy that she could hope to reach that ideal state of equable relationships with all and sundry. The Germans, it seems, knew nothing of the Anglo-French military discussions but they had a pretty shrewd suspicion that the *entente* and the conventions were embryo alliances and that their own behaviour could determine whether or not a fully fledged Triple Entente would be hatched. Their complaints of encirclement were not without foundation. This does not mean, of course, that Britain should not have embarked upon the tasks of improving her relations with France and Russia but it does mean that she should, at the same time, have made an equally determined effort to improve her relations with Germany. Her opposition to the Baghdad railway was only one of the many instances when she endeavoured to put a spoke in the Kaiser's wheel. It would have been rather more useful if she had, for the sake of Anglo-German friendship, made some genuine sacrifices: there is no reason to believe that they would have been ungraciously received. As it was, however, she battled hard on every front where her interests were threatened, with the result that Germany grew more frustrated, jealous and bitter. The naval rivalry was only a symptom of a general struggle for supremacy and Britain would have been well advised to have responded with rather more alacrity to Bethmann Hollweg's overtures of 1909: his proposals, however impertinent they might seem, offered plenty of scope for discussions. During the latter half of 1910 there was, admittedly, a feeling at the Foreign Office that an attempt should be made to settle all outstanding Anglo-German grievances, but Hardinge's replacement by Nicolson did not result in the prolongation of that feeling. If Britain, so the argument ran in domestic circles, were to reach a private agreement with Germany she would automatically forfeit the friendship of France and Russia. If, on the other hand, she endeavoured to bring France and Russia into the discussions she would be tacitly admitting that she had certain obligations towards them and this was something that Britain did not care to admit to herself, let alone to the rest of the world. It can also be

M.P.s were entitled to question him. Writing to Nicolson on October 3rd, 1906, he had remarked that he was not looking forward to the autumn session—'the members have now acquired the art of asking questions and raising debates and there is so much in foreign affairs which attracts attention and had much better be left alone.'[44]

argued that Grey worried rather too much about the susceptibilities of these two countries, neither of whom had bothered to consult him about recent agreements which they themselves had concluded with Germany, and that Britain was forced to accept all the liabilities of an alliance with none of the benefits. "Splendid isolation" was no longer a tenable proposition, but a satisfactory alternative had yet to be found.

CHAPTER FIFTEEN

DOMESTIC AFFAIRS,
JANUARY–JULY 1910

(1)

The weeks which elapsed between the results of the general election of January 1910 and the opening of the first and, as it transpired, the only Session of the new Parliament, were among the most depressing and perplexing that the Government ever had to endure. Both Asquith and Lloyd George were exhausted and dejected, the former momentarily finding himself unable to cope with the situation, and the Cabinet as a whole could reach no agreement as to what their next step should be. Gone was the optimism of December, when their course of action had seemed clear and unmistakable: in a sense, indeed, the Unionists had triumphed, since a genuine majority in favour of the Budget no longer existed in the House of Commons. Instead of repeating their victory of 1906, or coming anywhere near it, the Liberal Party had plunged to disaster. Only with the support of the Labour Party and the Nationalists could they remain in office, and while the votes of the former could be safely relied upon those of the latter were far from certain. The peers would presumably accept the Budget if it were passed again by the Lower House, but this could only be done with Irish support and Irish support would only be given on the understanding that the veto of the House of Lords would be destroyed, or at any rate severely restricted, before the end of the Session and a measure of Home Rule introduced as quickly as possible. It was doubtful, however, whether the Government could satisfy this condition, since their opponents declared that the election had not provided them with a mandate for constitutional reform and King Edward was extremely reluctant to grant his Ministers the use of the royal prerogative. As it transpired, they did not yet feel entitled to request constitutional safeguards from the Crown, but this left them in a very difficult position. The Liberal rank and file, together with the

Nationalists and the Labour Party, were convinced that now or never was the time to launch an attack upon the House of Lords. Something would certainly have to be done if the Government were not to alienate their strongest supporters in the Commons, but they were far from clear what course to pursue.*

Asquith intensely disliked the idea of relying upon the Irish Nationalists for his majority in the Commons. Speaking at East Fife on January 19th he made it plain that the Government must be allowed a free hand in tackling the problem of the House of Lords before they embarked upon anything else. The Nationalists could not very well take exception to this, since the passing of a Home Rule Bill depended upon the removal of obstacles in the Upper House, but what did arouse their anger was a suggestion that the first item on the new Parliament's agenda would be the Budget. At Dublin, on February 10th, Redmond retorted that the Government's immediate concern ought to be the abolition of the Lord's veto. Once the Nationalists had helped the Finance Bill through all its stages in the Commons, what guarantee did they possess that the Ministry would not discover some pretext for indefinitely postponing constitutional reform? Asquith wrote to the King on the same day, informing him that the Irish were threatening to oppose the Budget unless they received an assurance that legislation dealing with the veto would be passed during this first Session. "The Cabinet," he concluded, "were of course agreed that no such assurance could or would be given. It is quite possible, therefore, that on the question of the enactment of last year's Budget, the Government may be defeated in the House of Commons by the combined votes of the Unionist and Nationalist Parties."[2]

This was, to say the least, an alarming prospect. Not since 1885, when Salisbury's first administration retained office under similar conditions, had a Government's life hung by so slender a thread and King Edward VII had no desire to see a repetition of those unhappy days. At Asquith's request, he approached Balfour with the suggestion that, if the Irish opposed the Budget when it reappeared in the Commons, the Unionists should support the Government by voting in its favour. It was a forlorn hope and Balfour, after giving polite consideration to this proposal, replied on February 15th that "great as would be the embarrassment to all parties which

---

* Sandars, writing to Balfour on February 3rd, said that an informant of his ("a responsible source") had recently asked Lloyd George what the Government intended to do. "I see no reason for making any secret of it," came the reply. "As the elections have turned out, it is obviously quite impossible for us to press the King over guarantees. If the results had been different, no doubt we should. But as it is, we must be content with legislative security. We shall pass the Budget and then a new Budget and then we shall bring in a Veto Bill, which of course the Lords will throw out, and there will be another election in the autumn."[1]

would follow upon an immediate defeat of the Government . . . it would be vain to ask the Unionist Party on tactical grounds to vote black where they had before voted white."[2]

There could be no help from this quarter, therefore, and for the moment the Government decided to continue in office and call Redmond's bluff.* Meanwhile what was to be done about the House of Lords? In the first place, it was now unlikely that the King would be willing to give an assurance to exercise his royal prerogative to ensure that ministerial proposals, if rejected by the peers, should eventually become law. Had the Liberal Party achieved a resounding triumph at the polls the Prime Minister would, perhaps, have felt entitled to ask for such a guarantee. Before the election, as Vaughan Nash's letter to Asquith of December 15th, 1909 shows, the King was unwilling to make any promises, although he was evidently very uncertain what his answer should be once the election was over. These uncertainties were communicated to Balfour† who, on January 9th, told Esher that he "could not believe that it was really intended to ask the King for a promise to create peers *before* a Bill was introduced dealing with the House of Lords. He was amazed at the impudence of the thing. He has no shadow of doubt that the King ought not under any circumstances to agree."[6]

It soon became evident, as the election results flowed in, that the Liberal majority in the House of Commons was melting away and Esher noted on January 23rd that " the King is less depressed than he was, because undoubtedly the fix in which Ministers now find themselves makes it impossible for them to bully him."[7] Two days later the King told Esher that he would not agree to any request to create peers. He repeated this decision to Haldane, declaring that a "much more definite expression of opinion from the country" was needed before he could consider such a thing.[8] In view, however, of the declaration which he had made on December 10th, Asquith was loath to abandon his hope of obtaining some sort of guarantee. To confess to the Commons that he did not, in fact, possess the

---

* On the face of it, the Nationalists had more to lose than gain by renouncing their alliance with the Liberals. Redmond told Blunt on February 13th, however, that "he did not see there was any good to be got by keeping Asquith in office if he did not give them Home Rule. . . . Unless the Liberal Party could abolish the Lords' veto there was as much to be hoped from the Tories. . . . In Ireland the defeat of the Government would be hailed with delight. . . . The alliance with the Liberals was very unpopular and the people wanted a fighting policy again."[4]

† Knollys asked Esher (December 29th) to see Balfour and ascertain whether the latter would form a Government if Asquith resigned because he could not obtain guarantees. He added (January 8th) that "even if the King knows beforehand that Balfour should decline to form a Government, I think that he (the King) ought to send for him, as he could then present a better front," and make it clear that he had "no possible option" but to give way to the Liberal demand.[5]

"safeguards" without which they would neither assume nor hold office was a humiliating and frightening prospect. Yet the King would obviously not grant them. Confused and unhappy, dreading to meet his sovereign as much as King Edward dreaded to meet his Prime Minister, he abruptly departed for a brief holiday abroad, much to the surprise of all concerned. "You will be amused to hear," wrote Esher to Balfour on January 23rd, "that after the King—with some difficulty—screwed himself up to ask Asquith here on Saturday, Asquith has refused. So Crewe and Grey are coming, and Morley on Monday. It is plain that so far the Government have not settled anything, and I should doubt of any of them knowing their own minds."9★

A few days later, presumably refreshed and reinvigorated, Asquith returned to England. On February 12th he informed the King of the Cabinet's decision not "to advise or request any exercise of the royal prerogative in existing circumstances, or until the Government have submitted their plans to Parliament. If in their judgment it should then become their duty to tender any such advice, they would do so when, and not before, the actual necessity may arise."11

As yet, there was still little agreement as to what these plans should be. Lloyd George and Harcourt were in favour of doing away with the Lords' veto, while Churchill thought that they should reform the House of Lords at the same time. Morley and Grey were strongly in favour of reform but not for abolition of the veto, and the latter protested to Asquith (February 7th) that the "so-called C.B. plan" would lose them the next election.12 Haldane thought that the right course was to proceed with the Budget and then produce "a well considered measure for the reconstruction of the Second Chamber."13 Asquith, no doubt, was more in sympathy with the views of Grey and Haldane than those of the Radicals. Like Grey, he disliked anything in the nature of a single-chamber constitution and, in any case, reform was a practical possibility whereas an attack on the veto was fraught with terrifying pitfalls. To remodel the Second Chamber on an electoral rather than a hereditary basis would be to retain the theoretical advantages of the old system while affording moderately progressive measures an opportunity of reaching the Statute Book. Vested interests would disappear, and with both Chambers ulti-

★ The King suggested to Crewe a possible scheme for breaking the deadlock whereby every peer in the existing House of Lords would retain the right to attend and speak but only one hundred members (fifty from each party) would be able to vote. Crewe was not enamoured of the idea, pointing out (a) that the fifty peers nominated by each side would probably be nonentities whose votes would follow strict party lines and (b) that prominent non-party members would be debarred from voting.10

mately responsible to the people genuine democratic government would at last exist.

Already, a hint had been thrown out to Lansdowne that the position of the moderates in the Cabinet would be considerably improved if the House of Lords were willing to undertake its own reform. "The only objections I can see to this course," wrote Balfour to Lansdowne on January 29th, "are (1) that it a little savours of panic, and (2) that we may not find it easy to agree upon a scheme of reform which would be agreeable to the House of Lords, which would meet the views of the Unionist doctrinaires in the constituencies and which would be workable. Still, if the announcement that you mean to try your hand at the problem would strengthen the hands of the King and of the moderates within the Cabinet in resisting pressure by the extremists, I see no reason why it should not be done."[14] Balfour was also at pains to emphasise, in his letter of February 15th to the King, "that no final or satisfactory solution of this constitutional issue could be obtained except through the co-operation of both parties in the State."

The Unionist leaders were now more or less reconciled to the idea of a mild dose of constitutional reform, but were not prepared to yield on the question of the veto.* It was thus clear from the outset that, if this issue were raised, the Government would find itself confronted with angry opposition from the Conservative Party and the House of Lords. Assuming that a measure limiting the powers of the Second Chamber were passed by the Commons, it would most certainly be rejected by the Lords. Asquith would then ask the King for a dissolution of Parliament in order that a general election might be held specifically on this issue and, at the same time, request a guarantee that, in the event of their return to office and the Lords' continued obduracy, the royal prerogative would be used for the creation of a sufficient number of peers to ensure that the Government's proposals became law. Whether the King would agree to such a request at this stage was doubtful: he would most probably reserve judgment until the election had taken place. If the Liberals were again victorious then the guarantee would presumably be given. If, however, the Liberals lost further seats the King might argue that the election had been inconclusive. This would give rise to a host of new complications.

It is as well to emphasise the seriousness of such a request. There were, as Asquith wrote at this time, "about 600 members of the House of Lords, of

* "Personally," wrote Lord Robert Cecil to Long on February 28th, "I do not think that any system short of an admission that no one should sit in the Second Chamber except on his merits would be satisfactory. This may be achieved either by election or by life peerage. . . . I greatly prefer the latter."[15]

whom twenty-six sit on the episcopal bench and are not ostensibly party politicians. Of the remaining 570 or 580, it is probably within the mark to say that 500 belong to the Conservative or Unionist Party. It is true that a considerable number of peers rarely attend or vote, but in an emergency they respond with a good deal of alacrity to the party whip."[16] If 500 members of the House of Lords supported the Unionist Party, then the passage of a measure to which all these members objected could only be accomplished by the creation of at least 500 Liberal peers.*

That Asquith shrunk from such a prospect is hardly surprising. Nor is it surprising, in view of his own feelings on the subject and the arguments put forward by Grey and Haldane, together with the possibility of Unionist co-operation, that he showed more interest in the idea of reconstructing the Second Chamber rather than destroying its powers. Two members of the Government who had been defeated at the general election and were now engaged in by-election contests, J. A. Pease and Colonel Seely, delivered speeches at this time which, presumably on the Prime Minister's instructions, concentrated on reform and virtually ignored the veto. There was considerable alarm at this omisson from all sections of the Liberal Party, not to mention the Nationalists and the Labour members: Dilke, on February 15th, led a deputation to Asquith, threatening to move when Parliament opened that the Government had no mandate from the electorate for reform or reconstitution of the House of Lords, and on February 24th a meeting of Liberal members for the Scotch and northern constituencies passed a resolution to the effect that the Government should confine its attention to the veto. Keir Hardie, for the Labour Party, declared that "Ministers were returned not to reconstitute but to destroy the House of Lords."†

In the face of this clamour Asquith was reluctantly driven to the conclusion that the veto issue should take precedence over that of reform, although he was far from happy at having to embark upon so perilous a course. Yet it was not altogether clear, even now, what they would be able to achieve in this sphere. The plan devised by Campbell-Banner-

---

* At least one hundred peers never voted under any circumstances: the Home Rule Bill of 1893 had been rejected by 419 to 41, the Licensing Bill of 1908 by 272 to 96 and the Budget by 350 to 75.

† The results of the general election had placed the Labour members in a curious position. They were, at first glance, ideally placed to benefit from the situation since, in company with the Nationalists, they held the balance between the two main parties. The Government's defeat, however, would not be to their advantage—MacDonald frankly admitted that the party "was not in a financial position to turn the Government out and go back to the constituencies and spend £50,000"—and they were therefore obliged to draw even closer to the Liberals. The Osborne judgment had thrown a spanner into the works so far as electioneering was concerned.[17]

man in 1907 for a suspensory veto offered more possibilities than any other, but Grey's objection (made in his letter of February 7th) that it was "overlaid with details" was true enough and something less elaborate would have to be devised. It was difficult to judge what the reaction of the Nationalists would be to a mere suspensory veto but the Government would press on regardless until they were actually defeated in the Commons.*

(2)

Parliament was formally opened by the King on February 21st.† Several ministerial changes had meanwhile taken place, Churchill succeeding Gladstone as Home Secretary,‡ Sydney Buxton taking charge of the Board of Trade, Herbert Samuel becoming Postmaster-General and J. A. Pease, hitherto Chief Whip, succeeding Samuel as Chancellor of the Duchy of Lancaster. Alexander Murray, the Master of Elibank, who had already served as Scottish Liberal Whip, Comptroller of the Royal Household and Under-Secretary for India, now filled the vacancy left by Pease and came to hold, within a very short time, a unique position in the counsels of the party.

The King's Speech was one of the shortest on record. After commenting upon the impending Union of South Africa, the new India Council, a further increase in the Navy Estimates and the need to rectify the irregular financial situation, it ran as follows:

My lords and gentlemen, recent experience has disclosed serious difficulties, due to recurring differences of opinion between the two branches of the legislature. Proposals will be laid before you, with all convenient speed, to define the relations between the Houses of Parliament, so as to secure the undivided authority of the House of Commons over finance and its predominance in legislation. These

---

* Churchill told Blunt on February 10th that the Government's policy depended "on two unknown factors, Redmond and the King. The Nationalist alliance with the Liberals is anything but popular in Ireland and O'Brien's success in getting ten of his men returned may force Redmond's hand. 'Of course,' said Winston, 'if they [the Nationalists] go, we're done for' but he does not really fear this. . . . What Winston anticipates is a new dissolution, when he thinks they would gain thirty more seats."[18]

† It had been opened by Royal Commission on February 16th. Joseph Chamberlain (who had been returned for Birmingham West with an increased majority) had made a pathetic reappearance in the Commons the following day, when Austen signed the roll on his behalf.

‡ Gladstone had been appointed Governor-General of the new Union of South Africa (see page 106). Before he left England, however, he entered into a rather acrimonious correspondence with his successor as to certain statements made by the latter on March 15th. These statements implied, so Gladstone felt, that Churchill's appointment had resulted in a welcome change in the treatment of suffragettes. Churchill, while claiming that his remarks had been inaccurately summarised by the Press, did not help matters by endeavouring to prove that a change *had* taken place. See pages 355–7 for the relevant correspondence

measures, in the opinion of my advisers, should provide that this House should be so constituted and empowered to exercise impartially, in regard to proposed legislation, the functions of initiation, revision and, subject to proper safeguards, of delay.

There are three points to be noted about the King's Speech. In the first place, it implied that the Budget would have to be dealt with before anything else. Secondly, it did not specify what form the Government's constitutional proposals would take, since the word "constituted" suggested that the idea of reform had not been completely abandoned. Thirdly, the phrase "in the opinion of my advisers" (although this was standard wording) suggested that King Edward VII himself did not approve of the decisions of his Cabinet.

Lansdowne, in the debate that followed, stated that the Unionist peers would not oppose the Budget if it were again sent up to them. They were willing to consider proposals for House of Lords reform and, if necessary, would bring forward a scheme of their own. Crewe replied that, although he could not yet reveal the Government's constitutional proposals, they were determined that the experiences of the past four years should not be repeated and only retained office in order to secure statutory safeguards to that effect. This was the first time that a Liberal spokesman had qualified the threat of guarantees with the word "statutory".

Asquith was meanwhile carrying out the painful duty of explaining to his shocked supporters in the Commons that no pledge had been secured from the King to create peers if the need arose. "I tell the House quite frankly," he declared, "that I have received no such guarantee and that I have asked for no such guarantee.* In my judgment it is the duty of responsible politicians in this country, as long as possible and as far as possible, to keep the name of the sovereign and the prerogatives of the Crown outside the domain of party politics. If the occasion should arise, I should not hesitate to tender such advice to the Crown as in the circumstances the exigencies of the situation appeared to warrant in the public interest. But to ask, in advance, for a blank authority, for an indefinite exercise of the royal prerogative, in regard to a measure which has never been submitted to, or approved by, the House of Commons, is a request which, in my judgment, no constitutional statesman can properly make and it is a concession which the sovereign cannot be expected to grant." They had, in other words, all been under a misapprehension as to the

---

* Asquith was quite correct when he declared that he had not asked the King for a pledge to create contingent peers: what he had most certainly done, however, was to ascertain from the King what his answer would be if he *did* approach him with this request.

meaning of his speech at the Albert Hall on December 10th, and the matter was now to be regarded as closed. Since, however, an overwhelming majority in the House of Commons demanded immediate action on the question of the Lords' veto, this subject must take precedence over everything else. In order to save time they would proceed by resolutions which would, later in the Session, be embodied in a Bill and sent to the Upper House. The Budget would not be dealt with until these had been approved.

The Liberals, Nationalists and Labour members refused to be mollified by these latter statements, and made it plain that they felt Asquith had deliberately misled them by his speech of December 10th: they were not going to be caught again. "In a week," wrote the Master of Elibank a short time later, "the Prime Minister's prestige fell to so low an ebb that at one moment I despaired of his ever recovering it."[19] Grey, his proposals for reform apparently abandoned, contemplated resignation, while Lloyd George felt that he himself ought to resign and lead the Radical section of the party on a parallel course with the moderates as the only way of saving the situation. Redmond once again declared that the Irish would only support the Budget if given a definite assurance that a Veto Bill would be passed during this Session. George Barnes, the new Chairman of the Labour Party,* urged the Government to deal immediately with the House of Lords, after which they would pass the Budget.

It need hardly be emphasised that the Unionists were overjoyed at this state of affairs. It was, as Austen Chamberlain wrote to his father on the first day of the Session, "a very different House from the last—our benches crowded and our men overflowing the gangway. The Labour Party now sit on the Government side and the two front benches below the gangway on our side are occupied by our men and by the Independent Nationalists. But it is a different House in spirit as well as in externals. Our men are keen and full of fight and spirits. The Government side is chastened. There will not be the same brutality as there was in the first Session of the last Parliament."[21]

---

* Henderson had decided at the end of December that he could no longer continue in this post. MacDonald was ready to succeed him but was much offended at receiving a letter from Hardie advising him not to do so since, in Hardie's opinion, he was not a suitable candidate. Hardie felt that a more militant leader was needed and suggested Barnes. MacDonald, in a bitterly worded reply dated February 1st, declared that he was not concerned with private ambitions and was therefore willing to stand aside but that he *was* concerned with the future of the Labour movement. "I do want the party to be led," he wrote. ". . . Let it be led to the devil if you like, but do not let it be the nerveless thing of the past Session." Hardie, not accustomed to having his own arguments thrown back at him in quite so brutal a fashion, was equally offended and Snowden doubted whether relations between them were ever quite the same again. Barnes thus became chairman but made it clear, much to Hardie's chagrin, that he was accepting the post only because MacDonald had been unwilling to come forward.[20]

A motion in favour of Tariff Reform was defeated by only 285 to 254, figures which contrasted significantly with the crushing condemnation of 474 to 98 in 1906.

None the less, the Unionists were very anxious to avoid taking office at such a juncture. Balfour, on February 23rd, announced that they would assist the Liberals in carrying on the King's government but that they would be forced to oppose them on the issues of the Budget and of the House of Lords. They did not wish, in other words, to defeat the Ministry in the Commons and were prepared to go to great lengths to avoid doing so, since it could be reckoned that Asquith, given half a chance, would resign and advise the King to send for Balfour. The Unionists would thus take office in a minority and at a very difficult moment from the viewpoint of financial and constitutional affairs. In order to obtain a majority in the Commons they would need to ask for another dissolution and the Liberals, meanwhile, would take the opportunity of whipping up enthusiasm among their supporters and allies on a Radical programme of the "People's Budget", reform of the House of Lords and social reform, perhaps sweeping back into office with a substantial majority. Balfour eventually decided that he *would* be prepared to accept the premiership under such conditions, but for the time being Unionist policy was that of supporting the Liberals against the Nationalists and opposing them only when the Nationalists voted in the Government lobby. The only exception to this policy would be the vote on the Budget.*

The Master of Elibank was now called upon to play a decisive rôle. "My main object at this time," he wrote two months later, "was to prevent the party getting completely out of hand. There is no doubt that the Cabinet in these early days was absolutely discredited. It was well known that they were wrangling amongst themselves . . . The Prime Minister . . . had lost his nerve, he had no grip on the situation, and at any moment the secession of important Ministers would have brought down the whole fabric. I pressed on Ministers, separately and individually, that a disappointed party in the country looked to the Cabinet to cease their internecine quarrels and to pull the country through its difficulties. In the House of Commons the position was intolerable. Groups of Liberals were meeting constantly, rebellion was in the air, the Irish . . . were, through that astute parliamentarian T. P. O'Connor, unceasingly stirring

---

* "Briefly," wrote Austen Chamberlain on February 27th, "you may summarise it thus: a financial situation of great difficulty and complexity, a parliamentary situation of unstable equilibrium, a Government which might at any moment be upset, an Opposition which is not ready to take office . . . and an electoral situation full of doubt and danger for all parties."[22]

up our militants to action. No sooner had I headed off one group than another was on me. Members were declining to stand for their seats in the event of a general election and . . . these groups were not led by mere irresponsibles."[23]

Since the beginning of February, moreover, the Master had been principally responsible for direct negotiations with the Nationalist leaders. "On the evening of the Prime Minister's official dinner," he writes, "when the King's Speech was read, Lloyd George and I went to a reception at Wimbourne House, but not to remain there long. We shook hands with our host and hostess and then immediately . . . left the house by means of dark and interminable downstair passages and passed out by the tradesmen's entrance, where we took a cab and drove to a house in Victoria to keep an appointment with the Irish leaders. We were ushered into an ill-lit house by an Irish servant girl, taken up several flights of stairs and entered an uninviting and coldly furnished room. In the room were Redmond and the sallow-faced, melancholy Dillon. . . . They were rather taken aback by our uniformed appearance, but we at once plunged into business. For an hour and a half we discussed the general situation and possible concessions in the Budget, but we could get nothing definite in return from the Irishmen in the shape of an assurance that, if we made concessions, they would support us on the Third Reading."[24] Redmond, at length, told the Master on February 24th that unless the Government brought forward their veto resolution in both Houses at once and, if they were defeated or not voted upon in the Upper House, postponed introducing the Budget and immediately asked the King for guarantees, then the Nationalists "would feel bound to vote against the Government and oppose them consistently in the House of Commons."[25]

"The Irish send us a fresh ultimatum every day," Churchill told Austen Chamberlain on February 25th. "We're at the fourteenth now! I don't see how we can last beyond April."[26] At a Cabinet that day it transpired, as Asquith afterwards informed the King, that "in view of the exorbitant demands of Mr Redmond and his followers, and the impossibility under existing circumstances of counting upon a stable Government majority, certain Ministers were of the opinion that the wisest and most dignified course for Ministers was at once to tender their resignation to your Majesty." Others, however, thought that "this would be lacking in courage; that the Government was pledged to produce and lay on the table their proposals with regard to the House of Lords and could not honourably retire unless they were defeated in the House of Commons before or upon the disclosure of their plans."[27] The Master of Elibank was consequently instructed to inform Redmond that the Irish Nationalists must do whatever they thought best.

The following day's Cabinet appears to have been an important one. Asquith informed the King, as soon as it was over, " that there could be no question of immediate or voluntary resignation."[28] From this point onwards, in fact, the Government regained control of the situation, stiffening in its resolve to ignore the threats of the Nationalists and agreeing, at last, that abolition of the veto must precede reform. Two days later (February 28th) Asquith moved the business of the House for the month that lay ahead. The first necessity, he declared, was the enactment of measures to alleviate the financial situation, but when the Commons reassembled after the Easter recess they would be asked to consider three resolutions. The first of these would exclude the Lords from control of financial legislation, the second would so restrict their veto on other legislation that the will of the Commons would prevail during a single Parliament, and the third would limit the duration of Parliament to five years. In another session the Government would bring forward a bill to reconstitute the Second Chamber on a democratic basis. These resolutions, when passed, would be submitted to the Upper House, but irrespective of whether or not the Lords assented the Government would regard the limitation of the veto as their first and paramount duty.

No date was given for the reintroduction of the Budget and the Nationalists, determined not to be hoodwinked, announced that they would abstain from voting on this motion. Redmond explained that support for the Budget would gladly be given so long as they could be certain that the Government meant to abolish the Lord's veto before the end of the Session. Supposing, however, that the Lords rejected the resolutions or did not bring them to a decisive vote: would Asquith then ask for guarantees and, if these were refused, would he resign? The Prime Minister did not answer these questions but Lloyd George, later in the debate, used words which suggested that guarantees would certainly be requested. Balfour, much to the irritation of his supporters, did not force a division and contented himself with noting the evident disagreements in the Cabinet and the Government's curious reluctance to reintroduce its Budget. For the moment, as we have seen, he did not wish to force a crisis and Asquith's proposals, in any case, chimed in happily enough with the Unionists' own plan of campaign for the next few weeks. While the Commons were engaged in voting Supply the Lords would be demonstrating, to all and sundry, their willingness (indeed, their positive eagerness) to reform themselves without assistance from any outside agency.

(3)

Three days after the opening of Parliament Rosebery had given notice that, on March 14th, he would move that the Lords resolve themselves into a committee to consider the question of reform, and a week or so later his lordship attended a meeting of Unionist leaders at Lansdowne House to discuss the proposals which he would put forward. He himself, together with Austin Chamberlain and Curzon, urged the adoption of the recommendations made by the peers' Select Committee in 1908, namely that the Second Chamber should be an assembly part hereditary, part elective and part nominated by the Crown. Balfour reluctantly supported these ideas but Lansdowne, Midleton and Salisbury were far from happy. Rosebery, undeterred, gave notice in the Lords on March 9th that, if his motion were carried, he would move (1) that a strong and efficient Second Chamber was essential to the well-being of the State and the balance of Parliament, (2) that such a Chamber could best be obtained by the reform and reconstitution of the House of Lords, and (3) that a necessary preliminary to such reform was acceptance of the principle that a peerage in itself did not confer the right to sit and vote in the Upper House.

Rosebery's original motion was passed on March 17th, after a very tepid debate in which Lansdowne, while in favour of going into committee, made it clear that he had no great desire to see Rosebery's ideas implemented. The latter, not surprisingly, was rather upset at this attitude. "I honestly think," he wrote to Lansdowne on March 18th, "that if you cannot go beyond the limits you laid down last night, the House of Lords plan will be stillborn. The great mass of the Lords are not solicitous about reform at all; if they must have it they will go for the minimum, and it is the minimum which their leader offers and declares to be sufficient."[29] The other three motions were carried without much difficulty the following week, the only positive opposition coming from a small group of Tory die-hards led by Halsbury, but the majority of the peers were lukewarm in their support and the Government showed little interest in the proceedings.

Support for Rosebery came from an unexpected quarter. Grey, whose doubts about the wisdom of the Government's policy had still not been resolved, took the rather surprising step of publicly declaring on March 14th that "to confine ourselves to a single-chamber issue and to leave the policy of reform of the Second Chamber for the other side would result for us, politically speaking, in disaster, death and damnation." He followed this up with a letter to Crewe the following day, in which he argued that "unless it is announced that the limitation of the veto (in C.B. form) is proposed and will be used only to secure the passage of a bill to establish a new Second Chamber . . . we steer straight on to the single-chamber rock."*[30] Crewe, however, was firmly convinced that the veto would have to be permanently restricted and he and Asquith eventually persuaded Grey to curb his public utterances on the subject.

The Commons were meanwhile struggling through the interminable details of legislation relating to Supply. The rejection of the Budget had prevented the collection of income tax, super-tax and certain other taxes, calculated in all at £30,036,000, but payments to the Sinking Fund had been suspended, loans had been obtained from various sources, and with the passage now of a Treasury (Temporary Borrowing) Bill and a War Loans Redemption Bill, the ultimate shortfall became no more than £1,300,000. One very interesting point arose on March 10th, however, when they were asked to vote £8 million for the Civil Service and Revenue Departments, a sum which would last six weeks as opposed to the usual four or five months. It could only be inferred, from this, that the Government felt it might be compelled to resign before the end of April: a Unionist administration, taking office in a hurry, would find itself forced to dissolve Parliament at once in order to obtain a majority so that Supply could be voted. Without Supply, of course, the business of administration could not be carried on and no Government could remain in office if the Commons refused to grant it.† Austen Chamberlain told his father (March 22nd) that "Bonar Law had got from Lloyd George last night in the smokeroom a statement that a dissolution in May was 'inevitable' and the strong impression that the Government would themselves dissolve and not resign."[33]

It was all very mysterious, and what made the situation even more exasperating was Asquith's bland rejoinder of "Wait and see" (first used on March 3rd) whenever Unionist members questioned him on his intentions.

(4)

On March 29th, after the Easter recess, the long-awaited attack on the House of Lords finally got under way. The Government's three resolu-

---

* He wrote to Asquith saying that he felt he ought to resign, a missive which the recipient described to Crewe as "a tiresome letter". Morley, from whom such letters came at regular intervals, also threatened to resign if 500 peers were created.[31]

† "The schemes of the financial matters worked out by the Govt. are very clever and intricate," wrote King Edward to his eldest son on March 16th; "and I am not sure that they have not stolen a successful march on the Unionists."[32]

tions were carried, amidst stormy but not particularly memorable debates, through Committee and Report by majorities of approximately a hundred. On April 14th, amidst loud cheers from ministerial benches, Asquith introduced the bill based upon these resolutions—the Parliament Bill.

To appreciate the significance of events at this time it is necessary to turn once more to the problem of the Liberal Party and the Irish. Since January, as we have noted, certain members of the Government had been in close contact with the Nationalist leaders. Redmond and Dillon had been adamant throughout on the point that they could not agree to support the Budget before the resolutions had been dealt with by the House of Lords. In the event of their being rejected, which seemed highly probable, they wanted an explicit assurance that the King would be asked for guarantees. The only condition on which their support could otherwise be given, before the Lords had considered the resolutions, would be in return for a promise of the Veto Bill becoming law during the Session. As late as April 3rd Redmond was clinging to these stipulations in a speech he made at Tipperary, yet ten days later Nationalist support for the Budget was assured, and by April 29th it would have been trundled triumphantly through both Houses and on to the Statute Book. So sudden a change of heart was, in the circumstances, surprising.

Contemporaries, at any rate, certainly believed that assurances had been given. Not since the days of Fox and North, it would appear, had there developed so infamous an alliance as that now established between Asquith and Redmond. Unionists throughout the country, shocked beyond all measure at this instance of an English political party reaching secret understandings with Irish Nationalists, could hardly find words scathing enough to condemn them. According to the *Annual Register*, "it was generally held that the Ministry had now completely agreed to the demand of the Nationalists that the Crown should be asked for guarantees" and, as will be seen in a moment, Asquith's speech of April 14th gave the final touch of confirmation to this belief. In vain did the personalities concerned deny, with much indignation, that a bargain had been struck; in vain did the Prime Minister take the unusual step of writing to *The Times* to emphasise that he had not been influenced by Nationalist pressure in any conceivable way; in vain did Liberal speakers throughout the country struggle to exonerate him from these charges and from accusations that he had capitulated. The Press, the public and, for the most part, subsequent historians, thought otherwise.

Yet Asquith, at this time, had no intention of entering into an agreement with Redmond: the Nationalists must do whatever they thought fit and leave the Government to pursue its own policies. Thus, should the occasion arise, he would be able to deny that bargaining had taken place and, technically, would be speaking the truth. On the other hand, however, he was certainly anxious for their support, while ostentatiously scorning to seek it, and he did nothing to discourage the conversations which took place between Elibank, Lloyd George and the Irish leaders. Until the very last moment it was doubtful whether this policy of masterly inaction would succeed: that it did so was simply due to the fact that the Nationalists, once their bluff had been called, had no option but to support the Government.

At first this fact was very far from clear and Lloyd George, in particular, remained convinced that the Irish would vote for the Budget only if their country was excluded from the operation of the proposed whisky tax. His attempt to secure her exclusion the previous summer had been vetoed by the Cabinet, but on or about March 12th he told O'Brien and Healy that he was now in a position to make important concessions if the Nationalist Party as a whole requested them. He would also, it seemed, press for a further improvement of the Land Act of 1903. O'Brien and Healy were greatly attracted by these proposals: both of them disliked the Budget and neither believed that bartering Ireland's welfare for the sake of a Veto Bill was the policy which ought to be followed. They promised Lloyd George, therefore, that they would persuade their colleagues to join together in asking for concessions, but much to their indignation found that Redmond and Dillon would have nothing to do with this scheme. On March 24th, therefore, they saw Lloyd George for a second time and were obliged to confess failure.

The Master of Elibank now pondered on a scheme of a very different nature, namely royal mediation between the two Houses resulting, perhaps, in a constitutional conference under the King's chairmanship. The Master was, fortunately, on very good terms with the Prince of Wales, with whom he had discussed the problem at the beginning of the Session and again on March 29th in the company of Sir Arther Bigge, the Prince's secretary, and Rufus Isaacs. There was every possibility that the Prince would persuade his father, in the event of a parliamentary deadlock, to propose such a conference, but the matter would have to be handled very carefully. Unfortunately, Elibank made the fatal mistake of letting Churchill know of these conversations. The latter was greatly attracted by the idea, and in a speech which he made in the Commons on March 31st implied that the Crown and the Commons were united against the Lords, a declaration generally thought to be in very bad taste. To make matters worse, however, he himself approached the King, appropriating Elibank's scheme and consequently arousing Edward VII's whole-hearted opposition. "This is Winston all over," wrote an exasperated Elibank on learning of Churchill's blunder. "In mining parlance, if he can jump another man's claim, you can trust him to do it. In this instance his premature and unauthorised action with the King has been extremely unfortunate and has upset my plans."[34]

For the time being, therefore, hope of royal mediation had to be abandoned, and the Master decided that the Government would have to brazen out the situation as best it could. On April 12th, however, he had an important conversation with Lloyd George which resulted in the latter agreeing to drop his efforts to exclude Ireland from the whisky duty, it being stipulated in return that if circumstances so warranted it they would secure a promise from the King to create peers. "On Tuesday night," runs Elibank's account, "I had a long conversation with Lloyd George and with Churchill. The Chancellor at that time had made up his mind to drop the spirit duties in the Budget to please the Irish. In my many interviews with the Irish I had come to the conclusion that all they really cared about was the question of the guarantees. . . . The Cabinet were at sixes and sevens on the question of proceeding with or dropping the whisky duties. Accordingly I went to see Lloyd George early, previous to the Cabinet, and urged upon him that he should insist upon the Cabinet coming to a decision. . . . A quarter of an hour after this conversation, Lloyd George attended the Cabinet and agreed to abandon his [resistance to the] whisky duties. But at the same time he made it clear to the Cabinet that, unless they came to an immediate decision on the subject of approaching the sovereign in respect of guarantees, he would leave the Cabinet and join the Irish".*[35]

Under pressure from Lloyd George, therefore, and not from the Nationalists, Asquith was obliged to begin the delicate task of tackling the

* "The Cabinet," wrote Sandars to Balfour on April 16th, "had meetings on Tuesday and Wednesday [i.e., April 12th and 13th] of the most momentous kind. . . . At the earlier . . . the most determined objection was taken against the policy of concessions to the Irish over the Budget. . . . This view . . . prevailed at the Cabinet on Wednesday, when it was decided that, in consideration of presenting the Budget to Parliament without modifications, there should be a considerable advance made in the matter of guarantees. Lloyd George was converted to this policy, and, with the ardour of a convert, he threw himself into violent opposition to Budget concessions to Redmond. He saw Redmond, and informed him that in this Budget the Irish would in no way be met. . . . Redmond left . . . in a very angry mood and then demanded an interview with Asquith. At this interview . . . he was told that the Government were prepared to meet him on the question of guarantees and that they were prepared to go further than what he, Redmond, would probably have anticipated. Nevertheless, Redmond, though to a certain extent pacified by this undertaking, professed himself still dissatisfied."[36]

King. He paved the way, on April 13th, by the despatch of the following telegram:

As a result of Cabinet during last three days the Government have resolved to make no changes in Budget except purely formal ones and refuse demand of Irish for reduced spirit duties. They will ask House of Commons to pass Budget in every substantial respect in the same form in which it passed in the late House of Commons.

It is possible and not improbable that in consequence of this decision the Irish Party will vote against the Government in the critical division in the closure to the Budget on Monday next. If they do Government will be defeated and crisis of extreme urgency will at once arise.[37]

He followed this up with a very long letter in which he explained that the Cabinet had felt it their duty, in view of the precarious political situation, "and not [from] any desire to prolong their own official life, which, under existing conditions, is far from being a bed of roses," to authorise an exchange of views with the two sections of the Nationalist Party. The Irish had made demands which were totally unacceptable, and this had led them to the conclusion that Nationalists support could only be retained if they were now to make it clear, beyond any shadow of doubt, that they would if necessary make use of the royal prerogative to ensure the passage of the Parliament Bill through the Upper House. If, in the meantime, the Lords rejected or refused to discuss the resolutions which the Commons had already approved in principle, it would be the Cabinet's duty "at once to tender advice to the Crown as to the necessary steps—whether by the exercise of the prerogative, or by a referendum *ad hoc*, or otherwise—to be taken to ensure that the policy, approved by the House of Commons by large majorities, shall be given statutory effect in this Parliament.* If they found that they were not in a position to accomplish that object, they would then either resign office or advise a dissolution of Parliament, but in no case would they feel able to advise a dissolution, except under such conditions as would secure that in the new Parliament the judgment of the people as expressed at the elections would be carried into law."[38]

(5)

We must now return to the House of Commons on that evening of April 14th when, after an eventful day, the Prime Minister rose to introduce the measure which soon became known as the Parliament Bill. It

* The possibility of a referendum was not mentioned directly in Asquith's speech of April 14th.

differed very little, in form and content, from the resolutions which they had just been discussing, and consisted of a preamble and four clauses. The preamble, evidently a sop to Grey and his supporters, declared the Government's ultimate intention of substituting for "the House of Lords as it at present exists a Second Chamber constituted on a popular instead of hereditary basis, but such a substitution cannot immediately be brought into operation." It also hinted that the powers of a reconstituted Upper House would be greater than those now to be allotted to the existing House of Lords, although the Government declined to be drawn on this. The first of the four clauses stated that if the Lords withheld their approval of a money bill for more than a month such a measure would automatically become law after receiving the royal assent; the second, that the Speaker would decide what constituted a money bill; the third, that if another kind of bill was passed by the Commons in three successive sessions (though not necessarily of the same Parliament) then it must, on its third rejection by the House of Lords, be presented to the King and become law with his assent, though two years must elapse between the bill's first introduction into the Commons and its final reading; and the fourth, that the maximum duration of a Parliament should be five years instead of seven.*

"If the Lords fail to accept our policy," said Asquith, ". . . we shall then either resign our offices or recommend a dissolution of Parliament. And let me add this: that in no case would we recommend dissolution except under such conditions as will secure that in the new Parliament the judgment of the people as expressed in the election will be carried into law."

This statement, reminiscent though it was of the declaration of December 10th, could only be taken to mean that, if the Lords refused to pass the Parliament Bill, the Government would request the King for a dissolution on condition that, if they were returned to power, he would guarantee the creation of peers if asked to make them. If this condition were not satisfied, then they would resign. The rage of the Unionists, who were already firmly convinced that a bargain had been struck with the Nationalist Party, could hardly be contained as they listened to these

---

* This scheme differed in several respects from the Campbell-Bannerman plan. First, the idea of joint sessions had been quietly abandoned; secondly, the three sessions stipulated did not have to be those of the same Parliament and, finally, the original plan had not envisaged shortening the length of Parliaments. These alterations were, however, all to the good. A joint sitting would inevitably be an unsatisfactory affair while, in the view of the Radicals, the existing Unionist predominance in the Upper House was an insurmountable obstacle to such a device. The second change meant that a Liberal Government need not fear to introduce contentious measures into a House of Commons which had only one or two years to live, while the third, in so far as it necessitated more frequent appeals to the electorate, could hardly be opposed.

words. Asquith, from this point onwards, replaced Lloyd George as the chief object of their animosity, while he was now restored to full favour with the Liberal rank and file. "Thursday night," wrote the Master of Elibank a few days later, "saw a great parliamentary triumph for the Prime Minister. All his lost prestige has been recovered. He played a great part on a great occasion, and he announced the decision of the Cabinet in that wonderful language of his and with a dignity that abashed some of the ruder spirits opposite who tried to interrupt. It was a stirring scene, not likely to leave the memories of those who witnessed it, nor the enthusiasm with which the crowded Liberal, Nationalist and Labour benches cheered the Prime Minister as he left the Chamber."*[39]

The Unionist leaders were now in a quandary. It will be recalled that in February Balfour had been extremely unwilling to have the Government defeated on any small issue and had, indeed, gone out of his way to avoid any division which might afford them an opportunity of resigning. By the end of March, however, he was reaching the conclusion that if such a resignation took place he would, after all, be ready to assume office. Austen Chamberlain argued that the Radicals, by refusing to vote Supply for more than a few weeks, had created a revolutionary situation and that a Unionist Government would be entitled to take steps of a drastic nature to bring the situation to an end. This could only mean, of course, arbitrary government, which had not been attempted since the days of James II. Such government, however, need only last for a brief period, after which they would go to the country on a programme of moderate reform of the House of Lords, Poor Law reform, admission of colonial wheat tax free and, since it was thought that Lloyd George's proposed land taxes had rallied the English towns against them in the recent election, a promise of rate reassessment.[41]

Balfour and Austen Chamberlain discussed the situation at some length on April 19th. Balfour was convinced that Asquith would follow one of two courses: the Lords having rejected the Government's proposals, he would ask the King for guarantees and, if these were refused, would either resign immediately or wait until January and then request a dissolution. In the first instance, Balfour would take office in the hope that the Liberals would agree to vote Supply. If they refused to do this, then he was not altogether sure that he could carry on. Lord Rothschild would loan them a substantial sum if asked,† but this would leave them open to the charge

---

* "Ministers are to remain in their offices for six weeks or two months more, whatever happens," wrote Morley to Minto on April 19th. "What dazzling chances for grand statesmanship!"[40]

† There was a Disraelian precedent for such action.

of overriding the authority of the House of Commons. It was eventually agreed that the Bank of England could be relied upon to advance the Government a million or so until the next election had resulted (all being well) in a Unionist majority. The only legal difficulty would be that of obtaining the assent of the Comptroller and the Auditor General, but since the latter had already exercised a dispensing power in the collection of taxes and had spent money in excess of that authorised by Parliament, this might not prove insuperable. Supposing, however, that the Unionists were beaten? Austen Chamberlain felt that much would then depend upon the size of the Liberal Party's majority. If it were less than at present, it could be argued that they had not secured the mandate necessary to justify the King's agreeing to their request. Asquith's demands could still be refused and Balfour could retain office. It would, in fact, be impossible for the Liberals to carry through a constitutional revolution with the basis of their support crumbling away.[42]

On Monday, April 18th, Asquith moved in the Commons a guillotine resolution alloting time to the various stages of the Finance Bill. He admitted that certain changes in the Budget were the result of private discussion with Redmond, but dismissed them as textual alterations designed to secure effective drafting and again repudiated all suggestions of collaboration with the Irish leader.* Redmond, for his part, while anxious to represent the alterations as "valuable concessions", pointed out that the Irish had never opposed the whole Budget and that, in any case, Home Rule was more important than whisky taxes. The resolution, in a slightly amended form, was passed by 345 to 252 and the following day Lloyd George produced his revised Budget statement for 1909–10. The final balance amounted to £2,962,000, which was less than £1,300,000 short of the original estimate of £4,200,000. The Finance Bill reappeared in the Commons on April 20th and passed its Third Reading a week later by 324 to 231. It was debated in the House of Lords the following day for three hours and then passed without a division. With the royal assent, on April 29th, the "People's Budget" finally became law.

On April 21st there had been a meeting at Lansdowne House, at which the Unionist leaders decided that the Lords would consider the Government's resolutions when Parliament reassembled after the spring recess. Balfour was now convinced that the Government would resign as soon as the Lords rejected these proposals. On April 26th he discussed the situation with the Archbishop of Canterbury, Knollys and Esher at

---

* The changes, apart from alterations in dates, simply exempted from taxation those tenancies indirectly created by the Irish Land Act of 1903.

Lambeth Palace. Esher, presumably with Elibank's proposal in mind, suggested that the King might be able to arrange a compromise, but Balfour did not think this feasible. Knollys then suggested a referendum, but it had been agreed at the Lansdowne House meeting that such a device would be cumbersome and perhaps dangerous: Balfour thus replied that he thought Asquith was now hostile to the idea. The Unionist leader did state, however, that he would be willing to form a caretaker administration if Asquith resigned as a result of not being granted guarantees by the King.[43]

On April 29th Parliament adjourned for the spring recess, it being generally agreed that the Ministry's position was now far stronger than it had been at the beginning of the Session. The Liberal Party, assured of Nationalist and Labour support and once more in a crusading mood, would theoretically be able to march from triumph to triumph. If the Lords rejected their proposals, the Government would either request a promise of immediate guarantees or (failing this) a promise of guarantees after another election had been fought and won. If King Edward VII refused either of these requests, then Ministers would resign and leave him the unenviable task of finding a new Government. If Balfour did come to the King's rescue, he would find himself in a very difficult position and one which might, in fact, do the Unionists immense harm at the next election. On the whole, therefore, the prospects seemed brighter than they had done for a very long time, and with the lessening of tension and the deepening of confidence Ministers at last felt entitled to desert their posts for a brief period of relaxation. Lloyd George, like Redmond, T. P. O'Connor and others, departed for Italy, while Asquith, together with McKenna, set off on a Mediterranean cruise on the Admiralty yacht *Enchantress*.

The *Enchantress* called at Portugal, where Asquith received a formal audience from Manuel II, and on May 4th King Edward telegraphed to his Prime Minister: "Very glad that you liked your stay at Lisbon and that the King was so pleasant." Two days later, however, messages of a very different nature were being cabled by Knollys and others: the King, it seemed, was ill with bronchitis. "Your telegram received," Asquith wired Knollys on May 6th, soon after the yacht had reached Gibraltar. "Am starting at once for home. In half an hour *Enchantress* will be under weigh for Plymouth, where I hope to be on Monday." There was, as he recorded later, nothing in the messages that seemed to call for immediate alarm, but at 3.0 a.m. on May 7th the following words were radioed to the *Enchantress*: "I am deeply grieved to inform you that my beloved father the King passed away peacefully at a quarter to twelve tonight (the 6th).—George."[44]

"I went up on deck," writes Asquith, "in the twilight before dawn, and my gaze was arrested by the sight of Halley's Comet blazing in the sky. It was the first and last time that any of us saw it."[45]

(6)

The death of King Edward VII did nothing to change the course of Great Britain's political history. What it did do, for better or worse, was delay continuation of the constitutional conflict for exactly six months. King George V, a conscientious and sensible man, was not without experience of public affairs and, in normal times, the accession of a new monarch would have made no perceptible difference to the despatch of parliamentary business. But to be called to the throne in the midst of a constitutional crisis, to be plunged into a situation where the monarch's personal decision could make or break a Government, to be faced with the threat of political upheaval and the certainty of condemnation by some sections of the community whatever the outcome of this whole sorry affair—such a situation could hardly be regarded as the customary inauguration of a new reign. It is, of course, very easy to exaggerate the predicament in which the new monarch found himself, but it was essential for the sovereign to maintain the highest degree of impartiality in his dealings with the politicians of the day and, even more important, that he should be seen to do so. One false step at the outset of his reign, especially in the highly-charged conditions of 1910, might very well blight it permanently. Only by acting in strict accordance with constitutional usage would the impending crisis be surmounted, yet opinions differed as to what was constitutionally correct in the present situation and the precedents of 1712 and 1832 offered little guidance. If so dextrous and confident a monarch as King Edward VII could discern no means of preserving the equilibrium of the Crown in the turmoil that lay ahead, what hope was there for his ingenuous successor?

King George V's accession was formally proclaimed on May 9th and next day Asquith had his first audience with the new monarch. Little was said about the political situation and it was clear, in any case, that Parliament could not be dissolved in the immediate future: a new Regency Bill would have to be passed, together with another Consolidated Fund Bill and a fresh Civil List. Harcourt, writing to Asquith at this time, pointed out that the Government would incur much odium if it were to force a crisis on the King and that it would be wise, for tactical reasons, to delay the veto issue until the end of the year.[46] "Winston is for pressing the fight at once," wrote Austen Chamberlain to his father on May 11th. "Crewe and others are for delay and perhaps an autumn session. Lloyd George talks as if he were not averse from compromise."[47]

Elibank, as we have noted, had enlisted the support of the new King (when Prince of Wales) for the idea of royal mediation between the two parties. There was now a good chance of this being revived and the *Observer*, under the editorship of J. L. Garvin, declared on May 8th that "if King Edward upon his deathbed could have sent a last message to his people, he would have asked us to lay party passion aside, to sign a truce of God over his grave, to seek . . . some fair means of making a common effort for our common country." Haldane and Loreburn were greatly attracted by this article and W. T. Stead reported to Garvin on May 18th that Lloyd George was also "much impressed" with the idea.*[48] According to one of his biographers,† the Chancellor of the Exchequer drew up a memorandum in support of the plan and sent it to Asquith. The latter showed it to Crewe, Grey and Haldane, who agreed with its sentiments. So the story runs.[50] On May 18th, at any rate, the Prime Minister told the King that he "would endeavour to come to some understanding with the Opposition to prevent a general election and he would not pay attention to what Mr Redmond said."[51]

Support for a "Truce of God" was far from unanimous, since party bitterness had been exacerbated rather than assuaged by the "Peacemaker's" death.‡ The Liberal rank and file, together with the Nationalists and Labour members, were opposed to the Government's entering into negotiations: it would appear a sign of weakness, and if it ended indecisively the Ministry would find it hard to recapture the crusading spirit which Asquith's speech of April 14th was thought to have kindled. Liberal supporters of the idea, however, argued that the Ministry would expose itself to much criticism and probable defeat at the polls if it were to pursue its original objectives with no consideration for the King's position. A constitutional conference, even if it did not solve the parliamen-

---

* The Poet Laureate, Alfred Austin, did his best to help things along by producing a dirge entitled 'The Truce of God, A King's Bequest', which was published in *The Times* a few days later. Austen Chamberlain thought it a "lamentable performance".[49]

† Mr Frank Owen.

‡ "The cock-and-bull stories that are going about as to the King having been killed by the Liberals are too amazing," wrote Edward Marsh on May 20th. "The Queen Mother is supposed to have taken the P.M. and McKenna into the room and said, 'Look at your work'!!!" The Kaiser, who came to England for the funeral, informed Bethmann-Hollweg that "the Government is throughly hated. . . . During the lying-in-state the Prime Minister and his colleagues were publicly hissed in the streets, and . . . expressions like 'You have killed the King' were heard."[52]

tary deadlock, would at least give them time to consolidate their strength in the country. Exploited in the right way, failure to come to terms might very well win them additional support. This factor was also taken into account by many Unionists, of course, who felt that the Government would simply play for time and terminate discussion at the moment most favourable for an election.

For the moment, battles raged in the Cabinet. "Ll. G., Churchill and the Master still adhere strongly to the taking up of the veto issue in July," wrote T. P. O'Connor to Redmond on June 4th; "but Ll. G. says that the majority of the Cabinet are the other way; and Ll. G. fears that they will carry their plan at Monday's Cabinet."*53 Two days later he issued a further bulletin.

O'Connor to Redmond, June 6th, 1910

Here is how the matter with regard to the conference stands. The King was anxious for it and Balfour would have been ready for it immediately after the King's death.† Now, however, Balfour has cooled and the Tory Party as a whole is against it. The young bloods are all cursing Garvin for advocating it so violently in 'The Observer'. Ll. G. and C. both think it was a mistake of Asquith not to have jumped at the proposal when it was first made. This change of attitude on the part of the Tories has produced a corresponding change in the attitude of the King.‡ The King now will not suggest a conference himself; but Ll. G.—and W. C. rather, though not quite so hotly, agrees with him—believes it is good business for the Liberals to force a conference on the Tories. Ll. G. thinks such a conference may end in the acceptance of such a compromise as may by a different method get all we should get by the C. B. resolutions. Churchill is not so confident. The Master thinks the conference will be abortive. But they all think that the conference should be offered, mainly because public opinion in England demands it and, secondly, because it gives an excuse for the postponement of the general election.§55

* Why the Chancellor of the Exchequer should apparently advocate, according to Mr Frank Owen, the suspension of hostilities for a constitutional conference and yet be pressing for the introduction of the Parliament Bill into the Lords as originally planned, is not altogether clear: one cannot help feeling that Mr Owen's account of Lloyd George's behaviour at this time is not entirely accurate.

† Balfour told Esher at the beginning of the month that he was willing to meet Asquith and discuss a compromise settlement if the King wished it. "It is true," noted Esher, "that he sees no basis for accommodation but then, as he truly says, when the leaders of the parties get into a room together something is sure to be achieved."54

‡ For King George V the situation had been complicated by the fact that his two private secretaries, Bigge and Knollys, were in acute disagreement as to what he should do. Knollys was sympathetic towards the Government and felt that a promise of guarantees should, if requested, be given; Bigge, on the other hand, was anxious for the Crown to remain strictly impartial until it was unmistakably clear that the Ministry's policy really did represent the wishes of the nation.

§ According to Garvin, writing to Northcliffe on June 13th, "the question was submitted to two rather tempestuous Cabinet Councils. The motion to invite Balfour to confer was at length carried by a strong majority. Winston as I hear from both sides was dead against &

L

On June 9th (when Parliament reassembled) the die was cast and Asquith wrote to Balfour proposing that, in the interests of the nation, they should enter into private discussions to see if a satisfactory solution could be found to the problems confronting them. Balfour responded amicably and on June 16th Asquith was able to announce that four representatives of the two main parties would meet together to explore the prospects of a settlement, the Liberals being represented by himself, Lloyd George, Crewe and Birrell and the Unionists by Balfour, Lansdowne, Austen Chamberlain and Cawdor. The meetings would be held in strict privacy and no representatives of the Nationalist or Labour Parties would attend.

Thus, hesitantly, reluctantly and yet, perhaps, not altogether unhopefully, the leaders of the two great political parties of the day withdrew into seclusion in an attempt to solve the constitutional problem which had baffled and infuriated Liberal statesmen for more than half a century. Parliament continued to sit until July 30th, but the Session which had begun in so turbulent a manner now proceeded in a curious atmosphere of unreality. The Government had no desire, at such a juncture, to introduce any legislation which might be termed contentious and party conflict, if not ceasing altogether, was largely absent from the scene.*

remains dead against. Lloyd George was against the thing thinking it was not wise policy. When it was decided upon he said he would go in with it & do his best to make it succeed—a perfectly fair attitude. Lord Crewe was earnest for the Conference."[56]

   * Lloyd George's second Budget, introduced on June 30th, proved, to the relief of all members, a much milder affair than its predecessor. What attracted most attention at this time was a Parliamentary Franchise (Women) Bill: its Second Reading was carried (299 to 189) by a free vote on July 13th, but the Government refused to make time available for further debate.

CHAPTER SIXTEEN

DOMESTIC AFFAIRS, JULY–NOVEMBER 1910

(1)

It was, until comparatively recently, not altogether clear what happened at the Constitutional Conference of 1910. No official records were kept and the Press, though informed when meetings had taken place, received no information concerning the items discussed. From June 17th until November 10th, in short, the political arena fell into a strange state of disuse. The giants of the scene disappeared from the eyes of mortal men, deliberating together in undisturbed seclusion, and a mysterious calm succeeded to what had hitherto been chaos and confusion. The first six months of the new reign thus slipped away with scarcely a ripple. At the end of that time, however, the giants emerged from seclusion, confessing their inability to co-operate but unwilling to enlarge upon this brief admission. They returned to their respective camps. The flag of truce was hauled down and the abandoned offensives were hurriedly resumed. Within a matter of days it seemed that nothing had ever happened to disturb the customary tenor of political warfare and not until another twenty years or so had rolled on did the public gain some idea of what had taken place. Now, half a century later, it is possible to reconstruct with tolerable accuracy both the official and unofficial negotiations of those months. Together, they constitute one of the most remarkable episodes in modern British politics.

We must first consider the attitude of the participants. The Government representatives were, on the whole, more anxious for a negotiated settlement than a resumption of hostilities and throughout the Conference they were ready to make substantial concessions to the Unionist viewpoint. Asquith, admittedly, had hesitated before approaching Balfour but his doubts had centred upon his own backbenchers rather than the Opposition. If there were a possibility of his being extricated from the deep waters in which he now found himself, then it would most certainly be examined.

Crewe, though equally cautious, was convinced of the necessity for negotiations and hoped that they would lead to something.* Birrell was accommodating at all times and Lloyd George seems to have been favourably inclined to discussions. Of the Unionist representatives, Balfour had agreed to the Conference from a sense of duty but his interest was genuine enough once the talks actually began. He was no doubt always aware that a settlement would not be reached, but there were moments when he came very near to bargaining in real earnest. Chamberlain, to judge from his subsequent actions, was not averse to a compromise agreement but Lansdowne and Cawdor were, from the outset, unwilling to negotiate or to make any concessions.

The Government representatives proposed that the Conference should discuss the relations of the two Houses in regard to finance, the provision of machinery to deal with persistent disagreement on this and other subjects and, finally, the possibility of reforming the Second Chamber so that it could function as a non-partisan assembly. The Unionists produced, in reply, a memorandum which ignored the last of these requirements but concentrated on the first two, dividing legislation into three categories: financial, ordinary and constitutional. The Liberals accepted this memorandum and the talks (the first of which was held in Asquith's room at the House of Commons) then began.

With regard to finance, the Unionists were prepared to recognise that the House of Lords could not reject money bills but only on condition that such bills did not have "social or political consequences which go far beyond the mere raising of revenue." Tacking, in other words, would have to be prevented by the intervention of some authority acceptable to both sides. The Government spokesmen were reluctant to agree to the establishment of such an authority, and no progress was made on this subject for the time being.

The problem arising from ordinary legislation was, of course, that of deciding what should be done when proposals put forward by the Commons were repeatedly rejected by the unrepresentative assembly. It was clear that no Ministry could allow this situation to continue indefinitely, yet no solution had presented itself which did not envisage some restrictions on the power of the House of Lords to amend or reject. The Unionists had grudgingly admitted that some change in the composition of the

* "We have started on our negotiations . . . under good auspices," wrote Crewe to Gladstone on June 17th, "and, so far as I can judge, with a real wish on their side, as on ours, for a favourable issue." On August 5th he added that "we are all on both sides in a good mood over the Conference, some being more sanguine than others, but all of us determined to do our best to come to terms."[1]

Second Chamber was desirable, but they would not agree to restrictions. One idea which they did accept in principle was that of a joint sitting between the two Houses when a difference of opinion arose. Such a suggestion had been made by Campbell-Bannerman in his memorandum of May 31st, 1907 and it is possible, since the Parliament Bill was silent on this point, that the Government had been holding it in reserve as a useful bargaining point. In essentials it was simple enough: if a measure put forward by the Commons in at least two consecutive yearly sessions were rejected by the Lords on both occasions, then a joint sitting would take place between members of both Houses and the decision reached on this issue would be accepted as binding. The trouble was, however, that the Conference could not agree on details. Both sides agreed that all members of the Lower House should attend such a sitting and only a certain percentage of the Lords should be present, but they were unable to decide what the percentage should be or how it should be constituted.

The third category of legislation in the Unionist memorandum, that labelled constitutional or "organic", proved to be the ultimate stumbling-block. The Liberals refused to admit the existence of such a category, which they felt was simply another name for Home Rule, but the Unionists contended that any proposals affecting the Crown or the Protestant succession should, if rejected by the Lords, be submitted to a plebiscite after a second rejection rather than the device of a joint sitting. This was, perhaps, a reasonable suggestion, but the Government representatives felt unable to accept it. However, as this issue was not seriously discussed until October the twelve meetings held between June 17th and July 31st gave some colour to Asquith's report to the King that the Conference had "indicated a desire for 'rapprochement' ".[2]

(2)

There was no question of the Conference continuing its deliberations throughout the summer. The meeting of July 31st was to be the last for ten weeks and Balfour, indeed, writing to Lansdowne (from Cannes) a little while later expressed a wish that "the whole thing might be put off till November."[3] In neither camp, despite the unease which was constantly expressed, was there any real expectation of a settlement.* Birrell, addressing the Eighty Club on July 25th, suggested that a great scheme of federalism might be a means of overcoming the Home Rule obstacle, but

---

* The King, Balfour told Austen Chamberlain, "is said to think of nothing else but the Conference, and hopes for nothing so much as its success. I cannot conceive how he is to be gratified. But if the thing is to break down—as I fear it must—it becomes doubly important that the breakdown should not be attributed to us."[4]

the Unionist Press did not respond with much enthusiasm. Lansdowne, moreover, in a long and gloomy memorandum which he sent to Balfour on September 10th, pointed out that, quite apart from the question of constitutional legislation, no formula had yet been devised which would distinguish "pure finance from legislation partly financial but important quite as much from its political as from its financial effects."[5] Further progress seemed improbable.

Lloyd George, in particular, felt frustrated and baffled at this depressing state of affairs. It appalled him that, at a time when so much needed to be done in the fields of social reform, trade expansion and the encouragement of industry, they should find themselves bogged down in a mass of constitutional wrangling. Children might starve, old folk die from lack of attention and the canker of poverty feed ever more deeply upon the vitals of the nation before the Liberal and Unionist Parties, exhausted, bitter and jaded, brought their contest to a satisfactory conclusion and turned once more to consideration of that nation's welfare. It was surely a tragic waste of time and effort for all concerned. If only it were possible for them to unite on a common programme of reforms and agree that these should take precedence over all inter-party squabbles! Returning to his beloved Criccieth, he pondered upon these things. The Conference, it seemed, was doomed to failure. Something really imaginative was needed to save the situation—not simply a collection of half-hearted proposals which hardly dare venture beyond the confines of party policy but a scheme which swept away all petty restrictions at one fell swoop. What was wrong, therefore, with the formation of a National Coalition Government, composed of the most talented Liberals and Unionists and pledged to carry through a programme of reforms on which they all agreed? Excited by the possibilities of such a scheme he completed, on August 17th, a lengthy memorandum setting forth the advantages which would result from it.

"Parties," it ran, "will always disagree on certain vital issues affecting the government of this country . . . but at the present moment the questions which are of the most vital importance to the well-being of the great community are all questions which are not only capable of being settled by the joint action of the two great parties without involving any sacrifice of principle on the part of either, but which can be better settled by such co-operation than by the normal working of party machinery." No party would be able to tackle such questions alone since the extremists of each side, who usually exercised an influence out of all proportion to their numerical strength, would be sure to intervene: "joint action would make it possible to settle these urgent questions without paying too much attention to the formulae and projects of rival faddists." A Ministry of All the Talents, composed of "half a dozen first-rate men" from each side, would prove insurmountable.

Having emphasised the advantages of a Coalition Government, the memorandum passed to the problems it would have to tackle. Britain, it declared, was losing to foreign competitors in overseas trade and if she did not pull herself together would very soon be facing bankruptcy. Only by carrying through a programme of national reorganisation could she hope to survive. Social problems, moreover, were crying out for attention: there was need for more and better homes, a curb on excessive drinking, insurance against accidents and unemployment, reform of the Poor Law, settlement of the education controversy and expansion in the field of technology.

Next came the question of national defence. Breaking new ground with a vengeance, Lloyd George thought a Coalition would be able to introduce compulsory military service: "we might aim at raising 500,000 armed militia to supplement our regular army." On the subject of local government he showed himself an advocate of the federalist viewpoint: the Imperial Government had more than enough to cope with and some of its duties should be delegated to "local bodies on a large scale." Such bodies could enquire into "the various problems connected with State assistance to trade and commerce" and the case for Tariff Reform would be judged on its merits. The reorganisation of the nation's transport facilities was another problem needing attention. As for agrarian reform, he felt the only way to secure efficient use of the land would be for both parties to abandon their encouragement of smallholdings: big farms, plenty of capital and intelligent management were more use to the nation than innumerable small units struggling for independent existences.

Both on Imperial and foreign affairs a Coalition would be able to speak with far greater authority than a partisan administration. "Such a Government," concluded the memorandum, "representing as it would not a fragment but the whole nation, would undoubtedly enhance the prestige of this country abroad."[6]

Lloyd George was never afraid to advocate drastic and unprecedented steps in the face of a crisis, and the motives which inspired this remarkable document were admirable. The means he adopted to secure acceptance of his proposals, though unsuccessful, are equally deserving of praise. To accuse him, as certain writers have, of attempting to bring about Asquith's downfall by backstairs intrigue is to betray a fundamental ignorance both of Lloyd George's character and the political situation as it was in 1910. More than anything else, he was concerned with getting things done: if necessary he himself would resign from office in order that a Coalition might be formed. His ardour in this respect was perfectly genuine.

The memorandum was worded to appeal to both the main parties and, from a purely practical point of view, there was much to be said for a Coalition. The reflection that extremist minorities were capable of enforcing their will on the more moderate elements of a party was presumably intended for Balfour's especial consumption, although the belief that a Ministry of All the Talents would prove impregnable was not altogether correct: events in 1922 would show that a team of mediocrities was capable of dislodging and replacing such a Ministry. The case for social reform was couched in skilful language: the Liberals would agree that "the health, the vitality, the efficiency and the happiness" of the individual were of prime importance, while the Unionists would appreciate the necessity of an active and efficient labour force. As for the reforms themselves, Lloyd George did not make his proposals too specific, except in the case of insurance: time enough to decide on their character once a Coalition had actually been established. Unionists would, presumably, be in favour of compulsory military service if the Liberals also swallowed this pill and the memorandum's comments on agrarian reform, though unexpected, would certainly appeal to them. As for Imperial and foreign affairs, no one could take exception to the vague sentiments expressed by the writer. The Irish problem, incidentally, was mentioned only in passing: "parties might deal with it without being subject to the embarrassing dictation of extreme partisans". Tariff Reform would be judged impartially and, if necessary, would be adopted without delay: since 1907, if not earlier, Lloyd George had grown increasingly sceptical of the Free Trade gospel and was only too ready to jettison it without too much soul-searching.

Apart from Home Rule, Free Trade, education and licensing the differences between the Liberal and Unionist Parties at this time were not very great and, in some respects, a matter of habit rather than conviction. Assuming, therefore, that the Unionists could accept a federal solution to the Irish problem and the Liberals could survive a dose of Imperial Preference, there seemed no fundamental reason why the two parties should not unite. With the ablest men of both sides in control of the House of Commons, with a large Centre Party to support them and with a programme of national reforms on which they could all safely agree, such a combination would stand firm as a permanent barrier against Socialism and the disintegration of the British Empire. The Labour Party would be kept in its place and the Irish Nationalists would be no more than a pressure group.

This memorandum was completed on August 17th. The first person to whom Lloyd George showed it was Churchill, an ex-member of the Unionist Party, who was immediately attracted by the idea of a Coalition. They agreed that, before taking any other member of the Cabinet into their confidence (although something was said to Asquith at this stage) they should first ascertain what Unionist reaction was likely to be. Towards the end of September, therefore, Lloyd George explained his proposals to F. E. Smith and authorised him to discuss them with both Balfour and Bonar Law. The European situation, he declared, was dangerous and national security ought to be their paramount concern. Under the present system neither party could achieve great things, but a Coalition would be able to carry through conscription, build a strong navy (with "more economical working") and implement social reforms. So far as Tariff Reform was concerned, the Liberal Party could be persuaded to accept (a) a tariff for revenue purposes and (b) a remission of the duties paid by the colonies. Agreement on the education issue was almost in sight. On licensing both sides were in difficulties—the Liberals "with their teetotal faddists" and the Tories with the brewers, but an arrangement could be made on the basis of fair compensation and the reform of the public house system. The House of Lords (it was implied) would remain much the same while Home Rule would be granted in a moderate form. The advantage of a Coalition was that both parties would be able to shed their "duffers" (i.e., Burns) and share out the places equally between them, while the present situation meant a general election very shortly with a result much the same as the previous January. He gave Smith a copy of his memorandum (it seems that there were only two copies) and explained that, although it had not yet been shown to Asquith, the Prime Minister had raised no objection to exploratory talks and was, indeed, anxious to learn Balfour's views.*[7]

F. E. Smith, himself much attracted by the idea, hurried away to tell Balfour all about it. Lloyd George and Churchill (who had apparently

---

* This paragraph is based to a large extent on an undated "aide-mémoire" written by Sandars. The first part of this document runs as follows: "Winston wrote to F. E.—no answer. Lloyd George wrote proposing F. E. should see him in D. Street. F. E. went—thunderstruck by proposed Coalition. Do comment typewritten on Treasury paper. [Bonar] Law shown it [and] *the King* [and] Winston. Asquith not yet—going to. Anxious A. J. B. should see it. *No one else at present.* Asquith no opportunity for seeing A. J. B. personally."[8]

taken the King into their confidence) now awaited with great interest a speech while the Unionist leader was due to deliver at the Edinburgh Conservative Club on October 5th. If he showed himself conciliatory and ready to negotiate, all well and good; if, on the other hand, he adopted a belligerent attitude towards the Liberal Party, hopes for a settlement were at an end.

In the event, the speech did much to satisfy their expectations. Balfour commented optimistically on the progress made by the Conference, criticised Liberal policies in the mildest of terms and reserved his strongest words of condemnation for the Labour Party and its agitation over the Osborne judgment.* "On land too," wrote an elated Churchill to Lloyd George on October 6th, although not altogether accurately, "he marches in step with you. If we stood together we ought to be strong enough to impart a progressive character and policy, or by withdrawal terminate an administration which had failed in its purpose. Let us dine on Tuesday and talk to Grey about it all."[10] It was, however, on the following Monday, October 10th, that Lloyd George and Churchill first discussed the matter with Sir Edward, the latter expressing considerable interest in the proposal. The following day it seems that Lloyd George put the Master of Elibank in the picture and he also made a direct approach to Balfour for the first time. "I have," he wrote, evidently referring to a brief conversation which they had had after the Conference earlier that day, "some informal suggestions which I should like to put to you. You thought tomorrow at 4 would suit you. Don't you think dinner or lunch would be a more convivial opportunity for discussing things? If you agree it would give me great pleasure if you could dine with me tomorrow evening or failing that lunch with me after the Conference. The servants are Welsh and could not follow the conversation and the only other person present would be my little daughter of eight summers."[11]

It was presumably on October 12th, therefore, that Lloyd George explained his scheme in detail to the Unionist leader. Writing to Austen Chamberlain ten days later, Balfour recalled that "defence, education, licensing were the things on which he laid stress", although having no precise suggestions to make, while mentioning "(in his airy way) that something would have to be done for Ireland, probably as part of a gen-

---

* The mildness of this speech left some of the more extreme Unionists such as Leo Maxse in a disgruntled state, while Beatrice Webb thought that Balfour had "done for the chances of a Tory Party at the next election." It should be remembered, however, that Balfour was soft-pedalling on his utterances not so much from a desire to reach agreement with the Liberal Party as from his anxiety that the breakdown of the Conference should not be attributed to the Unionists.[9]

eral scheme of devolution" and suggesting that a commission should be appointed to enquire into the pros and cons of Tariff Reform.* This was, of course, all very vague but, as Balfour remarked, "we touched on so many questions, and the initial difficulty of forming a Coalition seemed so fundamental, that I did not think it worthwhile coming to close quarters as to the exact nature and limitations of the programme which a Coalition could carry out. . . . I think it quite possible, though perhaps improbable, that a 'modus vivendi' might be arrived at on the substance of a common policy if the enormous difficulties of a Coalition could be overcome. But I saw no object in a detailed discussion about the pattern of the wall-papers which are to adorn this new political structure when the foundations have not been laid." [13]

Lloyd George, notwithstanding, was left with the impression that Balfour "was by no means hostile; in fact, he went a long way towards indicating that personally he regarded the proposal with a considerable measure of approval.† He was not, however, certain of the reception which would be accorded to it by his party." [15] These words were written twenty years later but they do seem to be a fair reflection of Balfour's initial reactions. In the letter to Chamberlain quoted above, for instance, he remarked that he did not take up a 'non-possimus' attitude on any of the suggestions. He was, however, somewhat mystified as to the extent to which they had Asquith's support. Writing to Austen Chamberlain from Whittingehame on October 24th, with the Prime Minister "domiciled only half an hour by motor from here," he wondered whether "anything would be gained by my having a 'fishing' talk with him, and trying to find out where he stands in all this business? I am not keen on the idea, but I throw it out for your consideration. In many respects it would be far easier to promise our support to the Government if they were

---

* F. E. Smith, it seems, told Bonar Law that Lloyd George had stated that one of the first tasks of a Coalition would be to appoint a commission to enquire into the need for Tariff Reform. It would report within six months and the Government would abide by its recommendations, whatever they might be. Bonar Law dined with Austen Chamberlain on October 19th and told him of this proposal. Chamberlain, who was not himself directly approached by Lloyd George, was very interested and rather indignantly charged Balfour with having kept this information from him. Balfour (October 22nd) hurriedly explained that Lloyd George had mentioned the possibility of a commission, "*but he said nothing about reporting in six months, etc;* and as I have always resisted the appeal of our own Free Traders to hang up the subject until a commission had reported, I did not receive this part of the suggestion with any enthusiasm." [12]

† "In my conversations with B.," wrote Lloyd George to Crewe on October 20th, "I assumed that as a condition precedent to such an understanding, a compact on the constitutional issue was essential. I also gave it as my opinion that an agreement as to the lines of settlement of the education and Welsh Church questions was a necessary preliminary to any Coalition. The Nonconformists could not come in on any other terms. He raised difficulties about Home Rule; but he was quite ready to consider any proposals for a federal arrangement." [14]

prepared to defy the Irish and their own extremists than to offer to form a Coalition. Yet somehow I do not see how such an arrangement could be made to work satisfactorily." [16]

The Conference had resumed its deliberations on October 11th and met on each of the three days which followed, but very little progress was made. The Liberals, in an effort to break the Gordian knot, now made some substantial concessions as regards financial legislation,* but the breakdown came on the question of Home Rule. [18] The Unionists, it will be recalled, wanted a referendum after the second rejection of a Home Rule Bill by the House of Lords, but the Government were unable to accept this proposal. On October 14th, therefore, the Conference adjourn- ed until November 1st, Asquith informing the King that "the point of divergence . . . is the question whether organic and constitutional changes (such, e.g., as Home Rule, the franchise, redistribution) should be ex- cepted from the procedure of joint sessions, which, it is agreed, should be applicable to deadlocks between the two Houses in regard to ordinary legislation; and should (in cases of such difference) be submitted to a popular 'referendum ad hoc'. The representatives of the Opposition insist on this distinction; the representatives of the Government are opposed to it, not only on its merits, but because they know that it would be impossible to induce the Liberal Party to agree to it."†[19]

It was at this time that Lloyd George finally presented Asquith with a copy of his memorandum, although the Prime Minister had, of course, been aware of its existence (and its contents) for several weeks.‡ Asquith's reaction seems, on the whole, to have been one of private amusement, and thirteen years later he told Lucy Masterman that he was sure nothing would come of the scheme: "I just laughed at it." [22] He had no objection, however, to Lloyd George pursuing his discussions with the Unionist leaders for the time being and merely suggested that the memorandum

---

* Lloyd George proposed that a "Committee of Fourteen", composed of seven representa- tives from each House, plus the Speaker as chairman, should be elected for the duration of each Parliament. It would decide (in cases of disagreement) what constituted a genuine finance bill. The Speaker, if there were an equal division of opinion, would have a casting vote. This pro- posal was accepted by the Unionists, and the Conference got as far as drafting a formula on the subject. [17]

† "The condition that the new machinery is only to work after another general election," wrote Churchill to Lloyd George on October 14th, "means a fresh appeal to the people any- how on a disagreed Home Rule scheme and makes it necessary for us to have three general elections running in order to carry it. To say that even after the next election has been won on Home Rule by a majority big enough for a joint session, there is to be yet another election— the fourth—won running by the Liberals cannot conceivably be maintained by any people who wish to act fairly." [20]

‡ "Although I dictated it in the month of August," wrote Lloyd George to Crewe on October 20th, "I had no opportunity of showing it to the P.M. until last week." [21]

be shown to Crewe and Grey. This request was promptly complied with.

Both Crewe and Grey were impressed by the memorandum. The former, writing to Lloyd George on October 22nd, declared that he found the proposals attractive in view of the fact "that we have got pretty nearly to the end of our tether as regards great reforms on party lines. As you observe, they are bound to be unpopular in many quarters, and I don't see any signs of the driving force which is to carry them."[23] He wrote to Asquith in a similar vein, observing that the memorandum was a clever document but that he was disturbed at its novelty and the strange situation which had resulted from its appearing at so crucial a time.[24] Grey, who had a long talk with Lloyd George on October 25th, reported to Asquith the following day that (although appreciating the difficulties) he was attracted towards the idea of a Coalition. "If the Conference breaks up without agreement," he wrote, "I foresee the break-up of the Liberal Party and a time of political instability, perhaps of chaos, to the great detriment of the country. The other party is, of course, paralysed and useless, but behind us there are explosive and violent forces which will split our party, and I do not believe we can resume the old fight against the Lords by ourselves without division."*[25]

In selecting F. E. Smith and Bonar Law as his principal Unionist confidants Lloyd George had unconsciously been anticipating the course of future events. F. E. Smith, in particular, was very much smitten with the idea of a Coalition, as is clear from the letter that follows.

Smith to Chamberlain, October 20th, 1910

Compare what is attainable under this scheme with the result of defeat in January: (a) national service and adequate navy, (b) concessions to colonies on basis of existing duties and *a real and fair enquiry* of which Ll. G. has said that he will gladly follow if it recommends change. . . .

I am absolutely satisfied of Ll. G.'s honesty and sincerity. He has been taught much by office and is sick of being wagged by a Little England tail. But if he proved in a year or two "difficile" or turbulent, where is he and where are we? He is done and has sold the pass. We should still be a united party with the exception of our Orangemen: and they can't stay out long. . . .

A great sigh of relief would go up over the whole of business England if a strong and stable Government were formed. There is a general feeling that the new King should have a chance. Furthermore such a Government could (1) say to Redmond:

---

* "I have a letter from E. Grey," wrote Asquith to Crewe on October 27th, "from which it appears that Ll. G. has been extending his missionary operations into that quarter, and apparently not without producing an impression."[26]

thus far and no further, which Asquith standing alone cannot; and (2) absolutely refuse reversal of the Osborne judgment, which Asquith standing alone cannot.

I do not under all these circumstances believe that a Coalition would in any way shock the public conscience and it might at the best give us a national Government for ten years; at the worst it would enable us to fight against opponents whose most formidable leaders were discredited and under circumstances which might lead to another period of Tory ascendancy.[27]

Austen Chamberlain, in reply to this letter, agreed that Lloyd George appeared to be sincere in his desire for an all-party Coalition but pointed out the obstacles and emphasised the desirability of submitting Home Rule to the country rather than a joint session.* F. E. Smith, evidently pleased at the response his arguments had aroused, wrote an even more persuasive letter (October 21st) in which he again claimed that the Unionists had everything to gain and nothing to lose by throwing in their lot with the Liberal leaders. As for Home Rule, which he had gathered was the principal stumbling-block to a successful conclusion of the Conference, this would surely cease to be an issue once federalism had been accepted. "The present position," he declared, ". . . is that Asquith, Ll. George, Churchill, Haldane, Birrell and Crewe (Grey cannot be seen until Monday) are prepared to come into a Government in which the offices great and small will be precisely divided among our party and theirs . . . . I understand that Elibank counts upon 40 Radical dissentients, but says that he will carry the party machinery and of course the Irish. They are anxious that you should go to either the Admiralty or the colonies."[29]

Chamberlain's main reaction, on receiving this letter, was to take alarm at Smith's belief that the Home Rule issue was proving a stumbling-block to a settlement. He once again replied immediately, pointing out that the idea of devolution had not been brought before the Conference. "What we have been discussing there," he wrote, "is not *what changes* in our system of government should be made, but *how* such changes should be effected. . . . What we desire is not a guarantee against all change but security against changes in the machinery of government *which the people do not approve*."[30]

The chief result of Lloyd George's activity in the Unionist camp was to arouse enthusiasm for the idea of Home Rule on a federal basis. This meant, briefly, the establishment of an Imperial Parliament to deal with trade and defence and "domestic" parliaments to deal with the affairs of

---

* "What a world we live in," he wrote to Cawdor on October 21st, "and how the public would stare if they could look into our minds and letter boxes!"[28]

certain regions. He did not, of course, put this scheme forward as a novel proposal: Birrell's speech of July 25th showed that it was already being canvassed in Liberal circles and the Scottish National Committee had issued a manifesto in its support on August 5th. *The Times* (October 14th) cited these two incidents, together with a speech Lloyd George had made on September 20th, as indicative of a growing desire among Liberals and Nationalists for Irish independence under the guise of "Home Rule All Round". Two days later the *Observer* came out strongly in favour of federalism. Lyttelton reported to Balfour that there was "very great sympathy with Local Federation among the younger intellectuals. I mention F. S. Oliver, Brand, Kerr and Milner's kindergarten, Milner himself and Garvin."[31] From October 20th onwards a series of letters written by F. S. Oliver, under the pen-name "Pacificus", hammered home the case for Federal Home Rule to readers of *The Times*. The Liberal Press were equally enthusiastic and the *Morning Post* and the *Spectator* were the only Unionist publications to offer any opposition to the scheme. The Master of Elibank, speaking at Belfast on October 18th, declared that the Scottish and Welsh desires for local Home Rule had altered the situation and that the business aspect of the scheme would most probably advance the cause of federalism.

Balfour was anxious to quash this talk of an Irish settlement and, perfectly well aware in his own mind of the distinction between the official and unofficial negotiations, decided to make this distinction clear to his colleagues.

Balfour to Lyttleton, October 20th, 1910

The precise crisis on which we separated last Friday related to *every* form of constitutional change. We contended that constitutional change as such should be distinct both from ordinary and financial legislation and that the proper method of dealing with it if the two Houses differed in two successive sessions was not to refer it to a giant sitting but to a plebiscite. This, it seemed to me then and seems to me still, is in itself both logical and expedient; and it has the merit of giving to the other side a remedy against deadlocks and to ask for security against rash innovation by a new and reckless House of Commons.

On the question of "devolution" or "provincialism" or "Home Rule All Round" (or by whatever name it is to be known) I say nothing at this moment. I doubt whether most of those who talk about it have thought it out; certainly I am not prepared to dogmatise upon the subject. It never came up in any practical shape at the Conference and the rumour to the contrary is a pure invention of 'The Times' correspondent.[32]

The Ulster Unionists, led by Carson since January, were nevertheless well aware that secret negotiations for an Irish settlement were in progress. Sir Edward wrote to Balfour on October 25th informing him that he was being much pressed "to state publicly my disapproval and opposition to the rumoured proposals for a settlement on the Home Rule question."[33] Balfour did not reply for a few days and Carson told Lady Londonderry (October 29th) that he was "sick to death of this Home Rule tragedy": "It will split the party to pieces and, should it turn out to be true, I earnestly hope the Conservatives will never be in office again during my life. How can anyone suppose that those of us who have fought all our lives to prevent a separate parliament [could] now turn round and allow so base a surrender! We are all drifting and where to I don't know. I hate the whole situation. . . . 'F. E.' is very full of himself and seems to approve of the Home Rule proposals. What next!"[34]

The Ulster Unionists need not have worried. Balfour was never, at any time, in favour of the Lloyd George scheme and by November 6th Carson could write that "my own belief is that there is no fear of A. J. B. being likely to concede anything on Home Rule."[35] In order to understand the outcome of this whole curious episode it is necessary to study the Unionist leader's behaviour a little more closely.

(3)

There were, in a narrow context, three dominant factors governing Balfour's behaviour at this time: opposition to Home Rule *per se*; a reluctance to abandon the position which he had taken up on Ireland in 1886 and maintained ever since, and finally a determination not to betray the trust placed in him by the Unionist Party. The responsibilities of a party leader were always to the fore in his considerations and, despite his enviable reputation as a skilled parliamentarian, first-rate administrator and statesmanlike strategist, his conduct was invariably governed by the desire to satisfy as many Tory gentlemen at one fell swoop as was humanly possible. On a wider front, moreover, was the fact that the Liberal Party was in a very difficult position and presumably only too willing to be extricated from its predicament by an agreement of this nature.

Esher noted on October 16th that the Unionist leader suspected "some intrigue between the Government and Redmond" and on October 22nd, in response to a long and persuasive letter from Garvin, Balfour made it plain in a letter of equal length that he was not yet ready to countenance any change in the Act of Union. By this time, of course, he would have studied Lloyd George's memorandum of August 17th and on October 29th he received yet another. This second document, which the Master of

Elibank had helped to draw up, contained proposals of a rather more specific nature and evidently reflected the discussions which Lloyd George had had with various Unionists. It suggested, to begin with, a careful enquiry into the whole question of defence and went on to propose that Ireland should be granted a measure of self-government "which might form a nucleus for the federation of the Empire ar some future date." The objectives on which this memorandum laid special emphasis were disestablishment of the Church in Wales, reform of the Poor Law and of national education, a remodelling of the taxation system and the establishment of national insurance. It proved, however, of little importance.[36]

On November 1st Balfour discussed the whole question of a Coalition with Lloyd George, but what took place at this meeting is far from clear. Politicians are notoriously forgetful when it comes to writing their memoirs and Lloyd George's account of the talks between himself and the Unionist leader at this time, written twenty years later, cannot be accepted as trustworthy evidence. All we can be sure of, in fact, is that Balfour politely but firmly rejected the idea of a Coalition, presumably with as much apparent reluctance as he could decently muster. According to Lloyd George, he put his hand on his forehead and, more or less soliloquising, said: "I cannot become another Robert Peel in my party!" After a short interval he added: "Although I cannot see where the Disraeli is to come from, unless it be my cousin Hugh, and I cannot quite see him fulfilling that rôle!"[37] Balfour certainly appears to have had a Robert Peel complex at this time and the words which he is supposed to have used can be taken as a good representation of his feelings.* The true function of a political leader, he felt, was to give expression to the views held by the majority of his party at any one time and not to march them into pastures new and unreconnoitred, however attractive they might appear to those in the van. He did suggest, however, that he might be prepared to reconsider his views if Asquith himself were to indicate his willingness to coalesce with the Unionists. This was, as both he and Lloyd George knew quite well, an unlikely eventuality. The latter agreed to approach Asquith, although holding out little hope of a favourable reply. "I have just seen the P.M. as to your suggestion," he wrote the following day. "For the reasons I gave to you he thinks it undesirable *at*

---

* "Peel," he told his niece eighteen years later, "twice committed what seems to me the unforgivable sin. He gave away a principle on which he had come into power—and mind you, neither time had an unforeseen factor come into the case. He simply betrayed his party. I have at no time been possessed by a desire to emulate him in this."[38]

this stage to take part in the negotiations. But he asked me to say that all I did was with his full concurrence."*39

Here the matter ended, therefore, and the Coalition project was gently laid to rest. Superficially, at any rate, it had been a close thing since, of the Liberal leaders, Lloyd George himself, Churchill, Crewe, Grey, Birrell and Elibank had been attracted by the idea, while in the Tory camp Austen Chamberlain, F. E. Smith and Bonar Law had responded with interest. Yet it was a plan doomed to failure. Neither Asquith nor Balfour (despite the latter's initial hesitation) had welcomed it and in any case, when it came to examining the policies on which this Ministry of All the Talents was to unite, the fundamental basis for a Coalition simply did not exist. The "half a dozen first-rate men" of both parties probably had more in common with one another than they did with the humbler members of their respective rank and files, but real political power nevertheless resided with the latter. Even supposing that the leaders had dared to fling caution and principles to the winds and gone through with the proposals, they would not have been creating an all-party administration but a new party altogether. There was certainly no reason to suppose that Liberal backbenchers would support Liberals who had gone Tory or that Unionists would delight in seeing their leaders troop off to join the erstwhile enemy. The policies of such a Coalition would, moreover, have been so trimmed to suit both sides that they would finally cease to be distinctive innovations and become a nullified hotchpotch. The extremist rumps remaining would retain the old party machineries and the Coalition would gradually find itself squeezed out of existence, no matter how brilliant its individual members might be. Lloyd George's blueprint simply provided for a combination of personalities: it did not, and could not, provide for a combination of principles.

(4)

With visions of "the big settlement" (as F. E. Smith described it) having abruptly evaporated, the Conference resumed on November 1st the sittings which had been suspended on October 14th.† The unofficial

---

* Churchill subsequently told Austen Chamberlain in 1913 that Asquith had been kept fully informed of the progress of Lloyd George's conversations, but until Crewe and Birrell (presumably he meant Grey) had been consulted he "had maintained an attitude of strict reserve and aloofness." Nothing had been said to any other members of the Cabinet—"How could we tell them? Some of them would have had to go!"40

† It is important to remember that the Conference and the Lloyd George plan were two completely separate things, the Jekyll and Hyde of the constitutional discussions of 1910, and that, although two sets of negotiations had been in operation between the same two sets of people, the twain were never allowed to meet.

negotiations had been tried and found wanting: there remained the none too hopeful prospect of an agreement on Home Rule.

The Liberals now proposed a compromise on Ireland. Asquith, while not admitting any distinction between "organic "and "ordinary" legislation, was prepared to agree that, if the next Home Rule Bill were rejected by the Lords, a general election should at once be held. If the Bill were supported by the electorate, it would thenceforth be treated as ordinary legislation and eventually be carried through both Houses. On the other hand, if they were not supported on this occasion the Liberals would *not* pledge themselves to another general election should a fresh Home Rule Bill be eventually introduced by them and rejected by the Lords.

The Unionists did not view this proposal with much enthusiasm. "Though preferring our own scheme," states Balfour in a memorandum dictated a week or so later, "we should have raised no very serious objection to this alternative method of dealing with Home Rule had it been applicable to all Home Rule Bills, whenever proposed. This, however, our Government colleagues felt unable to concede. It was only the next Home Rule scheme which they proposed to safeguard; and to us it seemed impossible to accept a plan which required us to admit that the Union was a part of the constitution which only required temporary defence. We fully recognised that the suggestion was offered as a compromise . . . [but] we could not make ourselves responsible for a scheme which seemed to imply that, since the people had on three separate occasions expressed their hostility to Home Rule, it was high time to withdraw the subject from their cognisance and to hand it over to the unfettered discretion of the House of Commons and the joint sitting."[41]

On November 3rd, in an effort to "save time and conduce to clearness," Asquith sent Balfour a brief summary of the position as he and his colleagues understood it. "We regard the concession which we have provisionally agreed to in respect of finance," he wrote, "as of the most substantial character, and extremely difficult for us to defend against the criticism of our own supporters. To defend it at all would, we feel, become an impossibility if it were accompanied by the exclusion from the new machinery for preventing deadlocks of what is called organic or constitutional legislation. The distinction now suggested is entirely unknown to our constitution: it discriminates between legislative projects on the ground not of their real merit and the seriousness of their consequences, but according as they do or do not touch the law-making machinery; and it would render the new system totally inapplicable to a large number of the proposed changes to which our supporters attach the greatest value, and

in respect of which deadlocks are most likely to occur. We are prepared
to deal specially with Home Rule, on the lines of the Chancellor of the
Exchequer's suggestion. But we do not feel that we can maintain our
weakened position in regard to finance, unless (*a*) the new machinery is
made applicable to all legislation and (*b*) we can come to a satisfactory
agreement in regard to the interpretation of 'X' [i.e., the Unionist definition of 'organic or constitutional legislation'].''[42]

Balfour thought that this represented a change of front of Asquith's
part. "I had understood," he replied, "that you were prepared to treat
Reform Bills as belonging to a class of 'organic' legislation which might
have special safeguards attached to it; that you were more than willing to
treat the monarchy and the Protestant succession as 'organic' parts of the
constitution, and that you thought it vitally necessary that any legislation
based upon an arrangement come to at the Conference should be protected by a power of applying to the people (by plebiscite, or otherwise)
against any attempt to modify or repeal it. I need not assure you that I am
not for a moment suggesting that you have not an absolute right to
qualify or withdraw any provisional proposals or admissions made in the
course of our long—and I think useful—discussion. I only think it desirable
just to note that, if I rightly interpret what you say, your letter of this
afternoon represents a somewhat altered standpoint."[43]

Asquith responded promptly to this imputation. "When I referred in
my letter to 'organic' laws (as proposed to be put in a separate and specially protected category)," he wrote, "I had in mind Lansdowne's definition: 'projects of law which affect the law-making machine'. If it were
merely a question of the Crown and the Protestant succession, I should not
object (tho' I think it wholly unnecessary) to some special safeguard. So,
again, if we were happily to arrive at an agreement on the constitutional
question, and that agreement was embodied by consent in an Act of Parliament, it might be right and indeed expedient (as is proposed in Lloyd
George's clause) to give to the pact so concluded peculiar sanctions. But
the proposal now under consideration would include in the same category all Reform Bills, big or small (including the abolition of plural
voting), all forms of Home Rule from pure Parnellism to the most modest
schemes of devolution, and indeed practically all measures of *political*, as
distinguished from social or economic, change. It is here where the shoe
pinches so acutely that the party foot would in our judgment reject it as a
misfit."[44]

There had meanwhile been hectic discussions in the Cabinet as to the
number of Tory peers who could be present at a joint sitting. If a joint

sitting of both Houses were to be held in a literal sense, then the Liberals would always be at a disadvantage: they would have to have control of every seat in the Commons in order to out-vote the 500 Unionists in the Lords. The Government representatives had suggested, therefore, that a joint sitting should be composed of all the members of the Lower House together with a hundred peers. Twenty of the latter would be members of the Government* and the remaining eighty would be selected on a basis of proportional representation, namely twenty-five Liberals and fifty-five Unionists. At a joint sitting the Unionist peers would thus outnumber their Liberal counterparts by forty-five, which meant that the Government would have to be certain of a majority of at least fifty in the House of Commons. Lloyd George thought forty-five peers more than enough but Churchill, at one point in the proceedings, passed him a note scribbled on the back of an envelope: "I am going to suggest sixty." "Anything over forty I resign," came the reply, and Churchill evidently reconsidered his decision. In fact, according to Lucy Masterman, Lloyd George had selected fifty as his limit.[45]

After fruitless discussions at the Conference the Unionist representatives secured, on November 4th, permission to hold a meeting of their principal members to consider the situation. This took place at Lansdowne House on November 8th and lasted more than three hours.† Balfour opened the proceedings with a brief account of the progress so far made and explained that the question was, quite simply, whether it was worthwhile to continue these negotiations. He gave the impression that he himself was not prepared to go on, while Lansdowne, Cawdor and Austen Chamberlain made it clear that they personally were definitely opposed to further discussion. Long was inclined to agree with them while Lyttelton remained undecided. None of those present would agree to forty-five being the limit of a Unionist majority in a House of Lords delegation at a joint sitting, the number most favoured being in the region of eighty: Londonderry, Curzon and Halsbury were especially adamant on this point. The prevailing opinion was, in fact, that further negotiations would prove useless and that the Government's Home Rule proposals were an insurmountable barrier.[46] Esher, meeting Balfour later in the day, found him in low spirits. "He is most anxious." noted his lordship, "that the Conference should not be abortive. He sees no immediate hope of party advantage in a general election, and believes that for the country's sake a

---

* The Government did not contain more than thirteen peers at this time, but another seven would presumably have been created.

† Attendance at this meeting was (rather oddly) restricted to ex-Cabinet Ministers, which meant the exclusion of both Bonar Law and F. E. Smith.

compromise on the lines almost agreed to is the right thing. But his 'stalwarts' and young wreckers are opposed to him, and he does not fancy the rôle of Sir Robert Peel. . . . He is inclined—if he finds persuasion hopeless—to resign the leadership of the party."[47]

Balfour and his colleagues were empowered to make one last attempt at a settlement and, if this failed, to bring negotiations to an end. Later that day they met the Government representatives and put forward their minimum demands. It soon became clear that these would not be accepted. "Today's meeting of the Conference brought matters to a head," wrote Asquith to the King. "The proposed exclusion from the new machinery for settling deadlocks of Home Rule and other so-called organic changes was exhaustively discussed. The result showed an apparently irreconcilable divergence of view. But it was agreed that each side should carefully review in consideration the whole situation. A further, and possibly a final meeting, will be held tomorrow."[48]

The Prime Minister was vaguely optimistic to the last. Balfour, however, as the following note shows, was anxious not to prolong the agony.

Balfour to Asquith, November 8th, 1910

I am afraid that under existing circumstances there is little use continuing our meetings. I had at one moment greatly hoped for better things.

We must, I suppose, foregather to discuss exactly what is to be said to the public.[49]

The Conference met on November 10th for the twenty-first and last time. "It will be a disappointment if we fail." Asquith had written to his wife before the final meeting, "but nobody's fault. We all agree that A. J. B. is head and shoulders above his colleagues. I had a rather intimate talk with him before the Conference this morning. He is very pessimistic about the future and evidently sees nothing for himself but chagrin and a possible private life."[50]

In sorrow, rather than anger, the combatants parted. A statement was issued to the Press, declaring that no agreement had been reached and that the peculiar nature of the negotiations precluded any disclosure of what had been discussed. Many rumours were current and several versions of what had taken place prove, in retrospect, to have been remarkably accurate. These, however, were neither confirmed nor denied. The Nationalist and Labour Parties greeted the news with satisfaction. Liberals throughout the country breathed more freely.* Tension relaxed in Unionist circles. Thus, in an atmosphere of widespread relief, the Constitutional Conference of 1910 came to an end.

* "The Conference," wrote Harcourt to Gladstone on November 21st, "broke down—as I always felt sure it must do—because there was no possible ground of agreement."[51]

(5)

Minor changes had meanwhile taken place in the Government. Morley, it will be remembered, had only condescended to serve under Asquith so long as it was tacitly understood that he waived his claim to higher office.[*] He was, in consequence, very ready to take offence should the slightest opportunity for doing so arise and had threatened to resign on many occasions. Relations between himself and Asquith were uneasy and on September 13th, to quote Esher's account, "sore at not being invited to Balmoral, inclined to think that he was not being treated with consideration, he wrote to the Prime Minister saying that he was tired out and unable to go on."[53] Much to his surprise, Asquith raised no objections to this conclusion and simply offered the India Office to Crewe. Morley, in fact, was rather startled to find that he had been taken at his word, and during the next few weeks he postponed his departure in the hope that he would be pressed to stay. No pressure being exerted, however, he was obliged to carry his threat into execution, but one person at least was not content to let matters rest at this.

Churchill to Asquith, October 22nd, 1910

It is with some diffidence that I write to you on a matter which you may consider outside my province.

I had a talk with Morley yesterday and found a distinct undercurrent of feeling in his mind that he has been somewhat easily let go. He would of course be very much vexed with me for coming to such a conclusion, still more for repeating it to you. But I do so because I am strongly of opinion that Morley's complete detachment from the Government at this stage might prove very disadvantageous to us, and secondly because I have a deep personal affection for him and am proud to sit in Council by his side. . . .

Please do not be offended by my addressing you on such a subject. Only its importance and my wish to see your administration successful has prompted me. In no case let Morley know I have written.[54]

This letter, an instance of the new Radicals coming to the rescue of the old, may well have done the trick. On November 1st we find Asquith telling his wife that he had "seen a string of people, including J. M., whose vanity has been wounded by the supposed readiness with which I accepted his resignation of the India Office, as though it meant his complete retirement from the Cabinet. We had a very agreeable interview, in

---

* See footnote on page 154. Asquith told Crewe (September 14th) that Morley had announced his determination to be relieved of India "on grounds of age, weariness, advent of a new Viceroy, etc. I shall, of course, ask him to reconsider, but I don't think he will do so."[52]

the course of which I stroked him down, and in the end I have little doubt that he will stay on in some light office such as President of the Council."[55] A few days later it was announced that Crewe would take charge of the India Office and hand over colonial affairs to Harcourt. Morley became Lord President of the Council and remained a member of the Cabinet for another four years.

(6)

The Cabinet met a few hours after the breakdown of the Constitutional Conference and agreed that a general election should be held without delay. The following day, Friday, November 11th, Asquith journeyed to Sandringham in order to inform the King of these latest developments. He arrived at 6.30 p.m. and had two long talks with His Majesty, reporting, so the King noted in his diary, "that the Conference had failed & he proposed to dissolve & have a general election & get it over before Xmas. He asked me for *no guarantees*. I suggested that the Veto resolutions should first be sent up to the H. of L. & if they rejected them, then he could dissolve. This he agreed to do."[56]

King George V was understandably relieved at not having to face the question of guarantees. He did not realise, unfortunately, that this particular interview was not intended as an occasion for proffering advice and one can therefore appreciate his dismay at what followed.* On November 14th Knollys visited Downing Street and found, to his surprise, that what the Prime Minister "now advocated" were immediate guarantees for the next Parliament. The King was shocked and indignant when he heard this and Bigge despatched the following telegram to Asquith's private secretary: "His Majesty regrets that it would be impossible for him to give contingent guarantees and he reminds Mr Asquith of his promise not to seek for any during the present Parliament."[58] This time, however, the Cabinet stood firm. If the King would not pledge himself to a possible creation of peers, then his Ministers would resign. Asquith's declaration of April 14th was the deciding factor: there could be no second betrayal of

---

* Asquith, acting with typical circumspection, was working towards the subject of royal pledges very cautiously and regarded this meeting as nothing more than a preliminary reconnaisance. He pointed out to the King, so he afterwards recorded, that if the Government were returned to office and the Lords refused to give way, a final settlement could only be secured "by the willingness of the Crown to exercise its prerogative to give effect to the will of the nation. The House of Lords cannot be dissolved, and the only legal way in which it can be brought into harmony with the other House is either by curtailing, or adding to, its members. In theory, the Crown might conceivably adopt the former course, by withholding writs of summons. But this has not been done for many centuries: it would be a most invidious practice: and it is at least doubtful whether it can be said to be constitutional."[57]

the principles enunciated therein, as there had been of the Albert Hall speech of December 10th.*

Parliament reassembled the following day and the Prime Minister at once moved its adjournment. After some heated discussion it was agreed that he should postpone his statement on the constitutional issue until the 18th and the Commons contented themselves with discussing the use of troops in recent Welsh disturbances† and the effects of the new land taxes. The Cabinet meanwhile drew up the following Minute and sent it to Knollys:

> The Cabinet has very carefully considered the situation created by the failure of the Conference, in view of the declaration of policy made on their behalf by the Prime Minister in the House of Commons on the 14th of April, 1910.
>
> The advice which they feel it their duty to tender to His Majesty is as follows:
>
> An immediate dissolution of Parliament, as soon as the necessary parts of the Budget, the provision of old age pensions to paupers and one or two other matters have been disposed of.
>
> The House of Lords to have the opportunity, if they desire it, at the same time (but not so as to postpone the date of the dissolution) to discuss the Government resolutions.
>
> His Majesty's Ministers cannot, however, take the responsibility of advising a dissolution, unless they may understand that, in the event of the policy of the Government being approved by an adequate majority in the new House of Commons, His Majesty will be ready to exercise his constitutional powers (which may involve the prerogative of creating peers), if needed, to secure that effect should be given to the decision of the country.
>
> His Majesty's Ministers are fully alive to the importance of keeping the name of the King out of the sphere of party and electoral controversy. They take upon themselves, as is their duty, the entire and exclusive responsibility for the policy which they will place before the electorate.

---

* This was an argument which the Master of Elibank urged upon the King's private secretaries. "If there is a feeling in the country," he wrote to Knollys on November 14th, "that he [Asquith] is in any way flinching from his duty now that the crisis is upon us again, it would only serve as help and encouragement to the Socialist and extreme forces."[59]

† Early in November some 30,000 miners in the Rhondda and Aberdare Valleys had downed tools in protest against their conditions of labour. Feelings ran high, there were frequent clashes between strikers and police, and rioters ran amok in the village of Tonypandy on November 8th, looting and demolishing several shops. The Chief Constable of Glamorgan felt unable to cope and applied to the local army depot for assistance, but Churchill, after consulting with Haldane, refused to authorise the use of troops and sent instead a strong force of Metropolitan police. General Sir Nevil Macready, Director of Personal Services at the War Office, was placed in control of both the civil and military forces in the area. Riots continued and Churchill at last agreed to the movement of troops into the Rhondda Valley, but he made it clear that they were there solely for the protection of the police and orders were given that they were to take no part whatsoever in breaking the strike. On one occasion, after a group of policemen had been ambushed by strikers and pelted with stones, Macready's men intervened, but at no time were shots fired and the troops were eventually withdrawn. Churchill was nevertheless strongly criticised by Labour members for allowing them to be used.

His Majesty will doubtless agree that it would be undesirable, in the interests of the State, that any communication of the intentions of the Crown should be made public, unless and until the actual occasion should arise.[60]

The following day (November 16th) the King travelled to London and saw Asquith and Crewe at Buckingham Palace. "After a long talk," he wrote that evening, "I agreed most reluctantly to give the Cabinet a secret understanding that in the event of the Government being returned with a majority at the general election, I should use my prerogative to make peers if asked for. I dislike having to do this very much, but agreed that this was the only alternative to the Cabinet resigning, which at this moment would be disastrous."[61] This last was, indeed, the decisive factor. "It is obvious," wrote Asquith to Crewe a few weeks later, "that our resignation in such circumstances, with a dissolution following, would have been in every way more damaging to the authority of the Crown [than the King's promise to create contingent peers] and this consideration may well have weighed with him."[62]

Yet there had remained, perhaps, one last loophole. It would have been theoretically possible for the King to refuse the Cabinet's request on the grounds that he could not anticipate the result of a general election and, if they put their threat of resigning into effect, to send for Balfour. It will be recalled that this was precisely the idea discussed by Balfour and Chamberlain on April 19th and the Unionist leader had made it clear to Knollys on April 27th that he would be prepared to form a Government under such conditions. As things turned out, however, the King does not appear to have given this idea much consideration: with a Unionist defeat at the ensuing general election more than probable he would have been extremely ill-advised to embark on such a course. It would simply be a repetition of William IV's *faux pas* in 1834 with consequences far more damaging. The failure of Knollys to inform the King of Balfour's readiness to intervene has been justly censured by modern writers, but his lordship's curious lapse of memory should not be elevated to too great an importance. "The part to be played by the Crown in such a situation as now exists," wrote Asquith at this time, "has happily been settled by the accumulated traditions and the unbroken practice of more than seventy years. It is to act upon the advice of the Ministers who for the time being possess the confidence of the House of Commons, whether that advice does or does not conform to the private and personal judgment of the sovereign."[63]

From this precept there could, in the end, be no escape, yet it is still a moot point whether the Cabinet was justified in the decision it had forced upon the King. The Parliament Bill, it must be remembered, had not yet entered the Upper House when the Minute of November 15th was drawn up. An election on this specific issue had not been held. Strictly speaking, therefore, the question of guarantees ought not to have been raised at this stage of the proceedings. If the Lords rejected the Bill, an appeal to the country would automatically follow: if the Government were returned to office it would be able to reintroduce its Bill and, if the Lords remained adamant, to consider other means of ensuring that its will would prevail. Then, and only then, would it be necessary to approach the King for an assurance that he would create a certain number of peers if the Government requested him to do so. At the best, what Asquith had done was to cut a long story short; at the worst, he was treading on very dubious ground.

(7)

The parliamentary arena was once again the scene of much activity. In the Upper House the Parliament Bill was read for the first time on November 16th and the resolutions on reform which Rosebery had tabled in April were debated the following day (the first of them being agreed but the second being withdrawn by its sponsor). In the Commons, on November 18th, Asquith announced that the King had been advised to dissolve Parliament once all essential business had been settled. The Lords would have an opportunity of discussing the Parliament Bill, but there was no question of their being allowed to amend it and no one doubted what their views would be. Balfour declared himself amazed at this cavalier treatment of parliamentary procedure, while Barnes was annoyed at the prospect of yet another dissolution and thought that the Government should create peers without further ado—"plenty of unemployed would be glad of the job."

On November 21st the Parliament Bill was brought forward for its Second Reading in the Upper House. Crewe's introductory speech contained no fresh points and Lansdowne, after complaining of the unreality of the debate, examined the Government's proposals in detail. The financial safeguards, he thought, were inadequate: the Speaker was bound to defend the interests of the House of Commons. So were the clauses dealing with ordinary legislation: a conference on equal terms (though this, incidentally, was not mentioned in the Bill) would be impossible if legislation were eventually to be passed over their lordships' heads. The Opposition, since it could move no amendments, could only put on record its own alternative proposals, and these he produced later that day after the debate on the Bill had been adjourned. The scheme which he outlined was designed, so he claimed, to settle differences between the Commons and a "reduced and reconstituted House of Lords" and it bore some resemblance to the ideas which had been discussed at the Constitutional Conference. A difference on ordinary legislation which arose during two successive sessions and within an interval not less than one year would be settled at a joint sitting of members of both Houses, but if it related to a matter of grave concern which had not yet been adequately submitted to the judgment of the people it should first be presented to the electorate for a referendum. As for money bills, the Lords would forego their constitutional right to reject or amend provided that tacking was effectively prevented and that any question arising from such a bill should be referred to a joint committee of both Houses with the Speaker as chairman with, if necessary, a casting vote. Should the committee decide that the relevant provisions were not financial, they would be referred to the joint sitting.*

On November 23rd the Lords debated these proposals. Viscount St Aldwyn was very enthusiastic and only wished that they had been put forward earlier. They provided a fair settlement and he thought the Government ought to give them consideration instead of having an election. The Archbishop of Canterbury, who favoured a negotiated settlement, thought they had some points in common with the Government's own ideas. The Archbishop of York condemned the Ministry's haste in appealing to the country. Crewe, however, objected that the two Houses were too large to sit together and that it would be difficult to select the members of delegations. A referendum would be costly and it was, in any case, uncertain what questions would be settled by it—a tariff, for example, would be treated as a financial measure. In short, Liberal proposals would be submitted to a referendum, but Conservative not. As for money bills, the abandonment of the right of rejection was not much of a sacrifice and the right of amending had not been exercised for many years: the Commons, moreover, had never recognised either of them. After several more speeches, however, Lansdowne's proposals were agreed, ministerial supporters holding aloof, and it was decided that they should be communicated to the Lower House.

---

* Asquith, speaking at Hull on November 25th, attacked Lansdowne's scheme as "crude and complex". The referendum would allow the Lords to enforce a general election whenever they wished and would destroy the concept of representative government. It appears that King George V was none too keen on the scheme put forward by Lansdowne. "I think," wrote Esher on November 25th, "that the King is satisfied that the Veto Bill will do less harm than abolition of the hereditary principle and a complete break with the history of England."[64]

In the Commons, meanwhile, a truncated Finance Bill for 1910–11 was being rushed through its final stages. Asquith gave a hint of things to come when, on November 22nd, he declared that if the Government were in power for the next Parliament, it would introduce legislation for the payment of members while, at the same time, compelling unions to establish separate political funds to which contributions would be voluntary. Labour M.P.s received this news with mixed feelings. It was also announced that facilities would be provided for the passage of a Women's Suffrage Bill. On November 28th, all loose ends having been tidied up, Parliament was prorogued and dissolved.*

So ended one of the most remarkable Parliaments that this century has ever witnessed. Its one achievement, apart from the passing of the 1909 Budget, had been an Education (Choice of Employment) Act. Yet Asquith, speaking at Ladybank on October 29th, described 1910 as an *annus mirabilis* in British politics and his claim can hardly be denied. Two general elections, the death of a monarch, the introduction of a Parliament Bill, the Constitutional Conference and the proposed Coalition, not to mention the pledge which had finally been extracted from a King whose reign had barely begun, combined to make those twelve months some of the most fateful of modern English history. It had been a crucial time for the Liberal Government, and one from which it had not emerged altogether unscathed.

---

* "We are in for very serious times," Loreburn had written to Robson on September 20th, "domestic certainly, and perhaps also foreign. Woman's suffrage, Osborne judgment, working of the land taxes, to say nothing of increasing expenses, the territorial army and trade quarrels. Toryism kept us idle for twenty years when we ought to have been placing our house in order and all now comes with a rush. We have not the machinery to do the work with deliberation and care, and it will end, or perhaps almost begin, with Home Rule all round."[65]

CHAPTER SEVENTEEN

THE GENERAL ELECTION
OF DECEMBER 1910

(1)

For the second time in twelve months Great Britain found herself confronted with a general election. This was thought, by the standards of the day, to be rather too much of a good thing, and it soon became evident that there was none of that excitement in the country at large which had made the struggle for reform in 1832 so national an undertaking. The great majority of the people were bored and exhausted by the wrangling at Westminster and were more concerned with their Christmas shopping than with the outcome of the constitutional struggle. Unionists were able to argue, with some success, that political controversy ought to have been given a rest during the festive season, but with the failure of the Constitutional Conference the Government had been left with no option but to secure a renewal of their mandate at the earliest possible moment, since this was the only means available to them of demonstrating that the Parliament Bill commanded popular support. Not until the absolute veto of the Lords had been destroyed could schemes for national insurance, payment of members and, above all, Home Rule for Ireland be introduced into Parliament, and the support of the Nationalist and Labour Parties could only be relied upon so long as there was no relaxation of the pressure. Time was at a premium and a third election in the space of five years, however irksome, was a regrettable necessity for the Liberal Party. The Government's case, as Asquith made plain at the National Liberal Club on November 19th, was that the Lords had systematically thwarted the wishes of the House of Commons elected in 1906, an eminently representative body of the forces of progress, and that for five years the Government had been obliged to suffer the reckless destruction of their most carefully planned measures by a Second Chamber which was no more than a partisan assembly.* The time had come to put an end to this state of affairs.

* Carrington, the next speaker, rather spoilt his leader's argument by emphasising the number of reforms which the Liberals had so far introduced. Lansdowne, giving due publicity

Parliament was not dissolved until November 28th, but the signal for electioneering to begin was given, in effect, when Redmond, after a triumphant tour of the United States, returned to Ireland on November 12th. He had collected two hundred thousand dollars for the Nationalist cause and his arrival was heralded with bonfires and fireworks on the Irish coast. "No such reception," noted the *Annual Register*, "had been given to an Irish leader since Parnell's return from America in 1880." The *Observer* set the pace for Unionist invective by announcing, the following day, that Redmond had landed at Queenstown "with the money of America to wipe England out. He comes with the money of protected millionaires. . . . He comes with his republican cash to extort from the British Government his guarantees." Unionist speakers throughout the country took up the refrain and Balfour, in one of his less inspired moments, proclaimed that "the Government are going to destroy the constitution at the will of American subscribers."*

A Unionist election programme was produced at the annual conference of Constitutional and Conservative Associations on November 17th. The items which figured most prominently were reform of the House of Lords, based on the scheme put forward by Rosebery; Tariff Reform; an unassailable naval supremacy; repeal of the land and licensing clauses of the 1909 Budget; maintenance of the optional nature of trade union levies; State-aided small proprietorships and a State insurance scheme worked in conjunction with the friendly societies. Balfour was at pains to emphasise that it was only the composition, and not the powers, of the Second Chamber which needed to be changed, and Lansdowne, speaking four days later, gave, as we have seen, a more detailed account of what the Unionist reforms entailed.†

Asquith, at Hull on November 25th, hailed with delight the Unionist

---

to this divergence of views, told the annual conference of the Liberal Unionist Council on November 25th that the Lords had rejected only six of the 250 ministerial measures introduced into Parliament since January 1906.

* It was left to Lloyd George, speaking at Mile End on November 21st, to point out that it ill-became the British aristocracy to cast aspersions at Transatlantic subsidies. "Many a noble house," he declared, "tottering to its fall, has had its foundations underpinned, its walls buttressed, by a pile of American dollars." The Duke of Marlborough, who had married an American heiress, took this as a personal affront.

† "Balfour at Nottingham and Lansdowne in the House of Lords," wrote Harcourt to Gladstone on November 21st, "have at the eleventh hour—and as a deathbed repentance—launched a brand new scheme of House of Lords reform as a counter-proposal to ours. Whether it will please their own people or secures them any support from men of middle view remains to be seen, but at all events it gives away the whole case of the *existing* House of Lords." Harcourt thought that the Liberals would "come back again about as we are now—perhaps twenty stronger or weaker as the case may be."[1]

leaders' sudden desire for reform. "Ah, gentlemen," he exclaimed, "what a change eleven short months have wrought! This ancient and picturesque structure has been condemned by its own inmates as unsafe. The parricidal pickaxes are already at work, and constitutional jerry-builders are hurrying from every quarter with new plans. . . . In a single sitting, not unduly prolonged, the venerable institution which has withstood the storm and stress of ages, was transformed—in principle, of course, some of the details are still withheld—into a brand-new modern senate. There has been nothing like it since the memorable night of August 4th, 1789. . . . And what is this new Second Chamber which is now presented to the country as the real solution of our constitutional difficulties? It is a nebulous body of uncertain size, composed in undefined proportions of hereditary peers of official and qualified peers 'chosen'—not necessarily elected, but 'chosen'—chosen by somebody, somewhere, somehow. I said a moment ago that some of the details are lacking and the authors of this ingenious proposal seem to think it unreasonable that at this stage they should be called on for further particulars. . . . It is no answer to our demand for an immediate and effectual removal of the obstacle that blocks the road of progress to say that, in course of time, it may be found possible to evolve a Second Chamber, better fitted than the House of Lords, to exercise the true functions of such a body. I have always hoped and thought that it would. But I have got to deal—you have got to deal—the country has got to deal—with things here and now. We need an instrument that can be set to work at once, which will get rid of deadlocks, and give us the fair and even chance in legislation to which we are entitled and which is all that we demand. The plan of the Government will do so, and it is the only one before the country which even pretends to meet the necessities of the case."

Elsewhere, electioneering followed colourful but predictable lines. Healy and O'Brien accused Redmond of selling the Irish vote to the Liberal Party and thus blocking land-purchase reform. Redmond replied that fifty Budgets were as nothing compared to Ireland's liberty. The Unionists attacked the Government for its dependence on Nationalist support, declaring that the British constitution was to be destroyed because the Irish wanted Home Rule and arguing, moreover, that the Second Chamber was quite ready to reform itself at the earliest opportunity. The Liberals pointed indignantly to the defeat of their Education and Licensing Bills and the rejection of the Budget: the voice of democracy, they proclaimed, had been stifled by that of property and vested interests. The reformers of the Lower House had been overruled by the reactionaries of the Upper. Now, at long last, the balance would be redressed.

(2)

The Liberals were able to face the electorate as a united party and with a relatively clear conscience, but the Unionists were troubled from the outset with the awkward problem of what part Tariff Reform should play in their campaign. Some thought it might be wiser to concentrate solely on the constitutional issue, arguing that the results of the previous contest had made it plain that the country was not yet ready to countenance taxes on food and that it would do more harm than good to raise the banner of Imperial Preference at such a time as this. Others, however, refused to believe that Tariff Reform was really such a liability and argued that any attempt to dilute the Birmingham gospel would shock and dismay the Dominions and colonies and be a betrayal of all their labours during the past five years. Balfour himself was convinced that retention of the food taxes spelt certain disaster for the third time in succession but only the stricken Joseph Chamberlain could have carried through a major change of front. "I am not the man," Balfour is reported to have said, and it was decided at a meeting of Unionist leaders at the Constitutional Club on November 14th that no alteration should be made. Garvin, Carson and Sandars were the only dissentients and Sandars, of course, could not object too strongly for fear of compromising Balfour. Bonar Law was opposed to the food duties in principle but felt that it would be bad policy to change course so late in the day.

The rank and file of the Unionist Party, however, were far from pleased with this decision. "Just now," wrote a bitter Austen Chamberlain to his father on November 16th, "we are all flooded with letters from 'ardent' but wobbly Tariff Reformers begging us to play hankypanky somehow with the food taxes, to run away from them that we may live to fight for them again, etc., etc. . . . Here is G[arvin] promising Balfour the support of the whole Unionist Press except 'The Morning Post' and the 'B[irmingham] D[aily] P[ress]' if only he will promise that no new taxes on food shall be imposed, if we win this election, until we have yet another election, and explaining that we would then keep the counties, because they would believe that they would get agricultural protection after all, and win the towns because *they* would believe that they wouldn't!"[2] Sandars, five days later, told Garvin that "the cries of candidates and constituencies are still about the food taxes and they will increase," adding that "the Chief frankly admitted to me this morning that he thought we might have

M

won the country without them and that he regretted that the party had not accepted the policy of his famous Edinburgh speech years ago; but Highbury is Highbury, and Joe is the only man who could have done the business."[3]

Curiously enough, it was Lansdowne's speech of November 21st, with its suggestion that a referendum was the only means of settling matters of grave concern on which the two Houses could not agree, which provided Balfour with a means of ridding himself of the food taxes incubus. Liberal speakers attacked the referendum as a costly and unsatisfactory device which, in Lloyd George's words, would be "a prohibitive tariff against Liberalism", since Unionist administrations would (as usual) be able to pass all their bills without any difficulty. Several Ministers challenged Balfour to state whether he would be prepared to submit Tariff Reform proposals to a referendum if he were elected, confident that no reply would be forthcoming. Left to himself the Unionist leader would probably have gratified their expectations, but Bonar Law and Garvin, intent upon winning Lancashire, felt that such a challenge should not go unheeded. On November 27th, under a heading of 'Trust the People', the *Observer* came out in favour of a referendum on Tariff Reform and Garvin wrote to Sandars urging him to persuade Balfour to pledge himself to that effect. Sandars, who needed no encouragement, saw Lansdowne that same Sunday and found his lordship equally keen to accept the Liberal challenge.

Bonar Law had meanwhile written to Balfour urging that a declaration in favour of a Tariff Reform referendum should be made as quickly as possible. The Unionist leader was due to speak at the Albert Hall on the Tuesday and it was essential to reach a speedy decision. Balfour was tempted by Bonar Law's arguments, but felt that he should first consult with Austen Chamberlain, who was at that time campaigning in Scotland. He dictated a letter to Chamberlain on the 28th, asking him to cable his observations on Bonar Law's suggestion, but before sending it had a talk with Lansdowne. The latter made it clear that he was strongly in favour of accepting the Liberal challenge and Balfour then added a decisive postscript to his letter. "I am convinced," he wrote, "at least a large minority of our party will find themselves pledged to the new project before they know where we are. We shall then be in exactly the position we were in about letting in colonial corn free. In other words, the unpledged portion of the party can never hope to be strong enough to resist the pledged portion *plus* the Radicals. On the whole I am disposed to think that I cannot be silent about the matter tomorrow—that I cannot wisely plead for delay and further consideration—that I had better therefore . . . say that we do *not* shrink from an appeal to a referendum in the case of Tariff Reform."[4]

Austen Chamberlain, on receiving this letter, immediately cabled his strong disapproval of Balfour's decision and wrote to him in the same vein, arguing that there was no need to make this concession and that a change of front at the last moment would do more harm than good. All this was of no avail, however. The tide was now definitely on the turn. At Liverpool, that evening, F. E. Smith stated that he personally would be willing to submit Tariff Reform to a referendum and at the Albert Hall next day Balfour contemptuously accepted the Liberal challenge. The audience, at this point, rose to its feet in prolonged applause. Balfour waited until it had died down and then launched a counter-challenge: would the Liberal Party be equally prepared to submit Home Rule to the judgment of the people?

Lansdowne, speaking at Plymouth the following day, endorsed this pronouncement and so did other leading Unionists, including Lyttelton and Cromer, while Northcliffe's *Daily Mail* gave its jubilant support to this new policy. Milner and Goulding repudiated it, however, and the *Morning Post* declared that Tariff Reformers should keep to their original objective of introducing fiscal reform as soon as possible. Austen Chamberlain, it seems, was in a cold fury and the following correspondence speaks for itself.

Chamberlain to Balfour, November 30th, 1910 (telegram)

See 'Daily Mail'. Tariff Reform not an issue. Doing much mischief in doubtful seats here where electors care for nothing else. Has probably lost us one seat already. Please stop this misrepresentation of your speech.[5]

Balfour to Chamberlain, November 30th, 1910 (telegram)

Will do what I can with 'Daily Mail'. So far as I am concerned shall make it quite clear that Tariff Reform is one of the greatest issues.[6]

Balfour to Chamberlain, November 30th, 1910

I kept Lansdowne here till 7 o'clock, when your letter arrived, and we anxiously discussed it in the short time then available. I am fully impressed with the important arguments you use, and unquestionably the difficulties of a referendum are great. At the same time, had I refused the referendum we should have had to meet a broad line of argument of peculiar plausability at a time like this—I mean the contention that while we provided a machinery for preventing a House of Commons elected, as all Houses of Common are, on a mixed issue, from deciding some great new departure against the people's wishes when the majority in the House of Commons was Radical, we refused to provide any such machinery when the majority in the House of Commons happened to be Unionist. To this I believe there is no really effective electoral answer, and my own personal conviction—right or wrong—is that we could venture upon a Tariff Reform Budget with a narrow majority in much greater security if there were a referendum behind it than we could under any other conditions.[7]

The Liberal Party, meanwhile, were rather taken back by this unexpected acceptance of their challenge. The official attitude, after a momentary hesitation, became one of derision, ministerial supporters declaring that this new departure was simply a dodge to gain Lancashire and that, together with the proposed reform of the Second Chamber, it amounted to what Asquith described as "the largest reported experiment in vote-catching." So far as Balfour's counter-challenge was concerned, they were at pains to emphasise that the Liberals had never supported the idea of a referendum and that the question did not therefore arise of submitting Home Rule to one.

(3)

Polling began on Friday, December 2nd. The results of the first day showed that it was unlikely that the Unionists would gain the sixty-two seats needed to ensure them a bare majority: the Liberals held their own in London and defeated Bonar Law at north-west Manchester. They also won south-west Manchester, Rochester, Exeter and Peckham. The Unionists, however, gained four Lancashire seats as well as Grimsby, Darlington and King's Lynn. As the days slipped by, it became steadily apparent that the Liberals would be returned to office for a third time in succession and recriminations in the Unionist camp were long and bitter. From this point on, in fact, the battle between the Chamberlainites and the Balfourites was once again in full swing, although Austen Chamberlain was at pains to emphasise in private correspondence that he did not wish to supplant Balfour as leader of the party.*

The last election results were announced on December 20th and the following table shows the final position of the parties, compared with the situation after the January election.

* The Balfourites were not altogether dismayed at the results. Sandars, writing to Garvin on December 11th, thought that the party had gained a "fair measure of success" despite the "peevish moanings of Highbury". Balfour, attempting to mollify the indignant Austen in a letter dated December 13th, declared himself "convinced that if I had taken a different line the Government anticipations would have been fulfilled and we should have lost heavily." Chamberlain, however, remained unconvinced and at Buxton on December 14th grumbled that "great inconveniences" had been caused by Balfour's referendum pledge, which had formed "no part of the original plan of the Unionist Party."[8]

	January 1910	December 1910
Liberal Party	275	272
Labour Party*	40 ⎬ 397	42 ⎬ 398
Nationalists	82	84

Unionists (Including Speaker)	273	272

The distribution of seats (with the January distribution shown in brackets) was as follows:

	England	Scotland	Wales	Ireland	Totals
Liberal	190 (191)	58 (59)	23 (24)	1 (1)	272 (275)
Labour	35 (34)	3 (2)	4 (4)	– (–)	42 (40)
Nationalist	1 (1)	– (–)	– (–)	83 (81)	84 (82)
Unionist	239 (239)	11 (11)	3 (2)	19 (21)	272 (273)
Totals	465	72	30	103	670

The two major parties were now exactly equal in their representation in the House of Commons, although the general situation remained unchanged. The Liberals increased their strength a little in London and won two seats in Sunderland and regained several in East Anglia, but they lost seats in Devon, Cornwall and Lancashire. The Unionist gains in the latter county were regarded, by Tariff Reformers and referendum supporters alike, as vindication of their respective causes. In Wales the Unionists captured Cardiff, a seat which Lloyd George had loftily declined to fight in the previous election. The Nationalists gained two seats from the Independents, although the latter remained a contingent of ten in the new Parliament, while six "Unionist working men" financed by the *Standard* proved singularly unsuccessful. "Broadly speaking," remarked the *Annual Register*, "industrial England returned Liberals, except the Birmingham area, while the chief ports, except London, Liverpool and Plymouth, and the 'pleasure' and 'residential' towns were Unionist." The Government's real strength once again lay in Scotland and Wales.

Opinion, in the last analysis, was fairly evenly divided: the total votes cast for the Unionists amounted to 2,232,265 as opposed to 2,525,648 for the Ministry. This was enough to give the Liberals and their allies another

---

* The Labour Representation Committee had sponsored 56 candidates, of whom only 11 faced opposition from Liberals as well as Unionists.

majority over the Tories, yet it could scarcely be termed a decisive response to the Government's appeal for support against the Lords and Balfour, speaking at Dartford on December 12th, warned Ministers that they
must not think that the country would acquiesce in the Parliament Bill.
Even if the measure reached the Statute Book, which he was not prepared
to admit, it would certainly not remain there. It was simply a device to
get Home Rule through after the existing constitution had been destroyed
and before it had been remodelled on new and necessary lines. "On the
constitutional question," he was reported as saying, " the decision would
not be final; the relations between the two Houses, and between those
Houses and the people, could and would be remodelled on Unionist lines;
but Home Rule, once given, could not be withdrawn, and its passage over
the head of the people and against their wills would be one of the greatest
crimes in history."

The battle between the two Houses had not yet ended but it had been
decided so far as the Liberals were concerned. "The [constitutional] position," as Asquith wrote at this time, "becomes exceptionally clear and
simple, when—as the case now is—a ministry has appealed to the country
upon the specific and dominating issue of the day and upon that issue
commands a majority of more than one hundred in the House of Commons."[9] In contrast to the painful indecision of February and March he
was now, as the following memorandum indicates, in full command of the
situation.

Memorandum by the Master of Elibank, December 21st, 1910

The Prime Minister has seen the King. The interview was of a very cordial
nature and eminently satisfactory.

Asquith pointed out that the majority obtained at the election was formidable
and cohesive and had been in effect in the nature of a referendum on the House of
Lords question.

In the course of the conversation the King made a passing reference to the Tory
arguments which had been used to the effect that the Government would be secured
in office by the Irish vote. The Prime Minister, however, at once demolished those
arguments and laid emphasis upon the British majority which the Government
had obtained, quite apart from the Irish vote.

The King is very anxious that the Parliament Bill should be passed before the
coronation. I have told the Prime Minister that we will certainly try and do this if
we can, but that the absolutely necessary business to be taken will make it very
difficult.

The King also intimated that he wished to send Knollys to sound Arthur Balfour
as to the latter's intentions, but Asquith dissuaded him from this course—much to
the relief of Knollys as the latter told me![10]

On the morrow of this latest general election, therefore, the Government could face the future with a greater assurance than had been possible for many a long month. Once more they had been returned to power and, despite the decline in the Liberal Party's fortunes since that glorious January of 1906, they could still count on a substantial majority in the House of Commons. Their enemies were once again in a state of bitter disarray and their goal of constitutional reform was finally in sight: the King had guaranteed the creation of peers if the Upper House refused to accept the Parliament Bill and, whatever the Unionist Party might say or do, ultimate victory lay within their grasp. The Lords would go on to fight a rearguard action and the political arena would still resound with the cries of battle, but from now onwards the Ministry would have the consolation of knowing that it was only a matter of time. Thus, with five years of office and three general elections already behind them, the Liberals braced themselves for the conflicts that lay ahead.

CONCLUSIONS

All in all, it would not be unfair to conclude that the Liberal Government had received no more than the mandate it deserved, but this thought does not appear to have crossed any Minister's mind. That they should continue to be dependent upon the support of the Nationalist and Labour Parties for their continuance in office was simply the luck of the game, and they were able to console themselves with the reflection that their plight was no worse than it had been in January 1910.

The parliamentary party were, of course, disappointed by their leaders' inability to call a halt to expenditure on armaments, but beyond this they were moderately satisfied with the Ministry's performance. So far as the Empire was concerned they could claim that Liberal policies had been put into effect. "Chinese slavery" had been abolished and freedom had been granted to South Africa, while a start (however timid) had been made in reforming the organs of government in India. Foreign affairs were, admittedly, cloaked in a veil of secrecy, but the understanding reached with Russia (despite the widespread detestation of Czardom) and the closer relationship with France were presumably good things and would no doubt keep Germany in her place. Not until 1912 would the rank and file attempt to exercise some control over the conduct of foreign policy, and even then no one would appreciate quite the extent to which Sir Edward Grey, the luckless but well-meaning mouthpiece of the Foreign Office, had groped his way into paths from which there could be no return.

Hardly any members of the party appreciated, when it came to domestic affairs, that the Government (even when allowance has been made for the activities of the House of Lords and the exceptional circumstances of 1910) had precious little to show for five years of office. Some useful and humane measures had been put into effect and a cautious start had been made on the task of alleviating poverty in Britain, yet by and large the Ministry's objectives, such as they were, were curiously irrelevant to the needs of the time. The Education and Licensing Bills, even if they had reached the Statute Book, would not have made any great impact on the life of the nation. The implementation of old age pensions, however inadequate, the establishment of labour exchanges and the allocation of special funds for roads, railways and docks, from 1909 onwards, were perhaps the three most important achievements of this period, but by and large the Government had steered clear of radical changes. Home Rule was at last on the agenda (simply because it could no longer be kept off), but nothing had been done about the suffragettes—an issue which had been shunted into a siding whenever it showed signs of gathering momentum—and the episode of Tonypandy had suggested (unfairly) a certain lack of sympathy with the grievances of the working classes. The Trade Disputes Act, as passed, resulted solely from Campbell-Bannerman's anxiety not to offend the Labour Party. Even the "People's Budget", luridly depicted by both its supporters and opponents as a Radical measure in every sense of the word, owed more to the need for Dreadnoughts than a desire to invade the bastions of Property, and the grandiose schemes of national insurance which Lloyd George was now hastily devising would be firmly based on the principle of weekly contributions from the nation at large.

One should beware of applying later standards to the world of the 1900s but it is nevertheless wellnigh incredible that at none of the three general elections fought during this period had a Liberal programme of social reforms been put forward for consideration by the electorate. Such a programme was often referred to, in familiar terms which implied that there was no need to spell out the details, but the plain fact is that (except, perhaps, for those who vaguely recalled the "Newcastle programme" of 1891) it simply did not exist. In January 1906 the Government's immediate aims were both negative and conservative. A hotchpotch of measures was hastily assembled for the first Session of the new Parliament, most of which could quite cheerfully have been passed by a Unionist administration, but by 1907 the Government had run out of ideas. A comfortable lethargy descended upon Ministers, and it was only Haldane's schemes of army reform which saved the Session of that year from being a complete waste of time. Another election was, admittedly, not due until 1913 (although in practice no Parliament in the nineteenth century had gone the full length of seven years and only three—if that of 1900–6 is included—had gone as far as six) and Ministers could no doubt claim that they were contemplating the means whereby Utopia could be created. A steady stream of by-election defeats sounded a warning note, and in 1908, with the introduction of the Licensing Bill, the Eight Hours Bill and old age pensions, an attempt was made to save the situation. The first of these measures, however, was defeated, the second was emasculated and the third satisfied nobody except its sponsors.

Until 1909, in short, the Government existed on a hand-to-mouth basis. Somebody had a pet scheme, or a Royal Commission made a recommendation that could be safely accepted, or pressure was applied from the Nationalist or Labour benches, and the Government promptly brought in a bill. Reforms of a sort were thus carried through in a piecemeal, sporadic fashion.

The "People's Budget" proved a turning point. It was, as we have seen, brought about more by the force of events than the forces of Radicalism (although its custodians certainly contrived to settle some old scores), but it did show an awareness of the nation's need to put its house in order. With the rejection of the Budget the control of events passed out of the Government's hands, and 1910 was devoted solely to the question of the House of Lords. To call the constitutional dispute a godsend would, perhaps, be something of an exaggeration, but the Liberals nevertheless sallied forth to do battle against the peers with feelings of relief rather than fury. The Upper House, as Morley remarked, gave them something to swear at and swear by, and the furtive negotiations over Lloyd George's Coalition proposal showed that the line of division between the leaders of the two main parties—if not their respective ranks and files—was wearing perilously thin.

Liberalism as a genuine political force was on its last legs. The failure to devise a clear-cut programme of reforms reflecting a basic Liberal philosophy (always assuming, of course, that this was possible) meant that the life of the party had to be prolonged by periodic stimulants. In 1906 it had been the maintenance of Free Trade and the abolition of "Chinese slavery", in 1910 it had been the abolition of the Lords' veto and in 1912 it would be Home Rule. Lloyd George was, admittedly, aware that a great many things (not necessarily "Liberal") needed to be done in a great many fields. His memorandum of August 17th 1910 had pinpointed some of the glaring deficiencies which needed to be made up, but the programme which he proposed was one that could only be carried out by a Government with a rock-firm majority in the House of Commons. After 1909 the Liberals (even if they had adopted the greater part of Lloyd George's programme) did not possess such a majority.

The glorious opportunity of 1906 had been muffed. Whether the situation could still be saved was something which remained to be seen.

SELECTED LETTERS

INDEX

(1)

Gladstone to Campbell-Bannerman, November 30th, 1905

I had a long talk with Spender, who had been to the Durdans. R. is in a savage and despairing mood. He denounced A. & G. in unmeasured terms, accusing them of having abandoned him, saying he had done with public life, having no party and no friends. He had consulted those with him in Cornwall and they all agreed that your Stirling speech meant Home Rule. His brain was not good enough to interpret the language of a speech, and he was not fit therefore to take a leading part in politics. Of course, now he is "sorry he spoke", but he sees no way of unsaying it. . . .

G. and A. are now both on the right side and it is of enormous importance to keep them there. The advanced H. R.s and Radicals are of course all right and entirely with you, whatever turn you give to H. R. utterances either to or from it.

345

But the vote which will make or mar our majority is composed of Unionist Free Traders and Educationalists, and anti or weak H. R. Liberals.

Your Stirling speech was accepted by all till R.'s monstrous outbreak. Since then letters have been coming to me from all parts of the country reporting disturbed minds. What the best of them say is that the party is open to suspicion because you won't say in [clear] terms that a big H. R. scheme will not or cannot be brought forward in the next Parliament.

(2)

Grey to Campbell-Bannerman, December 7th, 1905

Asquith has told me of your decision, as to the alternative proposal, which I made yesterday, which would have left existing arrangements in the House of Commons unconditionally as they are, and would have placed authoritative declaration of policy in the House of Lords in hands in which I should have had complete confidence. When I wrote to you on Monday that under present conditions (viz., the absence of Rosebery) it was vital to me that Asquith should lead in the Commons, this possible alternative of supplying Rosebery's place in the Lords had not occurred to me or I would have suggested it then. I am very sorry that this too is not acceptable.

There are only two persons whose declarations of policy are accepted by the public as of full authority. One is the leader of the House of Commons; the other is the leader in the House of Lords.

I was, as I said on Monday at the beginning of our conversation, very reluctant to enter any government of which Rosebery could not be a member and about which (as I inferred) he could not even be consulted. I could not take office without a complete surrender of that independence which I have sometimes exercised in opposition and without undertaking a loyal obligation to defend the whole policy of the government; to do this I felt that in one House or the other the declarations of policy must be in the hands of one of those with whom I have been most closely associated. . . .

I did not raise any questions of policy the other day. On practical policy for the next Parliament I believe we are agreed, though I had asked for a public statement that Rosebery's interpretation of your Stirling speech was wrong; but I felt that it was not fitting or possible to go into questions of policy unless there was complete confidence as to the form which the declaration of policy would take.

It would be most undesirable for me to take office feeling that my resignation might become necessary in a short time.

I have always regarded the prospect of political office with great personal reluctance; it would be intolerable to be in office without giving complete and absolute support to all that was said by the head of the Government in both Houses; and as things are it is better for me to stay outside, retaining my freedom but with every intention of giving public support to Liberal policy as long as I retain any public position.

(3)

Campbell-Bannerman to King Edward VII, December 20th, 1905

The main subject of [today's Cabinet] discussion was the question of the Transvaal Colony in relation to (*a*) its representative constitution and (*b*) Chinese labour. On the former there is need of further information before any decision is arrived at. As to Chinese labour, it is to be borne in mind that the present system has always been treated as experimental with 50,000 as an extreme limit of number: also that the late Govt. tried to procure a voluntary cessation of importation when the number employed was about 30,000 but failed. It appears that there are now about 48,000 coolies in the Transvaal and that the startling number of 14,000 licences for the recruitment of additional Chinese have been issued. It was therefore resolved that the fresh recruitment and importation of coolies must be forthwith stopped, and orders to that effect will be given.

(4)

Campbell-Bannerman to Knollys, December 22nd, 1905

The decision of the Cabinet was taken with very full knowledge of the actual number of Chinese and the prospects of increase: and we had means of knowing the views of Lord Selborne on the larger question of Chinese labour generally. On that larger question we have come to no decision. . . .

At present all that has been done is to prevent [an] increase in the number . . . and the Cabinet was quite unanimous that it must be stopped. It may cause an outcry at the Cape but (whatever may be the ultimate settlement of the general question) we are sure that it is a necessary thing to do.

(5)

Chamberlain to Long, February 5th, 1906

Many thanks for your kind letter. The situation is indeed most difficult and critical. Balfour seems to me to have read the lessons of the election in altogether a different sense from what we do. He seems to me to have gone back and not forward in his views and to be entirely wrong as to the real feeling of the party as a whole.

One and perhaps the only advantage of a party meeting, to which by the way he is strongly opposed, would be to bring him into closer touch with the new members. I do not pretend to know what their exact position is, but if it represents the enormous correspondence with which I am burdened it would certainly open his eyes.

Nothing would induce me to take the leadership in his place and I have told all my friends, some of whom are no doubt almost as indiscreet as his supporters, that it is no use suggesting me for a position which would be entirely opposed to my personal sentiments and must inevitably lead to disaster. The leader of a party mainly composed of Conservatives ought to be, and I think must be, a Conservative. But unless Balfour moves in our direction the result of the full acceptance of his leadership by Tariff Reformers would be to place our subject on the shelf for five or more years, and then if by that time the Government fell to pieces we should not know what to do with out victory but should be in the same position which we have been obliged to occupy during the last two years. Against that I protest as the most dishonest of all the suggestions that have been made.

I agree with you that there must be an immense amount of popular education before Tariff Reform can be carried but how can we possibly even begin the work with our organisations driving one against the other and none of the teachers knowing what they are to teach?

I am told, though I do not think the matter was mentioned when I saw Balfour, that he is as much opposed to the suggestion of a third leadership (which would be quite acceptable to me) as he is to a definite platform or a union of organisations.

In fact he is "non possimus" everywhere and I confess I do not see my way out of the difficulty in which we are placed.

(6)

Campbell-Bannerman to Ripon, April 7th, 1906

We found on Friday at the H. of C. that there was much alarm among our people, on two grounds, over the Education Bill.

These are:

1st.   An explicit forbidding of tests for teachers. This we have most of us been proclaiming as one of our conditions—and unless it is included in terms great hostility will be created.

2nd.   That the "facilities" in non-provided schools should be out of school hours, so as not to be defrayed by public money.

It appears that "school hours" begin at 9 and not, as we had been led to understand, at 9.45.

Asquith, Morley, George and I talked the matter over, being all the members of the Cabinet who could be laid hold of—and as a result, I decided that we must have a Cabinet before Birrell made his speech: and I sent out summonses for Monday.

(7)

Campbell-Bannerman to King Edward VII, July 10th, 1906

The Cabinet met today mainly to consider navy policy with a view to an early statement in the House of Commons. The Board of Admiralty on the advice of the Sea Lords proposed as a main feature the laying down of four battleships of the Dreadnought type. The Chancellor of the Exchequer adduced figures to show that even the combination of France and Germany as the two greatest naval powers—a combination practically out of reason—would not justify such an addition to our fleet. The Cabinet unanimously invited Lord Tweedmouth to reconsider the matter and appointed the Prime Minister, the Chancellor of the Exchequer and Sir E. Grey to confer with him and Sir John Fisher and arrive at some conclusion.

(8)

Campbell-Bannerman to King Edward VII, July 18th, 1906

The Cabinet met today and agreed to the altered navy programme put forward by the Sea Lords, viz. that in the present financial year three large battleships (instead of four as originally proposed) should be laid down . . . and that in the following year (1907–8) two only should be commenced at the end of the year. If the Hague Conference, which by that time will have sat and published its results, has not secured general adhesion to a slackened rate of shipbuilding we should be free to lay down a third ship: if on the other hand there is a substantial and earnest engagement on the part of the great powers to diminish prospective increases it will be for us to consider whether the two ships will be necessary.

(9)

Knollys to Campbell-Bannerman, December 3rd, 1906

The King desires me to point out to you that Mr Lloyd George brought in His Majesty's name in the speech which he made against the House of Lords at Oxford on Saturday.

The King sees it is useless to attempt to prevent Mr Lloyd George from attacking, as a Cabinet Minister, that branch of the legislature, though His Majesty has more than once protested to you against it. He believes that at his request you remonstrated with Mr Lloyd George as to these attacks, and it is difficult for the King to understand why he has paid no attention either to the wish of his Sovereign or to the warning addressed to him by the head of the Government.

But his Majesty feels he has a right, and it is one on which he intends to insist, that Mr Lloyd George shall not introduce the Sovereign's name into these violent tirades of his, and he aks you, as Prime Minister, to be so good as to take the necessary steps to prevent a repetition of this violation of constitutional practice and of good taste.

(10)

Campbell-Bannerman to Knollys, December 4th, 1906

I deeply regret to learn that the words of one of the King's Ministers have been such as to give offence to His Majesty, and on receipt of your letter I took the earliest occasion to see Mr Lloyd George.

As you are aware, I had previously remonstrated with him as to his previous utterance, in which he seemed to exceed the usual limits in condemning the action of the House of Lords and in assailing the constitutional position of that House. In his speech at Oxford on Saturday I do not observe that he repeated the latter line of argument or said anything that was disrespectful of the Upper House, but he did speak, partly by way of banter (founded on the parable of the Good Samaritan), partly in strong direct reprobation of the manner in which the Education Bill has been treated. When he spoke before his diatribe was not justified, as the Bill had not been considered in detail; but I venture to submit that, whether his language be thought exaggerated or not, he had at least some excuse for fault-finding, when we have seen the Bill—in Committee, and even more in Report—not only seriously amended but turned upside down. I may add that an amendment wantonly introduced into the Bill last night seems to me to show, not only by its effect but by its spirit, that compromise is almost, if not quite, impossible, and indeed is not intended by the Opposition in the House of Lords.

If this be so, I fear that we must be prepared for forcible language being employed generally, and even by Ministers; for it will be hard to restrain the feelings certain to be legitimately aroused when a Bill so largely supported in the country, and passed in the Lower House by such a majority, is deliberately converted by the House of Lords into a measure whose purpose is the exact opposite. . . .

Mr Lloyd George begged me to lay before the King the expression of his profound regret if he had inadvertently offended, and I would humbly express the hope that His Majesty will, in view of the great tension of opinion and feeling which this keen controversy has evoked, look with indulgence on any indiscretion that may have been committed.

(11)

Gladstone to Birrell, December 8th, 1906

I found myself last night alongside Lord St Aldwyn at the Speaker's table.

He is strong for a settlement and thinks it quite possible—of course on the teacher point. The H. of L. Tories are many of them violent but he is confident that a compromise could be carried. He declared the Tory peers were by no means under the thumb of the party in the H. of C.

He thought, and he volunteered this, that we ought to reject *en bloc*, but to indicate conciliatory views on the points involved in a compromise.

He said he was most anxious for the Bill to pass. I know you must not let slip any chance. Personally I fail to see why the Bill should be wrecked on the country teachers question—for everyone agrees about town teachers—which seems to me a matter of small practical importance. It is dominated by the public control of the local authority.

I told the P.M. what Lord St A. said and he asked me to let you know. I am certain Ld. St A. is ready to do all he can for a settlement.

Lloyd George (and not Burns), I think, fairly described the general feeling. There might be a concentrated outburst of Liberal protests in London, as he said, but I am pretty sure the mass of reasonable Liberals would accept the situation as inevitable and as being not unsatisfactory. Massingham came to me on Thursday and having regard to the violence of the D[aily] N[ews] letters I was astonished when he said that there was no violent or strong feeling against compromise in the country. I have 10,000 people, roughly, in my constituency and my 9,000 voter supporters are nearly all Nonconformists and Non-Anglicans. I have not had a single line from them against compromise.

(12)

Morley to Campbell-Bannerman, January 3rd, 1907

I came here [the India Office] today and *Winston* sent in word to see me if possible. I reluctantly agreed, and he came. He evidently had got a good idea from somewhere how the land lies, and was extremely reticent. He and McK., I think, must have had some conversations in which each supported the claims of the other to [the] Cabinet. I told him that I did not know what your decision would be, either about Ireland or any consequential vacancies. He then said very emphatically and explicitly that he would cheerfully acquiesce in being left where he is, if you think it best for the Government that he should be so left: you had to think of your Government, and no personal wishes or claims should count for anything. I said, "Do you authorise me to tell the P.M. so?" He replied: "I not only authorise, but I shall be extremely obliged. The tension is rather severe, and I only should be grateful if I might be told whether I am likely to face re-election: my constituents are pressing me." When I asked him about his election chances, he spoke with infinite confidence, for which he gave me sound electioneering reasons. . . . But the delay raises expectations and injures him, so he said. I should like to add that his whole tone was most *handsome*.

I told him frankly, though cordially his friend, that he was not fit for Education. Rather ruefully, he thought I might be right. . . .

Forgive me if I have done amiss in promising him that I would write to you. Of course, you are quite free to use this letter as a peg on which to hang a letter to him, if you think fit.

(13)

Churchill to Campbell-Bannerman, October 15th, 1907 (from H.M.S. Venus, Gulf of Suez)

I am having a most delightful and prosperous voyage in this comfortable ship; and both at Malta and at Cyprus I learned a very great deal. I worked almost without a break the whole time I was on shore, visited nearly all the public institutions, conversed with all the official heads of departments, inspected the prisons most thoroughly and received every deputation and every person of consequence who desired to see me. In the result I have formed several conclusions about Malta, about its institutions and about some of its laws on which I am writing to Elgin.

But it is about Cyprus that I want to write to you.

Do you realise that we have drawn from this island, exhausted as it was with three centuries of odious misgovernment, upwards of £1,800,000 since our occupation? I confess that I had not mastered that fact. I thought that Cyprus was indebted to us for regular assistance through the readiness of the Grant in Aid. But that is only a Treasury fiction. This is what happens. By the Convention of 1878 we agreed that the Sultan should receive £92,000 a year as a tribute. The islanders were not themselves consulted; and the British Government of that day was of course activated by material motives and wished to secure—almost on any terms—a territory [?] in the Levant. Just about the same time as this convention was signed, the Sultan repudiated the 1855 Turkish debt. As this debt was guaranteed by Great Britain and France and secured on the revenues of the Turkish Empire, and as no portion of these revenues at any date were accessible to us, we intercepted the Cyprus tribute and devoted this money to paying the interest on the loan—which, but for the fact of having Cyprus in our grip, we should have been forced and bound to pay ourselves; and which was an obligation of our own, incurred solely for purposes of high policy, with none of which Cyprus was even remotely connected.

This may seem a very convenient transaction from our point of view. But look at it from the point of view of the Cypriots- *they* never agreed to the tribute. *We* pledged them to that. They were a wretched community living in a distant island, which happened for a time to be used as a pawn in Disraeli's curious confiscations. All they see is that their hard earned, pitifully scraped together money drains away out of the island year after year, without any return of any kind to them, for an object in which they are no degree concerned, which is not even the object specified in the treaty, and in virtue of no other right than superior force.

It is quite true that saddled with this enormous burden Cyprus collapsed. Even with the most grinding economies the administration could not be carried on, nor the whole tribute wrung from the people. Therefore it was the policy of the Treasury (1) to cut down the local administration to the bare necessities; (2) to debit the island with its cost plus the whole tribute; (3) to capture . . . every surplus, however petty, at the end of each financial year; (4) and then to make a refund of just so much as was necesssary to balance the accounts under guise of Grant in Aid, and lastly pose before the House of Commons as the generous benefactors of the Cypriots.

These infamous arrangements so unworthy of the British name were severely modified at the beginning of last year when Asquith arranged to give a fixed Grant in Aid of £50,000, and to allow the islanders the benefit of any surpluses they could secure, or any economies they could effect upon that basis; or in other words by an action of remarkable magnanimity we consented not to take from the island in any one year the sum of £42,000: and that is what we are doing now.

Have we any moral right to do this? We do not do it to any other island under the control of the Colonial Office. On the contrary, to many of them we pay large subscriptions. From Cyprus we exact monetary tribute—for our own profit. . . . To my mind—and I am sure you will agree with me—the oppression of a small community by a great one for the purposes of direct and undisguised pecuniary profit is an odious act. Can we wonder when we perpetrate it, that our rule in Cyprus . . . takes no hold upon the hearts of the people? . . . Everywhere I travelled in the island I was received with wild demonstrations in favour of Greek unity. . . . What a pity and folly it all is. . . .

I hope you will forgive me for writing as strongly on this subject as I feel. But I know we are not doing our duty to this island. We are not acting up to our standards as a nation. We have no right whatever to profit by a single penny of the tributary money. The whole revenue of Cyprus should be left to the Cypriots to spend in restoring their own island: and we should pay our own debts ourselves out of our own money.

(14)

Campbell-Bannerman to King Edward VII, January 29th, 1908

As originally framed by the Admiralty, these [the Navy Estimates] showed an increase of about two millions over the current year: and as such a result was difficult to reconcile with the general views of the Government. . . the Admiralty was instructed to bring the amount down.

The causes of the increase did not lie in the shipbuilding programme but in the continuance of expenditure on works which were formerly paid for out of loans, but are now charged to the Estimates, in the increasing charges in repayment of such loans; in the higher cost of coal; in improvements to victualling and to a higher scale of comfort; and above all in a necessary demand for stores which had been for the last two years largely supplied out of reserves and available stores on hand.

This last cause of increase is the most important, because it comes to this—that for three years not only Parliament, but the Cabinet of the day and the First Lord himself, have been misled as to the real expenditure. For one reason or another large amounts of stores have been available, and used, to the relief of the Vote; and in the coming year there is no such surplus to be drawn upon, and the Votes must bear nearly the full charge.

Mr McKenna, the late Secretary to the Treasury and Mr Runciman, the present Secretary, together with Mr Robertson, Secretary to the Admiralty, have gone fully into this matter; and it has become clear that the half-million due to this cause must be provided (it will be still greater next year) and they have suggested an alteration being made in the Votes which will keep Parliament informed in future. It is abundantly evident that the great saving claimed in 1904 from the extensive policy of "scrapping" the smaller vessels of the fleet, was in great part illusory, and this has now to be paid for.

The result of the examination is to show an increase—seemingly unavoidable —in the Estimates for next year of a million and a quarter.

(15)

Gladstone to Mrs Ennis Richmond, September 22nd, 1909

It is quite obvious that to carry women's suffrage a Government must be formed *ad hoc*. It is simply a delusion to think that a Government divided on a question by root differences can deal with it as a Government. All these militant tactics, at any rate in their later development, are not only lost labour, but now are most seriously putting obstacles in the way of a solution. I am afraid the outlook is thoroughly bad. . . .

Our position has been stated over and over again. It is the best we can do. Assuming a general election to come early, or following the failure of the Prime Minister's proposal, what will be the position at the general election? It will be chaotic, because men will not be bullied solely by the action of a few hundred women. Honestly, I believe the great majority of both political parties are willing and ready to co-operate for the solution of this question. But no one will lift a finger now because of these absurd tactics, which are intensely exasperating without being effective. If the danger from individual action increases, so will the difficulty of dealing with the political issue.

I own I cannot see [a way] through it. I say it with very deep regret, for I know the real mischief and danger of the present situation, which I look upon as deplorable.

(16)

Mrs Ennis Richmond to Gladstone, September 24th, 1909

I believe that every single one of us, in whatever Union or League, feels that it is Mr Asquith and Mr Asquith *alone* who is responsible for the present state of things. We are not asking and never have asked Mr Asquith to give us the vote; we have only asked him to give Parliament, at his own time, a proper and *genuine* opportunity of deciding in a constitutional manner whether they will give women the vote. The rage against Mr Asquith has its roots entirely in the fact that he has treated the matter with contempt and ignored the personal appeal—this last especially.

It is shameful and disgraceful that the Prime Minister of England should go about guarded like the king of an anarchist country; it is shameful and disgraceful that, in England, educated and refined women should be lying in prison, having food forced into them and enduring every hardship and indignity for having tried to force this guard. And the whole unbearable situation has been forced upon the country by Mr Asquith's refusal to treat the women as civilised people, worthy of his notice as Prime Minister. We must know—all of us who think at all—that this unnatural and horrible state of affairs could have been prevented.

(17)

Vaughan Nash to Asquith, December 15th, 1909

Lord Knollys asked me to see him this afternoon and he began by saying that the King had come to the conclusion that he would not be justified in creating new peers (say 300) until after a second general election and that he, Lord K., thought you should know of this now, though, for the present, he would suggest that what he was telling me should be for your ear only. The King regards the policy of the Government as tantamount to the destruction of the House of Lords and he thinks that before a large creation of peers is embarked upon or threatened the country should be acquainted with the particular project for accomplishing such destruction as well as with the general line of action as to which the country will be consulted at the forthcoming elections.

When it came to discussing this in detail the following points emerged:

1. That if the plan adopted for dealing with the veto follows the House of Commons resolutions coupled with shorter parliaments (the King prefers four years to five) the King would concur, though apparently he would still hesitate to create peers.

2. That his objection to the creation of peers would be "considerably diminished" if life peers could be created. (I pointed out to Lord Knollys that this would involve legislation to which the House of Lords might object.)

As to the first point, I said that your speech at the Albert Hall indicated that the plan to be adopted would follow the general lines of the C.B. plan.

Lord Knollys went on to say that it was in view of the objections which the King was likely to raise that he had advocated the introduction of legislation dealing with the Lords before supplies were dealt with by the new Parliament as by this means a lever might be brought to bear which would obviate the necessity of creating peers. I replied that whatever the merits of such a procedure might be, the practical difficulties were, as I understood, serious, the greatest being the short time available for getting the Finance Bill through. Moreover the onus as regards a financial deadlock would, in the circumstances, be held to rest not on the Lords but on the Government. And he quite saw the force of this.

Lord Knollys was very anxious that some alternative method of coercion should be devised. For instance, was there anything in the idea of summoning only such peers as would give a majority to the Finance Bill? I said I would ask your opinion, but I thought you would regard such a scheme as fantastic and impracticable, apart from its bearing on the monarch.

Before coming away I thought I had better ask Lord Knollys whether the King realised that at the next general election the whole question of the Lords would be fully before the country, and that the electors would know they were being invited to pronounce, not indeed on the details, but on the broad principles which were involved in the Government's policy. I also asked what he thought would be the position as regards the creation of peers if it turned out that the House of Lords refused to accept legislation forbidding them to touch finance. From the vague answers he gave I came away with the impression that the King's mind is not firmly settled and that it might be useful if you saw him some time before the elections, possibly on the 8th, the day of the Dissolution Council.

(18)

Gladstone to Churchill, March 16th, 1910

I am glad you are acting on my proposals as regards prison rules. . . .

The form of the announcement in the House of Lords, however, to me is a matter of rather more than surprise. Apart from the merits of the proposals two deductions will initially be made—first that you initiated the changes and I did not; secondly that you have done the obviously right thing and that I from foolishness and inhumanity did not. Whereas as you know I asked Byrne a long time ago to draw up proposals for consideration.

(19)

Churchill to Gladstone, March 17th, 1910

I am sorry you consider that you have reason to complain. The fault—if any there be—lies with the newspapers which have commented upon the change, and not with my answer which clearly associated you with it. As, however, you feel that you have been insufficiently referred to, I will arrange to have a question put to me in order to make your position clear. I have asked Troup to frame this and I enclose his suggestion for your information.

I may add that I decided to make a special code for political offenders as soon as I was appointed Home Secretary, and I dictated a memorandum on the subject in the first two or three days I was here. It was not until the matter had reached its final stage that I learned with pleasure from the official files how nearly we were in accord.

It has often happened to me when I left the Colonial Office to find much of the work, which I had quarried out laboriously, used with advantage by my successors. And I have always been very glad that they should do so.

In this case however I acted with entire independence of your views and gave instructions upon my own initiative for a reform which I have felt very strongly should have been carried out three years ago, and might have been carried out at any time.

(20)

Gladstone to Churchill, March 18th, 1910

Thanks for your letter. But I did not see any reference to "my predecessor" in your answer as reported in *The Times*. I assumed the report to be verbatim. The answer, I take it, was as usual supplied.

Two things struck me. First that you declined to admit *political* motive as ground for interfering with sentences. I do not therefore understand that part of your letter in which you say that you decided as soon as you became Home Secretary to make a special "code" for "political offenders". I have not seen the text of the new rules, but I imagine that you propose, as I did, to go far beyond "political offenders" whatever that term may mean. Secondly, the alterations seemed to follow my minutes in details, and were based on the same principles.

I don't in the least agree that these changes could have been properly made in the midst of disorderly actions designed to defy the administration of the law. . . .

During the last three years the suffragette question came frequently before the Cabinet. The concession was never suggested by anyone, not even by you. In fact the only suggestion you made to me—last December—was that to safeguard Cabinet Ministers and their meetings, I should proceed to lock up the suffragettes wholesale. I don't remember on that occasion any advocacy for the improvement of their prison treatment. . . .

But all this is a small matter, and I am sorry to have troubled you. I am very glad that you acted and it is not my intention to claim credit which rightly belongs to the responsible man. Perhaps however if you had been through three years of a vexatious and nasty movement which I faced with a minimum of public support from my colleagues, you would understand that I felt nettled at the invidious comparisons drawn at my expense in consequence of the form of your answer as reported in *The Times*.

SOURCES

Note

All the numbers used in this list of sources (i.e., 41,211 and 43,542) refer to volumes of additional manuscripts in the Department of Manuscripts in the British Museum. I have dispensed with the usual practice of quoting the prefix "B.M. Add. MSS".

The primary sources in question are the Campbell-Bannerman papers (41,208, 41,210, 41,211, 42,213, 41,214, 41,217, 41,218, 41,222, 41,223, 41,225, 41,230, 41,246, 52,512, 52,513, 52,514, 52,516, 52,518 and 52,521), the Balfour papers (49,692, 49,766, 49,767, 49,774 and 49,736), the Herbert Gladstone papers (45,986, 45,988, 45,995 45,996, 45,997, 46,019, 46,064, 46,065, 46,066, 46,067 and 46,068) and the Ripon papers (43,518, 43,541, 43,542, 43,543 and 43,552). The Balfour papers have not received their final classification, and the note "(prov.)", where it occurs, indicates that the particular volume concerned has only been provisionally numbered.

I have not given any source references for speeches, whether parliamentary or public, since accounts of these can be found either in *Hansard* or *The Times*.

For five works which are referred to frequently, I have used the following abbreviations:

BD *British Documents on the Origins of the War, 1898–1914*, ed. G. P. Gooch, D.Litt., F.B.A. and Harold Temperley, Litt.D., F.B.A.

Esher *Journals and Letters of Reginald, Viscount Esher*, vol. II, 1903–10 (1934), edited by Maurice V. Brett and vol. III, 1910–15 (1936), edited by Oliver, Viscount Esher

P from I *Politics from Inside, an Epistolary Chronicle, 1906–1914* by Sir Austen Chamberlain (1936)

S & A *The Life of Herbert Henry Asquith, Lord Oxford and Asquith* (vol. only) by J. A. Spender and Cyril Asquith (1932)

Spender, CB. *The Life of the Right Hon. Sir Henry Campbell-Bannerman, G.C.B.* (vol. II only with the exception of item 33 in Chapter Four) by J. A. Spender (1924)

Prologue
1. C. F. G. Masterman, *The Condition of England* (1960 edition, p. 166)

Chapter One: The Prelude, 1902–5
1. Blanche E. C. Dugdale, *Arthur James Balfour, First Earl of Balfour, K.G., O.M., F.R.S., etc.* (two volumes, 1936), vol. I, p. 354 (15/9/03)

2. Ibid., p. 412. For the importance of the 18-pounder gun in Balfour's calculations, see Kenneth Young, *Arthur James Balfour* (1963), p. 232 and *Sixty Years of Power* (1966) by the Earl of Swinton, in collaboration with James D. Margach, p. 31

3. See R. B. Haldane, *An Autobiography* (1929), p. 159, Sir Frederick Maurice,

Haldane, 1856–1915 (1937), pp. 147 and 151, G. W. Monger, *The End of Isolation: British Foreign Policy, 1900–1907* (1963), p. 258, Roy Jenkins, *Asquith* (1964), p. 147 and R. F. V. Heuston, *Lives of the Lord Chancellors, 1885–1940* (1964), p. 198

4. Margot Asquith, *Autobiography* (1922) (vol. II only), p. 67
5. 52,518
6. Ibid.
7. Sidney Low and Lloyd C. Sandars, *The History of England during the Reign of Victoria* (1907), p. 438
8. 45,988 (25/11/05)
9. Ibid. (30/11/05)
10. See Robert James, *Rosebery* (1963), p. 455
11. 52,521
12. Sir Charles Petrie, *Walter Long and his Times* (1936), p. 101 (letter from Acland Hood to Long dated 27/11/05)
13. Viscount Chilston, *Chief Whip, the Political Life and Times of Aretas Akers-Douglas, First Viscount Chilston* (1961), p. 331

Chapter Two: *Forming a Government, December 1905*
1. 41,210
2. See Jenkins, *Asquith*, p. 150
3. 41,225
4. Ibid.
5. 45,988
6. 46,019
7. Spender, CB, p. 193
8. 52,521
9. J. A. Spender, *Life, Journalism and Politics* (1927), vol. I, p. 126
10. See 41,207 for Knollys's letter. For the interview between Grey and Campbell-Bannerman, see Grey's letter of 7/12/05, quoted on page 346, Margot Asquith, op. cit., p. 71, Lord Shaw of Dunfermline, *Letters to Isabel* (1921), p. 263, and Spender, CB, p. 193. Grey's letter to his wife is quoted in *Grey of Fallodon* (1937) by G. M. Trevelyan,

p. 100, and his letter to Asquith is quoted in Heuston, op. cit., p. 199
11. 41,218
12. See Trevelyan, op. cit., p. 100, Margot Asquith, op. cit., p. 71 and Spender, CB, p. 194
13. Trevelyan, op. cit., p. 100
14. See Margot Asquith, op. cit., p. 72
15. 41,223
16. Margot Asquith, op. cit., p. 74. See 41,210 for Asquith's letter of 22/11/05 and see also Heuston, op. cit., p. 142
17. Ibid., p. 75. See also Spender, CB, p. 195
18. Ibid.
19. 41,210
20. 52,518
21. 41,217 (7/12/05)
22. S & A, p. 174
23. Haldane, op. cit., p. 169
24. Ibid., pp. 171 and 177–8
25. 52,518 (Acland to Campbell-Bannerman 17/12/05)
26. Haldane, op. cit., p. 180
27. Ibid., p. 172
28. Ibid.
29. Margot Asquith, op. cit., p. 75
30. 52,518 (Acland to Campbell-Bannerman 17/12/05)
31. Ibid.
32. Shaw, op. cit., p. 262
33. Trevelyan, op. cit., p. 100 (Grey to his wife 6/12/05)
34. Ibid.
35. 41,218
36. S & A, p. 175
37. 52,518 (30/11/05)
38. George W. Keeton, *A Liberal Attorney-General, The Life of Lord Robson of Jesmond (1852–1918)* (1947), p. 147
39. Beatrice Webb, *Our Partnership* (1948) (ed. Barbara Drake and Margaret Cole), p. 326
40. 52,518 (Acland to Campbell-Bannerman 17/12/05)
41. 46,019
42. 52,518
43. Ibid.

SOURCES

44. Ibid.
45. William George, *My Brother and I* (1958), p. 206, for Lloyd George's letter, and 52,518 for Harcourt's note of 5/12/05. McKenna's remark is quoted by Lord Riddell, *More Pages from My Diary, 1908–1914* (1934), p. 177
46. For Elgin's Home Rule stipulation see his letter to Campbell-Bannerman of 7/12/05, 41,214; for Harcourt's influence, see his note dated 8/12/05, 41,230, and for the "Bravo!" story see William Kent, *John Burns: Labour's Lost Leader* (1950), p. 145
47. George, p. 206

Chapter Three: The Liberal Triumph, December 1905–January 1906
1. See Haldane, op. cit., p. 182
2. Randolph S. Churchill, *Lord Derby, "King of Lancashire", The Official Life of Edward, Seventeenth Earl of Derby, 1865–1945* (1959), p. 91
3. Sir Sidney Lee, *King Edward VII, A Biography* (1927) (vol. II only), pp. 448–9
4. Heuston, op. cit., p. 200
5. Trevelyan, op. cit., p. 103
6. Margot Asquith, op. cit. p. 80
7. 41,217
8. Dugdale, op. cit., vol. I, p. 438 (re Lady Salisbury); Sir Charles Petrie, *The Life and Letters of the Right Hon. Sir Austen Chamberlain, K.G., P.C., M.P.* (1939) (vol. I only referred to in these source notes), p. 176 (re Chamberlain); Lee, op. cit., p. 449 (re Knollys) and Churchill, *Lord Derby*, p. 91 (re Stanley)
9. For full details of these negotiations see F. Bealey and H. Pelling, *Labour and Politics, 1900–1906* (1958) and Philip P. Poirier, *The Advent of the Labour Party* (1958). Letter of 14/3/00, 45,986; Gladstone's letter of 7/8/03, Poirier, pp. 186 and 192
10. Poirier, op. cit., p. 266
11. 41,217
12. Robert Blake, *The Unknown Prime*

Minister, *The Life and Times of Andrew Bonar Law, 1858–1923* (1955), p. 51

Chapter Four: The New Parliament
(*Note* For the earlier history of both the Liberal and Conservative Parties, see *Politics in the Age of Peel* (1953) and *Reaction and Reconstruction in English Politics, 1832–1852* (1965), both by Mr Norman Gash, and Mr H. J. Hanham's *Elections and Party Management; Politics in the Time of Disraeli and Gladstone* (1959).

Mr. John Vincent has carried out some preliminary spadework on the early history of the parliamentary Liberal Party in *The Formation of the Liberal Party, 1857–1868* (1966),while Mr Peter Stansky has described its internal upheavals in the 1890s in *Ambitions and Strategies* (1964). There has been no detailed study of its history in the 1870s and 1880s, although *The Passing of the Whigs* (1962) by Donald Southgate is useful and Sir Philip Magnus's biography of Gladstone (1954) contains much that is valuable.

The Conservative Party in its own right lacks a historian for the period after 1832 (apart from Mr R. B. McDowell's short study), although Mr Robert Blake's biography of Disraeli (1966) goes some way towards filling the gap.

The Irish Nationalist Party has been much better served. Mr David Thornley has dealt with its early history in *Isaac Butt and Home Rule* (1964), Mr Conor Cruise O'Brien has covered the 1880s in *Parnell and His Party, 1880–90* (1957) while Mr F. S. L. Lyons has dealt with the twenty years which followed in *The Fall of Parnell* (1960) and *The Irish Parliamentary Party, 1890–1910* (1951). *The Shaping of Modern Ireland* (1960), edited by Mr O'Brien, is useful.

The Labour Party has also been well

served by historians. In addition to the works by Bealey and Pelling and by Poirier referred to above, Mr Pelling has covered its earlier history in *The Origins of the Labour Party, 1880–1900* (1954).)

1. Roy Jenkins, *Mr Balfour's Poodle* (1954), pp. 7 and 8

2. Ibid., p. 8. For a very detailed analysis of this Parliament (largely in tabular form) see *The House of Commons, 1906–1911* (1958) by J. A. Thomas

3. 41,222

4. Quoted in *Fifty Years of Parliament* (1926) by the Earl of Oxford and Asquith, vol. II, p. 50

5. 41,223

6. Winston S. Churchill, *Great Contemporaries* (1947 edition), p. 195

7. See Leo Amery, *My Political Life* (1953), vol. I, p. 391 and Lloyd George's *War Memoirs* (1938 edition), vol. I, p. 601

8. Jenkins, *Mr Balfour's Poodle*, p. 44

9. *Beatrice Webb's Diaries, 1924–1932* (1956), edited by Margaret Cole, p. 71

10. See Heuston, op. cit., p. 198

11. Maurice, op. cit., pp. 164, 165 and 168 for remarks about Asquith, Morley, Grey and Lloyd George; Haldane, op. cit., p. 217 for remark about Churchill

12. See Poirier, op. cit., p. 158

13. Personal recollection

14. See *New Statesman* 17/8/62 for Paul Johnson's remark

15. R. C. K. Ensor, *England, 1870–1914* (1936), p. 388

16. Jenkins, *Mr Balfour's Poodle*, p. 7

17. Sir Philip Magnus, *Gladstone, A Biography* (1954), p. 381, and Keith Feiling, *The Life of Neville Chamberlain* (1946), p. 178

18. Churchill, *Great Contemporaries*, p. 188

19. Frank Owen, *Tempestuous Journey, Lloyd George, His Life and Times* (1954), p. 43

20. Philip Snowden, *An Autobiography* vol. I, p. 128

21. Julian Amery, *The Life of Joseph Chamberlain* (1951), vol. IV, p. 275

22. *The Shaping of Modern Ireland* (1960), edited by Conor Cruise O'Brien, p. 85. See also two articles in *Irish Historical Studies*, vol. XV, Nos. 58 (September 1966) and 59 (March 1967) respectively—"The unionist party and Ireland, 1906–10" by J. R. Fanning and "The southern Irish unionists, the Irish question, and British politics, 1906–14" by P. J. Buckland. The latter argues that the influence wielded by the southern Irish Unionists in the Unionist Party was rather more important than that of the Ulster Unionists

23. See Denis Gwynn, *Life of John Redmond* (1932), p. 115

24. 52,521

25. See Dorothy Macardle, *The Irish Republic* (1951 edition), p. 59

26. 41,211

27. Ibid.

28. F. S. L. Lyons, *The Irish Parliamentary Party, 1890–1910* (1951), p. 173

29. Snowden, op. cit., p. 71

30. Bealey and Pelling, op. cit., p. 211

31. Webb, *Our Partnership*, p. 132

32. *The Letters of Queen Victoria (3rd Series), vol. II, 1891–1895* (1931), p. 384

33. See Spender, CB (vol. I), p. 171

34. Dugdale, op. cit., vol. I, p. 335

Chapter Five: The Rise of the Opposition, February 1906

1. Petrie, *Walter Long*, p. 109

2. Lord Newton, *Lord Lansdowne, a Biography* (1929), p. 348

3. Ibid., p. 349

4. Young, op. cit., p. 259

5. Newton, op. cit., p. 351

6. Reginald Pound and Geoffrey Harmsworth, *Northcliffe* (1959), p. 298

7. 49,774 (prov.)

8. Ibid.

9. Ibid.

10. Ibid.
11. Lucy Masterman, *C. F. G. Masterman, a Biography* (1939), p. 174
12. Newton, op. cit., p. 352
13. Ibid.
14. Dugdale, op. cit., vol. I, p. 354
15. Feiling, op. cit., p. 46
16. H. Montgomery Hyde, *Carson, the Life of Sir Edward Carson, Lord Carson of Duncairn* (1953), p. 212
17. Sandars's letter of 14/5/06 is quoted in an article by R. B. Jones ("Balfour's Reform of Party Organisation") in the *Bulletin of the Institute of Historical Research*, vol. XXXVIII (May 1965), p. 96

Chapter Six: Domestic Affairs, February –December 1906
1. Snowden, op. cit., p. 122
2. 52,512
3. Wilfred Scawen Blunt, *My Diaries, Being a Personal Narrative of Events, 1888–1914* (single-volume edition, 1932), p. 557
4. G. K. A. Bell, *Randall Davidson, Archbishop of Canterbury* (3rd edition, 1952), p. 517 (This note followed a meeting with Morant.)
5. Sir Philip Magnus, *King Edward the Seventh* (1964), pp. 349, 353 and 354
6. Lee, op. cit., p. 459
7. Ibid.
8. Newton, op. cit., p. 353
9. Ibid., p. 354
10. 52,512
11. 43,543
12. Ibid.
13. Blake, op. cit., p. 54
14. Spender, CB, p. 295
15. Lee, op. cit., p. 456
16. 52,513
17. 43,552
18. Ibid.
19. Ibid.
20. Lee, op. cit., p. 462 and Spender, CB, p. 302 (27/11/06)
21. Bell, op. cit., p. 525
22. Spender, CB, p. 314 (4/12/06)

23. Bell, op. cit., p. 526
24. Ibid. and 52,512
25. 43,552
26. Ibid.
27. Bell, op. cit., p. 529
28. Newton, op. cit., p. 356
29. 52,512
30. Ripon to Campbell-Bannerman 12/10/06, 41,225; Campbell-Bannerman to Gladstone, Spender, CB, p. 225
31. 41,211

Chapter Seven: The Empire, 1905–10
(*Note* For South Africa, see L. M. Thompson, *The Unification of South Africa, 1902–1910* (1960) and G. H. L. Le May, *British Supremacy in South Africa, 1899–1907* (1965). For India, in addition to the works mentioned elsewhere, see Syed Razi Wasti, *Lord Minto and the Indian Nationalist Movement, 1905–10* (1964) and M. N. Das, *India under Morley and Minto, Politics behind Revolution, Repression and Reforms* (1964). For the British Empire generally, see the *Cambridge History of the British Empire, vol. III, The Empire-Commonwealth, 1870–1919* (1959).)
1. "Britain's part in world affairs", *The Listener*, vol. LXXVII No. 1994 (June 15th, 1967), p. 776
2. Quoted by G. P. Gooch, *Under Six Reigns* (1958), p. 103. See also *The Milner Papers, vol. II, South Africa 1899–1905*, edited by Cecil Headlam (1933), p. 410
3. Knollys to Elgin 22/12/05, Lee, op. cit., p. 479; Elgin to Ripon 24/12/05 and Ripon's reply, 43,552
4. 41,210
5. 41,214
6. L. M. Thompson, *The Unification of South Africa, 1902–1910* (1960), p. 25
7. Sarah Gertrude Millin, *General Smuts* (1936), vol. I, p. 212
8. Riddell, op. cit., p. 144
9. 52,521 and Spender, CB, p. 238
10. 43,552

11. Janet Adam Smith, *John Buchan* (1965), p. 159
12. 52,512
13. Lee, op. cit., p. 481 (28/3/06)
14. Magnus, *King Edward*, p. 351 (26/3/06)
15. Ibid., p. 380
16. Margot Asquith, op. cit., p. 86
17. *The Milner Papers, vol. II*, p. 534
18. 52,516
19. Ibid.
20. *Cambridge History of the British Empire, vol. III, The Empire–Commonwealth, 1870–1919* (1959), p. 451
21. Lord Hankey, *The Supreme Command, 1914–1918* (1961), p. 127
22. John, Viscount Morley, *Recollections* (1917) (vol. II only), p. 171 (11/5/06)
23. Mary, Countess of Minto, *India, Minto and Morley, 1905–1910* (1935), p. 49
24. Morley, op. cit., p. 154
25. Ibid., p. 175
26. Ibid., p. 176
27. *The Evolution of India and Pakistan, 1858 to 1947, Select Documents* (1962), edited by C. H. Phillips, p. 76
28. Lady Minto, op. cit., p. 222
29. Morley, op. cit., p. 287
30. Minto's letter of 10/4/07, Lady Minto, op. cit., p. 118; letter of 5/7/10, John Buchan, *Lord Minto* (1924), p. 312
31. Blunt, op. cit., p. 640
32. R. P. Masani, *Britain in India: an account of British Rule in the Indian Sub-Continent* (1960), p. 235
33. Morley, op. cit., pp. 323 and 325
34. Masani, op. cit., p. 235
35. Thompson, op. cit., p. 72
36. Ibid., p. 400
37. Ibid., pp. 408 and 416

Chapter Eight: Domestic Affairs, January–December 1907
1. 43,552
2. 52,512

3. 45,986
4. 41,230
5. Esher, vol. II, p. 215
6. See 41,223 for Morley's letters of 22/12/06 and 23/1/07 and 41,230 for Campbell-Bannerman's letter of 30/1/07
7. Lady Minto, op. cit., p. 116
8. For Sandars's letter of 2/4/07 see the article by R. B. Jones referred to above (*Bulletin of the Institute of Historical Research*, vol. XXXVIII, p. 98); for Balfour's letter to Chamberlain of 23/10/07 and Chamberlain's reply, see 49,736 (prov.)
9. Petrie, *Walter Long*, p. 123
10. Petrie, *Austen Chamberlain*, p. 203
11. Dugdale, op. cit. vol. II, p. 43
12. See P. from I, pp. 48–52
13. Esher, vol. II, p. 222
14. Lee, op. cit., p. 467 and 468
15. 41,230
16. 43,552 (21/3/07)
17. Ibid., (19/3/07)
18. Spender, CB, p. 353
19. 41,208
20. Jenkins, *Mr Balfour's Poodle*, p. 33
21. Dugdale, op. cit., vol. II, p. 49
22. 43,552
23. Ibid.
24. 52,513
25. Morley, op. cit., p. 226
26. Snowden, op. cit., p. 174
27. Owen, op. cit., p. 154
28. See George, op. cit., p. 212 for Lloyd George's letters
29. 41,208 (6/11/07)
30. A. J. P. Taylor, *Politics in Wartime* (1964), p. 131
31. George, op. cit., p. 213
32. Chilston, op. cit., p. 337
33. Ibid., p. 340
34. Viscount Cecil of Chelwood, *All the Way* (1949), p. 109
35. H. Montgomery Hyde, op. cit., p. 240
36. See Petrie, *Walter Long*, pp. 129 and 130 and Chilston, op. cit., p. 339

Chapter Nine: Prelude to Home Rule, 1906–8

1. Gwynn, op. cit., p. 121
2. Ibid., p. 126
3. Ibid.
4. Ibid., p. 130
5. Ibid., p. 123–4
6. 41,211
7. Ibid. (8/10/06)
8. Gwynn, op. cit., p. 142
9. 41,211 (10/10/06)
10. Gwynn, op. cit., p. 135
11. See 41,230 (Sinclair to Campbell-Bannerman 8/1/07) and 41,223 (Morley to Campbell-Bannerman, 20/1/07)
12. 41,223
13. Stephen Gwynne and G. M. Tuckwell, *Life of the Right Hon. Sir Charles W. Dilke, Bart* (1917), p. 466
14. 43,542
15. H. A. L. Fisher, *James Bryce* (1927), vol. I, p. 357
16. 52,513
17. Gwynn, op. cit., p. 144
18. 43,542
19. 43,552
20. Lyons, op. cit., p. 116
21. 43,542
22. 52,512
23. Lyons, op. cit., p. 246
24. Gwynn, op. cit., p. 154
25. Lyons, op. cit., p. 249

Chapter Ten: Domestic Affairs, January–December 1908

1. Fisher, op. cit., vol. II, p. 92
2. 41,218
3. 41,213 (Crewe's letter); 41,217 (Gladstone's letter)
4. Petrie, *Austen Chamberlain*, p. 213 and Esher, vol. II, p. 278
5. Esher, vol. II, pp. 256 and 284
6. 41,208
7. Morley, op. cit., p. 250
8. Spender, CB, p. 381
9. Ibid., p. 382
10. 43,518
11. 41,225
12. S & A, p. 195
13. 41,208
14. 43,552
15. 41,208
16. Ibid.
17. 41,218
18. P from I, p. 98
19. Spender, CB, p. 386
20. James Pope-Hennessy, *Lord Crewe, 1858–1945, The Likeness of a Liberal* (1955), p. 63
21. Lee, op. cit., p. 578
22. Ibid., p. 579
23. Ibid.
24. Spender, CB, p. 388
25. Maurice, op. cit., p. 225
26. Pope-Hennessy, op. cit., p. 60
27. Morley, op. cit., p. 250
28. Lee, op. cit., p. 581
29. Margot Asquith, op. cit., p. 98 (Also S & A, p. 197)
30. Ibid., p. 99 (Also S & A, p. 197)
31. 41,218
32. Christopher Hassall, *Edward Marsh, Patron of the Arts* (1959), p. 41. See also the interview with Baroness Asquith of Yarnbury in *The Listener*, vol. 78, No. 2002 (August 17th, 1967), p. 197
33. Margot Asquith, op. cit., p. 107
34. Churchill, *Great Contemporaries*, p. 107
35. Pope-Hennessy, op. cit., p. 64
36. George, op. cit., p. 220
37. Esher, vol. II, p. 303; Jenkins, *Asquith*, p. 184
38. See Lady Violet Bonham Carter (now Baroness Asquith), *Winston Churchill as I Knew Him* (1965), p. 165
39. Jenkins, *Asquith*, p. 182
40. Riddell, op. cit., p. 109
41. Churchill, *Great Contemporaries*, p. 108
42. Owen, op. cit., p. 162
43. Sir Harold Nicolson, "Prime Ministers at Close Range", published in the *Observer* 12/11/61. This paragraph has been based, to a large extent, on the account given by Mr Roy Jenkins in his

biography of Asquith (p. 181). See Baroness Asquith's book (p. 154) for a slightly different version of events
44. Morley, op. cit., p. 251; Lady Minto, op. cit., p. 207
45. Morley, op. cit., p. 255
46. 45,986
47. P from I, p. 109
48. George, op. cit., p. 220
49. Lee, op. cit., p. 653
50. *Lloyd George's Ambulance Wagon: the Memoirs of William J. Braithwaite, 1911–12* (1957), p. 71
51. George, op. cit., p. 221
52. P from I, p. 127 (2/7/08)
53. 43,518
54. Elie Halévy, *The Rule of Democracy, 1905–1914* (2nd edition, 1952), p. 243
55. 45,986
56. Newton, op. cit., p. 368
57. 43,552
58. Newton, op. cit., p. 370
59. Riddell, op. cit., p. 10
60. S & A, p. 238 (15/12/08)
61. 43,518
62. Ibid.
63. 43,543
64. 46,018
65. 43,518
66. Ibid.
67. Ibid.
68. Ibid. (Asquith to Ripon 20/9/08 and 30/9/08)
69. 43,543
70. Jenkins, *Asquith*, p. 192
71. See 46,065 for the details of this episode
72. 43,552
73. Henry Pelling, *A Short History of the Labour Party* (1961), p. 21
74. S & A, p. 235
75. Viscount Samuel, *Memoirs* (1945), p. 56
76. S & A, p. 240
77. Alfred M. Gollin, *Proconsul in Politics, a study of Lord Milner in Opposition and in Power* (1964), p. 152
78. J. W. Mackail and Guy Wyndham,

Life and Letters of George Wyndham (1925), p. 619
79. Jenkins, *Asquith*, p. 188
80. Lucy Masterman, op. cit., p. 114
81. George, op. cit., p. 222
82. Ibid.

Chapter Eleven: Foreign Affairs and Defence, 1905–8
(*Note* I must acknowledge, so far as my account of events in 1906 and 1907 is concerned, the invaluable assistance I have received from *The End of Isolation: British Foreign Policy, 1900–1907* (1963) by Mr G. W. Monger. The works of Professor G. P. Gooch, although now dated to some extent, have also proved extremely useful. Unless otherwise stated, the information on which this chapter is based is taken from *British Documents on the Origins of the War, 1898–1914*, edited by Professor Gooch and Harold Temperley.)
1. BD, vol. III, p. 169
2. Trevelyan, op. cit., p. 128
3. BD, vol. III, p. 178
4. Monger, op. cit., p. 239
5. 43,543
6. 52,518
7. See Spender, CB, p. 253
8. 52,514
9. 52,512
10. Monger, op. cit., p. 270
11. BD, vol. III, p. 174
12. A. J. P. Taylor, *The Struggle for Mastery in Europe, 1848–1918* (1954). p. 437
13. Spender, CB, p. 257
14. (Sir) Harold Nicolson, *Lord Carnock, A Study in the Old Diplomacy* (1930), p. 175
15. Viscount Grey of Fallodon, *Twenty-five Years, 1892–1916* (three-volume edition, 1928), p. 197
16. See Monger, op. cit., p. 274
17. BD, vol. III, pp. 249 and 266
18. Nicolson, *Lord Carnock*, p. 191 and 41,218

19. Monger, p. 277 and 278
20. Ibid., p. 278
21. Trevelyan, pp. 143 and 182 (letter to Cecil Spring-Rice 19/2/06)
22. BD, vol. IV, p. 381
23. Nicolson, *Lord Carnock*, p. 222
24. BD, vol. IV, p. 277
25. Ibid., p. 549
26. Quoted by Julian Amery, op. cit., p. 176
27. Arthur J. Marder, *From the Dreadnought to Scapa Flow, The Royal Navy in the Fisher Era, 1904–1919, vol. I, The Road to War, 1904–1914* (1961), p. 106
28. See Julian Amery, op. cit., p. 197 and Marder, op. cit., p. 112–13
29. Monger, op. cit., p. 268
30. Trevelyan, op. cit., p. 115
31. See Dudley Sommer, *Haldane of Cloan, His Life and Times, 1856–1928* (1960), p. 181; Winston S. Churchill, *Thoughts and Adventures* (1947 edition), p. 52 and Monger, op. cit., p. 303
32. Monger, op. cit., p. 301 and BD, vol. III, p. 389
33. Sommer, op. cit., p. 180
34. BD, vol. III, p. 392
35. See 41,213
36. Ibid.
37. Ibid. and Marder, op. cit., p. 71
38. BD, vol. VIII, pp. 287 and 299 for comments of Crowe (11/10/07) and Reay (22/10/07) respectively
39. 41,210
40. Maurice, op. cit., p. 158
41. Haldane, op. cit., p. 187
42. 41,218
43. Haldane, op. cit., p. 182
44. 41,230
45. 41,218
46. 41,230
47. 41,213
48. BD, vol. III, p. 397
49. Ibid., p. 421
50. BD, vol. VI, p. 24
51. See Monger, op. cit., pp. 328 and 329

52. Esher, vol. II, p. 281
53. For the battle over the 1908–9 Navy Estimates see ibid.; Spender, CB, p. 378; Marder, op. cit., p. 138 and Alfred M. Gollin, *"The Observer" and J. L. Garvin, 1908–1914, A Study in a Great Editorship* (1960), p. 52
54. See Magnus, *King Edward*, p. 375
55. George, op. cit., p. 221
56. See Halévy, op. cit., p. 432 and Maurice, op. cit., p. 225
57. Sommer, op. cit., p. 213
58. P from I, p. 127
59. Owen, op. cit., p. 161
60. Esher, vol. II, p. 326
61. 43,541
62. Magnus, *King Edward*, p. 411
63. Trevelyan, op. cit., p. 152
64. Lucy Masterman, op. cit., p. 129
65. George, op. cit., p. 253
66. BD, vol. IV, p. 280
67. BD, vol. V, p. 384
68. See BD, vol. IV, pp. 280 and 290
69. See Grey, op. cit., p. 278 and Nicolson, *Lord Carnock*, p. 282
70. BD, vol. V, p. 494
71. BD, vol. VI, p. 150
72. Ibid., p. 779
73. Trevelyan, op. cit., p. 154
74. BD, vol. VII, p. 110
75. Young, op. cit., p. 217
76. George, op. cit., p. 247
77. BD, vol. VI, p. 167
78. BD, vol. VIII, p. 375
79. Ibid., p. 377
80. 41,230
81. Monger, op. cit., p. 246
82. Ibid., p. 251
83. *The History of "The Times": vol. III, The Twentieth Century Test, 1884–1912* (1947), p. 612
84. Magnus, *King Edward*, p. 369
85. See Marder, op. cit., p. 387 for an account of this incident. He points out that the dating of 3/12/08 is suspect
86. BD, vol. V, p. 494
87. Stephen McKenna, *Reginald McKenna, 1863–1943* (1948), p. 71

Chapter Twelve: Domestic Affairs, January–December 1909
1. Jenkins, *Asquith*, p. 196
2. Gwynn, op. cit., p. 159
3. Riddell, op. cit., p. 65
4. Jenkins, *Asquith*, p. 193
5. Petrie, *Austen Chamberlain*, p. 228
6. Lucy Masterman, op. cit., p. 129
7. 46,067
8. 46,068
9. Jenkins, *Asquith*, p. 197
10. P from I, p. 177
11. George, op. cit., p. 226
12. Ibid., p. 227
13. See Owen, op. cit., p. 182
14. George, op. cit., p. 230
15. Pope-Hennessy, op. cit., p. 72
16. See ibid., p. 75, and Owen, op. cit., pp. 180 and 181
17. George, op. cit., p. 230
18. Ibid., p. 30
19. See Gwynn, op. cit., pp. 162–5
20. Ibid., p. 162
21. Jenkins, *Asquith*, p. 200
22. 49, 766
23. Blunt, op. cit., p. 689
24. George, op. cit., p. 230 (8/9/09)
25. Lady Minto, op. cit., p. 328
26. P from I, p. 182
27. Esher, vol. II, p. 409
28. Newton, op. cit., p. 376
29. Ibid., p. 378
30. Esher, vol. II, p. 406
31. S & A, p. 263
32. Ibid.
33. Lucy Masterman, op. cit., p. 137
34. Blunt, op. cit., p. 692
35. Esher, vol. II. p. 410
36. Gollin, *The Observer, etc*, p. 125
37. Newton, op. cit., p. 377
38. Jenkins, *Asquith*, p. 200
39. S & A, p. 257
40. See Jenkins, *Mr Balfour's Poodle*, p. 59 and Magnus, *King Edward*, p. 437
41. Jenkins, *Mr Balfour's Poodle*, p. 61
42. George, op. cit., p. 232
43. Margot Asquith, op. cit., p. 124
44. Ibid., p. 128

45. Gwynn, op. cit., p. 166
46. Ibid., p. 168

Chapter Thirteen: The General Election, December 1909–January 1910
1. Jenkins, *Asquith*, p. 202
2. S & A, p. 261
3. Newton, op. cit., p. 363
4. Ibid.
5. Ibid., p. 385
6. Morley, op. cit., p. 326
7. 49,736 (prov.)
8. Ibid.
9. Ibid.
10. Jenkins, *Asquith*, p. 205
11. Morley. op. cit., p. 227 (23/8/07)

Chapter Fourteen: Foreign Affairs and Defence, 1908–10
(*Note* Unless otherwise indicated, this chapter is based on information taken from *British Documents on the Origins of the War, 1898–1914*.)
1. 41,210
2. McKenna, op. cit., p. 65
3. George, op. cit., p. 222
4. McKenna, op. cit., p. 72
5. Marder, op. cit., p. 120
6. BD, vol. VI, pp. 237 and 239
7. Gollin, *The Observer, etc*, p. 66 and Marder, op. cit., p. 159
8. See Jenkins, *Asquith*, p. 194 and Esher, vol. II, p. 370
9. Lucy Masterman, op. cit., p. 124
10. George, op. cit., p. 223
11. Trevelyan, op. cit., p. 213
12. Ibid., pp. 214 and 215
13. S & A, p. 254
14. Lucy Masterman, op. cit., p. 125
15. S & A, p. 254
16. Lucy Masterman, op. cit., p. 127
17. BD, vol. vol. VI, pp. 240–1
18. P from I, pp. 160
19. Trevelyan, op. cit., p. 213
20. McKenna, op. cit., p. 82
21. Marder, op. cit., p. 170
22. Ibid., p. 101
23. Ibid., p. 201

24. BD, vol. V, p. 560
25. BD, vol. VI, p. 231
26. BD, vol. V, p. 736
27. Nicolson, *Lord Carnock*, p. 309
28. BD, vol. V, p. 771
29. Nicolson, *Lord Carnock*, p. 307
30. BD, vol. IX, p. 6
31. *The History of "The Times,"* vol. III, p. 682
32. BD, vol. IX, p. 14 and vol. V, p. 809
33. BD, vol. VI, p. 278
34. Ibid., p. 288
35. Ibid., p. 284
36. Ibid., p. 294
37. Winston S. Churchill, *The World Crisis, 1911–1918* (1938 two-volume edition), vol. I, p. 25
38. BD, vol. VI, p. 303
39. Monger, op. cit., p. 323
40. BD, vol. VI, p. 368
41. Ibid., p. 408
42. Marder, op. cit., p. 215
43. BD, vol. VI, p. 478
44. Monger, op. cit., p. 287

Chapter Fifteen: Domestic Affairs, January–July 1910
1. 49,766 (prov.)
2. S & A, p. 272
3. Newton, op. cit., p. 389
4. Blunt, op. cit., p. 702
5. Magnus, *King Edward*, pp. 444 and 445
6. Esher, vol. II, p. 435
7. Ibid., p. 439
8. Ibid., p. 442 and Maurice, op. cit., p. 260
9. Esher, vol. II, p. 439
10. See Pope-Hennessy, op. cit., p. 77 and Lee, op. cit., p. 695
11. S & A, p. 273
12. Jenkins, *Asquith*, p. 206
13. Sommer, op. cit., p. 229
14. Newton, op. cit., p. 386
15. Petrie, *Walter Long*, p. 140
16. Asquith, *Fifty Years of Parliament*, vol. II, p. 41

17. Snowden, op. cit., p. 214
18. Blunt, op. cit., p. 701
19. Arthur Murray, *Master and Brother: Murrays of Elibank* (1945), p. 39
20. See Pope-Hennessy, op. cit., p. 77 and Lee, op. cit., p. 695
21. P from I, p. 202 (21/2/10)
22. Ibid., p. 208
23. Murray, op. cit., p. 40
24. Ibid., p. 47
25. Gwynn, op. cit., p. 174
26. P from I, p. 208
27. Lee, p. 701 and S & A, p. 274
28. S & A, p. 274
29. Newton, op. cit., p. 392
30. Trevelyan, op. cit., p. 173
31. See Jenkins, *Asquith*, p. 206
32. Magnus, *King Edward*, p. 450
33. P from I, p. 235
34. Murray, op. cit., p. 47
35. Ibid., p. 45
36. 49,767 (prov.)
37. S & A, p. 278
38. Magnus, *King Edward*, p. 451 and Jenkins, *Asquith*, p. 209
39. Murray, op. cit., p. 45
40. Lady Minto, op. cit., p. 398
41. See P from I, pp. 255–9
42. Ibid.
43. Ibid., p. 263 and Esher, vol. II, p. 456
44. Asquith, *Fifty Years of Parliament*, vol. II, pp. 86 and 87
45. Margot Asquith, op. cit., p. 139
46. See Jenkins, *Asquith*, p. 213
47. P from I, p. 268
48. Gollin, *The Observer, etc*, p. 186
49. Ibid.
50. Owen, op. cit., p. 190
51. John Gore, *King George V, a Personal Memoir* (1941), p. 243
52. Hassall, op. cit., p. 156 and S & A, p. 283
53. Gwynn, op. cit., p. 176
54. Esher, vol. III, p. 8
55. Gwynn, op. cit., p. 178
56. Gollin, *The Observer, etc*, p. 190

Chapter Sixteen: Domestic Affairs, July–November 1910

1. 45,996
2. Sir Harold Nicolson, King George V (1952), p. 131
3. Pope-Hennessy, op. cit., p. 118
4. Petrie, Austen Chamberlain, p. 255
5. Newton, op. cit., p. 398
6. See Petrie, Austen Chamberlain, p. 381
7. 49,767 (prov.) See also P from I, p. 577
8. 49,767 (prov.)
9. Webb, Our Partnership, p. 461. See also Esher, vol. III, p. 24
10. Malcolm Thomson, David Lloyd George, the Official Biography (1948), p. 195
11. 49,692 (prov.)
12. See P. from I, p. 287 and 49,736 (prov.)
13. 49,736 (prov.)
14. Thomson, op. cit., p. 196
15. Lloyd George, op. cit., p. 22
16. 49,736 (prov.)
17. See P from I, pp. 295 and 303
18. See the article by P. J. Buckland, "The southern Irish unionists, the Irish question, and British politics, 1906–14", in Irish Historical Studies, vol. XV, No. 59 (March 1967), p. 229
19. S & A, p. 290
20. Thomson, op. cit., p. 196
21. Ibid.
22. Lucy Masterman, op. cit., p. 172
23. Thomson, op. cit., p. 197
24. See Gollin, The Observer, etc, p. 207
25. Jenkins, Asquith, p. 217
26. Ibid.
27. Lord Birkenhead, Frederick Edwin, Earl of Birkenhead (1933), vol. I, p. 205
28. P from I, p. 287
29. Birkenhead, op. cit., p. 206
30. P from I, p. 283 (21/10/10)
31. Dugdale, op. cit., vol. II, p. 77 (16/10/10). See also the article by Alan J. Ward, "Frewen's Anglo-American campaign for federalism, 1910–21" in

Irish Historical Studies, vol. XV, No. 59 (March 1967), p. 256
32. Young, op. cit., p. 296
33. H. Montgomery Hyde, op. cit., p. 279
34. Ibid.
35. Ibid., p. 280
36. Esher, vol. III, p. 27 and Gollin, The Observer, etc, pp. 215 and 226
37. Lloyd George, op. cit., p. 23
38. Dugdale, op. cit., vol. II, p. 75
39. 49,692 (prov.)
40. P from I, p. 577
41. Dugdale, op. cit., vol. II, p. 62
42. 49,692 (prov.)
43. Ibid.
44. Ibid.
45. Lucy Masterman, op. cit., p. 175
46. See P from I, p. 295
47. Esher, vol. III, p. 30
48. S & A, p. 291
49. 49,692 (prov.)
50. S & A, p. 291
51. 45,997
52. Pope-Hennessy, op. cit., p. 85
53. Esher, vol. III, p. 27
54. Churchill, Great Contemporaries, p. 75
55. S & A, p. 292
56. Nicolson, King George, p. 133
57. Ibid., p. 134
58. Ibid.
59. Murray, op. cit., p. 60
60. Nicolson, King George, p. 136
61. Ibid., p. 138
62. Pope-Hennessy, op. cit., p. 122
63. S & A, p. 305
64. Esher, vol. III, p. 37
65. Keeton, op. cit., p. 222

Chapter Seventeen: The General Election of December 1910

1. 45,997
2. Petrie, Austen Chamberlain, p. 267
3. Gollin, The Observer, etc, p. 255
4. 49,736 (prov.)
5. Ibid.
6. Ibid.

7. Ibid.
8. Gollin, *The Observer, etc*, p. 272 and 49,736 (prov.)
9. S & A, p. 306
10. Murray, op. cit., p. 68

Selected Letters
1. 45,988
2. 41,218
3. 52,512
4. Ibid.
5. Petrie, *Walter Long*, p. 110
6. 43,518
7. 52,512

8. Ibid.
9. Spender, CB, p. 314
10. Ibid.
11. 46,064
12. 41,223
13. 52,516
14. 52,513
15. 46,067
16. Ibid.
17. S & A, p. 261
18. 45,986
19. Ibid.
20. Ibid.

WORKS CONSULTED

Contemporary Publications
Annual Register (1906–10)
Winston S. Churchill, *Liberalism and the Social Problem* (1909)
Dod's Parliamentary Companion (1906–10)
C. F. G. Masterman, *The Condition of England* (1909) (reprinted 1960)
The Times (1905–10)

Histories
W. S. Adams, *Edwardian Heritage, A Study in British History, 1901–1906* (1949)
W. Ashworth, *An Economic History of England, 1870–1939* (1960)
F. Bealey and H. Pelling, *Labour and Politics, 1900–1906* (1958)
The Cambridge History of the British Empire, vol. III, The Empire–Commonwealth 1870–1919 (1959)
Sir John Clapham, *An Economic History of Modern Britain: Machines and National Rivalries (1887–1914) with an Epilogue (1914–1929)* (1938)
H. A. Clegg, Alan Fox and A. F. Thompson, *A History of British Trade Unions since 1889 (vol. I: 1889–1910)* (1964)
Margaret Cole, *The Story of Fabian Socialism* (1961)

T. P. Conwell-Evans, *Foreign Policy from a Back Bench, 1904–1918, A Study based on the papers of Lord Noel-Buxton* (1932)
Colin Cross, *The Liberals in Power, 1905–14* (1963)
George Dangerfield, *The Strange Death of Liberal England, 1910–1914* (1935)
M. N. Das, *India under Morley and Minto, Politics behind Revolution, Repression and Reforms* (1964)
Major John K. Dunlop, *The Development of the British Army, 1899–1914* (1938)
Sir Robert Ensor, *England, 1870–1914* (1936)
P. and G. Ford, *A Breviate of Parliamentary Papers, 1900–1916: The Foundation of the Welfare State* (1957)
Roger Fulford, *Votes for Women, The Story of a Struggle* (1957)
Alfred M. Gollin, *"The Observer" and J. L. Garvin, 1908–1914, A Study in a Great Editorship* (1960)
Alfred M. Gollin, *Balfour's Burden: Arthur Balfour and Imperial Preference* (1965)
G. P. Gooch, *Before the War, Studies in Diplomacy* (1936)
G. P. Gooch, *Recent Revelations of European Diplomacy* (1940)

G. P. Gooch, *Studies in Diplomacy and Statecraft* (1942)

G. P. Gooch, *Historical Surveys and Portraits* (1966)

Elie Halévy, *The Rule of Democracy, 1905–1914* (2nd edition, 1952)

Roy Jenkins, *Mr Balfour's Poodle, An Account of the Struggle between the House of Lords and the Government of Mr Asquith* (1954)

Sidney Low and Lloyd C. Sandars, *The History of England during the Reign of Victoria (1837–1901)* (1907)

G. Lowes Dickinson, *The International Anarchy, 1904–1914* (1926)

F. S. L. Lyons, *The Irish Parliamentary Party, 1890–1910* (1951)

Dorothy Macardle, *The Irish Republic* (4th edition, 1951)

S. Maccoby, *English Radicalism, 1886–1914* (1953)

Arthur J. Marder, *From the Dreadnought to Scapa Flow, The Royal Navy in the Fisher Era, 1904–1919; vol. I, The Road to War, 1904–1914* (1961)

Sir Ruston Pestonji Masani, *Britain in India: an account of British Rule in the Indian Sub-Continent* (1960)

R. B. McCallum, *The Liberal Party from Earl Grey to Asquith* (1963)

Mary, Countess of Minto, *India, Minto and Morley, 1905–1910* (1935)

B. R. Mitchell and Phyllis Deane, *Abstract of British Historical Statistics* (1962)

G. W. Monger, *The End of Isolation: British Foreign Policy, 1900–1907* (1963)

Kenneth O. Morgan, *Wales in British Politics, 1868–1922* (1963)

Simon Nowell-Smith (editor), *Edwardian England, 1901–1914* (1964)

Conor Cruise O'Brien, *Parnell and His Party, 1880–90* (1957)

Conor Cruise O'Brien (editor), *The Shaping of Modern Ireland* (1960)

Henry Pelling, *A Short History of the Labour Party* (1961)

Sir Charles Petrie, *The Powers behind the Prime Ministers* (1958)

Philip P. Poirier, *The Advent of the Labour Party* (1958)

Peter Stansky, *Ambitions and Strategies, The Struggle for the leadership of the Liberal Party in the 1890s* (1964)

A. J. P. Taylor, *The Struggle for Mastery in Europe, 1848–1918* (1954)

A. J. P. Taylor, *The Trouble Makers, Dissent over Foreign Policy, 1792–1939* (1957)

A. J. P. Taylor, *Politics in Wartime* (1964)

J. A. Thomas, *The House of Commons, 1906–1911* (1958)

F. M. L. Thompson, *English Landed Society in the Nineteenth Century* (1963)

L. M. Thompson, *The Unification of South Africa, 1902–1910* (1960)

The History of "The Times": vol. III, The Twentieth Century Test, 1884–1912 (1947)

Herbert Tracy (editor), *The British Labour Party, Its History, Growth, Policy and Leaders* (1948)

Syed Razi Wasti, *Lord Minto and the Indian Nationalist Movement, 1905–10* (1964)

Sir Llewellyn Woodward, *Great Britain and the German Navy* (1935)

Memoirs

L. S. Amery, *My Political Life, vol. I, England Before the Storm, 1896–1914* (1953)

Earl of Oxford and Asquith, *Fifty Years of Parliament* (1926)

Earl of Oxford and Asquith, *Memories and Reflections, 1852–1927* (1928)

Margot Asquith, *Autobiography* (1922). (Also the abridged, one-volume edition, 1962, with an introduction by Mark Bonham Carter)

Margot Asquith, *More Memories* (1933)

Margot Asquith, *Off the Record* (1943)

Arthur James, First Earl of Balfour, *Chapters of Autobiography* (1930)

Lord Beveridge, *Power and Influence* (1953)

Augustine Birrell, *Things Past Redress* (1937)

Wilfred Scawen Blunt, *My Diaries, Being a Personal Narrative of Events, 1888–1914* (1932, single-volume edition)

William J. Braithwaite, *Lloyd George's Ambulance Wagon: the Memoirs of William J. Braithwaite, 1911–1912* (1957)

Viscount Cecil of Chelwood, *All the Way* (1949)

Sir Austen Chamberlain, *Down the Years* (1935)

Winston S. Churchill, *The World Crisis, 1911–1918* (two-volume edition, 1938)

Winston S. Churchill, *My Early Life* (1947 edition)

Winston S. Churchill, *Thoughts and Adventures* (1947 edition)

J. R. Clynes, *Memoirs* (1937)

Sir Almeric Fitzroy, *Memoirs* (1925)

William George, *My Brother and I* (1958)

G. P. Gooch, *Under Six Reigns* (1958)

Viscount Grey of Fallodon, *Twenty-Five Years, 1892–1916* (three-volume edition, 1928)

R. B. Haldane, *An Autobiography* (1929)

Lord Hankey, *The Supreme Command, 1914–1918* (1961)

Lord Hardinge, *Old Diplomacy, The Reminiscences of Lord Hardinge of Penshurst* (1947)

T. M. Healy, *Letters and Leaders of My Day* (1928)

David Lloyd George, *War Memoirs* (two-volume edition, 1938)

John, Viscount Morley, *Recollections* (1917)

Arthur Murray, *Master and Brother: Murrays of Elibank* (1945)

Lord Newton, *Retrospection* (1941)

Lord Riddell, *More Pages from My Diary 1908–1914* (1934)

Viscount Samuel, *Memoirs* (1945)

Lord Shaw of Dunfermline, *Letters to Isabel* (1921)

Philip, Viscount Snowden, *An Autobiography* (1934)

J. A. Spender, *Life, Journalism and Politics* (1927)

Earl of Swinton, in collaboration with James D. Margach, *Sixty Years of Power, some memories of the men who wielded it* (1966)

Beatrice Webb, *Our Partnership* (1948), edited by Barbara Drake and Margaret Cole

Henry Wickham Steed, *Through Thirty Years, 1892–1922* (1924)

Earl Winterton, *Orders of the Day* (1953)

Biographies (Arranged Chronologically under Name of Subject)

J. A. Spender and Cyril Asquith, *The Life of Herbert Henry Asquith, Lord Oxford and Asquith* (1932)

R. B. MacCallum, *Asquith* (1936)

Roy Jenkins, *Asquith* (1964)

G. M. Young, *Stanley Baldwin* (1952)

A. W. Baldwin, *My Father: The True Story* (1956)

Blanche E. C. Dugdale, *Arthur James Balfour, First Earl of Balfour, K.G., O.M., F.R.S., etc* (1936)

Kenneth Young, *Arthur James Balfour, The Happy Life of the Politician, Prime Minister, Statesman and Philosopher, 1848–1930* (1963)

Rear-Admiral W. S. Chalmers, *The Life and Letters of David, Earl Beatty* (1951)

Robert Blake, *The Unknown Prime Minister, The Life and Times of Andrew Bonar Law, 1858–1923* (1955)

H. A. L. Fisher, *James Bryce* (1927)

William Kent, *John Burns: Labour's Lost Leader* (1950)

J. A. Spender, *The Life of the Right Hon. Sir Henry Campbell-Bannerman, G.C.B.* (1924)

Edward Majoribanks, *The Life of Lord*

Carson (1932). (This is volume one of a three-volume work, the second and third volumes being completed by Ian Colvin)

H. Montgomery Hyde, *Carson, The Life of Sir Edward Carson, Lord Carson of Duncairn* (1953)

Sir Charles Petrie, *The Life and Letters of the Right Hon. Sir Austen Chamberlain, K.G., P.C., M.P.* (1939)

Julian Amery, *The Life of Joseph Chamberlain, vol. IV, 1901–1903* (1951) (N.B. The fifth and final volume of this work, dealing with the Tariff Reform campaign, was scheduled for publication in the autumn of 1967.)

Peter Fraser, *Joseph Chamberlain* (1966)

Keith Feiling, *The Life of Neville Chamberlain* (1946)

Eric Alexander, Third Viscount Chilston, *Chief Whip, the Political Life and Times of Aretas Akers-Douglas, First Viscount Chilston* (1961)

Philip Guedalla, *Mr Churchill* (1941)

Virginia Cowles, *Winston Churchill, the Era and the Man* (1953)

Charles Eade (editor), *Churchill by his Contemporaries* (1953)

Peter de Mendelssohn, *The Age of Churchill, Heritage and Adventure, 1874–1911* (1961)

An *Observer* Appreciation, "Churchill by his Contemporaries" (1965)

Lady Violet Bonham Carter, *Winston Churchill as I knew Him* (1965)

Malcolm Thomson, *The Life and Times of Winston Churchill, 1874–1965* (1965)

Randolph S. Churchill, *Winston S. Churchill: Volume I, Youth 1874–1900* (1966) (N.B. The second volume of this work, covering the period 1901–1914, was published in the autumn of 1967, after this book had gone to press.)

James Pope-Hennessy, *Lord Crewe, 1858–1945, The Likeness of a Liberal* (1955)

Leonard Mosley, *Curzon: The End of an Epoch* (1960)

G. K. A. Bell, *Randall Davidson, Archbishop of Canterbury* (3rd edition, 1952)

Randolph S. Churchill, *Lord Derby, "King of Lancashire", The Official Life of Edward, Seventeenth Earl of Derby, 1865–1945* (1959)

Stephen Gwynne and G. M. Tuckwell, *Life of the Right Hon. Sir Charles W. Dilke, Bart* (1917)

Roy Jenkins, *Sir Charles Dilke, a Victorian Tragedy* (1958)

Sir Sidney Lee, *King Edward VII, A Biography* (1927)

Sir Philip Magnus, *King Edward the Seventh* (1964)

John Gore, *King George V, A Personal Memoir* (1941)

Sir Harold Nicolson, *King George the Fifth, His Life and Reign* (1952)

Sir Philip Magnus, *Gladstone, A Biography* (1954)

G. M. Trevelyan, *Grey of Fallodon* (1937)

Sir Frederick Maurice, *Haldane, 1856–1915, The Life of Viscount Haldane of Cloan* (1937)

Dudley Sommer, *Haldane of Cloan, His Life and Times, 1856–1926* (1960)

Emrys Hughes, *Keir Hardie* (1956)

Mary Agnes Hamilton, *Arthur Henderson* (1938)

Lady Victoria Hicks Beach, *Life of Sir Michael Hicks Beach, Earl St Aldwyn* (1932)

Lord Newton, *Lord Lansdowne, A Biography* (1929)

Herbert du Parcq, *Life of David Lloyd George* (1912)

W. Watkin Davies, *Lloyd George, 1863–1914* (1939)

Malcolm Thomson, *David Lloyd George, the Official Biography* (1948)

Thomas Jones, *Lloyd George* (1951)

Frank Owen, *Tempestuous Journey, Lloyd George, His Life and Times* (1954)

Richard, Earl Lloyd George of Dwyfor, *Lloyd George* (1960)

Donald McCormick, *The Mask of Merlin, A Critical Study of David Lloyd George* (1963)

Kenneth Morgan, *David Lloyd George* (1963)

Sir Charles Petrie, *Walter Long and his Times* (1936)

N. Macneill Weir, *The Tragedy of Ramsay MacDonald* (1938)

Christopher Hassall, *Edward Marsh, Patron of the Arts* (1959)

Lucy Masterman, *C. F. G. Masterman, A Biography* (1939)

Stephen McKenna, *Reginald McKenna, 1863–1943* (1948)

John Evelyn Wrench, *Alfred Lord Milner, The Man of No Illusions, 1854–1925* (1958)

Alfred M. Gollin, *Proconsul in Politics, a study of Lord Milner in Opposition and in Power* (1964)

John Buchan, *Lord Minto* (1924)

(Sir) Harold Nicolson, *Lord Carnock, A Study in the Old Diplomacy* (1930)

Reginald Pound and Geoffrey Harmsworth, *Northcliffe* (1959)

Denis Gwynn, *Life of John Redmond* (1932)

Lucien Wolf, *Life of the First Marquess of Ripon* (1921)

George W. Keeton, *A Liberal Attorney-General, The Life of Lord Robson of Jesmond (1852–1918)* (1947)

Marquess of Crewe, *Lord Rosebery* (1931)

Robert Rhodes James, *Rosebery* (1963)

John Bowle, *Viscount Samuel* (1957)

Asa Briggs, *A Study of the Work of Seebohm Rowntree, 1871–1954* (1961)

Second Earl of Birkenhead, *Frederick Edwin, Earl of Birkenhead* (1933)

Second Earl of Birkenhead, *F. E., The Life of F. E. Smith* (1960)

Sarah Gertrude Millin, *General Smuts* (1936)

W. K. Hancock, *Smuts, vol. I: The Sanguine Years, 1870–1919* (1962)

Colin Cross, *Philip Snowden* (1966)

J. W. Mackail and Guy Wyndham, *Life and Letters of George Wyndham* (1925)

Collected Biographies

W. S. Adams, *Edwardian Portraits* (1957)

Winston S. Churchill, *Great Contemporaries* (1947 edition)

Dictionary of National Biography

Second Supplement, vol III (1912) (edited by Sir Sidney Lee)

1922–1930 (1937) (edited by J. R. H. Weaver)

1931–1940 (1949) (edited by L. G. Wickham Legg)

1941–1950 (1959) (edited by L. G. Wickham Legg and E. T. Williams)

R. F. V. Heuston, *Lives of the Lord Chancellors, 1885–1940* (1964)

Collected Documents (arranged under Subject)

BRITISH *Documents on the Origins of the War, 1898–1914* (edited by G. P. Gooch and Harold Temperley)

vol. III, *The Testing of the Entente, 1904–6* (1928)

vol. IV, *The Anglo-Russian Rapprochement, 1903–7* (1929)

vol. V, *The Near East, The Macedonian Problem and the Annexation of Bosnia, 1903–9* (1928)

vol. VI, *Anglo-German Tension, Armaments and Negotiation, 1907–12* (1930)

vol. VII, *The Agadir Crisis* [1907–11] (1932)

vol. VIII, *Arbitration, Neutrality and Security* [1887–1914] (1932)

vol. IX, *The Balkan Wars* [1909–14] (1933)

CHAMBERLAIN—*Politics from Inside, An Epistolary Chronicle, 1906–1914*

N

(1936), the collected letters of Austen Chamberlain to his father and stepmother during this period, together with others, introduced by himself.

ESHER—*Journals and Letters of Reginald, Viscount Esher, vol. II, 1903–10* (1934) (edited by Maurice V. Brett) and *vol. III, 1910–15* (1936) (edited by Oliver, Viscount Esher)

INDIA—*The Evolution of India and Pakistan, 1858 to 1947, Select Documents* (1962) (edited by C. H. Phillips)

MILNER—*The Milner Papers, vol. II, South Africa 1899–1905* (1933) (edited by Cecil Headlam)

SOUTH AFRICA—*Select Documents relating to the Unification of South Africa* (1924) (edited by A. P. Newton)

WEBB—*Beatrice Webb's Diaries, 1924–1932* (1956) (edited by Margaret Cole)

Articles

P. J. Buckland, "The southern Irish unionists, the Irish question and British politics, 1906–14", *Irish Historical Studies*, vol. XV, No. 59 (March 1967)

M. B. Cooper, "British Policy in the Balkans, 1908–9", *The Historical Journal*, vol. VII, No. 2 (September 1964)

J. R. Fanning, "The unionist party and Ireland, 1906–10", *Irish Historical Studies*, vol. XV, No. 58 (September 1966)

R. B. Jones, "Balfour's Reform of Party Organisation", the *Bulletin of the Institute of Historical Research*, vol. XXXVIII (May 1965)

Sir Harold Nicolson, "Prime Ministers at Close Range", a series of articles published in the *Observer* (November 1961)

Alan J. Ward, "Frewen's Anglo-American campaign for federalism, 1910–21", *Irish Historical Studies*, vol. XV, No. 59 (March 1967)

Beryl J. Williams, "The Strategic Background to the Anglo-Russian Entente of August 1907", *The Historical Journal*, vol. IX, No. 3 (November 1966)

INDEX

Note

The following abbreviations are used for the names of five of the principal characters—HHA for Asquith, AJB for Balfour, CB for Campbell-Bannerman, WSC for Churchill and LG for Lloyd George. Other abbreviations used are: Irish Nat(s). (Irish Nationalists), Lab. (Labour), Lib(s). (Liberal(s)), Lib.–Un. (Liberal–Unionist) and Un(s). (Unionist(s)). (The term Lib-Lab is, of course, used in its own right.) The two Houses of Parliament are referred to as H of C and H of L and other straightforward abbreviations (such as Govt. for Government, and Parlty. Sec. for Parliamentary Secretary) are also used where appropriate.

Abdul Hamid II (1842–1918), *Sultan of Ottoman Empire until April 1909*: 182, 199, 201–2, 260, 270
Aberdeen and Temair, 1st Marquis of (1847–1934), *Lib. peer, Lord-Lieut. of Ireland from Dec. 1905*: 20, 64
Acland, Sir Arthur (1847–1926): 14–16, 18–19, 38
Acland-Hood, Sir Alexander (1853–1917), *Chief Un. Whip*: 7, 72f, 111, 248
Acts of Parliament (See also "Bills")
  Before 1906: Catholic Emancipation Act, 1829, 163; Budget, 1861, 168; Peace Preservation Act, 1881, 134; Crofters' Act, 1886, 114; Crimes Act, 1887, 130, 134; Budget, 1894, 168; Congested Districts Act, 1897, 114; Education Act, 1902—see separate entry; Irish Land Act, 1903, 130, 215; Licensing Act, 1904—see separate entry; Aliens Act, 1905, 109f, 154f
  1906: Agricultural Holdings Act, 87; Education Acts, 87; Expiring Laws Continuing Act, 134; Justices of the Peace Act, 87; Labourers' (Ireland) Act, 130–1; Merchant Shipping Act, 87; Town Tenants (Ireland) Act, 87; Trade Disputes Act, 87, 124, 343; Workmen's Compensation Act, 87
  1907: Evicted Tenants (Ireland) Act, 138; Patents Act, 122; Qualification of Women Act, 113; Small

Holdings and Allotments Act, 122; Territorial Army Act, 122, 190
  1908: Children Act, 166; Coal Mines Regulation Act, 160, 166; Education (Scotland) Act, 166; Evicted Tenants (Ireland) Act, 166; Irish University Act, 166; Old Age Pensions Act, 161, 165f, 166; Port of London Authority Act, 166; Prevention of Crimes Act, 166
  1909: Housing and Town Planning Act, 238; Indian Councils Act, 103, 104; Irish Land Act, 238; Labour Exchanges Act, 238; Road Development and Improvements Fund Act, 226f; South Africa Act, 106; Trade Boards Act, 238
  1910: Education (Choice of Employment) Act, 331
Admiralty: calculations as regards German navy programme, 192–3; and 1908–9 Estimates, 193; alarmed at rate of Germany's shipbuilding, 212, 251–2, 251f; and Beresford's allegations, 258–9; and Estimates for 1910–11 and 1911–12, 272; fears about German navy not realised, 275
Aehrenthal, Count von (1854–1912), *Austro-Hungarian Foreign Minister from Oct. 1906*: 199–201, 211, 260–2, 266
Afghanistan: 179, 180–1
Aga Khan: 103

377

INDEX 393